Helping Children and Families Cope with Parental Illness

A Clinician's Guide

Maureen Davey, Karni Kissil, and Laura Lynch

Routledge
Taylor & Francis Group

NEW YORK AND LONDON

First published 2016
by Routledge
711 Third Avenue, New York, NY 10017

and by Routledge
2 Park Square, Milton Park, Abingdon, Oxon, OX14 4RN

Routledge is an imprint of the Taylor & Francis Group, an informa business

Library of Congress Cataloging-in-Publication Data
Names: Davey, Maureen P., author. | Kissil, Karni, author.
Title: Helping children and families cope with parental illness : a clinician's guide /
    Maureen Davey, Karni Kissil, and Laura Lynch.
Description: New York : Routledge, 2016.
Includes bibliographical references and index.
Identifiers: LCCN 2015036916 | ISBN 9781138823983 (hbk. : alk. paper) |
    ISBN 9781138823990 (pbk. : alk. paper) | ISBN 9781315741741 (ebk)
Subjects: LCSH: Families—Health and hygiene. | Sick—Family relationships.
Classification: LCC RA418.5.F3 .D38 2016 DDC 362.82—dc23
LC record available at http://lccn.loc.gov/2015036916

ISBN: 978-1-138-82398-3 (hbk)
ISBN: 978-1-138-82399-0 (pbk)
ISBN: 978-1-315-74174-1 (ebk)

Typeset in Sabon
by Apex CoVantage, LLC

Helping Children and Families Cope with Parental Illness

When a parent or parental figure is diagnosed with an illness, the family unit changes, and clinical providers should consider using a family-centered approach to care and not just focus on the patient coping with the illness. *Helping Children and Families Cope with Parental Illness* describes theoretical frameworks, common parental illnesses and their courses, family assessment tools, and evidence-supported family intervention programs that have the potential to significantly reduce negative psychosocial outcomes for families and promote resilience. Most interventions described are culturally sensitive, for use with diverse populations in diverse practice settings, and were developed for two-parent, single-parent, and blended families.

Maureen Davey, PhD, LMFT, is an Associate Professor in the Department of Couple and Family Therapy at Drexel University. She has 20 years of clinical and research experience working with individuals, couples, and families coping with parental and childhood illnesses.

Karni Kissil, PhD, LMFT, is an AAMFT licensed clinical member with 20 years of experience as a clinician working with individuals, couples, and families in diverse practice settings.

Laura Lynch, PhD, is the Collaborative Healthcare Clinical Practice Educator in the Department of Couple and Family Therapy at Drexel University. She has worked with individuals, couples, and families within multiple medical and outpatient mental health settings, and most recently she completed the Families, Illness, and Collaborative Healthcare Fellowship at the Chicago Center for Family Health.

Developing and writing this book was both challenging and enjoyable. We are very grateful for all of the help and support of our editors at Taylor & Francis, especially Elizabeth Graber. We could not have done this without her. We also want to acknowledge the steady administrative support from Brianna Bilkins who helped us format and edit all of the chapters.

CONTENTS

ACKNOWLEDGMENTS

I would like to thank and acknowledge the many people who helped to make this book possible. I would like to first acknowledge my mother, Gladys Grund Semans, who was and continues to be an inspiration for me personally and professionally. My mother coped with breast cancer for 3.5 years while caring for three children between the ages of 2 and 12. Although my mother lost her battle with breast cancer when I was 9 years old, before she died she surrounded me and my two siblings (Rafael and Anne) with family (Grandma Esther Semans, Aunt Helen, Aunt Carole, Benita and Itsak Peretz, Aunt Liz, and Uncle Phil), her friends, the Jewish community (Rabbi Rudavsky), and neighbors (The Neals) who always looked out for us. As a provider and family researcher, my mother continues to inspire me to help other families like ours so children are acknowledged and parents are supported while they navigate illness and caring for their children. I want to also acknowledge my father, Phillip Miller Semans, who, despite coping with an affective disorder all of his life, always unconditionally loved his children and grandchildren (Dylan, Garrett, Gabriela, and Noah); he taught me how to be kind and forgiving. I also want to acknowledge my supportive and caring husband, Adam. He encouraged me to write this book 2 years ago when I was approached by a publisher (Marta Moldavi) during my presentation on parental illness at a national family therapy conference. At that time I was hesitant to write this book because of the competing demands of career and family; however, Adam encouraged me to make a difference in children's lives by helping providers. I also want to acknowledge my daughter, Gabriela, for helping me carve out the time necessary for writing this book. Finally, I want to acknowledge my two co-authors, Karni and Laura, for their steady support and encouragement; thank you for helping me bring this project to fruition.

Maureen Davey

I would like to express my gratitude to Maureen Davey, who invited me to co-author this book. This has been a meaningful journey for me. I am dedicating this book to my mother, Elinoar Horkin, who died of cancer at the age of 39. Her untimely death and the long years we as a family struggled with her illness have made me sensitive to the impact of parental illness on families and especially the pain of the children. She would have been proud to know that I used my personal struggle to help others.

Karni Kissil

I would like to first thank Maureen Davey, the driving force behind this project. Thank you for your incredible mentorship and for giving me the opportunity to write with you. I am also so grateful to my husband, Phil; words cannot express how much I appreciate your unconditional love and constant support. Finally, I would like to acknowledge my parents, James and Darlene, and my siblings, Amy and Ben; together we have faced challenges and experienced great joy, and I am privileged to call you my family.

Laura Lynch

PART I

INTRODUCTION AND THEORETICAL FRAMEWORKS

CHAPTER 1

INTRODUCTION

Maureen Davey, Karni Kissil, and Laura Lynch

We are passionate about this book because of our own experiences with parental illness, our clinical work, and clinical research with parents and their families. As children, we were each significantly impacted by parental illness. Two of us (M.D. and K.K.) lost a mother to cancer when we were school-age children. One of us (L.L.) experienced a father struggling to manage type 1 diabetes. Reflecting back on our experiences as adults and providers, we realized how family-centered approaches to medical care could have made our parents' and families' struggles easier and reduced feelings of isolation and distress. We each remember feeling invisible and overlooked by healthcare providers when our parents were coping with their chronic (diabetes) or life-threatening (cancer) illnesses. Experiences with parental illness in our own families inspired us to study and develop culturally sensitive prevention programs to help other families like ours. Thus, our shared desire to help providers improve the lives of the millions of children currently coping with parental illness is what motivated us to write a book to help providers better meet the needs of these vulnerable families.

This book was written for mental healthcare providers (e.g., behavioral healthcare providers, clinical psychologists, social workers, family therapists, counseling psychologists, nurses) who work with families coping with parental illness in diverse practice settings (e.g., primary care, specialty care, community mental health, private practice). We describe theoretical frameworks (attachment theory: Bowlby, 1969/1982, family systems illness model: Rolland, 1999, 2005), seven types of prevalent parental illnesses and their impact on parents and their children (e.g., depression, cancer, HIV, multiple sclerosis, lupus, diabetes, cardiovascular diseases), experiences of grandparents raising grandchildren, psychosocial and family assessment tools, general clinical guidelines to help families cope with parental illness, evidence-supported prevention programs that facilitate family resilience, parental death and grief interventions, and ethical considerations. Additionally, we consider the importance of adapting interventions so they are more culturally relevant (e.g., tailored for different cultures, ethnicities, and races) and can be used in diverse practice settings (e.g., primary care, specialty medical clinics, outpatient mental health clinics, and private practice settings).

History of Helping Families Cope with Parental Illness

From the late 1950s until the mid-1980s, children living with ill parents were rarely mentioned in the literature, except noting that these children might have more responsibilities at home (e.g., Arnaud, 1959; Romano, 1976). At this time, most clinical providers and researchers focused on patients' and spouses' needs, rather than on their children at home. In the late 1980s, clinical researchers began focusing on specific parental illnesses with regard to how they impact children, adolescents, and parents. Yet despite this focus on children and adolescents in the last 30 years, most medical clinics (primary and specialty) and mental health and private practice clinics are not routinely assessing and attending to the needs of children who have ill parents, and they are not providing culturally sensitive, evidence-supported prevention programs. More often, peer or parent-only cognitive behavioral or psychoeducational approaches are offered to families in lieu of prevention programs that are more interactive and focus on parent–child attachment and improved parent–child communication (Campbell, 2003; Shields, Finley, & Chawla, 2012).

Families are networks of reciprocal relationships. When a parent is diagnosed with an illness like depression, cancer, HIV, or diabetes, although the course of the particular illness will differ, it affects the family system, for example, marital relationships, parenting practices, family roles and routines, children and adolescents, household management, work responsibilities, and social relationships (e.g., Aldridge & Becker, 1999; Masten, 2001; Rolland, 1994, 1999). When a parent or primary caregiver (e.g., grandparents who are raising grandchildren) is ill, depressive mood and distress may be experienced by both the ill parent and his or her partner or spouse (Armistead, Klein, & Forehand, 1995; Armsden & Lewis, 1993; Burton, 1992). Noteworthy, there are more symptoms of distress among single parents with lower incomes because they tend to have less family support (Cross, 1989; Evans & Kim, 2013; Sue, 2003; Whaley & Davis, 2007). Additionally, many parents experience impaired parenting because of the illness, side effects of treatment, and understandable emotional distress (Beardslee, Gladstone, Wright, & Cooper, 2003; Beardslee, Versage, & Gladstone, 1998). Consequently, some parents coping with an illness are less psychologically available to their children, have poorer communication and supervision, provide inconsistent discipline, experience more irritability, and use more coercive parenting practices. Parental illness, whether physical or mental, can stress even the strongest of families.

Impact of Parental Illness

Parental illnesses are common and can affect all levels of the family system: patient, spouse/partner, and their children. Parental illnesses can also cause depressive mood and distress in both the afflicted parent and his or her partner or spouse (Compas, Worsham, Ey, & Howell, 1996). In turn, this can result in impaired parenting as described previously (Beardslee et al., 1998, 2003). This impairment of parenting has been linked to poorer adaptability among children, for example, behavioral, social, and self-esteem problems (Armistead et al., 1995; Lewis, 2004; Pederson & Revenson, 2005; Weaver, Rowland, Alfano, & McNeel, 2010). Clinical researchers have reported that children may experience physical symptoms, family conflict, and less family cohesion (Bogosian, Moss-Morris, Hadwin, 2010; Pakenham, Bursnall, Chiu, Cannon, & Okochi, 2006). Older school-age children report that their lives are often complicated by their parent's diagnosis and treatment. Clinical researchers suggest that among children of all ages whose parents have an illness, older school-age children (ages 10 to 18) tend to report the highest levels of psychological symptoms and are at most risk for experiencing anxiety and depression (Armsden & Lewis, 1993; Beardslee et al., 2003).

Since parental illness can have a profound impact on children and adolescents with regard to their development, physical and mental health, and overall well-being (Pakenham & Cox, 2012), a family-centered approach to care is needed in our healthcare system. Access to information and a range of practical and emotional support services are essential for families experiencing parental illness (Chelsa, 2010). Psychosocial support should be part of the routine practice of all healthcare providers who have direct contact with children and families.

Yet, our current healthcare system does not routinely support families, children, and adolescents when a parent has a serious, chronic, or life-threatening illness (Blank, 2012; Johnson, 2000). Many of today's behavioral health therapists and mental healthcare providers lack training regarding how to interview, intervene, and respond to more than the ill parents who are their patients (Martire, 2005; Martire, Lustig, Schulz, Miller, & Helgeson, 2004). Families frequently describe difficulty meeting the demands of a parental illness. They may have limited financial resources, inadequate respite support, limited communication with the education and healthcare systems, and competing work and family commitments (Evans & Kim, 2013). Some families become socially isolated at a time when they most need supportive social relationships. Helping providers routinely use psychosocial assessments and family interventions at the front end and throughout treatment could help these families receive the support they need (Chelsa, 2010). We hope our book helps providers working in diverse practice settings with families who are coping with parental illness.

Audience for the Book

Designed for prevention and intervention, this book was written for two groups of professionals. The first group includes clinical supervisors who train providers (such as counselors, psychologists, nurses, physicians, social workers, marriage and family therapists) who work in medical settings, community mental health clinics, and private practice, to help them utilize a family-centered approach to care with families coping with different types of parental illnesses.

The second group includes program administrators and other decision-makers involved in developing curricula and implementation in various helping professional programs. This book can be used as a primary or supplemental textbook for graduate classes dedicated to the clinical preparation and development of clinicians such as clinical practicum, medical family therapy, or health psychology courses. It is applicable across mental health and physical health disciplines including psychology, sociology, nursing, public health, social work, and medicine.

Overview of Book Chapters

This book is divided into three parts. Part I continues with Chapter 2, "Maintaining a Family Focus: Utilizing Attachment Theory and the Family Systems Illness Model," in which we review two frameworks, attachment theory (Bowlby, 1969/1982) and the family systems illness model (Rolland, 1999), that guided the development of this book. Bowlby (1969/1982) emphasized the importance of accessibility and responsiveness between children and adolescents and their primary caregivers, which has been linked to better social and emotional adjustment; we believe this can help shield children and adolescents who are coping with an ill parent. Attachment theory assumes that a child's sense of security in life depends on parents being available and protective. Although attachment is essential in infancy, it is also important throughout the life cycle (Bowlby, 1969/1982). Parental illness is a stressful life event that can lead to family instability and parental depression, which are associated with less parental supervision and sometimes more coercive parenting. The strength of the parent–child attachment bond can shield children from the negative effects of coping with a parent's illness. Secure attachments can help to protect children so that when adversity is present, they can better cope and adapt.

Rolland's family systems illness model (1999, 2005) provides a systemic framework for working with families who are facing any chronic illness. Rolland's model acknowledges the effect of the "psychosocial types of illness" (Rolland, 1999, p. 244), which refers to categorizing and understanding the impact of the illness based on its: (1) type of onset, (2) type of course it takes, (3) outcome of an illness, (4) how much incapacitation the illness causes, and (5) level of uncertainty related to the illness. We applied this model to each of the illnesses described in Part II of our book to provide a systemic framework for identifying clinically relevant and culturally sensitive clinical interventions.

Part II, Parental Illnesses, consists of eight chapters describing seven different types of parental illnesses (Chapters 3 to 9) and the experiences of grandparents coping with illness and raising grandchildren (Chapter 10). Chapter 3 through 9 are all organized in the following way: (1) prevalence, prognosis, and associated medical outcomes, as well as a description of illness according to Rolland's (1999) categorization; (2) effects of the illness on parents and children; (3) cultural considerations and consideration of cultural differences and presentations based on the clinical context (e.g., primary care, specialty clinics, outpatient mental health, private practice), age of child, race, ethnicity, family structure, which parent or grandparent is ill, and class; (4) clinical vignette illustrating how a family coping with the specific parental illness could present; and (5) additional resources. The seven illnesses reviewed in Part II are reflected in the respective chapter titles: "Parental Depression" (Chapter 3), "Parental Cancer" (Chapter 4), "Parental HIV" (Chapter 5), "Parental Multiple Sclerosis" (Chapter 6), "Parental Systemic Lupus Erythematosus" (Chapter 7), "Parental Diabetes" (Chapter 8), and "Parental Cardiovascular Diseases" (Chapter 9). We end Part II with a chapter describing the experiences of grandparents raising grandchildren (Chapter 10). We included this chapter because there has been a steady increase in the number of grandparent-headed households in the United States since the 1990s. Unfortunately, grandparents who have the primary responsibility of raising their grandchildren tend to have poorer self-reported mental health outcomes, including experiencing greater parenting stresses, depression, family strain, and anxiety compared to those grandparents not serving in this capacity. This is particularly so for those of lower socioeconomic status (SES) who tend to have fewer material resources and poorer networks of social support (Burton, 1992).

Part III, Interventions and Clinical Considerations, includes five chapters. In Chapter 11, "Needs Assessments and Clinical Tools," we review valid and reliable adult, child/adolescent, and family assessment tools that can help providers utilize a family-centered approach to care. We describe the importance of doing needs assessments on adult patients to determine if they have school age children at home and if these children are struggling because of a parent's illness. In Chapter 12, "Clinical Guidelines for Working with Parental Illness," we review available literature and offer clear, step-by-step guidelines for effective and culturally sensitive treatment in diverse practice settings. We also describe how to help parents have more open communication about their illness, so children do not worry alone, and how parents can provide updates to children in developmentally appropriate ways. Finally, we provide tips to help parents prepare children for any hospital visits by describing in advance what a child will see and hear; debrief with children after medical visits to allay any worries, fears, or concerns; and provide other forms of communication (e.g., cards, drawings, videos) when visits are not possible while in treatment. In Chapter 13, "Evidence-Supported Treatments for Parental Illness," we review some evidence-supported family treatment programs for depression, cancer, and HIV. We also consider the importance of culturally adapting treatments for diverse populations and becoming a culturally sensitive provider.

The purpose of this book is to help providers support families coping with parental illness. Sadly, for some families, illness will lead to the death of the ill parent. Providers working with families coping with parental illness have an important role and can help families work through both anticipatory grief before the loss and mourning after the death. In Chapter 14, "Parental Death and Grief Interventions," we describe how children at different ages tend to grieve the loss of a parent and when grief becomes complicated. We also describe factors that can affect children's adjustment following parental loss, and we offer interventions that can be used by professionals to facilitate healthy grieving.

In the last chapter, Chapter 15, "Ethical Considerations," we review legal and ethical issues that could arise when working with families who are coping with parental illness. We use two case examples to illustrate issues such as collaborating with medical providers, confidentiality and informed consent, working with the family as a unit of treatment, and contacting school personnel.

This book was written for a clinical audience so it could be used as a practical, hands-on resource. All of the illness chapters follow the same format to make it easier to find relevant information. We included text boxes with salient take-home points in most chapters, for those readers who do not have time to thoroughly read each chapter. We also included additional resources in each chapter to help providers expand their knowledge beyond the scope of this book. We hope providers use this book as a resource to help them provide family-centered approaches to care to children coping with parental illness and their parents.

References

Aldridge, J., & Becker, S. (1999). Children as carers: The impact of parental illness and disability on children's caring roles. *Journal of Family Therapy, 21*, 303–320.

Armistead, L., Klein, K., & Forehand, R. (1995). Parental physical illness and child functioning. *Clinical Psychology Review, 15*(5), 409–422.

Armsden, G. C., & Lewis, F. M. (1993). The child's adaptation to parental medical illness: Theory and clinical implications. *Patient Education and Counseling, 22*(3), 153–165. doi:10.1016/0738-3991(93)90095-E

Arnaud, S. H. (1959). Some psychological characteristics of children of multiple sclerotics. *Psychosomatic Medicine, 21*, 8–22.

Beardslee, W. R., Gladstone, T. R. G., Wright, E. J., & Cooper, A. B. (2003). A family-based approach to the prevention of depressive symptoms in children at risk: Evidence of parental and child change. *Pediatrics, 112*(2), e119–e131. doi:10.1542/peds.112.2.e119

Beardslee, W. R., Versage, E. M., & Gladstone, T. R. (1998). Children of affectively ill parents: A review of the past 10 years. *Adolescent Psychiatry, 27*(11), 1134–1141.

Blank, R. H. (2012). Transformation of the US healthcare system: Why is change so difficult? *Current Sociology, 60*(4), 415–426.

Bogosian, A., Moss-Morris, R., & Hadwin, J. (2010). Psychosocial adjustment in children and adolescents with a parent with multiple sclerosis: A systematic review. *Journal of Clinical Rehabilitation, 24,* 789–801.

Bowlby, J. (1969/1982). *Attachment and loss: Vol. 1: Attachment.* New York: Basic Books.

Burton, L. M. (1992). Black grandparents rearing children of drug-addicted parents: Stressors, outcomes, and social service needs. *The Gerontologist, 32*(6), 744–751. doi:10.1093/geront/32.6.744

Campbell, T. L. (2003). The effectiveness of family interventions for physical disorders. *Journal of Marital and Family Therapy, 29,* 263–281.

Chelsa, C. C. (2010). Do family interventions improve health? *Journal of Family Nursing, 16,* 355–377.

Compas, B. E., Worsham, N. L., Ey, S., & Howell, D. C. (1996). When mom or dad has cancer: II. Coping, cognitive appraisals, and psychological distress in children of cancer patients. *Health Psychology, 15,* 167–175.

Cross, T. L. (1989). *Towards a culturally competent system of care: A monograph on effective services for minority children who are severely emotionally disturbed.* Rockville, MD: National Institute of Mental Health (DHHS) Child and Adolescent Service System Program.

Evans, G. W., & Kim, P. (2013). Childhood poverty, chronic stress, self-regulation, and coping. *Child Development Perspectives, 7*(1), 43–48.

Johnson, B. H. (2000). Family-centered care: Four decades of progress. *Families, Systems, & Health, 18*(2), 137.

Lewis, F. (2004). Family-focused oncology nursing research. *Oncology Nursing Forum, 31*(2), 288–292.

Masten, A. (2001). Ordinary magic: Resilience processes in development. *American Psychologist, 56,* 227–238.

Martire, L. M. (2005). The "relative" efficacy of involving family members in psychosocial interventions for chronic illness: Are there added benefits to patients and family members? *Families, Systems, and Health, 23,* 312–328.

Martire, L. M., Lustig, A. P., Schulz, R., Miller, G. D., & Helgeson, V. S. (2004). Is it beneficial to involve a family member? A meta-analysis of psychosocial interventions for chronic illness. *Health Psychology, 23,* 599–611.

Pakenham, K. I., Bursnall, S., Chiu, J., Cannon, T., & Okochi, M. (2006). The psychosocial impact of caregiving on young people who have a parent with an illness or disability: Comparisons between young caregivers and noncaregivers. *Rehabilitation Psychology, 51*(2), 113–126.

Pakenham, K. I., & Cox, S. (2012). Test of a model of the effects of parental illness on youth and family functioning. *Health Psychology, 31*(5), 580.

Pederson, S., & Revenson, T. A. (2005). Parental illness, family functioning, and adolescent well-being: A family ecology framework to guide research. *Journal of Family Psychology, 19*(3), 404–419.

Rolland, J. S. (1994). *Families, illness, and disability: An integrative treatment model.* New York: Basic Books.

Rolland, J. S. (1999). Parental illness and disability: A family systems framework. *Journal of Family Therapy, 21,* 242–266.

Rolland, J. S. (2005). Cancer and the family: An integrative model. *Cancer, 104*(S11), 2584–2595. doi:10.1002/cncr.21489

Romano, M. D. (1976). Preparing children for parental disability. *Social Work in Health Care, 1,* 309–315.

Shields, C. G., Finley, M. A., & Chawla, N. (2012). Couple and family interventions in health problems. *Journal of Marital and Family Therapy, 38*(1), 265–280.

Sue, S. (2003). In defense of cultural competency in psychotherapy and treatment. *The American Psychologist, 58*(11), 964–970.

Weaver, K. E., Rowland, J. H., Alfano, C. M., & McNeel, T. S. (2010). Parental cancer and the family. *Cancer, 116*(18), 4395–4401.

Whaley, A. L., & Davis, K. E. (2007). Cultural competence and evidence-based practice in mental health services. *American Psychologist, 62,* 563–574.

CHAPTER 2

MAINTAINING A FAMILY FOCUS
Utilizing Attachment Theory and the Family Systems Illness Model

Laura Lynch

The Institute of Medicine has recognized the important role families play in individual healthcare practices and clinical outcomes and has recommended their inclusion in primary and tertiary care clinical settings (IOM, 2001). A family-centered approach to care describes a philosophy that places the patient *and* his/her family at the center of health care; advocates for collaboration between the patient, family members, and the healthcare team; and facilitates collaborative relationships (Martire et al., 2004). Family-centered care is responsive to families' strengths and needs, cultural contexts regarding views about health and illness, and the need for long-term continuity of care (McDaniel, Campbell, Hepworth, & Lorenz, 2005).

Although many researchers and providers have reported that family and social support are powerful untapped resources for improving treatment adherence to chronic medical conditions, primary and specialty care providers have not consistently found a way to utilize family-centered approaches to assessment and care (e.g., Johnson, 2000; Peterson, Takiya, & Finley, 2003). Some of the reasons providers struggle to implement family-centered approaches to care, especially with adult patient populations, is because of financial (billing for family visits and for multiple providers), clinical (lack of knowledge about how to work with families), and administrative barriers (see Peek, 2008).

Despite these barriers, family-centered care has been recommended because positive family support is associated with better medication and treatment adherence; more open and positive communication between patients, family members, and their treatment teams; and treatment retention (DiGioia, Greenhouse, & Levison, 2007). Family members influence the patient's psychological adjustment and management of chronic illnesses, including the adoption of healthy behaviors (Martire, Lustig, Schulz, Miller, & Helgeson, 2004). The family is the primary social context for patients; it is a naturally occurring support system through which to provide health-related prevention and intervention programs (Duke & Scal, 2011; Pakenham & Cox, 2014).

Involving family members in each other's care can be efficient, informative, and influential to the success of treatment plans (Ødegård, 2005). Family inclusion can range from acknowledging the family's influence on individual health to incorporating family, friends, and caregivers as part of routine care (IOM, 2001; McDaniel et al., 2005). Although this clinical approach is more common among providers who work with pediatric (e.g., partnering with parents to help an ill child) and geriatric (e.g., partnering with caregivers of elderly patients) populations, we recommend using a family-centered approach to care with adult patients who are parenting children at home.

In this chapter, we review John Bowlby's attachment theory (Bowlby, 1973, 1980) and John Rolland's family systems illness model (Rolland, 1999) to help providers utilize a family-centered approach to care with parents who are coping with an illness and caring for children at home. Bowlby (1969/1982) emphasized the importance of accessibility and responsiveness between children, adolescents, and their primary caregivers, which has been linked to improved social and emotional adjustment among children. Parental illness is a stressful life event that can lead to family instability and parental depression (see Chapter 3), which is associated with less parental supervision and, for some parents, more coercive parenting (e.g., Beardslee et al., 1998). The strength of the parent–child attachment bond can shield children and adolescents from the negative effects of coping with a parent's illness. Secure attachments can help to protect children so that when adversity is present (a parent's illness), they can better cope and adapt (Feeney, 2000).

Additionally, in this chapter we summarize John Rolland's FSI model (1999, 2005), which is a systemic framework for working with families who are facing chronic illness. We chose this model because it focuses on family strengths and "attends to the expected psychosocial demands of a disorder through its various phases, family systems dynamics that emphasize family and individual life cycles, multigenerational patterns, and belief systems" (Rolland, 1999, p. 244). The family systems illness model acknowledges the effect of the "psychosocial types of illness" (Rolland, 1999, p. 244), which refers to categorizing and understanding the impact of an illness based on the following: (1) type of onset, (2) type of course it takes, (3) outcome of the illness, (4) how much incapacitation the illness causes, and (5) level of uncertainty related to the illness.

Theory provides a framework to guide clinical work with individuals, couples, and families; it helps providers develop case conceptualizations, interpret new issues that emerge a case, and develop treatment goals. In this chapter we review one theory (attachment theory; Bowlby, 1969) and one theory-based model (family systems illness model; Rolland, 1994a,b, 1999) to help providers utilize a family-centered approach to care with families who are coping with parental illness.

Attachment Theory

An understanding of attachment theory is essential for working with parents and children, because this theory provides a foundational framework for understanding parent–child relationships. John Bowlby (1988), a psychiatrist, developed attachment theory to explain the consequences of parent–child separations during World War II. Existing theories explaining children's ties to their mothers did not fit with what he observed and experienced as a provider working with institutionalized and hospitalized children (Bowlby, 1988), so he developed a theory to better explain parent–child dynamics. Bowlby (1988) posited that attachment to significant others is an individual and primary source of human motivation, and is instinctual, like the innate drive for food and sex.

Attachment theory assumes that a child's sense of security depends on parents being available, attuned, and protective. Although attachment is essential during infancy, it is also important throughout the life cycle (Bowlby, 1969/1982). Researchers have reported that attachment issues in childhood can have long-term negative effects in adulthood (Ainsworth et al., 1978; Armistead et al., 1995; Armsden & Lewis, 1993; Bowlby, 1969/1982; Rolland, 1999; Simpson, Collins, Tran, & Haydon, 2007; Walsh, 2002), such as anxiety, anger, depression, trouble making secure attachments in adult relationships, and substance abuse, among other negative outcomes. Attachment begins in infancy; infants have an innate need to connect to a primary caregiver who can protect them and meet their basic needs (e.g., food, shelter).

During infancy, the primary attachment figure is typically the mother, but a child can have more than one attachment figure (e.g., mother and father; grand-parents). When children experience physical or emotional distress, they tend to seek out their primary attachment figures in order to feel safe and to receive comfort (Bowlby, 1969/1982); they do this by exhibiting attachment behaviors. "Attachment behaviour is any form of behaviour that results in a person attaining or maintaining proximity to some other clearly identified individual who is con-ceived as better able to cope with the world" (Bowlby, 1988, p. 26). For example, an infant will do this through crying, while young children look for or move toward their attachment figures.

When an attachment figure is consistently available, attuned, can comfort the child, and meet practical, emotional, and social needs, then a secure attachment is developed. If a parent is unavailable, or inconsistently available, insecure attach-ments tend to develop because children learn they cannot depend on their attach-ment figures (Bowlby, 1988). The type of response and consistency of attachment figures also affects children's internal working models. Bowlby (1988) defines "internal working models" as children's views of themselves and others, formed through interactions and experiences with attachment figures. This in turn affects how children anticipate and respond to attachment figures and their surroundings (Bowlby, 1969/1982). These early attachment experiences and related internal working models continue to affect how individuals view and act in close rela-tionships during adolescence and later in adulthood (Caffery & Erdman, 2003).

Attachment theory was expanded by Bowlby's colleague, Dr. Mary Ainsworth, who was a developmental psychologist. Her most renowned research was conduct-ing "the strange situation" experiment, in which she observed infants' behaviors in the presence and absence of their mothers and in the presence of a stranger (Ainsworth et al., 1978). When the stranger was present, children felt threat-ened and attachment behaviors (seeking contact with mother) were heightened (Ainsworth et al., 1978). Ainsworth hypothesized that parents act as a foundation of safety and security, a "secure base" from which children can confidently explore their surroundings (Ainsworth et al., 1978). Yet, this only occurs if there is secure attachment between the child and parent (Rajecki, Lamb, & Obmascher, 1978).

In her seminal research with children and their primary caregivers, Ainsworth and Bell (1970) identified three main attachment patterns: (1) secure, (2) ambiv-alent, and (3) avoidant. The latter two are insecure attachment styles. Securely attached children were distressed when first separated from their mothers, but then were able to self-soothe and explore. When reunited, these children imme-diately sought contact with their mothers and then returned to exploring their surroundings. These mothers were consistently warm, attuned, and responsive to their babies' social and emotional needs (Ainsworth & Bell, 1970).

Ambivalent attachment was characterized by distress upon separation from attachment figures, but ambivalence when reunited with them. Mothers of ambivalently attached infants were inconsistent with their responsiveness (e.g., sometimes warmly responding to their cries, sometimes ignoring their children)

(Ainsworth et al., 1978). Avoidant attachment was characterized by infants who did not exhibit much distress when separated from their mothers and were avoidant of their mothers when reunited. Mothers of these infants tended to reject them and be emotionally unresponsive (Ainsworth et al., 1978).

Later, Main and Solomon (1990) described a fourth type of attachment pattern: disorganized (also an insecure attachment). Infants with this type of attachment did not have any predictable attachment behaviors. Disorganized attachment forms when attachment figures are unpredictable themselves and children cannot anticipate how they will react (Lyons-Ruth & Jacobvitz, 1999).

Parental Illness and Attachment

Parental illness is a stressor that can activate attachment behaviors in children at all ages. The illness can lead to physical separations between the ill parent and children, for example, because ill parents might need to be hospitalized for varying periods of time (Feeney, 2000; Feeney & Ryan, 1994). Even if a child is able to visit the parent in the hospital, the parent is not as readily available to the child and is unable to be as attuned and responsive and care for the child's needs in the same way. Additionally, having a chronic illness can make it difficult for parents to be as emotionally and physically attuned and responsive to their children, even when they are not hospitalized (e.g., needing to rest at home because of side effects from treatment) (Meijer, Oort, Visser-Meily, & Sieh, 2014).

Thus, physical separations and decreased parental responsiveness can trigger attachment behaviors in the children/adolescents of chronically ill parents. Attachment behaviors will vary based on whether the child is securely or insecurely attached and the age of the child (Diareme et al., 2007). Armsden and Lewis (1993) noted that "children with a history of secure attachment might show a more intense behavioral reaction to a real separation threat than children who have experienced chronic unresponsive parenting" (p. 155). Yet, securely attached children are able to more easily cope will the stressor because of their abilities to seek out assistance from trusted attachment figures and because positive attachment experiences have shaped a more resilient and positive internal working model (Armsden & Lewis, 1993). Attachment behavior of a child with an ill parent will also look different depending on the child's age and culture; these differences are further explored in Chapter 13.

Parental illness itself does not necessarily lead to the development of an insecure attachment. Rather, the illness can activate existing attachment patterns between parents and their children. For example, Sieh, Visser-Meily, and Meijer (2013) compared a sample of Dutch families who were parenting adolescents who had healthy parents to a sample of families with adolescents who had parents coping with a chronic medical condition. They found no differences in the quality of parent–child attachment between the two groups of adolescents. Sieh et al. (2013) said, "it may be argued that children [of parents with chronic medical conditions] require . . . highly secure parent attachment to buffer the risk for adjustment difficulties" (p. 216).

Children's attachment security affects how they will react to and experience parental illness. Ireland and Pakenham (2010) examined the adjustment of youth to parental illness or parental disability in a sample of 81 Australian children who were 10 to 25 years old. They reported associations between the participants' attachment security and caregiving of their ill parents; more attachment security was associated with less distress providing care to their ill parents and greater confidence providing care to their parents. According to their results, attachment security was not associated with adjustment to the parental illness. Yet, the authors noted that attachment between children and the parent who was not ill was not measured; secure attachment to the healthy parent may reduce the negative effects of insecure attachment to the ill parent (Ireland and Pakenham, 2010).

It is important to mention that if a parental illness is severe enough to cause repeated and long-term ruptures in the parent–child relationship and to interfere with the ill parent's responsiveness, a child's previously secure attachment with the ill parent could become compromised (Pakenham & Cox, 2014). Armsden and Lewis (1993) said "dramatic and consistent positive or negative alterations in parental availability, for example, may result insignificant changes in the child's view of the relationship" (pp. 154–155). Bowlby (1988) also suggested that significant changes in parental behavior toward a child can change the quality of attachment, although attachment style tends to become more static as a child ages (p. 127). Next, we summarize John Rolland's family systems illness model (Rolland, 1999, 2005) to help mental healthcare providers use a family-centered approach to care.

Family Systems Illness Model

Rolland's family systems illness (FSI) model (1984, 1987a,b, 1988, 1994a,b, 1999, 2005) is a systemic framework to help providers work with families facing a chronic illness. Rolland developed this model based on family systems theory and his own clinical experiences as a psychiatrist working with families coping with illness (Rolland, 2005). His model emphasizes family strengths and "attends to the expected psychosocial demands of a disorder through its various phases, family systems dynamics that emphasize family and individual life cycles, multigenerational patterns, and belief systems" (Rolland, 1999, p. 244). Rolland (1999) noted that family belief systems are informed by the family's culture, ethnicity, and gender. Undoubtedly, individuals and the family systems they are embedded in are recursively affected by these salient contextual variables.

The FSI model also acknowledges the effect of "psychosocial types of illness" (Rolland, 1999, p. 244), which refers to categorizing and understanding the impact of an illness based on the following factors: (1) the type of illness onset (acute or sudden, gradual), (2) the course the illness takes (progressive, constant, relapsing), (3) the outcome of an illness (nonfatal, shortened life span, fatal), (4) the extent of incapacitation caused by illness (none, mild, moderate, severe), and (5) the level of uncertainty related to the illness. Rolland notes that the level of uncertainty is a factor that is affected by all of the previous factors (e.g., onset, course) and is better understood as a "metacharacteristic" of the others (1994a, p. 33). For instance, some illnesses have an unpredictable course (e.g., multiple sclerosis) and/or outcome (e.g., advanced stage cancer), and sometimes the rate at which an illness develops or changes over time can be unpredictable.

Illnesses can have an acute or gradual onset; an acute onset tends to have a more negative effect on the family because it is unexpected and sudden (Rolland, 1999). Rolland (1999) broke down the course of an illness into the following three categories: (1) "progressive" or steady deterioration over time, (2) "constant" or "a semi-permanent change that is stable and predictable over a considerable time span," and (3) "relapsing or episodic," in which stability or symptom intensity varies (Rolland, 1999, p. 245).

Rolland (1999) also described the importance of the "time phases of illness" (p. 246), which refers to the development of an illness over time. He identified three salient time phases: (1) crisis (prediagnosis with symptoms, diagnosis, and adjustment period), (2) chronic (the long haul during treatment), and (3) terminal (preterminal, death, mourning, and resolution of loss). The crisis phase occurs when symptoms are present but a diagnosis has not yet been made, and it describes the period of adjustment right after a patient receives a definitive diagnosis. Rolland (1999) notes that during the crisis phase, mental health and healthcare providers can have a significant impact on how family members view the illness. The chronic phase is the ongoing experience of coping with the illness (e.g., treatment, monitoring) post crisis phase. If an illness reaches the terminal phase, "the inevitability of death becomes apparent and dominates family life" (p. 248).

Parental Illness and the FSI Model

Rolland (1994a,b, 2005) wrote about the FSI model in the context of parental illness and disability. He emphasized the importance of attending to the family's life cycle phase; for example, parental illness while raising young children is not a normative or expected occurrence. Thus, families are likely to experience additional stress if the demands of the parental illness interfere with typical developmental tasks and family routines (e.g., having children, guiding children through their own milestones, preparing to launch children) during this phase (Rolland, 1999). The ill parent may not be able to fully share parenting responsibilities with the healthy parent the same way he or she could before the illness; single parents may struggle if they do not have help from other family members for support. The illness could also affect a couple's timeline for having children or the number of children they have.

As children become adolescents and begin to individuate from their parents, they may feel conflicted because of a desire to spend more time with peers versus the parent and the corresponding needs of the family (Rolland, 1999). Rolland (1999) also said that how a couple handles and communicates about the illness can affect how their children are able to cope with the illness; when parents have more open communication about the illness and their relationship, children are better able to adapt as well. Open communication between parents and children benefits children who are coping with a parent's illness; children's anxiety can be decreased when parents provide age-appropriate information about the illness and its impact (Rolland, 1999) (see Chapter 13 for more details).

Families coping with parental illness may have the tendency to see the illness as the sick parent's issue; however, it is more adaptive and beneficial for all family members when it is reframed as a family challenge so everyone can work together (Rolland, 1999). Nonetheless, it is important that the familial relationships (couple, parent–child, siblings) do not become defined by the illness. Rolland (1999) notes that "therapists can help family members to learn how to circumscribe the time and space occupied by the condition in their relationships . . . [and] keep the illness in its place" (p. 259) (see Chapter 13 for more details).

Providers using FSI should first consider who (couple, parent–child, patient/family–healthcare team) should be included in therapy sessions or excluded and why. They should first meet with parents to find out what topics are off limits with children at home and why, as well as explore the communication and parenting styles with children and adolescents at home (Rolland, 1999). For example, there is no evidence that children or youth are hurt by gradual age-appropriate information about the parent's illness; blocked communication is associated with feelings of isolation, anxiety, and depression for family members. Additionally, older youth might benefit from meeting with the healthcare team so they are better informed and feel less anxious about the course of the parent's treatment, especially with single parents who rely on older children to care for younger children at home and help out with family routines. Rolland (1999) recommends a range of family consultations depending on the presenting issues in the family. For instance, he suggests meeting with family during crucial transition points (such as a change in prognosis) and conducting psychosocial check-ups with family members throughout treatment.

It is important to understand multigenerational family patterns regarding past experiences with illness (Rolland, 1987a), such as individual and family development; multigenerational experiences with illness and loss, including stories of resilience; current timing of the parental illness with regard to the family's life cycle (newly formed couple, new parents, parenting school age/adolescent children, launching adult children); and the impact of the illness on future individual and family life cycle planning. Rolland recommends asking families the following questions to understand the multigenerational experiences with illness: (1) How did the family organize itself as a system in response to any prior illness, loss, and crisis, and how did this system evolve over time? (2) What did family members learn from those experiences? (3) What are learned differences among key family members (Rolland, 1999)? Providers should also illicit family members' health beliefs to understand how the family creates meaning for the parental illness experience, and then try to facilitate competency and mastery. Some beliefs to examine among family members are: (1) mind–body relationship, (2) control and mastery, (3) beliefs about the cause of the parental illness (e.g., punishment for sins, blame on self or family member, genetic link to parent, injustice, bad luck), (4) course and outcome, (5) ethnic and cultural beliefs (e.g., control, appropriate sick role, kind and degree of open communication, who is in caretaking system, normative illness rituals), (6) spirituality, and (7) communication style among family members (Rolland, 1999).

Sieh, Dikkers, Visser-Meily, and Meijer (2012) conducted a study with Dutch families coping with parents' chronic medical conditions using the FSI model (Rolland, 1984, 1987a,b, 1988, 1994a,b, 1999, 2005). The researchers explored the link between adolescents' stress levels and parental illness type. Sieh et al. (2012) noted the FSI model views illness with regard to illness type and family functioning; different chronic illnesses differ from each other in terms of onset, course, disability, level, outcome, and stage of illness. Their results support the FSI model; family functioning (based on quality of the marital relationship, parent–child interaction, and parent–child attachment) was significantly associated with adolescents' stress levels, but the parents' illness types were not associated with stress level. This latter finding may be due to the fact that only families in the chronic phase were included in this study, and "the stressors associated with the crisis stage of a less severe condition could easily generate more strain on a family system than the chronic phase of a more serious condition" (Sieh et al., 2012, p. 603).

Conclusions

Attachment theory, the FSI model, and a family-centered approach to care complement each other. The FSI model focuses on family functioning and parent–child relationships, which are important factors regarding how families adapt to chronic illnesses, whereas attachment theory more deeply considers the nature of children's relationships to their parents. The FSI model adds to attachment theory by acknowledging the larger family system that the parent–child relationship is part of, as well as the context of the various dimensions of the chronic illness and time (the family life cycle, culture, spirituality). By using attachment theory and the FSI model, providers can better understand and attend to the complex dynamics among families who are coping with an ill parent and utilize a family-centered approach to care.

References

Ainsworth, M. D. S., & Bell, S. M. (1970). Attachment, exploration, and separation: Illustrated by the behavior of one-year-olds in a strange situation. *Child Development, 41*, 49–67.

Ainsworth, M. D. S., Blehar, M. C., Waters, E., & Wall, S. (1978). *Patterns of attachment: A psychological study of the Strange Situation.* Hillsdale, NJ: Erlbaum.

Armistead, L., Klein, K., & Forehand, R. (1995). Parental physical illness and child functioning. *Clinical Psychology Review, 15*(5), 409–422.

Armsden, G. C., & Lewis, F. M. (1993). The child's adaptation to parental medical illness: Theory and clinical implications. *Patient Education and Counseling, 22*(3), 153–165. doi:10.1016/0738-3991(93)90095-E

Beardselee, W. R., Versage, E. M., & Gladstone, T. R. G. (1998). Children of affectively ill parents: A review of the past 10 years. *Journal of the American Academy of Child & Adolescent Psychiatry, 37*(11), 1134–1141. doi:10.1097/00004583-199811000-00012

Bowlby, J. (1969/1982). *Attachment and loss: Vol. 1: Attachment.* New York: Basic Books.

Bowlby, J. (1973). *Attachment and loss: Vol. 2: Separation.* New York: Basic Books.

Bowlby, J. (1980). *Attachment and loss, Vol. 3: Loss, sadness and depression.* New York: Basic Books.

Bowlby, J. (1988). *A secure base: Parent-child attachment and healthy human development.* New York: Basic Books.

Caffery, T., & Erdman, P. (2003). Attachment and family systems theories: Implications for family therapists. *Journal of Systemic Therapies, 22*(2), 3–15. doi:10.1521/jsyt.22.2.3.23346

Diareme, S., Tsiantis, J., Romer, G., Tsalamanios, E., Anasontzi, S., Paliokosta, E., & Kolaitis, G. (2007). Mental health support for children of parents with somatic illness: A review of the theory and intervention concepts. *Families, Systems, & Health, 25*(1), 98–118. doi:10.1037/1091-7527.25.1.98

DiGioia, A., Greenhouse, P. K., & Levison, T. J. (2007). Patient and family-centered collaborative care: An orthopaedic model. *Clinical Orthopaedics and Related Research, 463*, 13.

Duke, N. N., & Scal, P. B. (2011). Adult care transitioning for adolescents with special health care needs: A pivotal role for family centered care. *Maternal and Child Health Journal, 15*(1), 98–105.

Feeney, J. A. (2000). Implications of attachment style for patterns of health and illness. *Child: Care, Health and Development, 26*(4), 277–288. doi:10.1046/j.1365-2214.2000.00146.x

Feeney, J. A., & Ryan, S. M. (1994). Attachment style and affect regulation: Relationships with health behavior and family experiences of illness in a student sample. *Health Psychology, 13*(4), 334–345. doi:10.1037/0278-6133.13.4.334

Institute of Medicine. (2001). *Committee on quality health care in America. Crossing the quality chasm: A new health system for the 21st century.* Washington, DC: National Academies Press.

Ireland, M., & Pakenham, K. (2010). Youth adjustment to parental illness or disability: The role of illness characteristics, caregiving, and attachment. *Psychology, Health & Medicine, 15*(6), 632–645. doi:10.1080/13548506.2010.498891

Johnson, B. H. (2000). Family-centered care: Four decades of progress. *Families, Systems, & Health, 18*(2), 137.

Lyons-Ruth, K., & Jacobvitz, D. (1999). Attachment disorganization: Unresolved loss, relational violence, and lapses in behavioral and attentional strategies. *Infant Medical Health Journal, 25*(4), 318–335.

Main, M., & Solomon, J. (1990). Procedures for identifying infants as disorganized/disoriented during the Ainsworth Strange Situation. *Attachment in the preschool years: Theory, research, and intervention, 1*, 121–160.

Martire, L. M., Lustig, A. P., Schulz, R., Miller, G. E., & Helgeson, V. S. (2004). Is it beneficial to involve a family member? A meta-analysis of psychosocial interventions for chronic illness. *Health Psychology, 23*(6), 599–611.

McDaniel, S. H., Campbell, T. L., Hepworth, J., & Lorenz, A. (2005). *Family-oriented primary care*. New York: Springer Science & Business Media.

Meijer, A. M., Oort, F. J., Visser-Meily, J. M. A., & Sieh, D. S. (2014). Mediators for internalizing problems in adolescents of parents with chronic medical condition. *Journal of Developmental and Physical Disabilities, 26*(1), 67–82. doi:10.1007/s10882-013-9345-1

Ødegård, W. (2005). Chronic illness as a challenge to the attachment process. *Clinical Child Psychology and Psychiatry, 10*(1), 13–22. doi:10.1177/1359104505048787

Pakenham, K. I., & Cox, S. (2014). The effects of parental illness and other ill family members on the adjustment of children. *Annals of Behavioral Medicine, 48*(3), 424–437. doi:10.1007/s12160-014-9622-y

Peek, C. J. (2008). Planning care in the clinical, operational, and financial worlds. In R. Kessler & D. Stafford (Eds.), *Collaborative medicine case studies* (pp. 25–38). New York: Springer.

Peterson, A. M., Takiya, L., & Finley, R. (2003). Meta-analysis of trials of interventions to improve medication adherence. *American Journal of Health and Systemic Pharmacology, 60*, 657–665.

Rajecki, D. W., Lamb, M. E., & Obmascher, P. (1978). Toward a general theory of infantile attachment: A comparative review of aspects of the social bond. *Behavioral and Brain Sciences, 1*(3), 417–436. doi:10.1017/S0140525X00075816

Rolland, J. S. (1984). Toward a psychosocial typology of chronic and life-threatening illness. *Family Systems Medicine, 2*, 245–263.

Rolland, J. S. (1987a). Chronic illness and the life cycle: A conceptual framework. *Family Process, 26*(2), 203–221. doi:10.1111/j.1545-5300.1987.00203.x

Rolland, J. S. (1987b). Family illness paradigms: Evolution and significance. *Family Systems Medicine, 5*(4), 482–503. doi:10.1037/h0089735

Rolland, J. S. (1988). A conceptual model of chronic and life-threatening illness and its impact on the family. In C. Chilman, E. Nunnally, & F. Cox (Eds.), *Chronic illness and disability* (pp. 17–68). Beverly Hills, CA: Sage Publications.

Rolland, J. S. (1994a). *Families, illness, and disability: An integrative treatment model*. New York: Basic Books.

Rolland, J. S. (1994b). In sickness and in health: The impact of illness on couples' relationships. *Journal of Marital and Family Therapy, 20*(4), 327–347. doi:10. 1111/j.1752-0606.1994.tb00125.x

Rolland, J. S. (1999). Parental illness and disability: A family systems framework. *Journal of Family Therapy, 21*(3), 242–266. doi:10.1111/1467-6427.00118

Rolland, J. S. (2005). Cancer and the family: An integrative model. *Cancer, 104*(S11), 2584–2595. doi:10.1002/cncr.21489

Sieh, D. S., Dikkers, A. L. C., Visser-Meily, J. M. A., & Meijer, A. M. (2012). Stress in adolescents with a chronically ill parent: Inspiration from Rolland's family systems-illness model. *Journal of Developmental and Physical Disabilities, 24*(6), 591–606. doi:10.1007/s10882-012-9291-3

Sieh, D. S., Visser-Meily, J. M. A., & Meijer, A. M. (2013). Differential outcomes of adolescents with chronically ill and healthy parents. *Journal of Child and Family Studies, 22*(2), 209–218. doi:10.1007/s10826-012-9570-8

Simpson, J. A., Collins, W. A., Tran, S., & Haydon, K. C. (2007). Attachment and the experience and expression of emotions in romantic relationships: A developmental perspective. *Journal of Personality and Social Psychology, 92*(2), 355–367. doi:10.1037/0022-3514.92.2.355

Walsh, F. (2002). A family resilience framework: Innovative practice applications. *Family relations, 51*(2), 130–137.

PART II

PARENTAL ILLNESSES

CHAPTER 3

PARENTAL DEPRESSION

Laura Lynch

An estimated 7.5 million parents are currently coping with depression in the U.S., and approximately 15 million children have a parent who has depression (National Research Council and Institute of Medicine, 2009). It is important to note that depression does not automatically mean an individual cannot be a good parent; however, if the depression is not treated and the family is not supported, it can have long-lasting and negative effects on children. Although depression is a mental health condition, we decided to include it in our book because across all types of parental medical illnesses, comorbid depression is common for up to 2 years after diagnosis and can negatively impact both parents and their offspring. Providers working with families who are coping with parental illness will often encounter depressive symptoms or depression and should understand how it can affect families.

Depression: About the Illness

Prevalence

Depression is a mental health condition characterized by low mood and/or anhedonia, defined as the loss of interest or pleasure in previously pleasurable activities that persists for two or more weeks (APA, 2013); it affects many individuals in the U.S. and worldwide. According to the CDC's (2012) analysis of the National Health and Nutrition Examination Survey (NHANES) data from 2007 to 2010, almost 8% of individuals in the United States (ages 12 and above) met the criteria for "current depression." "Current depression" describes individuals who meet the criteria for depression based on their score on the Patient Health Questionnaire, which asks about depressive symptoms in the past 2 weeks (CDC, 2012). Approximately 4.1% of these individuals will be diagnosed with major depressive disorder criteria. According to the Substance Abuse and Mental Health Services Administration's (SAMHSA, 2013) 2012 National Survey on Drug Use and Health, approximately 16 million adults, or 6.9% of the U.S. population, have experienced one or more episodes of major depression in the past 12 months.

There are significant health disparities (e.g., age, gender, race, ethnicity, SES, marital status) in the incidence of depression. Young adults (ages 18–25) report the highest rates of major depressive episodes in the past year with a prevalence rate of 8.7% (SAMHSA, 2013). This age group is followed by 26- to 49-year-olds, who have a 7.6% prevalence, and then people aged 50 years and older, who have a 5.1% prevalence rate (SAMHSA, 2013). Racial minorities, particularly Black and Hispanic individuals, have a significantly higher incidence of depression compared to Whites (Pratt & Brody, 2014). According to SAMHSA (2013), individuals who identified as having two or more races have the highest incidence (11.4%) of a major depressive episode in the past 12 months. This group was followed in incidence rates by individuals who identified as American Indian or Alaska Native (8.9%), White individuals (7.3%), Hispanic individuals (5.8%), Black individuals (4.6%), Asian individuals (4.0%), and Native Hawaiian/Other Pacific Islander (1.6%).

There is a significantly higher incidence of depression among women compared to men (see Figure 3.1); in 2013, approximately 8.1% of women and 5.1% of men had a major depressive episode in the last 12 months (SAMHSA, 2013). There are also socioeconomic disparities related to depression. Individuals living below the poverty line are significantly more likely to experience depression than those living at or above the poverty line (Pratt & Brody, 2014). According to the National Center for Health Statistics (2012), from 2005 until 2010, adults living below the poverty level had an incidence of depression more than four times higher than adults whose family incomes fell at or above 400% of the poverty level. Noteworthy, low-income mothers have significantly high rates of depression compared to higher-income mothers (Beardslee, Versage, & Giadstone, 1998). Conversely, there is significantly less depression among adults who have college degrees compared to individuals with lower levels of education (including less than high school, high school, and some college levels of education) (SAMHSA, 2013).

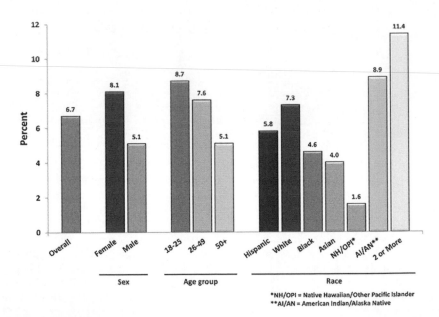

Figure 3.1 12-Month Prevalence of Major Depressive Episode among U.S. Adults (2013)

Source: U.S. Department of Health and Human Services, National Institutes of Health, National Institute of Mental Health. (2013). Major depression among adults. Data courtesy of SAMHSA. Retrieved from www.nimh.nih.gov/health/statistics/prevalence/major-depression-among-adults.shtml

Symptoms and Medical Outcomes

Depressive symptoms can include low mood, loss of interest or pleasure, appetite changes, weight changes, sleep changes, low energy, difficulty concentrating, feelings of guilt or worthlessness, restlessness, and suicidal ideation (APA, 2013). Depending on the severity and length of the depressive symptoms, an individual can be diagnosed with a depressive disorder, such as major depressive disorder. In the next section, the different types of depression are described according to the DSM-V (APA, 2013).

Types of Depression

There are different types of depressive disorders classified by the American Psychological Association's DSM-V (APA, 2013). In this chapter, we focus primarily on depressive disorders that tend to co-occur with parental medical illnesses.

Major Depressive Disorder

Major depressive disorder (MDD) is diagnosed when an individual has experienced depressed mood and/or anhedonia in addition to four other depressive symptoms almost daily for at least 2 weeks. An individual must have no history of manic or hypomanic episodes to receive this diagnosis. A manic episode is characterized by a period of abnormally and persistently elevated, expansive, or irritable mood lasting for at least 1 week with at least three additional related symptoms. A hypomanic episode is characterized by a distinct period similar to a manic episode but with less intense symptoms and a shorter duration of 4 days (APA, 2013). MDD can last indefinitely, or the major depressive episode can lead to periods of remission for at least 2 months with little to no symptoms (APA, 2013).

Persistent Depressive Disorder

In the DSM-V (APA, 2013), persistent depressive disorder is a newer diagnosis that combines the previous DSM-IV-TR (APA, 2000) diagnoses of chronic major depressive disorder and dysthymic disorder, which is a milder but chronic type of depression. A persistent depressive disorder diagnosis describes an individual who is experiencing depressed mood almost daily for most of the day, for a minimum of 2 years, along with at least two of the following symptoms: (1) increased or decreased appetite, (2) difficulty sleeping or sleeping too much, (3) decreased energy or tiredness, (4) low self-esteem, (5) poor concentration or indecisiveness, and (6) feelings of hopelessness (APA, 2013). Symptoms must have a significant impact on psychosocial functioning (e.g., work performance, close relationships). Additionally, if an individual has experienced a remission in symptoms during a 2-year or longer period, it cannot be for more than 2 months. If an individual meets the criteria for persistent depressive disorder and also meets the criteria for a major depressive disorder, then persistent depressive disorder is diagnosed, with the proviso that MDD is also present.

Depressive Disorder Due to Another Medical Condition

Depressive disorder due to another medical condition is diagnosed when there is significant and persistent depressed mood or anhedonia and when "there is evidence from the history, physical examination, or laboratory findings that this disturbance is the direct pathophysiological consequence of another medical condition" (APA, 2013, p. 180). In order to receive this diagnosis, symptoms cannot be exclusive to an episode of delirium, cannot be better explained by another mental health diagnosis, and have a negative psychosocial impact (APA, 2013). Examples of chronic illness that can result in this diagnosis are: (1) stroke, (2) Huntington's disease, (3) traumatic brain injury, (4) Parkinson's disease, and (5) hypothyroidism (APA, 2013).

Other Specified Depressive Disorder and Unspecified Depressive Disorder

Individuals can be given a diagnosis of other specified depressive disorder or unspecified depressive disorder if they experience depressive symptoms that are significant but do not fully meet the criteria for another depressive disorder because of the number and duration of symptoms (APA, 2013). The experience of significant depressive symptoms that fit a specific depressive disorder category has been described as minor depression in the co-morbid depression and illness literature.

Depression can have negative health consequences for patients. Patients coping with depression as well as a physical illnesses tend to have worse illness outcomes, such as lower levels of overall physical health, more illness burden, and higher mortality rates (Chiang et al., 2015; Katon, Lin, & Kroenke, 2007; McCusker, Cole, Ciampi, Latimer, Windholz, & Belzile, 2007; van Dijk et al., 2015). Co-morbid depression can also affect how individuals experience and cope with a chronic physical illness; depression can negatively impact patients' perceptions of their illness severity (Hurt, Weinman, & Brown, 2009; Walker, Lindner, & Noonan, 2009) and their healthcare utilization (Snell, Fernandes, Bujoreanu, & Garcia, 2014). Noteworthy, researchers report that depressed individuals are at a higher risk for developing physical illnesses in general (Holahan, Pahl, Cronkite, Holahan, North, & Moos, 2010; Patten et al., 2008).

Depression can also contribute to decreased overall self-care and poor adherence to medical treatment, which has negative consequences for health (Katon, 2003). For example, there is a significant link between depression and other unhealthy behaviors (e.g., smoking, lack of exercise, poor diet) (Appelhans et al., 2012; Chang, Lin, Wang, Fan, Chou, & Chen, 2013; Ellis, Orom, Giovino, & Kiviniemi, 2015; Husky, Mazure, Paliwal, & McKee, 2008; Rosal et al., 2001).

Suicide

Suicide is defined by the CDC as "death that has been caused by self-directed injurious behavior with any intent to die as a result of the behavior" (CDC, 2015a). Suicide is the 10th leading cause of death in the U.S. (National Center for Injury Prevention and Control, CDC, 2013), and depression is a significant risk factor for suicide (Mayo Clinic, 2015). Suicidal ideation is one of the symptoms of depression, and if it is not addressed, there is a risk that suicidal thoughts will escalate into a suicidal plan and/or action. From 2005 to 2009, the suicide rates were highest among American Indian/Alaskan Natives and non-Hispanic Whites (National Center for Injury Prevention and Control, CDC, 2013). In 2013, the age-adjusted suicide rate for Whites was 14.19 per 100,000, for American Indian/Alaskan Natives it was 11.65, for Asian/Pacific Islanders it was 5.82, and for Black individuals it was 5.39 (National Center for Injury Prevention and Control, 2013). (We want to note that these racial groups included all individuals who identified as Hispanic or non-Hispanic because Hispanic was not considered a separate racial category.)

In addition, despite the statistic that more women are diagnosed with depression compared to men, significantly more men commit suicide (CDC, 2015b).

Psychological Comorbidities

Depression often co-occurs with other psychiatric conditions. There is a significant association between mood disorders (e.g., major depressive disorder) and anxiety disorders, especially posttraumatic stress disorder, generalized anxiety disorder, obsessive-compulsive disorder, and social phobia (Brown et al., 2001). Depression often co-occurs with substance use (Currie & Wang, 2005; Mueller et al., 1994) and personality disorders (Fava, Fabbri, & Sonino, 2002; Luca, Luca, & Calandra, 2012). More than 30% of patients diagnosed with major depressive disorder have a comorbid substance use disorder, such as alcohol dependence (Davis, Uezato, Newell, & Frazier, 2008). Researchers also suggest that comorbid personality disorders can negatively affect depression treatment (Newton-Howes, Tyrer, & Johnson, 2006; Grilo et al., 2010).

Diagnosis and Prognosis

Depression is often diagnosed by primary care providers, but it can also be diagnosed by other healthcare or mental healthcare providers. Depression is diagnosed when specific criteria for depressive disorders are clinically observed or reported by a patient, as outlined in the fifth edition of the *Diagnostic and Statistical Manual of Mental Disorders* (APA, 2013); however, the course of depression can vary.

Multiple factors contribute to the course of depression. A younger age of onset of depression, a family history of mood disorders, and a longer length of depressive episodes are all risk factors for developing chronic depression, which is defined as long-term depression without periods of full remission (Hölzel, Härter, Reese, & Kriston, 2011). Individuals who experience trauma in childhood tend to have more chronic depression and fewer remissions (Barnhofer, Brennan, Crane, Duggan, & Williams, 2014; Kaplan & Klinetob, 2000). Additionally, the occurrence of negative life events (e.g., job loss, death of a loved one) is associated with a more chronic course of depression and a longer period of time to the first remission. Cronkite et al. (2013) reported that the severity of depression based on initial levels of depressive symptoms and course was common among individuals who had more chronic medical conditions, less psychological flexibility (e.g., low levels of happiness, calm, and positive disposition), and who tended to use avoidance to cope with stress.

Personality traits have a salient role in the development of depression and its course. For example, Cloninger, Svrakic, and Przybeck, (2006) reported that the trait of self-directedness ("a person's degree of cognitive coherence and reality testing which facilitate a person to be responsible, purposeful, resourceful, self-accepting, and hopeful," p. 41) was a protective factor for developing depression; a decrease in the level of self-directedness was associated with negative mood changes. Additionally, Steunenberg, Beekman, Deeg, and Kerkhof (2010) reported an association between depressive episode recurrence and high levels of the personality trait of neuroticism, which is characterized by a tendency toward negative emotions and thinking and low levels of the trait of mastery ("the extent to which individuals consider themselves to be in control of their own lives," p. 166).

Most individuals who have a major depressive episode will experience a remission of depressive symptoms within 12 months (Whiteford et al., 2013). Without any treatment for depression, it is estimated that approximately 23% of depressed individuals will experience remission of their symptoms within 3 months, 32% of individuals within 6 months, and 53% individuals within 12 months. Yet, each depressive episode increases the chance of a recurrence of depression, and the longer an episode lasts, the lower the likelihood of recovery from the depressive symptoms (Richards, 2011). The longer the remission period after a major depressive episode, the lower the likelihood of a recurrence (Solomon et al., 2000). Approximately 15% of individuals who experienced an episode of major depression later had subsequent episodes without experiencing even a single 12-month period of remission over the course of 23 years (Eaton et al., 2008). Yet, an estimated 50% of participants had no recurrences after their first episode of depression (Eaton et al., 2008).

Treatment

Recent meta-analyses suggest that episodes of depression can be prevented with treatment (Cuijpers, Beckman, & Reynolds, 2012; Cuijpers, Von Strategn, Smit, Miahlopoulous, & Beckman, 2008). There are many safe and effective strategies in a wide range of community and clinical settings (e.g., primary care, community mental health) for treating adults with elevated symptoms of major depression, including: (1) medication, (2) cognitive behavioral therapy, and (3) interpersonal therapy (Cuijpers et al., 2012). Depression is often treated with antidepressants, psychotherapy, or a combination of both. Electroconvulsive therapy is a treatment that can be used to treat more severe, treatment-resistant depression (NIMH, n.d.). Next, different types of treatments for depression are summarized.

Medication

Several classes of medications have been developed to treat depression. Approximately 10.8% of individuals in the U.S. over the age of 12 take antidepressant medications (Pratt, Brody, and Gu, 2011) (see Figure 3.2 for a breakdown by sex and age). Selective serotonin reuptake inhibitors (SSRIs) are the class of antidepressants most commonly prescribed by healthcare providers to treat depression. SSRIs prevent serotonin, a chemical released in the brain, from being reabsorbed in the brain, keeping an individual's serotonin levels higher; serotonin levels affect mood. Common drugs in this classification include: (1) citalopram, (2) escitalopram, (3) fluoxetine, (4) paroxetine, and (5) sertraline; these tend to have fewer side effects compared to other types of antidepressants (Mayo Clinic, 2013c). Individuals who experience side effects while taking SSRIs typically experience them temporarily. Side effects (see Table 3.1) can include: (1) nausea and/or vomiting, (2) nervousness or restlessness, (3) dizziness, (4) sexual issues, (5) drowsiness, (6) difficulty sleeping, (7) weight changes, (8) headache, (9) dry mouth, and (10) diarrhea (Mayo Clinic, 2013c).

Serotonin and norepinephrine reuptake inhibitors (SNRIs) are a newer class of antidepressant medications that are similar to SSRIs. They prevent the reabsorption of both norepinephrine (another chemical released in the brain affecting mood) and serotonin. Duloxetine, venlafaxine, desvenlafaxine, and levomilnacipran are SNRIs. They are similar to SSRIs and also tend to be well-tolerated with fewer side effects (www.mayoclinic.org/diseases-conditions/depression/in-depth/antidepressants/art-20044970). Side effects (see Table 3.1) for this class

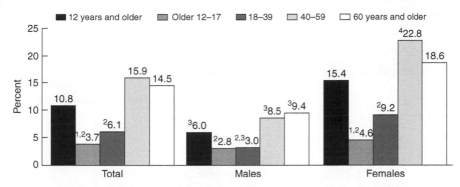

Figure 3.2 Percentage of Persons Aged 12 and over Who Take Antidepressant Medication, by Age and Sex: United States, 2005–2008

[1] Significantly different from age group 18–39.

[2] Significantly different from age groups 40–59 and 60 and older.

[3] Significantly different from females.

[4] Significantly different from age group 60 and older.

Source: Reprinted from Pratt, L.A., Brody, D.J., & Gu, Q. (2011). Antidepressant use in persons aged 12 and over: United States, 2005–2008. NCHS data brief, no 76. Hyattsville, MD: National Center for Health Statistics. Retrieved from www.cdc.gov/nchs/data/data briefs/db76.htm

of medication can include: (1) nausea, (2) dry mouth, (3) dizziness, (4) excessive sweating, (5) fatigue, (6) urination issues, (7) anxiety, (8) constipation, (9) difficulty sleeping, (10) sexual issues, (11) headaches, and (12) poor appetite (Mayo Clinic, 2013d).

Monoamine oxidase inhibitors (MAOIs) stop monoamine oxidase, which is an enzyme, from breaking down chemicals in the brain (norepinephrine, serotonin, and dopamine), leading to improved mood (Mayo Clinic, 2013b). MAOIs include: (1) tranylcypromine, (2) phenelzine, (3) isocarboxazid, and (4) selegiline. This was the first class of medications developed to treat depression, but they are now utilized to treat depression after all other types of antidepressants have failed (Mayo Clinic, 2013b). MAOIs tend to cause more severe side effects compared to other classes of medications, and they also require adherence to a special diet and the avoidance of some types of medications to prevent blood pressure from increasing (NIMH, n.d.).

Trycyclic antidepressants (TCAs) are an older class of antidepressants. Similar to SSRIs and SNRIs, TCAs prevent the reabsorption of mood-affecting chemicals in the brain, specifically serotonin and epinephrine. TCAs include: (1) amitriptyline, (2) amoxapine, (3) desipramine, (4) doxepin, (5) imipramine, (6) nortriptyline, (7) protriptyline, and (8) trimipramine (Mayo Clinic, 2013e). This class of medication tends to cause more side effects compared to SSRIs or SNRIs, which can include: (1) dry mouth, (2) blurred vision, (3) constipation, (4) urinary issues, (5) fatigue, (6) increased appetite, (7) low blood pressure, (8) sweating, (9) confusion, (10) tremors, (11) heart rate changes, (12) sexual issues, and (13) an increase in seizures in individuals with a seizure history (Mayo Clinic, 2013e).

Atypical antidepressants are those that do not fit under any other antidepressant drug class. These medications include: (1) buproprion, (2) trazodone, (3) mirtazapine,

Table 3.1 Side Effects and Medications

Side Effect	Medicines Most Likely to Cause This Side Effect
Nausea/vomiting	• Venlafaxine (Effexor®, Effexor XR®) • Paroxetine (Paxil®)
Weight gain o Between 2 and 7 pounds in 6 to 8 weeks	• Mirtazapine (Remeron®, Remeron SolTab®)
Diarrhea	• Sertraline (Zoloft®)
Sleepiness	• Trazodone (Desyrel®)

**Sexual problems (such as
   decreased sex drive or
   difficulty getting an erection)**
	• Paroxetine (Paxil®, Paxil CR®)
	• Escitalopram (Lexapro®), fluoxetine
	  (Prozac®, Prozac Weekly®), paroxetine
	  (Paxil®, Paxil CR®), and sertraline (Zoloft®)
	  had more sexual side effects than bupropion
	  (Wellbutrin®, Wellbutrin SR®, Wellbutrin XL®)

Source: Humphries, A., Smith, A., Workman, T., Jurdi R. A., & Fordis, M. (2012). Medicines for treating depression: A review of the research for Adults. Agency for Healthcare Research and Quality. Retrieved from http://effectivehealthcare.ahrq.gov/ehc/index.cfm/search-for-guides-reviews-and-reports/?pageAction=displayProduct&productID=1142. Reproduced with permission from Agency for Healthcare Research and Quality.

and (4) vortioxetine. They affect dopamine, serotonin, and norepinephrine levels; each type of medication has different side effects. Buproprion is often prescribed because it causes less sexual and weight side effects (Mayo Clinic, 2013a).

Electroconvulsive Therapy

Electroconvulsive therapy (ECT) is a treatment in which electrical impulses are administered to the brain. An individual receives this treatment under anesthesia. ECT treatment takes a few minutes to complete. An individual usually receives three treatments per week, and typically 6 to 12 treatments total (University of Michigan Department of Psychiatry, 2015). Side effects tend to be only temporary and can include confusion, disorientation, and memory loss (NIMH, n.d.).

Psychotherapy

Cognitive behavioral therapy (CBT) and interpersonal therapy (IPT) are two evidence-based psychotherapy models that help to treat depression (NIMH, n.d.). CBT clinicians use interventions to restructure individuals' negative thoughts and related behaviors to create more realistic, adaptive thoughts and positive behaviors (Sudak, 2012). IPT clinicians work with clients to identify and reframe the presenting issue as an interpersonal problem and then focus on increasing the client's social support, decreasing the client's interpersonal distress, helping the client process his or her emotions, and increasing the client's interpersonal skills (Lipsitz & Markowitz, 2013). Researchers have also reported that couples therapy is as effective as individual therapy for decreasing depressive symptoms (Barbato & D'Avanzo, 2008). There is also some support for the effectiveness of family therapy to treat depression, but randomized controlled trials are needed for it to be considered an evidence-based intervention for treating depression (Henken et al., 2007).

Level of Uncertainty about the Depression

Depression can lead to high levels of uncertainty for individuals diagnosed with it and their families. When the depression is first diagnosed by a medical or mental healthcare provider, many report feeling relieved to finally have a definitive diagnosis; many parents report feeling uncertain regarding what the depressive disorder diagnosis means for their quality of life and their families. The depressed individual and their family members often worry about the stigma of the diagnosis and treatment (e.g., psychotropic medication, therapy) (Latalova, Kamaradova, & Prasko, 2014; Oakley, Kanter, Taylor, & Duguid, 2012). Family members often feel confused about what is causing the depressive symptoms and how it will affect their relationships and current roles in the family (Knobloch & Delaney, 2012). Daily life may become unpredictable as family members are unsure how the depressed individual will feel or react (e.g., irritable, sad, unable to resume daily routines or parenting) (Ahlström, Skärsäter, & Danielson, 2009).

As previously described, an individual may experience one or multiple major depressive episodes throughout his/her lifetime; an individual can experience a period of remission after a major depressive episode. Persistent depressive disorder is a long-term course of depression. Depressive symptoms can be managed or resolved depending on the success of the medication and/or psychotherapy treatment. Unfortunately, there is no guarantee that depression will not reoccur or worsen, even after it has been successfully treated. Consequently, parents and families may worry about the recurrence of depressive symptoms, especially children at home and spouses/partners of depressed individuals. When a recurrence does occur, family members may be better prepared because they have a better understanding of depression and how it can be treated (if it was treated before), but they may now worry the depression will never fully be resolved. For more severe depression in which there is suicidal ideation and/or a self-harm history, family members may additionally experience significant distress and worry about the depressed individual's physical safety, as well as his or her mental health.

Impact of Parental Depression on Parents

Parental depression is a significant issue in the U.S.; approximately 15 million children in the U.S. live with parents who have significant symptoms of depression (National Research Council and Institute of Medicine, 2009). Depression can affect an individual's ability to work, maintain relationships, and manage household tasks. Given the psychological and physical symptoms of depression, depressed parents often experience some impaired functioning, less consistency, and lower levels of supervision (Ahlstrom et al., 2009; Brennan et al., 2002). Parenting is a challenging role at the best of times; depression can make it much more difficult and complex. Depressive symptoms such as low mood, feelings of guilt and hopelessness, and low energy can make it tough to carry out parenting tasks and be attuned to children's practical and emotional needs (National Research Council and Institute of Medicine, 2009). More severe depressive symptoms can make effective parenting difficult and lead to negative social, emotional, and behavioral outcomes among children (Jacobs, Warner, & Weissman, 2013; Kouros & Garber, 2010). For example, Geulayov, Metcalfe, Heron, Kidger, and

Gunnell (2014) reported that the number of maternal suicide attempts increased children's risks of suicide attempts and suicidal thoughts.

Mothers who are depressed tend to be more punitive and have lower levels of sensitivity and responsiveness to their children (Murray & Cooper, 2003). Maternal depression has also been associated with less responsiveness to infants (Flykt, Kanninen, Sinkkonen, & Punamäki, 2010); this can be harmful because infancy is a critical time for the development of secure parent–child attachment and child development. Parents who are depressed may also exhibit more inconsistent or extreme parenting styles; they could be overly permissive or highly reactive while parenting (Errázuriz Arellano, Harvey, & Thakar, 2012). Depressed parents may be more irritable and hostile, and they are often less engaged and attuned to their children (Lovejoy, Graczyk, O'Hare, & Neuman, 2000). Although this compromised parenting style can have negative consequences for offspring, parents often report feeling overwhelmed, guilty, and helpless and are unable to address their children's needs while coping with the burden of their own depressive symptoms.

Depression in one partner can also negatively affect marital satisfaction in couples (Kronmüller et al., 2011) and is associated with higher levels of conflict between parents (Fear et al., 2009). Among children with a depressed parent, conflict between parents has been linked to higher levels of anxiety and depression and more aggressive behaviors in children (Fear et al., 2009). Couple conflict is one pathway through which parental depression can affect children, but it is not the only one. Parental depression can also directly impact children (Hanington, Heron, Stein, & Ramchandani, 2012).

What Clinicians Need to Know about Depression

1   Comorbid depression can negatively affect chronic illness outcomes.
2   Depression is associated with poorer marital satisfaction.
3   Antidepressant medication and psychotherapy can decrease depression.
4   Family history of depression is a risk factor for depression.
5   Depressive symptoms include both physical and psychological symptoms.
6   Children and parents may experience or perceive stigma about experiencing parental depression.
7   Parents struggle to parent while coping with depression.

Impact of Parental Depression on Children
Effect on Child Mental Health and Behaviors

Parental depression can lead to an increased risk of children developing psychiatric disorders, including mood, anxiety, and substance abuse disorders, by the time they are young adults (Leis & Mendelson, 2010). Cummings, Cheung, and Davies (2013) reported parental depression increases parents' negative expressiveness toward their children, which in turn can negatively impact children's levels of emotional security and their likelihood of internalizing symptoms (e.g., of depression and anxiety). There is evidence that parental depression is also linked to children's risk of developing externalizing behaviors (e.g., aggressive and antisocial behaviors) (Kouros & Garber, 2010; Piché, Bergeron, Cyr, & Berthiaume, 2011).

Parents' experiences additionally support these findings. Langrock, Compas, Keller, Merchant, and Copeland (2002) examined depressed parents' views of their children's coping with their depression. Parents' reports suggest there was a high incidence of anxiety, depression, and aggressive behaviors among their children. Children also experienced stress related to parental withdrawal behaviors (not as available emotionally/physically to their children) and intrusiveness (e.g., parents who were upset, angry, or easily frustrated).

Paternal Versus Maternal Depression

Researchers and scholars have examined the relationship between maternal depression and negative behavior and mental health outcomes in children (Kim-Cohen, Moffitt, Taylor, Pawlby, & Caspi, 2005). Less frequently examined, although equally important, is the impact of fathers' depression on their children.

Kane and Garber (2009) reported a link between paternal depression and externalizing and internalizing behaviors in children, after controlling for maternal depression. They reported the level of conflict between fathers and children mediated children's externalizing issues; more conflict in relationships between depressed fathers and their children led to more externalizing symptoms in their children. Jacobs et al. (2013) also reported that both maternal and paternal depression are associated with greater risks of internalizing disorders in their children; noteworthy, fathers' depression had a more negative impact if the depression occurred when the child was aged 18 or older, while no difference in child's age at onset was reported for maternal depression.

Connell and Goodman (2002) conducted a meta-analysis to examine the impact of paternal versus maternal psychopathology on child behavior. Parental "psychopathology" in this study included parental depression, but it was combined with studies that included parents with alcohol or substance abuse or dependence, anxiety disorders, schizophrenia, antisocial personality disorder, bipolar disorder, or specific symptoms of mental distress (p. 751). They reported mothers' and fathers' psychopathology were equally associated with their children's externalizing behaviors. They also suggest mothers' psychopathology has a slightly stronger association with internalizing behaviors in children compared to fathers' mental health issues.

Brennan, Hammen, Katz, and Le Brocque (2002) conducted study with a large Australian community sample that examined maternal depression and paternal psychopathology and the impact on adolescents. They reported a link between maternal and paternal depression; when one parent is depressed, the other parent is more likely to also be depressed. When both parents were depressed, adolescent nondepressive externalizing disorders (including ADHD, conduct disorder, oppositional defiant disorder, and substance abuse disorders) significantly increased. Conversely, the impact on children when both mothers and fathers were depressed was no different than when only one parent was depressed.

Differences by Child Age and Gender

The risk for children varies based on age and gender of the child. The impact of parental depression can begin in the prenatal period, when the child is in utero.

Women who are depressed during pregnancy have a higher risk of premature delivery and slower fetal growth (Diego et al., 2009). In infancy and toddler-hood, when parent–child attachment is first developing, parents' depression can increase the likelihood of insecure child–parent attachment styles (Toth, Rogosch, Manly, & Cicchetti, 2006). School-age and adolescent children are also affected by negative parenting behaviors (e.g., lack of warmth, hostility), as discussed in the previous section, and compared to younger children are more likely to view their depressed parents' behaviors and lack of attunement as stressful (National Research Council and Institute of Medicine, 2009). Goodman et al. (2011), in their meta-analysis of studies on maternal depression and child psychopathol-ogy, found that the younger the children, the more they were affected (in terms of internalizing and externalizing problems or other psychopathology) by their mothers' depression.

Girls who grew up with a depressed parent are at a higher risk for experienc-ing depression in adulthood compared to boys (Morris, McGrath, Goldman, & Rottenberg, 2014). Adolescent girls of parents who have had a depressive episode are also more likely to experience depression after stressful life events compared to adolescent boys (Bouma, Ormel, Verhulst, & Oldehinkel, 2008). Yet, Essex, Klein, and Cho (2003) studied depressed mothers who also reported marital con-flict and reported that while female children had more internalizing behaviors, the male children had more externalizing behaviors.

Impact on Children's Views of Self

Parental depression can also negatively impact children's self-esteem. Goodman, Adamson, Riniti, and Cole (1994) reported that mothers with a history of depres-sion are more likely to have negative attitudes toward their children, which can result in children's lower self-esteem. Self-esteem is important, because children of depressed parents who have higher self-esteem are more likely to have long-term positive outcomes (e.g., high functioning, lack of psychiatric diagnosis) (Lewand-owski et al., 2014).

Impact on Parent–Child Attachment

The quality of attachment between depressed parents and their children plays a significant role in how parental depression affects children. There is evidence that children with higher levels of negative attachment to their depressed parents have a greater risk of developing depression themselves (Abela, Zinck, Kryger, Zilber, & Hankin, 2009).

Caretaking Behaviors by Children

As depressed parents become less emotionally and physically available to their chil-dren, their children could become parentified and take on the role of caregivers for their depressed parents (Champion et al., 2009; Van Parys & Rober, 2013). This can include doing more household chores, caring for younger siblings, and making sure a parent gets out of bed in the morning to go to work (Van Parys & Rober, 2013). Children could also become emotional caregivers for their depressed par-ents and withhold their own thoughts and feelings in order to protect their parents; parents may in turn feel guilty about their children assuming caregiving responsi-bilities (Van Parys & Rober, 2013). Champion et al. (2009) studied mothers with a depression history and their adolescent children. They reported adolescents' levels of emotional and instrumental (e.g., taking on household chores) support were associated with adolescents' levels of anxiety and depression; adolescents who assumed more household tasks tended to be distressed. Yet, caregiving behaviors by adolescents are not problematic if parents meet their offsprings' needs and children do not have burdensome levels of responsibilities (Jurkovic, Thirkield, & Morrell, 2001, as cited by Champion et al., 2009).

Abuse and Neglect Risk

Due to the physical and psychological impact of depressive symptoms, depressed parents are at risk for abusive or neglectful behaviors. Turney (2011) reported depressed mothers are more likely to self-report psychological aggression, physical assault, and lower levels of child engagement compared to mothers who were not depressed. Parental depression is also associated with excessive infant crying, which increases the risk of child abuse (van den Berg et al., 2009). In a sample of parents of 3- to 5-year-olds, paternal and maternal depression rates were approximately twice as high in families in which child neglect was present (Lee, Taylor, & Bellamy, 2012). Shay and Knutson (2008) reported "it is the [symptom of] irritability of the depressed mother that contributes to physical abuse" (p. 48).

Child Outcomes with Parental Depression Treatment

Given how parental depression can affect the diagnosed parent, the couple relationship, and the depressed parent's parenting ability, it is not surprising that parental depression can negatively impact children's mental health. On the other hand, effective treatment of parental depressive symptoms can improve child well-being and lower levels of distress. Wickramaratne et al. (2011) examined psychopathology among children of depressed mothers after remission of their depression symptoms and found that the children's symptoms and problem behaviors significantly decreased in the 1-year period after the mothers' depression went into remission. Garber, Ciesla, McCauley, Diamond, and Schloredt (2011) also reported that as parents' depressive symptoms remitted, their children's depressive symptoms also significantly improved.

Overall, prior research suggests clinicians should assess and treat a parent's depressive symptoms, the couple relationship, and the parent–child relationship to minimize the impact of parental depression on the child while providing relief and respite to the often overwhelmed depressed parent.

Impact of Depression on Parents and Children: Main Points

1   Children can be negatively affected by parental depression through increased marital conflict and dissatisfaction and decreased parenting abilities.
2   Children of depressed parents are at a higher risk for internalizing and externalizing behaviors.

(Continued)

3   Child gender and age differentially impact the experience of parental depression.
4   Parental depression can negatively affect parent–child attachment.
5   Parental depression increases the risk of child abuse and neglect.

Cultural Considerations

Similar to parents coping with physical illnesses, attending to the cultural backgrounds of patients and their families is important to consider while treating parental depression. How individuals understand, express, and want to treat depression will differ based on a family's cultural background. For example, Karasz (2005) reported that, compared to European Americans, South American individuals tend to believe depressed feelings are caused by life stress and social/relational issues and they are not perceived as an illness. South Americans tend to address depression by attending to the underlying issue or avoiding negative thoughts about the issue (Karasz, 2005).

Givens, Houston, Van Voorhees, Ford, and Cooper (2007) explored attitudes about depression and depression treatment in a large sample of White, African American, Asian/Pacific Islander, and Hispanic participants. They reported racial and ethnic minority (non-White) participants preferred counseling over medication for depression treatment and were less likely to believe there are biological causes of depression. All ethnic/racial groups were concerned about the stigma of depression; however, Pacific Islanders had more fears about stigma. Black, Gitlin, and Burke (2011) explored how older African Americans experienced depression; many did not view depression treatment as the best way to address it. Instead, most participants preferred to "[resolve] depression meshed with adaptive strategies they used throughout life to deal with negative circumstances, such as reliance on community, church, friendship, prayer, and aloneness" (Black et al., 2011, p. 655).

Depressive symptoms and the descriptions of depression can also vary depending on the culture. Chinese individuals, for example, may be more likely to endorse the physical (somatic) symptoms of depression compared to the psychological ones (Kleinman & Good, 2004; Ryder & Chentsova-Dutton, 2012). Compared to Eastern cultures, Western cultures tend to view positive emotions as healthy and depressed mood as more pathological (Tsai & Chentsova-Dutton, 2002). Western culture also tends to view depression as more biological in nature and as more of an individual/internal issue (Tsai & Chentsova-Dutton, 2002).

Thus, depressive symptoms, language, and meaning can vary across and even within cultural groups. Clinicians should increase their cultural competence by learning how depression is experienced and expressed cross-culturally while remaining curious and willing to learn from each patient's and family's unique story and perspective. Clinicians should try to be flexible enough to allow for "other constructions" of depression (Falicov, 2003, p. 385) so they can avoid overlooking depression in patients from diverse cultures. Dwight-Johnson and Lagomasino (2007) assert that clinicians should ensure that racial and ethnic minority patients are provided with accurate, updated information about treatment options in an understandable format (i.e., in their primary language if they speak a language other than English).

Clinical Context

Depressed patients are more likely to first be diagnosed in primary care medical settings versus mental healthcare settings. Clinicians working in primary care are on the front lines, where they can identify and treat (or refer for treatment) depressed individuals. Even though a depressed adult is likely to come alone to a primary care visit, clinicians should routinely ask about children of depressed patients and ensure the family is being supported, especially children at home and partners/spouses of the depressed patient. Clinicians in outpatient mental health settings and private practice may be referred individuals who have depression, but more often there will be other types of individual, couple, or family presenting problems. Consequently, we recommend that clinicians assess each client, especially all parents coping with medical illnesses, for any underlying depressive symptoms as part of their routine intake assessment. It is important to think about the impact of parental depression on all family members and to stay attuned to any development of depressive symptoms throughout the course of therapy.

Clinical Vignette

The following is a clinical vignette to help you consider how a family coping with parental depression might present clinically.

Tracy is a 27-year-old White single mother who came to her primary care provider's (PCP's) office for an annual well visit. On one of her screening forms, she indicated several depressive symptoms, including low mood most days, anhedonia, difficulty staying asleep, weight gain, low energy, and difficulty concentrating. Tracy's PCP, Dr. Lopez, is particularly concerned about Tracy's significant weight gain given that her BMI was already above average at her last appointment. When Dr. Lopez further assessed Tracy's mood during the appointment, Tracy became tearful. She reported she has been feeling depressed for the past few months. Tracy said she has experienced periods of depression in the past but that they didn't last as long, stating "I just can't shake it this time." Tracy is the primary caretaker for her daughter, Jasmine (age 4), and her boyfriend's daughter, Monique (age 12). Her boyfriend, Charlie (age 31), works the night shift as an airplane mechanic. Tracy reports that she often finds herself crying for no reason, and many days she finds it difficult to make herself get out of bed. She states "it's so hard to run around after Jasmine these days," and she explains that Monique has helped by taking care of Jasmine after school so Tracy can "just lie down." Tracy reports that Charlie is very emotionally supportive of her but that he is not often available to help her with the children due to working many overtime hours.

Tracy's PCP is especially concerned about Tracy's depression and her level of self-care because Tracy's bloodwork has indicated that she is prediabetic. These factors mean that Tracy is at very high risk for developing type 2 diabetes if she does not make significant changes in her diet and exercise. Tracy's PCP offers to prescribe her antidepressants to decrease her depression, but Tracy refuses. She reports that she does not believe in taking medications to help with mood, and she discusses how her family also shares this belief. When the PCP suggests psychotherapy as another means to address Tracy's mood, Tracy hesitantly agrees to try it.

Conclusions

Depression is a pervasive mental health issue in the U.S. and worldwide that has significant consequences for children of depressed parents. Depression and physical illness have a bidirectional relationship; depression increases an individual's risk for developing various physical illnesses, and physical illness increases an individual's risk for developing depression. It is very important for mental healthcare and medical professionals to be aware of this relationship and provide family-centered approaches to health care that attend to the needs of children at home. When working with families coping with a physical illness, psychoeducation should be provided to the parents about the risk and role of depression, and depression screenings should be administered regularly. Clinicians also need to attend to the cultural backgrounds of their clients when assessing for and discussing depression in session; we know that clients' conceptualization and beliefs about depression will vary greatly based on their cultures.

Test Your Knowledge: True or False

1 Depression is more common among men than women.
2 Depression has been associated with negative health outcomes.
3 There are no racial disparities in depression incidence in the U.S.
4 Psychotherapy treatment of depression should only be recommended if medication has failed to manage depressive symptoms.
5 Significant weight loss or gain, anhedonia, and suicidal ideation are all possible symptoms of depression.
6 Depression always co-occurs with a chronic physical illness.
7 Depression can negatively affect the couple relationship.
8 Individuals understandings of and attitudes toward depression are impacted by their cultural backgrounds.

Answers: 1-F, 2-T, 3-F, 4-F, 5-T, 6-F, 7-T, 8-T

Did You Know?

• More than 350 million people globally are coping with depression.
• Depression was historically referred to as "melancholia."
• In 1621, Robert Burton wrote a text called *Anatomy of Melancholy*, in which he explored psychosocial causes of depression.
• Sigmund Freud posited that melancholia was a result of actual or perceived loss.
• One of the first antidepressant medications discovered, iproniazid, was originally developed to treat tuberculosis.
• Antidepressant medications typically take 4 to 6 weeks to start working and improving mood.

Professional Readings and Resources

American Foundation for Suicide Prevention: http://afsp.org
Anxiety and Depression Organization of America: http://adaa.org
National Institute of Mental Health: http://nimh.nih.gov/health/topics/depression/index.shtml
National Research Council and Institute of Medicine. (2009). *Depression in parents, parenting, and children: Opportunities to improve identification, treatment, and prevention*. Washington, DC: National Academies Press.
World Health Organization: http://who.int/topics/depression/en/

References

Abela, J. R., Zinck, S., Kryger, S., Zilber, I., & Hankin, B. L. (2009). Contagious depression: Negative attachment cognitions as a moderator of the temporal association between parental depression and child depression. *Journal of Clinical Child & Adolescent Psychology, 38*(1), 16–26.

Ahlström, B., Skärsäter, I., & Danielson, E. (2009). Living with major depression: Experiences from families' perspectives. *Scandinavian Journal of Caring Sciences, 23*(2), 309–316. doi:10.1111/j.1471-6712.2008.00624.x

American Psychiatric Association. (2000). *Diagnostic and statistical manual of mental disorders* (4th ed., text rev.). Washington, DC: Author. doi:10.1176/appi.books.9780890423349

American Psychiatric Association. (2013). *Diagnostic and statistical manual of mental disorders* (5th ed.). Washington, DC: Author.

Appelhans, B. M., Whited, M. C., Schneider, K. L., Ma, Y., Oleski, J. L., Merriam, P. A., . . . Pagoto, S. L. (2012). Depression severity, diet quality, and physical activity in women with obesity and depression. *Journal of the Academy of Nutrition and Dietetics, 112*(5), 693–698. doi:10.1016/j.jand.2012.02.006

Barbato, A., & D'Avanzo, B. (2008). Efficacy of couple therapy as a treatment for depression: A meta-analysis. *Psychiatric Quarterly, 79*, 121–132. doi:10.1007/s11126-008-9068-0

Barnhofer, T., Brennan, K., Crane, C., Duggan, D., & Williams, J. M. G. (2014). A comparison of vulnerability factors in patients with persistent and remitting lifetime symptom course of depression. *Journal of Affective Disorders, 152–154*, 155–161. doi:10.1016/j.jad.2013.09.001

Beardselee, W. R., Versage, E. M., & Gladstone, T. R. (1998). Children of affectively ill parents: A review of the past 10 years. *Journal of the American Academy of Child & Adolescent Psychiatry, 37*(11), 1134-1141.

Black, H. K., Gitlin, L., & Burke, J. (2011). Context and culture: African-American elders' experiences of depression. *Mental Health, Religion & Culture, 14*(7), 643–657.

Bouma, E. M. C., Ormel, J., Verhulst, F. C., & Oldehinkel, A. J. (2008). Stressful life events and depressive problems in early adolescent boys and girls: The influence of parental depression, temperament and family environment. *Journal of Affective Disorders, 105*(1), 185–193. doi:10.1016/j.jad.2007.05.007

Brennan, P. A., Hammen, C., Katz, A. R., & Le Brocque, R. M. (2002). Maternal depression, paternal psychopathology, and adolescent diagnostic outcomes. *Journal of Consulting and Clinical Psychology, 70*(5), 1075–1085. doi:10.1037/0022-006X.70.5.1075

Brown, R. A., Kahler, C. W., Zvolensky, M. J., Lejuez, C. W., & Ramsey, S. E. (2001). Anxiety sensitivity: Relationship to negative affect smoking and smoking cessation in smokers with past major depressive disorder. *Addictive behaviors, 26*(6), 887–899.

Centers for Disease Control and Prevention (CDC). (2012, January). QuickStats: Prevalence of current depression among persons aged ≥12 years, by age group and sex— United States, national health and nutrition examination survey, 2007–2010. Retrieved from www.cdc.gov/mmwr/preview/mmwrhtml/mm6051a7.htm?s_cid=mm6051a7_w#x2013;%20United%20States,%20National%20Health%20and%20Nutrition%20Examination%20Survey,%202007-2010%3C/a%3F.

Centers for Disease Control and Prevention (CDC). (2015a, August). Definitions: Self-directed violence. Retrieved from www.cdc.gov/violenceprevention/suicide/definitions.html

Centers for Disease Control and Prevention (CDC). (2015b). Suicide: Facts at a glance. doi:10.1037/e572512009-001

Champion, J. E., Jaser, S. S., Reeslund, K. L., Simmons, L., Potts, J. E., Shears, A. R., & Compas, B. E. (2009). Caretaking behaviors by adolescent children of mothers with and without a history of depression. *Journal of Family Psychology, 23*(2), 156.

Chang, C., Lin, M., Wang, J., Fan, J., Chou, L., & Chen, M. (2013). The relationship between geriatric depression and health-promoting behaviors among community-dwelling seniors. *Journal of Nursing Research, 21*(2), 75–82. doi:10.1097/jnr.0b013e3 182921fc9

Chiang, H., Guo, H., Livneh, H., Lu, M., Yen, M., & Tsai, T. (2015). Increased risk of progression to dialysis or death in CKD patients with depressive symptoms: A prospective 3-year follow-up cohort study. *Journal of Psychosomatic Research, 79*(3), 228–32. doi:10.1016/j.jpsychores.2015.01.009

Cloninger, C. R., Svrakic, D. M., & Przybeck, T. R. (2006). Can personality assessment predict future depression? A twelve-month follow-up of 631 subjects. *Journal of Affective Disorders, 92*(1), 35–44.

Connell, A. M., & Goodman, S. H. (2002). The association between psychopathology in fathers versus mothers and children's internalizing and externalizing behavior problems: A meta-analysis. *Psychological Bulletin, 128*(5), 746–773. doi:10.1037/0033-2909.128.5.746

Cronkite, R. C., Woodhead, E. L., Finlay, A., Timko, C., Unger Hu, K., & Moos, R. H. (2013). Life stressors and resources and the 23-year course of depression. *Journal of Affective Disorders, 150*(2), 370.

Cuijpers, P., Beckman, A., & Reynolds, C. (2012). Preventing depression: A global priority. *JAMA, 307*, 1033–1034.

Cuijpers, P., Von Strategn, A., Smit, F., Miahlopoulous, C., & Beckman, A. (2008.) Preventing the onset of depressive disorders: A meta-analytic review of psychological interventions. *American Journal of Psychiatry, 165*, 1271–1280.

Cummings, E. M., Cheung, R. Y., & Davies, P. T. (2013). Prospective relations between parental depression, negative expressiveness, emotional insecurity, and children's internalizing symptoms. *Child Psychiatry & Human Development, 44*(6), 698–708.

Currie, S. R., & Wang, J. (2005). More data on major depression as an antecedent risk factor for first onset of chronic back pain. *Psychological Medicine, 35*(9), 1275–1282.

Davis, L., Uezato, A., Newell, J. M., & Frazier, E. (2008). Major depression and comorbid substance use disorders. *Current Opinion in Psychiatry, 21*(1), 14–18.

Diego, M. A., Field, T., Hernandez-Reif, M., Schanberg, S., Kuhn, C., & Gonzalez-Quintero, V. H. (2009). Prenatal depression restricts fetal growth. *Early Human Development, 85*(1), 65–70. doi:10.1016/j.earlhumdev.2008.07.002

Dwight-Johnson, M., & Lagomasino, I. T. (2007). Addressing depression treatment preferences of ethnic minority patients. *General Hospital Psychiatry, 29*(3), 179–181.

Eaton, W. W., Shao, H., Nestadt, G., Lee, B. H., Bienvenu, O. J., & Zandi, P. (2008). Population-based study of first onset and chronicity in major depressive disorder. *Archives of General Psychiatry, 65*(5), 513–520.

Ellis, E. M., Orom, H., Giovino, G. A., & Kiviniemi, M. T. (2015). Relations between negative affect and health behaviors by Race/Ethnicity: Differential effects for symptoms of depression and anxiety. *Health Psychology,* doi:10.1037/hea0000197

Errázuriz Arellano, P. A., Harvey, E. A., & Thakar, D. A. (2012). A longitudinal study of the relation between depressive symptomatology and parenting practices. *Family Relations, 61*(2), 271–282.

Essex, M. J., Klein, M. H., & Cho, E. (2003). Exposure to maternal depression and marital conflict: Gender differences in children's later mental health symptoms. *Journal of the American Academy of Child and Adolescent Psychiatry, 42*(6), 728.

Falicov, C. J. (2003). Culture, society and gender in depression. *Journal of Family Therapy, 25*(4), 371–387.

Fava, G. A., Fabbri, S., & Sonino, N. (2002). Residual symptoms in depression: An emerging therapeutic target. *Progress in Neuro-Psychopharmacology and Biological Psychiatry, 26*(6), 1019–1027.

Fear, J. M., Champion, J. E., Reeslund, K. L., Forehand, R., Colletti, C., Roberts, L., & Compas, B. E. (2009). Parental depression and interparental conflict: Children and adolescents' self-blame and coping responses. *Journal of Family Psychology, 23*(5), 762.

Flykt, M., Kanninen, K., Sinkkonen, J., & Punamäki, R.-L. (2010). Maternal depression and dyadic interaction: The role of maternal attachment style. *Infant and Child Development, 19*, 530–550.

Garber, J., Ciesla, J. A., McCauley, E., Diamond, G., & Schloredt, K. A. (2011). Remission of depression in parents: links to healthy functioning in their children. *Child Development, 82*(1), 226–243.

Geulayov, G., Metcalfe, C., Heron, J., Kidger, J., & Gunnell, D. (2014). Parental suicide attempt and offspring self-harm and suicidal thoughts: Results from the avon longitudinal study of parents and children. *Journal of the American Academy of Child and Adolescent Psychiatry, 53*(5), 509.

Givens, J. L., Houston, T. K., Van Voorhees, B. W., Ford, D. E., & Cooper, L. A. (2007). Ethnicity and preferences for depression treatment. *General Hospital Psychiatry, 29*(3), 182–191.

Goodman, S. H., Adamson, L. B., Riniti, J., & Cole, S. (1994). Mothers' expressed attitudes: Associations with maternal depression and children's self-esteem and psychopathology. *Journal of the American Academy of Child & Adolescent Psychiatry, 33*(9), 1265–1274.

Goodman, S. H., Rouse, M. H., Connell, A. M., Broth, M. R., Hall, C. M., & Heyward, D. (2011). Maternal depression and child psychopathology: A meta-analytic review. *Clinical Child and Family Psychology Review, 14*(1), 1–27. doi:10.1007/s10567-010-0080-1

Grilo, C. M., Stout, R. L., Markowitz, J. C., Sanislow, C. A., Ansell, E. B., Skodol, A. E., . . . McGlashan, T. H. (2010). Personality disorders predict relapse after remission from an episode of major depressive disorder: A 6-year prospective study. *The Journal of Clinical Psychiatry, 71*(12), 1629–1635. doi:10.4088/JCP.08m04230gre

Hanington, L., Heron, J., Stein, A., & Ramchandani, P. (2012). Parental depression and child outcomes–is marital conflict the missing link? *Child: Care, Health and Development, 38*(4), 520–529.

Henken, H. T., Huibers, M. J. H., Churchill, R., Restifo, K., & Roelofs, J. (2007). Family therapy for depression. *The Cochrane Database of Systematic Reviews,* (3), CD006728.

Holahan, C. J., Pahl, S. A., Cronkite, R. C., Holahan, C. K., North, R. J., & Moos, R. H. (2010). Depression and vulnerability to incident physical illness across 10 years. *Journal of Affective Disorders, 123*(1), 222–229.

Hölzel, L., Härter, M., Reese, C., & Kriston, L. (2011). Risk factors for chronic depression— a systematic review. *Journal of affective disorders, 129*(1), 1–13.

Hurt, C., Weinman, J., & Brown, R. (2009). Illness perceptions and depression in Parkinson's disease. *Parkinsonism and Related Disorders, 15*, S40–S40. doi:10.1016/S1353-8020(09)70165-8

Husky, M. M., Mazure, C. M., Paliwal, P., & McKee, S. A. (2008). Gender differences in the comorbidity of smoking behavior and major depression. *Drug and Alcohol Dependence, 93*(1), 176–179.

Jacobs, R. H., Warner, V., & Weissman, M. M. (2013). The impact of paternal and maternal depression on internalizing and externalizing disorders among offspring. *Comprehensive Psychiatry, 54*(1), E1–E14. doi:http://dx.doi.org/10.1016/j.comppsych.2012.07.028

Jurkovic, G. J., Thirkield, A., & Morrell, R. (2001). Parentification of adult children of divorce: A multidimensional analysis. *Journal of Youth and Adolescence, 30*, 245–257.

Kane, P., & Garber, J. (2009). Parental depression and child externalizing and internalizing symptoms: Unique effects of fathers' symptoms and perceived conflict as a mediator. *Journal of Child and Family Studies, 18*(4), 465–472. doi:http://dx.doi.org/10.1007/s10826-008-9250-x

Kaplan, M. J., & Klinetob, N. A. (2000). Childhood emotional trauma and chronic posttraumatic stress disorder in adult outpatients with treatment-resistant depression. *The Journal of Nervous and Mental Disease, 188*(9), 596–601. doi:10.1097/00005053-200009000-00006

Karasz, A. (2005). Cultural differences in conceptual models of depression. *Social Science & Medicine, 60*(7), 1625–1635.

Katon, W. J. (2003). Clinical and health services relationships between major depression, depressive symptoms, and general medical illness. *Biological Psychiatry, 54*(3), 216–226.

Katon, W., Lin, E., & Kroenke, K. (2007). The association of depression and anxiety with medical symptom burden in patients with chronic medical illness. *General Hospital Psychiatry, 29*(2), 147–155.

Kim-Cohen, J., Moffitt, T. E., Taylor, A., Pawlby, S. J., & Caspi, A. (2005). Maternal depression and children's antisocial behavior: Nature and nurture effects. *Archives of General Psychiatry, 62,* 173–181.

Kleinman, A., & Good, B. (2004). Culture and depression. *New England Journal of Medicine, 351,* 951–952.

Knobloch, L., & Delaney, A. (2012). Themes of relational uncertainty and interference from partners in depression. *Health Communication, 27*(8), 750. doi:10.1080/104102 36.2011.639293

Kouros, C. D., & Garber, J. (2010). Dynamic associations between maternal depressive symptoms and adolescents' depressive and externalizing symptoms. *Journal of Abnormal Child Psychology, 38*(8), 1069–1081. doi:10.1007/s10802-010-9433-y

Kronmüller, K. T., Backenstrass, M., Victor, D., Postelnicu, I., Schenkenbach, C., Joest, K., . . . & Mundt, C. (2011). Quality of marital relationship and depression: Results of a 10-year prospective follow-up study. *Journal of Affective Disorders, 128*(1), 64–71.

Langrock, A. M., Compas, B. E., Keller, G., Merchant, M. J., & Copeland, M. E. (2002). Coping with the stress of parental depression: Parents' reports of children's coping, emotional, and behavioral problems. *Journal of Clinical Child and Adolescent Psychology, 31*(3), 312–324.

Latalova, K., Kamaradova, D., & Prasko, J. (2014). Perspectives on perceived stigma and self-stigma in adult male patients with depression. *Neuropsychiatric Disease and Treatment, 10,* 1399–1405.

Lee, S. J., Taylor, C. A., & Bellamy, J. L. (2012). Paternal depression and risk for child neglect in father-involved families of young children. *Child abuse & neglect, 36*(5), 461–469.

Leis, J. A., & Mendelson, T. (2010). Intergenerational transmission of psychopathology: Minor versus major parental depression. *The Journal of Nervous and Mental Disease, 198*(5), 356–361.

Lewandowski, R. E., Verdeli, H., Wickramaratne, P., Warner, V., Mancini, A., & Weissman, M. (2014). Predictors of positive outcomes in offspring of depressed parents and non-depressed parents across 20 years. *Journal of Child and Family Studies, 23*(5), 800. doi:10.1007/s10826-013-9732-3

Lipsitz, J. D., & Markowitz, J. C. (2013). Mechanisms of change in interpersonal therapy (IPT). *Clinical Psychology Review, 33*(8), 1134–1147. doi:10.1016/j.cpr.2013.09.002

Lovejoy, M. C., Graczyk, P. A., O'Hare, E., & Neuman, G. (2000). Maternal depression and parenting behavior: A meta-analytic review. *Clinical Psychology Review, 20*(5), 561–592.

Luca, M., Luca, A., & Calandra, C. (2012). Borderline personality disorder and depression: an update. *Psychiatric Quarterly, 83*(3), 281–292.

Mayo Clinic. (2013a). Atypical antidepressants. Retrieved from www.mayoclinic.org/diseases-conditions/depression/in-depth/atypical-antidepressants/art-20048208

Mayo Clinic. (2013b). Monoamine oxidase inhibitors (MAOIs). Retrieved from www.mayoclinic.org/diseases-conditions/depression/in-depth/maois/art-20043992

Mayo Clinic. (2013c). Selective serotonin reuptake inhibitors (SSRIs). Retrieved from www.mayoclinic.org/diseases-conditions/depression/in-depth/ssris/art-20044825

Mayo Clinic. (2013d). Serotonin and norepinephrine reuptake inhibitors (SNRIs). Retrieved from www.mayoclinic.org/diseases-conditions/depression/in-depth/antidepressants/art-20044970

Mayo Clinic. (2013e). Tricyclic antidepressants (TCAs). Retrieved from www.mayoclinic.org/diseases-conditions/depression/in-depth/antidepressants/art-20046983

Mayo Clinic. (2015, May 19). Suicide and suicidal thoughts. Retrieved July 07, 2015, from www.mayoclinic.org/diseases-conditions/suicide/basics/risk-factors/con-200 33954

McCusker, J., Cole, M., Ciampi, A., Latimer, E., Windholz, S., & Belzile, E. (2007). Major depression in older medical inpatients predicts poor physical and mental health status over 12 months. *General Hospital Psychiatry, 29*(4), 340–348. doi:10.1016/j.genhosppsych.2007.03.007

Morris, B. H., McGrath, A. C., Goldman, M. S., & Rottenberg, J. (2014). Parental depression confers greater prospective depression risk to females than males in emerging adulthood. *Child Psychiatry & Human Development, 45*(1), 78–89.

Mueller, T. I., Lavori, P. W., Keller, M. B., Swartz, A., Warshaw, M., Hasin, D., . . . Akiskal, H. (1994). Prognostic effect of the variable course of alcoholism on the 10-year course of depression. *American Journal of Psychiatry, 151*(5), 701–706.

Murray, L., & Cooper, P. (2003). Intergenerational transmission of affective and cognitive processes associated with depression: Infancy and the pre-school years. In I. M. Goodyer (Ed.), *Unipolar depression: A lifespan perspective* (pp. 17–46). Oxford: Oxford University Press.

National Center for Health Statistics. (2012). *Health, United States, 2011: With special feature on socioeconomic status and health.* Hyattsville, MD: National Center for Health Statistics.

National Center for Injury Prevention and Control, CDC (2013). *NCHS vital statistics system for numbers of deaths.* Web-based Injury Statistics Query and Reporting System (WISQARS). NVDRS Reports

National Institute of Mental Health (NIMH). (n.d.). Depression. Retrieved from www.nimh.nih.gov/health/topics/depression/index.shtml#part_145399

National Research Council and Institute of Medicine. (2009). *Depression in parents, parenting, and children: Opportunities to improve identification, treatment, and prevention.* Washington, DC: National Academies Press.

Newton-Howes, G., Tyrer, P., & Johnson, T. (2006). Personality disorder and the outcome of depression: Meta-analysis of published studies. *British Journal of Psychiatry, 188*, 13–20.

Oakley, L. D., Kanter, J. W., Taylor, J. Y., & Duguid, M. (2012). The self-stigma of depression for women. *International Journal of Social Psychiatry, 58*(5), 512–520. doi:10.1177/0020764011409820

Patten, S., Williams, J., Lavorato, D., Modgill, G., Jetté, N., & Eliasziw, M. (2008). Major depression as a risk factor for chronic disease incidence: Longitudinal analyses in a general population cohort. *Generalized Hospital Psychiatry, 30*(5), 407–413.

Piché, G., Bergeron, I., Cyr, M., & Berthiaume, C. (2011). Interaction effects between maternal lifetime depressive/anxiety disorders and correlates of children's externalizing symptoms. *Journal of Child and Family Studies, 20*(5), 596–604. doi:10.1007/s10826-010-9433-0

Pratt, L. A. & Brody, D. J. (2014) *Depression in the U.S.-household population, 2009–2012.* NCHS data brief, no 172. Hyattsville, MD: National Center for Health Statistics.

Richards, D. (2011). Prevalence and clinical course of depression: a review. *Clinical Psychology Review, 31*(7), 1117–1125.

Pratt, L. A., Brody, D. J., & Gu, Q. (2011). *Antidepressant use in persons aged 12 and over: United States, 2005–2008.* NCHS data brief, no 76. Hyattsville, MD: National Center for Health Statistics. Retrieved from www.cdc.gov/nchs/data/databriefs/db76.htm

Rosal, M. C., Ockene, I. S., Ockene, J. K., Ma, Y., Hebert, J. R., Merriam, P. A., & Matthews, C. E. (2001). Behavioral risk factors among members of a health maintenance organization. *Preventive Medicine, 33*(6), 586–594. doi:10.1006/pmed.2001.0929

Ryder, A. G., & Chentsova-Dutton, Y. E. (2012). Depression in cultural context: "Chinese somatization," revisited. *Psychiatric Clinics of North America, 35*(1), 15–36.

Shay, N. L., & Knutson, J. F. (2008). Maternal depression and trait anger as risk factors for escalated physical discipline. *Child Maltreatment, 13*(1), 39–49. doi:10.1177/1077559507310611

Snell, C., Fernandes, S., Bujoreanu, I. S., & Garcia, G. (2014). Depression, illness severity, and healthcare utilization in cystic fibrosis. *Pediatric Pulmonology, 49*, 1177–1181. doi:10.1002/ppul.22990

Solomon, D. A., Keller, M. B., Leon, A. C., Mueller, T. I., Lavori, P. W., Shea, M. T., . . . Endicott, J. (2000). Multiple recurrences of major depressive disorder. *American Journal of Psychiatry, 157*, 229–33.

Steunenberg, B., Beekman, A. T., Deeg, D. J., & Kerkhof, A. J. (2010). Personality predicts recurrence of late-life depression. *Journal of Affective Disorders, 123*(1), 164–172.

Substance Abuse and Mental Health Services Administration. (2013). *Results from the 2012 national survey on drug use and health: Mental health findings*, NSDUH Series H-47, HHS Publication No. (SMA) 13–4805. Rockville, MD: Substance Abuse and Mental Health Services Administration.

Sudak, D. M. (2012). Cognitive behavioral therapy for depression. *Psychiatric Clinics of North America, 35*(1), 99–110. doi:10.1016/j.psc.2011.10.001

Toth, S. L., Rogosch, F. A., Manly, J. T., & Cicchetti, D. (2006). The efficacy of toddler-parent psychotherapy to reorganize attachment in the young offspring of mothers with major depressive disorder: A randomized preventive trial. *Journal of Consulting and Clinical Psychology, 74*(6), 1006–1016. doi:10.1037/0022-006X.74.6.1006

Tsai, J. L., & Chentsova-Dutton, Y. (2002). Understanding depression across cultures. In I. H. Gottlieb & C. L. Hammen (Eds.), *Handbook of depression* (pp. 363–85). New York: Guilford Press.

Turney, K. (2011). Labored love: Examining the link between maternal depression and parenting behaviors. *Social Science Research, 40*(1), 399–415. doi:10.1016/j.ssresearch.2010.09.009

University of Michigan Department of Psychiatry. (2015). How does ECT work? Retrieved from www.psych.med.umich.edu/ect/how-does-ect-work.asp

van den Berg, M. P., van der Ende, J., Crijnen, A. A. M., Jaddoe, V. W. V., Moll, H. A., Mackenbach, J. P., . . . Verhulst, F. C. (2009). Paternal depressive symptoms during pregnancy are related to excessive infant crying. *Pediatrics, 124*(1), e96–e103. doi:10.1542/peds.2008-3100

van Dijk, M. R., Utens, E., Dulfer, K., Al-Qezweny, M., van Geuns, R., Daemen, J., & van Domburg, T. (2015). Depression and anxiety symptoms as predictors of mortality in PCI patients at 10 years of follow-up. *European Journal of Preventive Cardiology.* doi:10.1177/2047487315571889

Van Parys, H., & Rober, P. (2013). Trying to comfort the parent: A qualitative study of children dealing with parental depression. *Journal of Marital and Family Therapy, 39*(3), 330–345.

Walker, K., Lindner, H., & Noonan, M. (2009). The role of coping in the relationship between depression and illness severity in chronic fatigue syndrome. *Journal of Allied Health, 38*(2), 91–9.

Whiteford, H. A., Harris, M. G., McKeon, G., Baxter, A., Pennell, C., Barendregt, J. J., & Wang, J. (2013). Estimating remission from untreated major depression: A systematic review and meta-analysis. *Psychological Medicine, 43*(8), 1569. doi:10.1017/S0033291712001717

Wickramaratne, P., Gameroff, M. J., Pilowsky, D. J., Hughes, C. W., Garber, J., Malloy, E., . . . & Weissman, M. M. (2011). Children of depressed mothers 1 year after remission of maternal depression: findings from the STAR* D-Child study. *American Journal of Psychiatry, 168*, 593–602.

PARENTAL CANCER

Maureen Davey

Cancer: About the Illness

Prevalence

Cancer develops when cells in the body are damaged, leading to their inability to have a normal programmed cell death (see Figure 4.1). Instead, cancer cells continue to grow and divide in an aggressive and often uncontrolled way, leading to large masses or tumors that can spread and destroy other parts of the body or organs where they are embedded (NCI, 2014). Cancer cells spread by getting into the blood stream or lymph vessels; when they spread to other parts of the body, they can grow and become new tumors. Many factors contribute to the development of cancer, including: (1) genetics or a family history of cancer, (2) tobacco use, (3) excess body weight, (4) alcohol abuse, (5) sun exposure, (6) radiation exposure, (7) environmental causes (e.g., pollution), (8) hormones, and (9) immune conditions (ACS, 2013). Although there is no definitive cause of cancer, these person-environmental factors can all contribute to the possibility of developing cancer in one's lifetime. If left untreated, cancer can lead to incapacitation and ultimately death.

There are over 100 types of cancer, and they vary by site of origin in the body (e.g., prostate, breast, bone marrow) and can differ in symptoms, staging, progression, and prognosis (ACS, 2014). Additionally, there are two main classifications of cancer: (1) solid tumor and (2) blood/liquid tumors. A solid tumor is an abnormal mass of tissue that does not have liquid areas (NCI, 2014), for example, breast, prostate and colon cancer. Blood or liquid tumors begin in blood-forming tissue, like bone marrow or cells in the immune system, for example, leukemia or lymphoma (NCI, 2014).

As of January 2014, the most common type among men in the U.S. was prostate cancer (approximately 2,975,970 survivors or 43%), followed by melanoma (621,430 or 9%), urinary bladder (455,520 or 7%), non-Hodgkin lymphoma (297,820 or 4%), testis (244,110 or 4%), kidney (229,790 or 3%), lung/bronchus (196,580 or 3%), oral cavity and pharynx (194,140 or 3%), leukemia (177,940 or 3%), and 6,876,600 for all other cancers (ACS, 2014). As of January 2014, the most common type of cancer among women in the U.S. was breast cancer (3,131,440 or 41%), followed by uterine (624,890 or 8%), colon/rectum (624, 340 or 8%), melanoma (528,860 or 7%), thyroid (470,020 or 6%), non-Hodgkin lymphoma (272,000 or 4%), cervix (244,180 or 3%), lung/bronchus (233,510

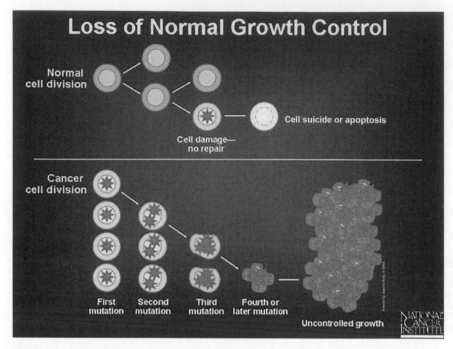

Figure 4.1 Development of a Cancer Cell
Source: National Cancer Institute. Retrieved from www.cancer.gov/about-cancer/what-is-cancer. Reprinted with permission.

or 3%), ovary (199,900 or 3%), kidney (159,280 or 2%), and 7,607,230 for all other cancers (ACS, 2014).

Additionally, there are significant health disparities in the incidence of cancer; older individuals and minorities are at a higher risk of being diagnosed with cancer. Black men and women have a higher incidence and increased mortality for most solid tumor cancers (ACS, 2013). For example, White women more often develop breast cancer, but Black women have a greater chance of being diagnosed with more aggressive, advanced-stage breast cancer and are more likely to be diagnosed at a younger age, leading to a worse prognosis (NCI, 2014). Black women and men have a higher incidence of colon cancer, and Black men have a higher incidence of prostate cancer at all ages. Hispanics have lower prevalence rates for all cancers combined when compared to Whites, but they have higher rates of infection-related types of cancer including uterine, cervix, liver, gallbladder, and stomach cancer. Thus, minority populations in the U.S. (e.g., African Americans, Hispanic Americans, Asian Americans, and Native Americans/Alaskan Natives) have a higher total incidence of cancer and a higher total death rate as compared to Whites (ACS, 2014). Noteworthy, for all cancers combined, the death rate is 25% higher for African Americans/Blacks compared to Whites (NCI, 2014).

Socioeconomic disparities also exist in the United States. Individuals living in areas where at least 20% of people are below the poverty line tend to have cancer mortality rates that are 13% higher compared to individuals who live in more affluent counties (Ward et al., 2004). Cancer patients who live in less affluent areas also have lower 5-year survival rates (Ward et al., 2004). Lack of medical coverage, barriers to early detection and screening, and unequal access to improvements in cancer treatment may be contributing to these differences in survival (NCI, 2014). Additionally, SES has been linked to negative health behaviors that can increase cancer risks. For example, individuals with lower SES are more likely to smoke, be obese, and have higher alcohol intakes, and they are less likely to get screened for cancer (ACS, 2013). Approximately half of all cancer survivors (46%) are 70-years-old, because cancer is more often diagnosed in older individuals. Of note, cancer is steadily increasing among minorities (ACS, 2014).

Prognosis and Medical Outcomes

Medical providers tend to first perform a biopsy (the removal of a sample of tissue or cells so it can be examined under a microscope) of any abnormal cells detected during physical exams or regular screenings (e.g., mammogram) to determine the stage of cancer. For example, the stages of breast cancer are determined by the following four factors: (1) whether it is invasive, (2) tumor size, (3) number of lymph nodes affected, and (4) whether it has metastasized or spread to areas other than the breast (ACS, 2014). Breast cancer stages include stage 0, IA, IIA, IIB, IIIA, IIIB, IIIC, and IV. It is beyond the scope of this chapter to describe the different stages for all types of cancer, but for most tumors, stage 0 refers to when the cancer cells have not spread outside of where they initially developed in the breast, whereas in stage IV, the cancer has spread beyond the breast itself to other areas of the body such as the bones or brain (ACS, 2013).

Each type of cancer has a different type of staging (with more advanced stages associated with worse prognoses because the cancer has spread from its site of origin), and each type has a varying course of treatment, a different prognosis, and different outcomes, which is again beyond the scope of this chapter. Most treatment regimens last between four and eight months (ACS, 2013), but this will vary based on the type of cancer, staging, and treatment regimen. Some types of cancer, when caught in earlier stages, tend to have better survival rates (e.g., colon, leukemia), whereas other types of cancer (e.g., pancreatic) have poorer survival rates.

Most providers agree that a cancer diagnosis and the treatment significantly affect patients and their family members because of the significant side effects of treatment (e.g., fatigue, nausea, pain). Treatment can include surgery, chemotherapy, radiation, hormone therapy, and frequent visits to the doctor. In addition, there are many physical and emotional demands of the illness. Healthier eating habits are important during cancer treatment (NCI, 2014) because some treatments work better when patients get enough calories and protein in their diets. Oncology providers report that patients who eat healthier tend to have better prognoses and quality of life (NCI, 2014).

The most common types of cancer treatments are surgery, chemotherapy, and radiation therapy (ACS, 2014). Surgery is used to diagnose, treat, or prevent cancer and can offer the greatest chance for cure, if the cancer has not spread to other parts of the body. Chemotherapy describes the use of medications to kill cancer cells; however, it also tends to kill the healthy cells, which can lead to negative side effects (e.g., loss of hair, fatigue). Radiation therapy uses high-energy particles or waves to destroy or damage cancer cells and is one of the most common treatments for cancer, either by itself or with other types of treatment (NCI, 2014). Targeted therapy is a newer type of cancer treatment that uses drugs to more precisely identify and attack cancer cells, to prevent the damage of normal cells (NCI, 2014). Targeted therapy is becoming a part of many cancer treatment regimens. Immunotherapy is a treatment that uses the body's own immune system to help fight cancer. For example, in some blood cancers, such as leukemia, bone marrow transplants and other types of stem cell transplants are used to treat cancer (ACS, 2014).

Many patients report struggling with chemotherapy treatment because it can lead to nausea, vomiting, and diarrhea. Medication may be prescribed to patients to help reduce symptoms of nausea and vomiting. Cancer-related pain can also be caused by the treatment (e.g., surgery, radiation, chemotherapy). Typically providers assess for the level of cancer pain and then decide how to best help each patient feel more comfortable (e.g., medication, mindfulness meditation, biofeedback) (Koch, Jansen, Brenner, & Arndt, 2013). Additionally, cancer-related fatigue is a common problem that affects many patients' quality of life.

Psychological Comorbidities

Cancer patients tend to experience high rates of depressed mood during the acute phase of treatment and for two or more years after diagnosis (ACS, 2012; Bottomley, 1998; Brown, Kroenke, Theobald, Wu, & Tu, 2010; Caplette-Gingras & Savard, 2008; Carlson et al., 2004; Fann et al., 2008; Harris & Zakowski, 2003; Hoffman, McCarthy, Recklitis, & Ng, 2009; Massie, 2004; Meyerowitz, Kurita, & D'Orazio, 2008). Even in absence of depressed mood, treatment demands or preoccupation with the cancer can lead to patients feeling anxious and physically or emotionally unavailable to family members at home (Davey, Kissil, Lynch, Harmon, & Hodgson, 2012, 2013; Lewis, 2004, 2006).

Coping with the diagnosis and treatment of cancer changes daily routines, schedules, activities, self-esteem, self-worth, sexuality, self-perception, and life priorities (Compas et al., 1994; Leedham & Meyerowitz, 1999; Lewis & Hammond, 1996). The initial diagnosis can be a shocking and traumatic time for patients. "Why me?" and "Why now?" are common questions asked by patients in response to cancer diagnosis. Patients may also suffer from a loss of income, the financial stress of medical bills, and fears (real or anticipated) of losing their jobs and insurance. As a result of the cancer, many patients lose some level of social interaction and the ability to do previous activities. As these patients search for meaning and try to adapt to the psychosocial transitions described, depressive symptoms and anxiety (for some) are often experienced.

Level of Uncertainty about the Illness

Cancer patients who complete their treatment regimens often report living with feelings of fear and uncertainty because they worry the cancer will reoccur. Many parents worry about whether they will be there for their children (Koch et al., 2013; Ness et al., 2013). Cancer patients who require surgery, chemotherapy, and radiation treatments are usually those who are diagnosed with more advanced stages of cancer which require more aggressive treatment, and thus they are more likely to have a cancer recurrence. Many cancer survivors report concerns after completing their cancer treatment because approximately 40% of all cancers have a less than 5-year survival rate (ACS, 2014).

Patients report worrying most right before their follow-up appointments when they are screened for any cancer recurrence (Ness et al., 2013). Common questions that patients tend to have for their providers are: (1) Will it come back? (2) What are the chances it will come back? (3) How will I know if it comes back? (4) What will I do if it comes back? and (5) When will it come back? (Koch et al., 2013). Some report trouble sleeping, excessive worrying, and depressive and anxiety symptoms because of their fears of recurrence. Some patients report obsessing about every ache and pain as signs the cancer has returned. Some symptoms of recurrence that patients and providers should be attuned to are: (1) return of the cancer symptoms (e.g., lump or new growth where the cancer first started); (2) new or unusual pain that does not dissipate; (3) weight loss without trying; (4) bleeding or unexplained bruising; (5) chills or fever; (6) headaches; (7) shortness of breath; (8) lumps, bumps, or swelling; (9) nausea, vomiting, and loss of appetite; and (10) any other unusual symptoms (ACS, 2014).

What Clinicians Need to Know about Cancer

1   Cancer can be treated by surgery, chemotherapy, radiation therapy, and hormonal therapy.
2   Nausea, vomiting, diarrhea, and pain can be caused by the cancer treatment; treatment of these symptoms should be addressed by providers so patients are more comfortable.
3   The initial diagnosis can be a shocking and traumatic time for patients with cancer.
4   Cancer patients tend to experience high rates of depressed mood during the acute phase of treatment and for two or more years after diagnosis.
5   Cancer patients who complete their treatment regimen often report living with feelings of fear and uncertainty because they worry the cancer will reoccur.

Each year, approximately 1.2 million parents of school-age children will be newly diagnosed with cancer in the U.S. (ACS, 2014). Assuming there are one to two children per household, this means that approximately 2.4 million children will be affected by the diagnosis and treatment of cancer in a parent (Lewis, 2006, 2007). Despite the recent advancements in cancer treatment, and even in cases with good prognosis for survival, patients may experience damage to their physical appearance and the loss of physical functioning and abilities to carry out their daily routines (Compas et al., 1994; Hoffman et al., 2009; Lewis, 2004). An estimated 25% of adults within two years of an initial cancer diagnosis are parenting children 18 years of age and younger (ACS, 2013; Niemelä et al., 2010; Osborn, 2007), which suggests that every year thousands of children will be affected by the diagnosis and treatment of cancer in a parent.

In addition to struggling to accept a cancer diagnosis, parents also report struggling with feelings of uncertainty about the future of their families and worry that they will not survive the cancer (Christ, Siegel, & Sperber, 1994; Compas et al., 1994). Parents often fear missing their children's traditional developmental milestones of graduation, marriage, and childbirth. They may also experience guilt and anxiety about not being able to parent their children and support their spouse or partner during the course of the illness (Johnson, Martin, Martin, & Gumaer, 1992; Lewis, 2007). Consequently, an ill parent's ability to adjust to the stress can affect the entire family system (Compas et al., 1994; Leedham & Meyerowitz, 1999;Lewis & Hammond, 1996).

The Effect of Cancer on Parenting

Cancer patients report that caring for their children is most difficult during the initial phase of diagnosis and treatment, when they often experience feelings of shock and uncertainty, and they regret not being able to parent their children the way they would like to (Billhult & Segersten, 2003; Buchbinder, Longhofer, & McCue, 2009; Davey, Niño, Kissil, & Ingram, 2012; Hoke, 2001; Lewis & Hammond, 1996). Cancer can cause distress and depressive symptoms in both the ill parent and his or her spouse or partner (Leedham & Meyerowitz, 1999; Lewis & Hammond, 1996). Depressed parents often show impaired parenting characterized by less psychological availability, less communication, decreased supervision, lack of consistency in discipline, as well as more hostility, irritability, and coerciveness (Armsden & Lewis, 1994; Christ et al., 1994; Compas et al., 1994). Even in the absence of depressive symptoms, cancer can lead to parental inaccessibility. The treatment demands or preoccupation with the illness can make a parent physically or emotionally unavailable to offspring. Overall, parental illness has been reported to cause parental withdrawal, indifference, unreliability, hostility, and coerciveness, and these characteristics have been linked to impaired adaptability of the child; for example, the child may have behavioral, social, and self-esteem problems (Armsden & Lewis, 1994; Christ et al., 1994; Compas et al., 1994).

Parental cancer can also affect parenting because of changes in the marital relationship (Baik & Adams, 2011). Parental cancer can cause marital tension, which may result in adjustment difficulties for children and adolescents in the family. Marital discord has been associated with more frequent punishment (Osborn, 2007). The parental atmosphere of marital strife may lead to anxiety in children and adolescents as well as to concerns about the future and the family's stability. Children and adolescents may misinterpret decreased parental accessibility and believe that they are not loved or valued (Compas, Worsham, Ey, & Howell, 1996; Lewis & Hammond, 1996).

The Effect of Parental Cancer on Children and Adolescents

It is estimated that 22–32% of school-age children who are coping with a parent diagnosed with cancer will reach the clinical range of depression and/or anxiety (Huizinga et al., 2003; Lewis & Darby, 2003; Lewis, 2004, 2006, 2007; Nelson & While, 2002). As described previously, treatment, disease-related symptoms, and parental depressed mood can all negatively affect children's physical and emotional access to the parent and affect the quality of parenting. Yet, children and adolescents often report relying on themselves to manage and to cope with their parent's cancer (Davey, Tubbs, Kissil, & Niño, 2011; Deshields, Zebrack, & Kennedy, 2013; Edwards et al., 2008; Forrest, Plumb, Ziebland, & Stein, 2006; Hoekstra et al., 2007; Grabiak, Bender, & Puskar, 2007; Kissil, Niño, Jacobs, Davey, & Tubbs, 2010).

Children whose parents are diagnosed with cancer may experience psychosocial stress (e.g., Lewis, 2004, 2006, 2007). For example, Compas and his colleagues (1994) assessed anxiety/depression and stress responses in adult cancer patients (n = 117), spouses (n = 76), and their children (n = 110, aged 6 to 30 years old) shortly after the patients' diagnoses to identify family members at risk for psychological maladjustment. Children, adolescents, and young adults reported moderate to high levels of emotional distress when their parents were diagnosed and treated for cancer. The authors reported that both the stress-response and anxiety/depression symptoms varied in children as a function of age, sex of the child, and sex of the parent who was ill. Adolescent girls whose mothers had cancer were the most significantly distressed.

Living with a chronically ill parent exposes children to the following psychosocial stressors: (1) the potential loss of the parent to death; (2) the temporary loss of the ill parent because of symptoms of the disease and side effects of treatment; (3) temporary loss of the healthy parent because he or she is preoccupied with taking care of the ill parent and is emotionally unavailable; and (4) the disruption of family roles and routines. Children's ways of coping with stress will play an important role in their emotional and psychological adjustments to this stressful experience. For example, Wellisch (1979) reported that among children whose parent had cancer, younger children displayed regressed behavior and older adolescent children displayed antisocial conduct, including acting out anger, drinking alcohol, and engaging in promiscuous sexual behavior.

Lewis and her colleagues (2004, 2006, 2007) examined how school-age children cope with their mother's breast cancer and how their families help them cope (Lewis et al., 2006). They conducted semistructured interviews with 81 children, 6 to 20 years old, from 50 families in which the mother had been diagnosed with breast cancer within the 2.5 years of the study. In their study, children were divided into the following three age groups: (1) young school-aged (7 through 10 years old), (2) older school-aged (11 through 13 years old), and (3) adolescents (14 through 18 years old). All children were asked to verbalize their concerns and feelings about their mothers' illness. Each group provided responses consistent with their stage of psychosocial and cognitive development. Lewis and her team reported that it was difficult for younger school-age children to understand the concept of cancer because of their concrete mode of thinking. They often described the illness as "it," and their emotional responses were concerned primarily with fear, loneliness, anger, and uncertainty about the future.

The older school-aged children acknowledged that they had to take on more responsibilities, such as household chores, which took time away from their own interests and activities. These children tended to display developmentally appropriate responses to their parents' cancer; they were more concerned with playing and their own activities than with empathizing and helping out at home. Therefore, they maintained an egocentric position on the process, relative to their own stage of cognitive and psychosocial development.

Since the cognitive abilities of adolescents are more advanced than those of younger children, they are better able to comprehend the illness and the treatment process and to identify the ramifications for current and future family life and relationships (Armsden & Lewis, 1994; Compas et al., 1994). Due to their developmental life stage, adolescents report feeling torn between the developmental tasks of adolescence (e.g., forming relationships outside the family) and the need to deal with the practical, psychological, and social tasks demanded by the illness. Adolescents report that their lives are often complicated by a parent's cancer. Adolescents, who are typically struggling for independence and the formation of their own identities, reported feelings of conflict between the desire to break away from the family of origin and the knowledge that they were needed at home both emotionally and physically. This particular age group often felt burdened with additional roles and responsibilities (Compas et al., 1996). Thus, a parent's cancer diagnosis and the demands of treatment can keep adolescents more closely aligned with the family at a time when developmentally they should be pulling away from the family to progress toward autonomy.

Parental Cancer and Adolescent Gender Differences

There are differences regarding how male and female adolescents cope when their mothers have cancer. Adolescent daughters report wanting to support their mothers during the course of the illness, yet they also feel anger and resentment and, consequently, they often withdraw from their mothers. These daughters may also fear the risk of inheriting the disease from their mothers who have cancer. Consequently, they could harbor resentment toward their mothers for contributing to their own genetic vulnerability or predisposition to cancer. Their anger is often expressed overtly through argumentativeness or covertly through emotional and physical distancing.

Adolescent sons may also have difficulty adjusting to parental illness, as they often avoid communication that directly addresses the illness and the situation. They may also want all information about the disease concealed from others outside the family. For adolescent sons, emotions are more likely to be acted out rather than expressed through open communication.

Similarly, in our studies with racially diverse families coping with parental cancer (Davey, Askew, & Godette, 2003; Davey, Gulish, Askew, Godette, & Childs, 2005; Davey et al., 2011), female and male adolescents seemed to adapt and cope in different ways. Female adolescents described experiencing fear of inheriting cancer when their mothers were diagnosed with breast cancer. They also tended to more readily express their feelings to others as a form of coping, as they reported experiencing sadness, fear, and anxiety. Adolescent males, when asked about their feelings at diagnosis and during treatment, used phrases like "hard inside" or they could not recall how they felt during those times. Overall, adolescent boys in our studies seemed less expressive and tried to deny or ignore their feelings during the family interviews; they more often reported feeling angry and numb rather than sad and fearful, and they more often coped by distracting themselves or blocking things out. These studies highlight the importance of considering gender differences and styles of coping when developing family interventions with this population of families and with adolescents in general.

Despite the gender differences, both female and male adolescents reported that their lives had been complicated by a parent's cancer. This particular age group often felt burdened with additional roles and responsibilities, especially the oldest child in the family (Armsden & Lewis, 1994). Additionally, researchers (e.g., Compas et al., 1996; Hoke, 1997; Leedham & Meyerowitz, 1999; Lewis & Hammond, 1996) have suggested that among children whose parents had a particular type of illness, adolescents whose parents have cancer report the highest levels of psychological symptoms (e.g., symptoms of anxiety and depression).

Children's and adolescents' developmental needs will in many ways determine how to best talk to them about the cancer and how to best help them (Leedham & Meyerowitz, 1999). For example, the way a younger child reacts is most often reflected in his or her behavior. Young children may appear to regress in behavior if their worlds are threatened. For example, children who are fully toilet trained may start having accidents. Two and three year olds, who typically are adventuresome in exploring their environments, may become unusually clingy and dependent. First graders who have adjusted well to starting school may resist going to school and display exaggerated separation anxiety. For children who cannot talk about their worries, these behaviors are clues for parents and clinicians regarding anxieties about changes in the household or in their relationships to their parents. During these times, parents may need to offer extra attention to their children. If a parent is feeling too ill, other family members may be called upon to temporarily help manage children.

School-age children have the advantage of being able to verbalize their feelings and also have more resources outside of their immediate families to help them cope. School personnel should be informed of the parent's cancer so the child's responses can be understood within that context. Parental illness can be particularly difficult for adolescents, who are in a developmental stage of separation from parental figures. It is typical for teenagers to test parental limits and to gradually achieve more self-confidence in their desire for independence. When this process is interrupted by cancer, teenagers can experience ambivalence and resentment, especially if they are called upon to take over parental responsibilities.

In cases where a parent is diagnosed with cancer, clinicians can provide emotional and social support to the family. A chronic illness such as cancer impacts all families, even those families with good coping and adaptation skills. When cancer strikes a family, parents might instinctively want to protect their children; however, children are good at sensing when something is wrong, and it is important for parents to talk over the issue with their children in developmentally appropriate ways. By keeping the cancer diagnosis a secret, many children experience even more anxiety because they might imagine something worse than what is actually happening in the family. When parents are ready to tell their children about the cancer, there are ways to help them discuss it.

The following suggestions were taken from several clinical articles on helping parents talk to their children about cancer (Leedham & Meyerowitz, 1999):

1 Help the parents practice their explanations to their children beforehand.
2 Have parents explain to their younger children that cancer is not contagious.
3 Help parents remove any blame; children at younger ages might think they caused the illness.
4 Help parents balance optimism and pessimism when sharing the news (e.g., offer a realistic but hopeful assessment of the situation).
5 If the ill parent is in the hospital for any extended period of time, encourage parents to stay in touch to reassure their children that the illness has nothing to do with how much they love them.
6 Encourage parents to take their children's/adolescents' feelings seriously. It is common for children to have many different reactions when they learn a parent has cancer; these can include anger, sadness, guilt, fear, confusion, and even frustration. All of these responses are normal, and children need to know it is healthy for them to have all kinds of feelings.
7 Encourage parents to answer questions honestly; for young children, the amount of information parents give them is usually less important than parents making them feel safe with what they say.
8 Encourage parents to help their children understand treatment. Children's greatest fears often spring from what they do not know; their imaginations can create pictures that are worse than that actual situation,

so explain the treatment process in a way that is appropriate for their ages.

9   Help parents prepare their children for the effects of treatment (physical changes like weight and hair loss can sometimes frighten them).

10   Encourage parents to let their children and adolescents help, but don't overburden them with responsibilities.

11   Encourage parents to be prepared to discuss death. (For more about preparing children for parental death, see Chapter 15.)

Some children and adolescents will not speak up and say that they are struggling, because they do not want to overload or worry their parents (Davey, Kissil, et al., 2012, 2013; Lewis et al., 2006; Osborn, 2007). Even after parents' cancer goes into remission, the fears about cancer can stay with a child. Support groups can be safe and supportive places for children to express their feelings about their parents' cancer without fearing that they will burden their families (Lewis et al., 2006; Muriel & Rauch, 2003; Niemelä et al., 2010).

Impact of Cancer on Parents and Children: Main Points

1   Parents with cancer are concerned about the impact on their children, and they experience many challenges in parenting their children.

2   Research suggests that female adolescents are most negatively affected by a mother's cancer.

3   Children's ways of coping with stress will play important roles in their emotional and psychological adjustment to parental cancer.

4   It is important for providers to consider age and gender differences and styles of coping among children dealing with parental cancer.

5   Children and adolescents often do not speak up and say that they are struggling, because they do not want to overload or worry their parents.

6   It is important to provide children with accurate information about the cancer and assess whether they attribute changes in the course of illness to their own behavior.

Cultural Considerations

Age is a primary risk factor for most cancers (most cancers are diagnosed in individuals aged 55 or older); however, as discussed earlier in this chapter, cancer incidence also varies by race and ethnicity, with some groups more likely to be diagnosed with certain types of cancers compared to others (ACS, 2014). The total projected cancer incidence will increase by 45%, from 1.6 million in 2010 to 2.3 million in 2030, because it has been estimated that cancer will be diagnosed more often among older adults and minorities (Smith, Cokkinides, & Brawley, 2009). Given these statistics, it is important to understand that there are differences in how individuals cope with cancer across racial and ethnic groups (Culver,

Arena, Wimberly, Antoni, & Carver, 2004; Deshields et al., 2013; Spencer et al., 1999).

Although all patients need to feel understood, reassured, and supported by providers, it is especially important for ethnic and racial minority cancer patients that providers instill trust, hope, and a fighting spirit because of possible cultural differences in health beliefs and behaviors and an understandable mistrust of larger systems, including the medical system (Deshields et al., 2013; Whaley & Davis, 2007). It is additionally important for providers to assess for barriers to treatment among low income patients (e.g., transportation and child care needs) and offer practical support to improve treatment appointment adherence (Whaley & Davis, 2007). More emphasis needs to be placed on how family members are interconnected and mutually influence each other and on how culture is essential in their lives to better help diverse families cope with cancer (see Part III of this book).

Mental healthcare providers who work in oncology clinics are more likely to encounter families who are coping with parental cancer because they have direct access to the oncology treatment team. It is important to first do a full needs assessment (see Chapter 12) with all adult cancer patients (both males and females, as well as older adults who may be raising grandchildren) to find out if they have any children at home. Providers who work in oncology clinics should ask all cancer patients about how they are coping with the cancer, their levels of social support, and whether they are able to maintain family recreation and leisure activities. It is important to maximize the child or youth's support system by helping him or her connect to other safe adult figures, have someone track school performance, and enable maintenance of peer activities to allow for a break from the parental cancer, as needed.

Providers should also help parents have more open communication about their cancer diagnosis and ongoing treatment so children do not worry alone; parents are encouraged to provide updates to children in developmentally appropriate ways. It is important to help parents prepare children for any hospital visits by describing in advance what a child will see and hear; debrief after medical visit to allay any worries, fears, and concerns; and provide other forms of communication (e.g., cards, drawings, videos) when visits are not possible while in treatment.

Mental healthcare providers who work in more traditional outpatient clinical settings (e.g., private practice, community mental health) need to be more intentional about collaborating with oncology providers who are involved in the care of parents diagnosed with cancer. During intake sessions with clients and families, the mental healthcare provider should do a full biopsychosocial spiritual assessment (see Chapter 12) and ask about any current illnesses that family members are managing. If a parent has been diagnosed with cancer, providers should explain that collaboration with oncologists is important to ensure that all of the providers and the family are on the same page. Mental healthcare providers should contact the oncology treatment team to: (1) establish open communication about treatment and (2) share relevant information to ensure best care for the cancer patient and the family.

Clinical Vignette

The following is a clinical vignette to help you consider how a family coping with parental cancer might present clinically.

Jake is an African American, 16-year-old adolescent whose mother has stage III breast cancer. Jake's mother and father are both 48 years old and are African American; they have been married for 19 years. His mother has a bachelor's degree and his father has a technical degree. Their income is between $40,000 and $60,000, and both parents report being Baptist. Jake is an only child, is in 11th grade, and is a B student. He considers himself religious. His mother was diagnosed with stage III breast cancer 6 months ago, and Jake was told about the cancer 2 weeks after the diagnosis; this is a first-time diagnosis for his mother. She has had a double mastectomy, and she is now in the middle of her chemotherapy treatment. The final stage of treatment will be radiation therapy, once the chemotherapy is completed. Jake was referred to therapy by his school counselor because his grades dropped and he has been distracted in school since his mother's cancer diagnosis.

Jake worries daily that his mother will not recover after the cancer treatment is completed. When he first found out about his mother's cancer diagnosis, he felt frustrated because a lot of other people are also sick in his family and are not available to provide support to his mother and his father at this time. Additionally, his grandmother had breast cancer 5 years ago, and she did not survive past 2 years, so he worries that his mother will also not recover. Often, he comes home to his mother resting on the couch or sleeping because of the fatigue after doing the chemotherapy treatment, especially the day after her treatment at the hospital. Jake and his father do not currently talk much to each other about their concerns, because they are both so overwhelmed and fearful about the future. Jake feels isolated and has not shared his mother's diagnosis and treatment with his friends because he feels they would not understand and he "does not like telling people his personal business." He is trying to stay focused on school, which is his parents' expectation for him, but it is difficult because he is keeping his feelings of distress to himself and he does not want to cry in front of his mother. He is trying to stay strong in front of his parents so he does not further burden them with his worries and concerns. Consequently, his grades have dropped from all Bs to Cs this past grading period.

Jake did not realize how much his life would change because of his mother's breast cancer diagnosis and treatment, and at this time he is unable to go out and have fun with his friends. As an only child at home, he tries to tell his mother to take it easy, but his mother does not listen to him because she wants to keep the family's routine as normal as possible. Jake's father is not as involved because he had to take a second job after his wife needed to take a leave from work in order to do the demanding treatment regimen. Jake does go to church with his family and has been trying to pray more often. He thought it might be helpful, but he finds it is not as comforting as he was hoping.

The psychosocial well-being of the children of cancer patients is a relatively new area of clinical research. Consequently, it is still more common to provide psychosocial support to the adult cancer patients and their spouses, but not to the offspring at home (Lewis, 2004; Niemalä, Hakko, & Räsänen, 2010). In the last decade, however, more family interventions have been developed and evaluated that will be discussed in detail in Part III of this book.

Conclusions

In this chapter, we described the prevalence of cancer and described the racial and socioeconomic health disparities associated with the incidence of cancer (older individuals and minorities are most at risk) and survival rates (ACS, 2014). Additionally, we discussed the psychological comorbidities (e.g., anxiety) and levels of uncertainty about the illness; for example, cancer patients tend to experience high rates of depressed mood during the acute phase of treatment and for two or more years after diagnosis (e.g., Caplette-Gingras & Savard, 2008). In addition, cancer patients who complete their treatment often report living with fear and uncertainty because of the fear of recurrence (Koch et al., 2013; Ness et al., 2013). Next we discussed how cancer affects parents (i.e., in their parenting roles) and their children, and we considered gender and developmental stage differences in children with regard to how they cope with parental cancer. For example, adolescent daughters of mothers coping with cancer are at the highest risk of experiencing emotional distress (e.g., Compas, Worsham, Ey, & Howell, 1996; Lewis, 2007). We described cultural factors to take into consideration (e.g., age, income, race, healthcare setting) while working with families coping with parental cancer. Finally, we provided a brief clinical vignette to illustrate how a family coping with parental cancer might clinically present.

Test Your Knowledge: True or False

1 Every year, hundreds of children will be affected by the diagnosis and treatment of cancer in a parent.
2 The most common type of cancer is prostate cancer.
3 Cancer patients tend to experience low rates of depressive symptoms up to 2 years after diagnosis.
4 Cancer patients who complete treatment are not worried about cancer anymore.
5 Cancer can cause distress in both the ill parent and his/her partner or spouse.
6 Younger children are more negatively affected by parental cancer than adolescents.
7 Among adolescents whose parents have cancer, there are differences in how male and female adolescents cope.
8 Children's and adolescents' developmental needs determine how to best talk to them about the cancer and how to help them.
9 Children and adolescents almost always speak up and tell their parents they are struggling with the parental cancer.
10 There are differences in how individuals cope with cancer across racial and ethnic groups.

Answers: 1-F, 2-T, 3-F, 4-F, 5-T, 6-F, 7-T, 8-T, 9-F, 10-T

Professional Readings and Resources

Harpham, W. S. (2011). *When a parent has cancer: A guide to caring for your children*. New York: Harper Collins.
Heiney, S. P. (2001). *Cancer in the family: Helping children cope with a parent's illness*. American Cancer Society.
Van Dernoot, P. (2006). *Helping your children cope with your cancer: A guide for parents and families*. Long Island, NY: Hatherleigh Press.

References

American Cancer Society. (2012). *Cancer facts and figures 2012*. Atlanta, GA: American Cancer Society.

American Cancer Society. (2013). *Cancer facts and figures 2013*. Atlanta, GA: American Cancer Society.

American Cancer Society. (2014). *Cancer facts & figures 2014*. Atlanta, GA: American Cancer Society.

Armsden, G. C., & Lewis, F. M. (1994). The child's adaptation to parental medical illness: Theory and clinical implications. *Patient Education and Counseling, 22*(3), 153–165. doi:10.1016/0738-3991(93)90095-E

Baik, O., & Adams, K. B. (2011). Improving the well-being of couples facing cancer: A review of couples-based psychosocial interventions. *Journal of Marital and Family Therapy, 37*, 250–266.

Billhult, A., & Segersten, K. (2003). Strength of motherhood: Nonrecurrent breast cancer as experienced by mothers with dependent children. *Scandinavian Journal of Caring Science, 17*, 122–128. doi:10.1046/j.1471-6712.2003.00219.x

Bottomley, A. (1998). Anxiety and the adult cancer patient. *European Journal of Cancer Care, 7*(4), 217.

Brown, L. F., Kroenke, K., Theobald, D. E., Wu, J., & Tu, W. (2010). The association of depression and anxiety with health-related quality of life in cancer patients with depression and/or pain. *Psycho-Oncology, 19*(7), 734–741. doi:10.1002/pon.162

Buchbinder, M., Longhofer, J., & McCue, K. (2009). Family routines and rituals when a parent has cancer. *Families, Systems, and Health, 27*, 213–227. doi:10.1037/a0017005

Caplette-Gingras, A., & Savard, J. (2008). Depression in women with metastatic breast cancer: A review of the literature. *Palliative and Supportive Care, 6*(4), 377–387. doi:10.1017/S1478951508000606

Carlson, L. E., Robinson, J., Simpson, J. S. A., Speca, M., Tillotson, L., Bultz, B. D., . . . Pelletier, G. (2004). High levels of untreated distress and fatigue in cancer patients. *British Journal of Cancer, 90*(12), 2297–2304. doi:10.1038/sj.bjc.6601887

Centers for Disease Control and Prevention (CDC). (2013, August 12). Retrieved from www.cdc.gov/cancer/prostate/statistics/race.htm

Christ, G. H., Siegel, K., & Sperber, D. (1994). Impact of parental terminal cancer on adolescents. *American Journal of Orthopsychiatry, 64*(4), 604–613.

Compas, B. E., Worsham, N. L., Epping-Jordan, J. E., Grant, K. E., Mireault, G., Howell, D. C., & Malcarne, V. L. (1994). When mom or dad has cancer: Markers of psychological distress in cancer patients, spouses, and children. *Health Psychology: Official Journal of the Division of Health Psychology, American Psychological Association, 13*(6), 507–515. doi:10.1037/0278-6133.13.6.507

Compas, B. E., Worsham, N. L., Ey, S., & Howell, D. C. (1996). When mom or dad has cancer: II. Coping, cognitive appraisals, and psychological distress in children of cancer patients. *Health psychology, 15*(3), 167–175

Culver, J. L., Arena, P. L., Wimberly, S. R., Antoni, M. H., & Carver, C. S. (2004). Coping among African-American, Hispanic, and non-Hispanic white women recently treated for early stage breast cancer. *Psychology & Health, 19*(2), 157–166. doi:10.1080/0887044031000165269

Davey, M. P., Askew, J., & Godette, K. (2003). Parent and adolescent responses to nonterminal parental cancer: A retrospective multiple-case pilot study. *Families, Systems, & Health, 21*(3), 245–258. doi:10.1037/1091-7527.21.3.245

Davey, M., Gulish, L., Askew, J., Godette, K., & Childs, N. (2005). Adolescents coping with mom's breast cancer: Developing family intervention programs. *Journal of Marital and Family Therapy, 31*(2), 247–258. doi:10.1111/j.1752-0606.2005.tb01558.x

Davey, M., Kissil, K., Lynch, L., Harmon, L. R., & Hodgson, N. (2012). Lessons learned in developing a culturally adapted intervention for African American families coping with parental cancer. *Journal of Cancer Education, 27*, 744–751.

Davey, M., Kissil, K., Lynch, L., Harmon, L. R., & Hodgson, N. (2013). A culturally adapted family intervention for African American families coping with parental cancer: Outcomes of a pilot study. *Psycho-Oncology, 22*, 1572–1580.

Davey, M., Niño, A., Kissil, K., & Ingram, M. (2012). African American parents' experiences navigating breast cancer while caring for their children. *Qualitative Health Research, 22,* 1260–1270.

Davey, M., Tubbs, C., Kissil, K., & Niño, A. (2011). "We are survivors too": African American adolescents' experiences of coping with parental breast cancer. *Psycho-Oncology, 20,* 77–87.

Deshields, T., Zebrack, B., & Kennedy, V. (2013). The state of psychosocial services in cancer care in the United States. *Psycho-Oncology, 22*(3), 699–703. doi:10.1002/pon.3057

Edwards, L., Watson, M., St James-Roberts, I., Ashley, S., Tilney, C., Brougham, B., . . . Romer, G. (2008). Adolescent's stress responses and psychological functioning when a parent has early breast cancer. *Psycho-Oncology, 17*(10), 1039–1047. doi:10.1002/pon.1323

Fann, J. R., Thomas-Rich, A. M., Katon, W. J., Cowley, D., Pepping, M., McGregor, B. A., & Gralow, J. (2008). Major depression after breast cancer: A review of epidemiology and treatment. *General Hospital Psychiatry, 30*(2), 112–126. doi:10.1016/j.genhosppsych.2007.10.008

Forrest, G., Plumb, C., Ziebland, S., & Stein, A. (2006). Breast cancer in the family: Children's perceptions of their mother's cancer and its initial treatment: Qualitative study. *BMJ: British Medical Journal, 332*(7548), 998–1001. doi:10.1136/bmj.38793.567801.AE

Grabiak, B. R., Bender, C. M., & Puskar, K. R. (2007). The impact of parental cancer on the adolescent: An analysis of the literature. *Psycho-Oncology, 16*(2), 127–137. doi:10.1002/pon.1083

Harris, C. A., & Zakowski, S. G. (2003). Comparisons of distress in adolescents of cancer patients and controls. *Psycho-Oncology, 12*(2), 173–182. doi:10.1002/pon.631

Hoekstra, H. J., Hoekstra-Weebers, J. E., van der Graaf, W. T., Gazendam-Donofrio, S. M., Visser, A., Wiel, H. B. v. d., & Huizinga, G. A. (2007). Family functioning and adolescents' emotional and behavioral problems: When a parent has cancer. *Annals of Oncology, 18*(12), 1951–1956. doi:10.1093/annonc/mdm373

Hoffman, K. E., McCarthy, E. P., Recklitis, C. J., & Ng, A. K. (2009). Psychological distress in long-term survivors of adult-onset cancer: Results from a national survey. *Archives of Internal Medicine, 169*(14), 1274–1281. doi:10.1001/archinternmed.2009.179

Hoke, L. A. (1997). A short-term psychoeducational intervention for families with parental cancer. *Harvard Review of Psychiatry, 5*(2), 99–103.

Hoke, L. A. (2001). Psychosocial adjustment in children of mothers with breast cancer. *Psycho-Oncology, 10*(5), 361–369. doi:10.1002/pon.515

Huizinga, G. A., van der Graaf, W. T., Visser, A., Dijkstra, J. S., & Hoekstra-Weebers, J. E. (2003). Psychosocial consequences for children of a parent with cancer: A pilot study. *Cancer Nursing, 26*(3), 195–202. doi:10.1097/00002820-200306000-00004

Johnston, M., Martin, D., Martin, M., & Gumaer, J. (1992). Long-term parental illness and children: Perils and promises. *School Counselor, 39,* 225–231.

Kissil, K., Niño, A., Jacobs, S., Davey, M., & Tubbs, C. Y. (2010). "It has been a good growing experience for me": Growth experiences among African American youth coping with parental cancer. *Families, Systems & Health: The Journal of Collaborative Family Healthcare, 28*(3), 274–289. doi:10.1037/a0020001.

Koch, L., Jansen, L., Brenner, H., & Arndt, V. (2013). Fear of recurrence and disease progression in long-term (≥5 years) cancer survivors: A systematic review of quantitative studies. *Psychooncology, 22,* 1–11.

Leedham, B., & Meyerowitz, E. (1999). Responses to parental cancer: A clinical perspective. *Journal of Clinical Psychology in Medical Settings, 6,* 441–461. doi:10.1023/A:1026228000254

Lewis, F. M. (2004). Family-focused oncology nursing research. *Oncology Nursing Forum, 31*(2), 288–292. doi:10.1188/04.ONF.288-292

Lewis, F. M. (2006). The effects of cancer survivorship on families and caregivers: More research is needed on long-term survivors. *Cancer Nursing, 29*(suppl), 20–25. doi:10.1097/00002820-200603002-0000

Lewis, F. M. (2007). Parental cancer and dependent children: Selected issues for future research. *Psycho-Oncology, 16*(2), 97–98. doi:10.1002/pon.1141

Lewis, F. M., Casey, S. M., Brandt, P. A., Shands, M. E., & Zahlis, E. H. (2006). The enhancing connections program: Pilot study of a cognitive-behavioral intervention for mothers and children affected by breast cancer. *Psycho-Oncology, 15*(6), 486–497. doi:10.1002/pon.979

Lewis, F. M., & Darby, E. L. (2003). Adolescent adjustment and maternal breast cancer: A test of the "faucet hypothesis". *Journal of Psychosocial Oncology, 21*, 81–104.

Lewis, F. M., & Hammond, M. A. (1996). The father's, mother's, and adolescent's functioning with breast cancer. *Family Relations, 45*(4), 456–465.

Massie, M. J. (2004). Prevalence of depression in patients with cancer. *Journal of the National Cancer Institute. Monographs, 2004*(32), 57–71. doi:10.1093/jncimonographs/lgh014

Meyerowitz, B. E., Kurita, K., & D'Orazio, L. M. (2008). The psychological and emotional fallout of cancer and its treatment. *Cancer Journal, 14*(6), 410–413. doi:10.1097/PPO.0b013e31818d8757

Muriel, A. C., & Rauch, P. K. (2003). Suggestions for patients on how to talk with children about a parent's cancer. *The Journal of Supportive Oncology, 1*(2), 143–145.

NCI (2014). Press releases, available at www.cancer.gov/news-events/press-releases/2014.

Nelson, E., & While, D. (2002). Children's adjustment during the first year of a parent's cancer diagnosis. *Journal of Psychosocial Oncology, 20*(1), 15–36.

Ness, S., Kokal, J., Fee-Schroeder, K., Novotny, P., Satele, D., & Barton, D. (2013). Concerns across the survivorship trajectory: results from a survey of cancer survivors. *Oncology Nursing Forum, 40*, 35–42.

Niemelä, M., Hakko, H., & Räsänen, S. (2010). A systematic narrative review of the studies on structured child-centred interventions for families with a parent with cancer. *Psycho-Oncology, 19*(5), 451–461. doi:10.1002/pon.162

Osborn, T. (2007). The psychosocial impact of parental cancer on children and adolescents: A systematic review. *Psycho-oncology, 16*(2), 101–126.

Smith, R. A., Cokkinides, V., & Brawley, O. W. (2009). Cancer screening in the United States 2009: A review of current American Cancer Society Guidelines and Issues in Cancer Screening. *CA Cancer Journal of Clinicians, 59*, 27–41. doi:10.3322/caac.20008

Spencer, S. M., Lehman, J. M., Wynings, C., Arena, P., Carver, C. S., Antoni, M. H., . . . Love, N. (1999). Concerns about breast cancer and relations to psychosocial well-being in a multiethnic sample of early-stage patients. *Health Psychology, 18*(2), 159–168. doi:10.1037/0278-6133.18.2.159

Ward, E., Jemal, A., Cokkinides, V., Singh, G. K., Cardinez, C., Ghafoor, A., & Thun, M. (2004). Cancer disparities by race/ethnicity and socioeconomic status. *CA: A Cancer Journal for Clinicians, 54*(2), 78. doi:10.3322/canjclin.54.2.78

Wellisch, D. K. (1979). Adolescent acting out when a parent has cancer. *International Journal of Family Therapy, 1*(3), 230–241.

Whaley, A. L., & Davis, K. E. (2007). Cultural competence and evidence-based practice in mental health services. *American Psychologist, 62*, 563–574, doi:10.1037/0003-066X.62.6.563

CHAPTER 5

PARENTAL HIV

Maureen Davey

HIV: About the Illness

Prevalence

The human immunodeficiency virus (HIV) is a retrovirus that uses CD4 T-cells (helper cells whose main purpose is to initiate the body's response to infections) to reproduce and attack the immune system, which then causes the acquired immunodeficiency syndrome (AIDS) (CDC, 2013; Weiss, 1993). Individuals diagnosed with HIV who have CD4 counts below 200 cells/mcL are diagnosed with AIDS (CDC, 2010). HIV/AIDS reduces the number of helper T-cells, which leads to a weakened immune system and an inability to fight opportunistic infections that would normally not significantly affect otherwise healthy individuals (CDC, 2012b). These infections are referred to as *opportunistic* because they take advantage of a weakened immune system and cause illnesses (e.g., pneumonia, central nervous system lymphoma, some types of cancer) that can lead to death (CDC, 2010). Without treatment, the average survival time after being infected with HIV is approximately 9 to 11 years; however, HIV is now manageable with treatment (e.g., HAART), but it is not curable (CDC, 2013).

Unfortunately, HIV continues to spread globally (e.g., Africa, Asia, Eastern Europe, Central Asia, Caribbean, Latin America) and in the U.S. (United Nations Programme on HIV/AIDS [UNAIDS], 2008). In 2007, there were 2.7 million new HIV infections; younger individuals (aged 15 to 24 years) made up half of all new HIV infections globally (UNAIDS, 2008). The CDC (2012a) estimates that more than 1 million individuals are currently living with HIV in the United States. The highest new rates of HIV infection in the U.S. are among 20- to 45-year-olds. In particular, young African American MSMs (men who have sex with men) and African American heterosexual females are the fastest growing groups because of unprotected intercourse.

There are significant health disparities in the incidence of HIV in the United States. Individuals of color who have lower SES tend to be disproportionately affected by HIV (CDC, 2012a,b,c; Schuster et al., 2000; U.S. Department of Health and Human Services, 2001). Noteworthy, when HIV was first recognized and diagnosed by medical providers, few women were diagnosed with it; however, currently women account for more than 25% of all new HIV/AIDS diagnoses, and women of color (e.g., African American, Latina) are disproportionately affected (CDC, 2012b,c). According to the CDC (2012a), high risk heterosexual contact is currently the source of 80% of newly diagnosed cases of HIV among women across all races in the U.S.

By race, African Americans face the most significant HIV burden (CDC, 2010, 2012a,b) (see Figure 5.1). For example, in 2010, African Americans accounted for approximately 44% of all new HIV infections among adults and adolescents aged 13 and older, yet they only represent 12% of the U.S. population (CDC, 2012a). The estimated rate of new HIV infections for African American women was 20 times that of White women and almost 5 times that of Hispanic/Latino women.

Latinos are also significantly affected by HIV. The estimated number of new HIV infections in 2010 was three times higher for Latinos than for Whites, likely due to poverty and language barriers that can affect access to health care and to a lack of health literacy regarding protective behaviors that can help to prevent the transmission of HIV (CDC, 2010). Among Latino MSMs, approximately 67% of new HIV infections occur under the age of 35 (CDC, 2010). HIV has also affected American Indians and Alaskan Natives, who have the highest number of individuals diagnosed with HIV out of all racial/ethnic groups because of contaminated needles and substance abuse (CDC, 2012c). Americans aged 50 and older have many of the same HIV risk factors as younger Americans. Individuals who are 55 years old and older account for 19% of the 1 million people living with HIV in the United States. HIV progresses more rapidly in older people (CDC, 2012a).

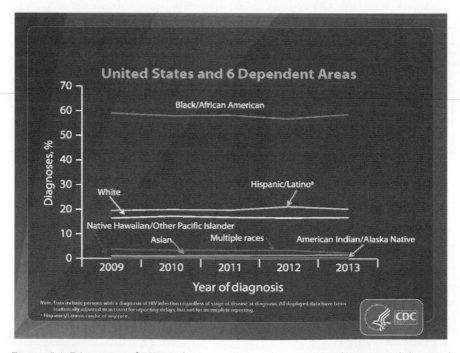

Figure 5.1 Diagnoses of HIV Infection among Adolescents and Young Adults Aged 13 to 24 Years, by Race/Ethnicity, 2009–2013

Source: National Center for Health Statistics (NCHS), Center for Disease Control. Retrieved from www.cdc.gov/hiv/pdf/statistics_surveillance_Adolescents.pdf

Socioeconomic factors impact how individuals are diagnosed and cope with HIV. According to the CDC (2011), poverty is a significant barrier to accessing HIV testing and HIV medications (HAART). For example, the CDC (2011) reported that individuals who live below the poverty line are twice as likely to be HIV infected (2.3%) compared to individuals who live in the same community but above the poverty line (1.0%), and the prevalence for both groups is higher than the national average (0.45%). Additionally, HIV infection is more prevalent among individuals who are unemployed and who have less than a high school education (CDC, 2012c).

Prognosis and Medical Outcomes

There are three main types of bodily fluids that can transmit HIV/AIDS: (1) blood products, (2) semen, and (3) vaginal fluids. Thus, the four main routes of HIV infection are: (1) blood transfusions, (2) unprotected sexual intercourse (including oral and anal), (3) sharing contaminated needles, and (4) mother to baby either before birth or during birth (referred to as *perinatal HIV*) or through breast milk. When HIV enters the bloodstream, it first attacks the white blood cells (CD4 cells). The immune system then produces antibodies to fight off infections. When an individual takes an HIV test, providers are looking for these antibodies, which will confirm that an HIV infection has occurred (www.amfar.org). It is important to get tested after potential exposure. Within a few weeks after being infected with HIV, many people develop temporary flu-like symptoms or swollen glands. Yet, some individuals report feeling healthy for a decade or more, and unfortunately, HIV-infected people who feel healthy can still transmit the virus to others (CDC, 2012b).

Most people develop detectable HIV antibodies within 3 months of the infection, with the average at 20 days; in rare cases, it can take 6 to 12 months. For this reason, the CDC (2012b) recommends HIV testing 6 months after the last possible exposure (e.g., unprotected vaginal, anal, or oral sex or sharing needles). Individuals can be tested at their doctor's office, the local health department, the hospital, and clinics (e.g., mobile) that provide HIV testing (www.amfar.org; CDC, 2012b). HIV test results are confidential and can only be shared with people who are authorized to see the medical records; anonymous testing sites are also available. Several HIV antibody tests are used today, and the most common are blood and oral fluid tests (CDC, 2014a). Unlike traditional tests, which can take from 3 days to several weeks, rapid HIV testing results are ready in 20 to 60 minutes. Although all tests are accurate, positive HIV results should be later confirmed with a follow-up test before a final diagnosis of HIV can be made (CDC, 2010).

There are several stages after an individual has been infected with HIV. The first stage, or acute stage, includes the following symptoms, which can occur 1 to 6 weeks after the HIV infection: (1) short, flu-like illness; (2) fever; (3) weight loss; (4) mouth sores or thrush; (5) headaches; (6) skin rash; and (7) nausea or vomiting (CDC, 2010). The second stage, an asymptomatic period, can last for an average of 10 years. This stage is usually free of symptoms; however, there may be swollen glands, and the level of HIV in the blood can drop to low levels but HIV antibodies are still detectable in the blood. The third stage is called the symptomatic stage, where the immune system significantly deteriorates leading to the development of opportunistic infections and cancers (CDC, 2012b). In the fourth and final stage, HIV becomes AIDS as the immune system weakens and CD4 cells decrease significantly in number (CD4 count below 200 cells/mcL).

People infected with HIV have a higher risk for developing the following types of cancer: (1) Kaposi sarcoma (a cancer that causes patches of abnormal tissue to grow under the skin in the lining of the mouth, nose, and throat or in other organs), (2) non-Hodgkin lymphoma (tumors develop from lymphocytes, which is a type of white blood cell), and (3) cervical cancer (NCI, 2014). A diagnosis of any one of these cancers typically means that the HIV has progressed to AIDS (NCI, 2014).

Regarding the progression of HIV/AIDS, individuals with CD4 counts of less than 500 are vulnerable to experiencing the following: (1) bacterial infections, (2) tuberculosis, (3) herpes simplex (genital herpes) and herpes zoster (shingles), (4) vaginal candidiasis (an infection of the vagina caused by a yeast, or fungus, referred to as *candida*), and (5) Kaposi sarcoma (pink or purplish skin lesions caused by the HHV-8 virus) (CDC, 2013). When CD4 counts drop below 200, then individuals are at risk of developing the following: (1) pneumonia, (2) toxoplasmosis (a parasitic disease), and (3) non-Hodgkin lymphoma. When CD4 counts drop below 50, individuals are at risk of developing: (1) disseminated mycobacterium avium complex infection or MAC (caused by inhalation or ingestion with symptoms such as fever, sweats, weight loss, and anemia), (2) histoplasmosis (known as "cave disease," a potentially fatal fungal disease), (3) CMV renitis (an inflammation of the retina caused by a CMV infection), (4) CNS lymphoma (cancer affecting the central nervous system), (5) progressive multifocal leukoencephalopathy (a viral infection of the brain), (6) HIV dementia, and (7) wasting syndrome (an unexplainable, profound weight loss accompanied by weakness and persistent diarrhea) (CDC, 2013).

The HIV/AIDS epidemic has changed from treating an illness that often led to death in the 1980s and early 1990s to now treating a chronic yet manageable illness due to the development of highly active antiretroviral therapies (HAART; Lightfoot, Rotheram-Borus, & Tevendale, 2007). HAART is the name given to the aggressive treatment used to suppress HIV viral replication and the progression of the HIV disease (Miller & Hays, 2000). The HAART regimen combines three or more different drugs developed to reduce the amount of active virus, and for some people it even lowers the numbers of active virus until it is undetectable using HIV blood testing. Yet, HAART often includes the following side effects that can negatively affect treatment compliance: (1) anxiety, (2) insulin resistance, (3) diarrhea, (4) nausea and vomiting, and (5) rashes (Kolbasovsky, 2008). Despite these uncomfortable side effects, HAART has significantly reduced the number of AIDS deaths in the U.S. and worldwide (CDC, 2013).

For most patients, near perfect (95%) medication adherence is needed to achieve full and durable viral suppression (Davey, Foster, Milton, & Duncan, 2009; Naar-King et al., 2006), so the introduction of HAART has led to many studies that examined factors that affect medication adherence (CDC, 2010; DiMatteo, Giordani, Lepper, & Croghan, 2002; Song, Lee, Rotheram-Borus & Svvendeman, 2006). Poor medication adherence to the HAART regimen has many more negative consequences for HIV compared to other illnesses (e.g., Johnson et al., 2006) and is the second strongest predictor of the progression to AIDS and death, after the CD4 count (Miller & Hayes, 2000). This degree of adherence requires a patient on a twice-daily regimen to not miss or delay more than three doses of antiretroviral medications per month, is far greater than that commonly associated with other chronic diseases, and is difficult for most patients to maintain over the course of a lifelong illness (Osterberg & Blaschke, 2005; Peterson, Takiyah, & Finley, 2003).

At some point, a healthcare provider may decide to change an individual's HIV treatment plan. Two of the most common reasons are: (1) drug toxicity and (2) treatment regimen failure or resistance to HAART (www.amfar.org). Drug toxicity refers to when HIV medications cause harmful side effects that make it too difficult for a patient to continue taking them. Regimen failure means that the medications are not working well enough to control the HIV because drug resistance has occurred. This can result from poor overall health, poor treatment adherence, drug resistance, alcohol or substance use, or medical conditions or illnesses other than HIV infection. Providers often change the combination of three antiretrovirals prescribed (there are over 25 FDA approved antiretroviral medications; CDC, 2013). Some providers have patients take a "drug holiday" from their HIV medicine, which is a structured treatment interruption; this can take place if the viral load is very low and the patient is asymptomatic or if the side effects are causing too much discomfort (DiMatteo et al., 2002; Miller & Hays, 2000). Once an individual's status has changed from HIV to AIDS, providers will treat the opportunistic infections and likely prescribe a different HAART regimen, with the hope that the amount of HIV in the blood will become suppressed again and the patient will convert back to having HIV (Miller & Hays, 2000).

Psychological Comorbidities

Many individuals who are coping with HIV/AIDS additionally experience depression, anxiety, post-traumatic stress disorder (PTSD), loneliness, and fear because they are also coping with the stigma of a disease that is often perceived as immoral by their families, communities, and larger society (Herek & Capitanio, 1993). HIV is different from the other types of parental illnesses described in this book because there are unique challenges, such as deciding how and when to disclose one's HIV status because individuals could be shunned verbally, physically, and financially by society (Dutra et al., 2000; Qiao et al., 2013; Schuster et al., 2000). Additionally, HIV/AIDS can affect multiple family members who could be ill at the same time (Kolbasovsky, 2008; Rotheram-Borus et al., 2005). Unfortunately, the stigma attached to HIV/AIDS often leads to secrecy and alienation from social support and resources and, for some, co-occurring distress (Herek & Capitanio, 1993; Rotheram-Borus, Robin, Reid, & Draimin, 1998; United Nations Programme, 2008).

Prior studies suggest that individuals who are coping with HIV tend to experience elevated rates of depressive symptoms, anxiety, and PTSD and are at an increased risk of engaging in substance abuse, intimate partner violence, and being homeless (Gaynes, Pence, Eron, & Miller, 2008; Leserman, 2003). The effects of HIV on the brain, the stigma of HIV, losing one's job, social isolation, and illness-related stressors can all predispose individuals to experience co-occurring mental health issues (Herek & Capitanio, 1993; Parry, Blank, & Pithey, 2007). Depression has been associated with poorer medication compliance, worse clinical outcomes, increased sexual risk taking, higher suicide risk, and a decreased quality of life (Gaynes et al., 2008). Individuals coping with HIV and PTSD tend to have poorer treatment compliance, more reports of pain and discomfort, and more alcohol/substance abuse (Leserman, 2003; Parry et al., 2007). Additionally, epidemiological studies suggest that the suicide rate is more than three times higher among HIV-positive individuals compared to the general population (Carrico, 2010). Consequently, these co-occurring issues can all negatively affect medication compliance and clinical outcomes (Osterberg & Blaschke, 2005).

Level of Uncertainty about the Illness

Patients report experiencing trauma and fears about the acute stage of the HIV illness returning, viral loads increasing, grief for the loss of one's physical health, and isolation and rejection from family members, friends, and the community (e.g., Serovich, Kimberly, Mosack, & Lewis, 2001). Many report feeling over-whelmed when they find out they are HIV positive, including feelings such as shock, fear, and anger. Often people feel helpless, sad, and anxious about the illness (CDC, 2012b,c). HIV can cause feelings of uncertainty because, even with good treatment adherence, opportunistic infections can still occur (e.g., pneumonia), and the viral load may increase because of resistance to the HAART regimen (United Nations Programme, 2008). Although with 95% treatment adherence to HAART many do live full lives without experiencing many of these negative psychosocial outcomes, prior studies suggest that worries about the HIV illness becoming more acute and converting to AIDS are common among most individuals who are coping with HIV (Rotherum-Borus et al., 2005, 2012).

What Clinicians Need to Know about HIV

1   HIV infection causes the immune system to begin to fail, which can lead to life-threatening opportunistic infections.
2   HIV is most often acquired through unprotected sexual intercourse, contaminated needles, and from an infected mother (perinatal).
3   The highest new rates of HIV infection in the U.S. are among 20- to 45-year-olds, in particular young African American MSMs (men who have sex with men) and African American heterosexual females.
4   Although there is no cure for HIV/AIDS, HAART, which is a highly active antiretroviral therapy developed to reduce the amount of HIV virus in the blood, has improved outcomes since the mid-1990s.
5   When working with individuals with HIV/AIDS, it is important to remember that they tend to have elevated rates of depression, which have been linked to poor self-care, poor medication adherence, and worse outcomes.
6   Depressive symptoms are likely caused by the stigma of HIV/AIDS, social isolation, and illness-related stressors.
7   Studies have also reported that anxiety and PTSD are elevated among individuals with HIV/AIDS.

Effects of Parental HIV on Parents and Children

Although HIV/AIDS is diagnosed in an individual, the entire family and community are affected (Rotheram-Borus, Rice, Comulada, Best, & Li, 2012). "As the epidemic has unfolded, the early focus on individuals has become inadequate: families live with HIV, not just individuals" (Rotheram-Borus, Flannery, Rice, & Lester, 2005, p. 978). Families may face psychological and interpersonal issues as they adapt to the diagnosis and long-term treatment of HIV/AIDS. Unlike other physical illnesses such as heart disease and cancer, HIV/AIDS is different because many family members can be ill at the same time, and there is often social stigma associated with this illness (Zhao, Li, Zhao, Zhang, & Stanton, 2012), which can lead to secrecy and experiences of isolation from other community supports. Families may additionally be coping with chronic poverty, multiple losses, trauma, and substance abuse (Lee et al., 2007). Additionally, there has been a profound negative impact of HIV on low-income African American and Latino families because they are disproportionately affected by HIV/AIDS in the U.S. (CDC, 2013).

It has been estimated that 200,000 children in the U.S. are living with a parent who has HIV, but this is likely an underestimate because approximately one-third of individuals who have HIV are not in care and another one-third do not yet know they are infected (CDC, 2012a). Women account for 24% of individuals living with HIV in the U.S., and many of these women are the primary caregivers of children (CDC, 2013; Murphy et al., 2015; Rotheram-Borus et al., 2012).

Medical advancements have led to people with HIV/AIDS living much longer (CDC, 2013), and as a result, it is more likely that the children of HIV-infected parents will not lose their parents until they reach adulthood (Bauman et al., 2006; Rotheram-Borus et al., 2006; Shuster et al., 2000). It is also possible that more HIV-infected individuals will decide to become parents. In a sample of HIV-positive adults receiving health care in the U.S., 28–29% of men and women wanted to have children in the future (Chen et al., 2001). Another study reported that 12% of the women and 2% of men in this sample had conceived and had their youngest child after being diagnosed with HIV (Schuster et al., 2000). Women and men coping with HIV can safely have children, which will be explained further in this chapter (CDC, 2012a).

Societal factors that can complicate the adjustment of families to HIV include: (1) the secrecy, (2) stigma, (3) social isolation, and (4) discrimination often experienced by families coping with parental HIV (CDC, 2013; Dutra et al., 2000; Zhao et al., 2012). Families may be additionally burdened with: (1) chronic poverty, (2) homelessness, (3) multiple losses, and (4) substance abuse (Bogart et al., 2008; Bor et al., 1993; Chi & Li, 2013). Navigating parenting in the context of illness can be challenging, as described in this book, but living with HIV as a parent is different than living with another type of chronic illness because of the societal stigma and discrimination that can lead to isolation and less social support (Dutra et al., 2000; Lee et al., 2007; Mitrani, Prado, Feaster, Robinson-Batista, & Szapocznik, 2003; Rotheram-Borus et al., 2005; Zhao et al., 2012).

Couples in which one partner is HIV positive and the other is HIV negative are referred to as either serodiscordant or mixed serostatus (CDC, 2012c; Fife, Scott, Fineberg, & Zwickl, 2008). Couples in mixed-status relationships may additionally be coping with the following issues: (1) the HIV-positive partner may focus on not infecting his/her partner and the HIV-negative partner may focus on caregiving, which can lead to an imbalance in the relationship; (2) HIV can lead to physical changes and HAART can also cause side effects that can lead to negative feelings about physical attraction and impact intimacy; and (3) fears about transmitting HIV to one's partner may lead to decreased or no sexual intimacy, even though precautions can be taken to not infect a partner (e.g., condoms and safe sex practices) (Fife et al., 2008; Martire, Schulz, Helgeson, Small, & Saghafi, 2010). Additionally, psychoeducation for couples is recommended because, although HAART cannot cure HIV, adhering to the medication regimen can reduce the chances of transmitting HIV to a partner (e.g., because of maintaining an undetectable viral load), as can regularly using condoms and avoiding sexual activity during infections (e.g., STDs, cold, or flu).

Women and men who are HIV positive can safely have biological children. Recent studies suggest that HIV-infected sperm can be "washed" and then used to have a healthy baby (Eke & Oragwu, 2011). Sperm washing describes when individual spermatozoa are separated from the seminal fluid. Sperm washing is used to prevent HIV transmission but allow conception in sero-discordant couples in which the male is HIV positive but the female is HIV negative. This procedure is feasible because HIV cannot attach itself to spermatozoa, but it can be found in the fluid and cells surrounding spermatozoa. Yet, not everyone can afford this procedure; it costs approximately $10,000, and medical insurance tends to not cover it. It can also be tough to find a clinic that has the medical equipment needed to wash sperm (Eke & Oragwu, 2011).

Approximately 35% of pregnant HIV-positive women can pass the HIV infection to their newborns, if they are not treated (CDC, 2012c). HIV transmission during pregnancy, labor, and delivery or breastfeeding is referred to as *perinatal transmission* and is the most common route of HIV infection in children. When HIV is diagnosed before or during pregnancy and treated with HAART (and breastfeeding does not occur), then, according to the CDC (2012c), the risk of passing HIV to a newborn drops significantly to 2% (CDC, 2012c). Fortunately, in the last 20 years, HIV testing and prevention efforts have resulted in a 90% decrease in the number of perinatal infections in the U.S. (CDC, 2012c).

The Effect of HIV on Parenting

Parents who are coping with HIV have reported many challenges while caring for their children, such as: (1) parenting ability, (2) disclosing HIV status to their children, (3) stigma associated with HIV, (4) children's emotional and behavioral reactions, (5) medical treatment and adherence, and (6) guardianship planning (Forehand et al., 2002; Rotheram-Borus et al., 2005, 2006). Yet, some of the positive changes parents reported are: (1) commitment to parenting and (2) strengthened parent–child relationships (Chi & Li, 2013; Murphy et al., 2015).

Parenting ability is often a struggle because parents report experiencing fatigue, side effects from the HAART treatment, and depressive symptoms (Gaynes et al., 2008; Leserman, 2003). Disclosure of HIV status to children is especially challenging because they report struggling with: (1) how to disclose to children, (2) what to tell their children, (3) when to disclose to their children, and (4) telling older children but not younger children (Qiao et al., 2013). Some of the challenges reported by parents are the possible community stigma (e.g., children's peers at school) associated with HIV, which can lead to them keeping it a family secret, isolation and peer rejection, and fears and misperceptions (Corona et al., 2006; Murphy et al., 2015).

Some of the parenting challenges regarding children's emotional and behavioral reactions are mixed according to prior studies on HIV disclosure (Qiao et al., 2013; Rotheram-Borus et al., 2005, 2012). Some children experience depressive symptoms and anxiety, engage in risky behaviors, have more family conflict, and experience role reversals as children become caregivers for their parents (Bauman et al., 2006; Stein, Riedel, & Rotheram-Borus, 1999). Other challenges parents have reported concern medication and treatment adherence regarding hiding medications from their children who do not know their HIV status and missing medical appointments because of child care issues (Osterberg & Blaschke, 2005; Qiao et al., 2013). Additionally, guardianship planning to decide, in the worst case scenario, who will care for their children can lead to family isolation and struggles with the legality of these plans (Rotheram-Borus et al., 1998, 2012). Despite these challenges, some parents have reported positive changes in their parenting; for example, qualitative studies suggest a renewed commitment to parenting, strengthened parent–child relationships, and some role reversals (parentification) that are adaptive for older children to assume more developmentally appropriate responsibilities at home (Bauman et al., 2006; Bogart et al., 2008).

Disclosure of HIV Status to Children

Parental HIV disclosure to children is a process, not a single event, that should change developmentally throughout a child's life (Lesch et al., 2007). Disclosure will likely involve multiple conversations that are informed by the child's cognitive development and gradually improve the child's age-appropriate understanding of HIV and its impact on his/her life (Qiao et al., 2013). Providers need to understand each family's unique cultural and family environment and start with a comprehensive assessment of caregivers' and children's needs and the factors (e.g., family, psychosocial, cultural, religious) that may affect HIV disclosure. It is recommended that providers first carefully discuss disclosure with the caregiver(s) to find out their beliefs and views about disclosure, for example, who needs to be told before the child can be told (Lester et al., 2002).

It is important to attend to cultural beliefs and practices (e.g., race, ethnicity, religion) regarding appropriate ways of discussing HIV with children and caregiver readiness to deal with the disease and disclose to their children (Plaff, 2004). Clinicians need to provide an environment that is supportive and open and that addresses caregivers' concerns and fears about disclosure (Waugh, 2003). Some precipitating factors for disclosure include: (1) illness progression and the appearance of visible signs of illness, (2) the child's persistent illness-related questions, and (3) parental illness or death (Lester et al., 2002). Disclosure patterns by caregivers can range from a full disclosure to partial disclosure to no disclosure (Nehring et al., 2000). Many parents report being afraid to disclose their HIV status to their children because they worry that their children will inadvertently disclose their status to others, who would then treat their children unfairly (Zhao et al., 2012). Unfortunately, three decades into the HIV/AIDS epidemic, disclosure of parental HIV infection is often delayed until children are older, and few empirically based interventions or guidelines are available for assisting parents and clinicians in making decisions about disclosure to children (Wiener et al., 2007).

The Effect of Parental HIV on Children and Adolescents

Like other children with a seriously ill parent, parental HIV-affected children and adolescents are vulnerable to emotional and behavioral issues (Bor, Miller, & Goldman, 1993; Corona et al., 2009; Forehand et al., 2002); however, prior research additionally suggests they face unique challenges because of their parents'

HIV status, including misconceptions about transmitting HIV, fear of prejudice and discrimination, family disruption, and lack of planning for their future care if parents are dying because of the progression from HIV to AIDS (Chi & Li, 2013; Qiao et al., 2013; Rotheram-Borus et al., 2005, 2006). HIV can lead to elevated levels of family stress if roles in the family are reorganized to compensate for the parent's illness (e.g., many adolescents assume caregiving responsibilities and household tasks to help out the ill parent) and if the needs of the uninfected child are overlooked because of the physical and emotional needs of the infected parent (Zhao et al., 2012).

According to two recent systemic reviews of the literature, many children and youth have symptoms of distress when their parents are coping with the more acute stages of HIV (Chi et al., 2013; Qioa et al., 2013). Longitudinal studies suggest that children and youth who are living with parental HIV will be negatively impacted with regard to their emotional and behavioral adjustment. Chi and Li (2013) conducted a recent systematic review of the literature and noted that four studies in the U.S. have examined the longitudinal effects of parental HIV/AIDS on children's psychological well-being. Their review suggests that these children are vulnerable to experiencing depressive symptoms, post-traumatic stress, and problems focusing in school.

Rotheram-Borus (2005, 2006, 2012) reported that psychological distress in children and youth (e.g., depression, anxiety, post-traumatic stress) peaks when parents' HIV is most severe (and becomes AIDS) and parents are struggling to manage their symptoms. Similarly, another longitudinal study was conducted by Forehand et al. (2002), who compared the psychosocial adjustment of non-infected children (ages 6 to 11 at first assessment) whose mothers are and are not HIV infected over 4 years. They examined changes in the two groups of children and examined how parenting impacts children's adjustment. Forehand et al., (2002) reported that children of HIV-infected mothers had more depressive symptoms across the four assessments compared to children whose mothers were not infected. Additionally, the quality of the mother–child relationship (clearer communication and closer relationship) was associated with improved child adjustment in both groups (Forehand et al., 2002).

Many HIV researchers and providers underscore the importance of addressing the stigma and the often resulting secrecy and lack of disclosure of parents' HIV status to children (Murphy et al., 2012; Qiao et al., 2013). Unfortunately, HIV is still stigmatized in the U.S. Many children and youth often understand that their parents' illness is a secret and consequently may experience feelings of shame about it. This can also reduce children's opportunities for garnering social support, because they are unable to openly talk about the parent's illness with peers (Lee et al., 2007). Many children and youth report experiencing fear, worries, and anxiety about their parents' HIV and concerns about their futures if their parents' HIV becomes AIDS (Rotherum-Borus et al., 2006, 2012; Schuster et al., 2000). Additionally, the child's age affects how much he or she understands HIV/AIDS. Younger children tend to have a limited understanding of HIV because of their cognitive development; they may only understand that their parent is ill and not the complexities of HIV and the treatment regimen. School-age children and adolescents, if the parent has disclosed his/her HIV status, are capable of understanding HIV and some even track parents' treatment and medical appointments (Corona et al., 2009).

Impact of HIV on Parents and Children: Main Points

1 Parenting ability is often a struggle because parents report experiencing fatigue, side effects from the HAART treatment, and depressive symptoms.

2 Parents with HIV are often concerned about disclosing their HIV status to children because they may tell others and then be treated unfairly and stigmatized.

3 Other challenges parents have reported concern medication and treatment adherence regarding hiding medications from their children who do not know their HIV status and missing medical appointments because of child care issues.

4 Guardianship and custody planning are common concerns among parents and children.

5 Younger children are not cognitively able to understand the complexities of HIV and the tough HAART treatment regimen.

6 Many adolescents assume caregiving and household tasks to help out their ill parent, leading to changing family roles.

7 Some children and youth understand that the parent's illness is a secret and consequently may experience feelings of shame about it.

8 Longitudinal studies suggest that living with parental HIV negatively impacts children's emotional and behavioral adjustment (e.g., depressive symptoms, post-traumatic stress, and school issues).

9 Children's feelings of shame can reduce their opportunities for garnering social support, because they are unable to openly talk about the parent's illness with peers.

Cultural Considerations

Because the most recent increase in HIV diagnoses is among 20- to 45-year-olds, in particular young African American MSMs and African American heterosexual females (CDC, 2013), culturally specific risk and protective factors should be attended to while working with families. Thus, culturally specific risk and protective factors (e.g., race, ethnicity, gender, SES) should be attended to while working with families who are coping with parental HIV (CDC, 2014b; Chi & Li et al., 2013; Dutra et al., 2000). Since individuals of color who have lower SES tend to be disproportionately affected by HIV in the U.S. (Schuster et al., 2000; U.S. Department of Health and Human Services, 2001), it is important to provide culturally sensitive care to improve treatment engagement and retention. Providers need to adapt their approaches to HIV care from primarily treating HIV-positive gay men in the earlier years of the epidemic to treating minorities and women, so the methods attend to patients' unique needs (Smedley, Stith, & Nelson, 2003). For example, since most new HIV cases diagnosed in African American and Hispanic women are due to high-risk heterosexual encounters, it is important for providers to attend to cultural differences. Depending on the racial/ethnic community, how gender and power impact safer sex practices, cultural and language barriers, poverty, and transportation issues likely need to be attended to and overcome (Squires, 2007).

Núñez (2000) suggests that reducing health disparities requires a shift from cultural competence (belief that a provider can ever become competent) to cultural efficacy (attitude of cultural humility) among providers. Cross-cultural efficacy implies that healthcare providers need to learn how to be effective with diverse patient populations where neither the culture of the provider or the patient is favored (Núñez, 2000). Núñez says that providers should attend to the influences of both individuality (patient-centered) and group factors (cultural group norms) because this will facilitate a more empathetic stance and trust during the clinical encounter, which will lead to improved patient engagement, treatment retention, and clinical outcomes.

HIV/AIDS is a chronic disease requiring long-term medical and psychosocial support to parents who are coping with HIV *and* their children. Most individuals are diagnosed in primary care, while having a routine visit, during gynecologic care, or in a clinic where anonymous testing is provided. After diagnosis, providers should make a referral to a specialty care clinic that serves HIV positive and exposed patients. In HIV clinics, routine care should include: (1) history taking, (2) physical examination, (3) prescription of HAART, (4) infant testing if the parent gave birth and was diagnosed with HIV at the birth, (5) adherence to medication support, and (6) risk reduction counseling (Rotherum-Borus et al., 2012). Additionally, many HIV clinics have medical case management onsite and also in collaboration with outside partners (e.g., Action AIDS) to help patients receive basic assistance with housing, insurance, and referrals to other agencies as needed. Finally, some HIV clinics have onsite therapy and support groups available for HIV positive patients and mental healthcare providers who can help patients navigate how to inform partners of their HIV status (CDC, 2012c; Davey et al., 2008, 2009).

Although most HIV/AIDS clinics include a behavioral component (e.g., case management to address insurance issues, behavioral health provider to help patients cope with treatment adherence and depressive symptoms), unfortunately family-centered approaches to care that routinely include children and family members are less common. An exception is an HIV family clinic in the northeastern U.S. that provides a one-stop shopping model for HIV positive parents and their children (Davey et al., 2008, 2009). This clinic provides the following services to the parent diagnosed with HIV and the entire family: (1) medical care, (2) case management, (3) nutritional counseling, (4) family therapy, and (5) psychoeducation support groups to parents and children. Our hope is that more HIV clinics consider including children so both parents coping with HIV/AIDS and their families are educated about prevention and how best to cope with parental HIV (e.g., disclosure of HIV status in the family, reducing feelings of shame and fears) and they can garner more social supports and cope as a family.

Clinical Vignette

The following is a clinical vignette to help you consider how a family coping with parental HIV might present clinically.

Donna is a 30-year-old, White mother who has HIV and is currently parenting two school-age children, Eve (12 years old) and Dan (8 years old). Donna recently developed a resistance to her HIV medications (HAART) from prior poor medication adherence, and she is now progressing to chronic renal failure and dialysis. She has a long history of trauma. Donna was infected with HIV in her mid-teens through sexual abuse by an older male in the neighborhood, and she had an HIV-positive baby from that assault who was placed in foster care and eventually adopted by another family. At 18, Donna had her second child (Eve) as a single mother, and then she had her son (Dan). She was a wonderful parent. She took the HAART medication and was compliant during the two pregnancies, so her children were born HIV negative. Unfortunately, after having her children, Donna struggled to take her HIV medication because she experienced resentment and anger due to being infected when she was sexually assaulted. In particular, swallowing the pills triggered PTSD because that reminded her of how she was sexually assaulted. Currently, Donna's CD4 counts are very low (below 50) and she has progressed to AIDS. She is now on dialysis because her kidneys have failed, and she needs to make a plan for her two children after she is gone. Donna could no longer go to the clinic, so hospice care was set up for her at home, but her two children still had no plan for guardianship and they were very fearful and concerned about the future. Donna kept hoping she would recover and keep caring for her children because she was dedicated as a mother. Donna's mother lives nearby, but they have a strained relationship; Donna is considering whether she could meet with her and help form a plan for who would care for her children in the future.

The psychosocial well-being of the children of HIV patients is a growing area of clinical research. In the last two decades, more family interventions have been developed and evaluated; these will be discussed in detail in Part III of this book.

Conclusions

Parental HIV/AIDS is a stressful condition for the infected individuals as well as for their families. Many parents report experiencing depressive symptoms, anxiety, PTSD, loneliness, and fear because they are also coping with the stigma of HIV. The stigma attached to HIV/AIDS often leads to secrecy and alienation of families from social supports. As extrafamilial support decreases, it can become more difficult for parents to provide children with nurturing, predictable, and consistent environments. Parents who are coping with HIV have reported many challenges while caring for their children (e.g., parenting ability, disclosing HIV status to their children, stigma associated with HIV, children's emotional and behavioral reactions, adherence to treatment, and guardianship planning).

Youth whose parents are diagnosed with HIV are vulnerable to emotional and behavioral issues and additionally face unique challenges because of their parents' HIV status, including misconceptions about transmitting HIV, fear of prejudice and discrimination, family disruption, and lack of planning for their future care if parents are dying because of the progression from HIV to AIDS. It is important to provide culturally sensitive care to improve treatment engagement and retention, because individuals of color who have lower SES tend to be disproportionately affected by HIV in the U.S. Finally, we recommend more family-centered HIV clinics that target not just the parent coping with HIV but also their children so families are educated about prevention and how best to cope with parental HIV (e.g., disclosure of HIV status in the family, reduce feelings of shame and fears) and they can garner more social supports and cope as a family.

Test Your Knowledge: True or False

1   HIV/AIDS interferes with the body's ability to fend off viruses, bacteria, and other disease-causing agents.
2   Kaposi sarcoma (pink or purplish skin lesions caused by the HHV-8 virus) is a type of cancer involving a tumor in the blood vessel walls. Although it is rare in people who are HIV negative, many people infected with HIV develop the condition, which causes skin lesions.
3   Disclosure of HIV status to others is an easy, straightforward process.
4   HIV is most prevalent among gay men today.
5   Parents are most concerned about how, when, and what to tell their children about their HIV status.
6   Children and adolescents often experience worries, fears, and concerns about their parents' HIV.
7   Most HIV clinics provide care to the entire family (the parent diagnosed with HIV and his/her children at home).

Answers: 1-T, 2-T, 3-F, 4-F, 5-T, 6-T, 7-F

Professional Readings and Resources

AIDS Alliance: Children, Youth, and Family. A resource to give voice to the needs of women, children, youth, and families living with and affected by HIV and AIDS. Retrieved from www.aids-alliance.org/

Kidd, R., & Clay, S. (2003). *Understanding and challenging HIV stigma: Toolkit for action.* Washington, DC: International Center for Women (ICRW).

National AIDS Hotline: 800-342-2437 (English), 800-344-7432 (Spanish)

Richter, L. (2010). An introduction to family-centered services to children affected by HIV and AIDS. *Journal of International AIDS Society, 13*(suppl 2), SI.

References

Bauman, L. J., Foster, G., Silver, E. J., Berman, R., Gamble, I., & Muchaneta, L. (2006). Children caring for their ill parents with HIV/AIDS. *Vulnerable Children and Youth Studies, 1,* 56–70.

Bogart, L. M., Cowgill, B. O., Kennedy, D., Ryan, G., Murphy, D. A., Elijah, J., & Schuster, M. A. (2008). HIV-related stigma among people with HIV and their families: A qualitative analysis. *AIDS and Behavior, 12,* 244–254.

Bor, R., Miller, R., & Goldman, E. (1993). HIV/AIDS and the family: A review of research in the first decade. *Journal of Family Therapy, 15,* 187–204.

Carrico, A. W. (2010). Elevated suicide rate among HIV-positive persons despite benefits of antiretroviral therapy: Implications for a stress and coping model of suicide. *American Journal of Psychiatry, 167,* 117–119.

CDC. (2010). Estimated lifetime risk for diagnosis of HIV infection among Hispanics/Latinos—37 states and Puerto Rico, 2007. *MMWR, 59*(40), 1297–1301.

CDC. (2011). Characteristics associated with HIV infection among heterosexuals in urban areas with high AIDS prevalence—24 cities, United States 2006–2007. *MMWR, 60,* 1045–1049.

CDC. (2012a). Estimated HIV incidence among adults and adolescents in the United States, 2007–2010. *HIV Surveillance Supplemental Report, 17*(4), 1–26.

CDC. (2012b). High-impact HIV prevention: CDC's approach to reducing HIV infections in the United States. Retrieved from www.cdc.gov/hiv/pdf/policies_funding_ps12-1201_HD_awards_media_factsheet.pdf

CDC. (2012c). Sexually transmitted diseases surveillance. Retrieved from www.cdc.gov/std/stats12/

CDC. (2013). Statistics Center, available at www.cdc.gov/HIV/statistics/.

CDC. (2014a). Caring for someone with AIDS at home: Providing emotional support. Retrieved from www.cdc.gov/hiv/living/treatment/index.html

CDC. (2014b). Progress along the continuum of HIV care among blacks with diagnosed HIV—United States, *MMWR*, *63*, 85–89.

Chen, J. L., Phillips, K. A., Kanouse, D. E., Collins, R. L., & Miu, A. (2001). Fertility desires and intentions of HIV-positive men and women. *Family planning perspectives*, *33*, 144–165.

Chi, P., & Li, X. (2013). Impact of parental HIV/AIDS on children's psychological well-being: A systematic review of global literature. *AIDS Behavior*, *17*, 2554–2574. doi:10.1007/x10461-012-0290-2

Corona, R., Beckett, M. K., Cowgill, B. O., Elliott, M. N., Murphy, D. A., Zhou, A. J., & Schuster, M. A. (2006). Do children know their parent's HIV status? Parental reports of child awareness in a nationally representative sample. *Ambulatory Pediatrics*, *6*, 138–144.

Corona, R., Cowgill, B. O., Bogart, L. M., Parra, M. T., Ryan, G., Elliott, M. N., . . . Schuster, M. A. (2009). Brief report: A qualitative analysis of discussions about HIV in families of parents with HIV. *Journal of Pediatric Psychology*, *34*, 677–680.

Davey, M., Duncan, T. M., Foster, J., & Milton, K. (2008). Collaboration in action: Keeping the family in focus at an HIV/AIDS pediatric clinic. *Families, Systems, and Health*, *26*, 350–355.

Davey, M., Foster, J., Milton, K., & Duncan, T. M. (2009). Collaborative approaches to increasing family support for HIV positive youth. *Families, Systems, and Health*, *27*, 39–52.

DiMatteo, M. R., Giordani, P. J., Lepper, H. S., & Croghan, T. W. (2002). Patient adherence and medical treatment outcomes: A meta-analysis. *Medical Care*, *40*, 794–811.

Dutra, R., Forehand, R., Armistead, L., Brody, G., Morse, E., Morse, P., & Clark, L. (2000). Child resiliency in inner-city families affected by HIV: The role of family variables. *Behaviour Research and Therapy*, *38*, 471–468.

Eke, A. C., & Oragwu, C. (2011). Sperm washing to prevent HIV transmission from HIV-infected men but allowing conception in sero-discordant couples. *Cochrane Database System Review*, (1), CD008498. doi:10.1002/14651858.CD008498.pub2

Fife, B. L., Scott, L. L., Fineberg, N. S., & Zwickl, B. E. (2008). Promoting adaptive coping by persons with HIV disease: Evaluation of a patient/partner intervention model. *Journal of the Association of Nurses in AIDS Care*, *19*, 75–84.

Forehand, R., Jones, D. J., Kotchick, B. A., Armistead, L., Morse, E., Morse, P. S., & Stock, M. (2002). Noninfected children of HIV-infected mothers: A 4-year longitudinal study of child psychosocial adjustment and parenting. *Behavior Therapy*, *33*, 579–600.

Gaynes, B. N., Pence, B. W., Eron, J. J., & Miller, W. C. (2008). Prevalence and comorbidity of psychiatric diagnoses based on reference standard in an HIV+ patient population. *Psychosomatic Medicine*, *70*, 505–511.

Herek, G. M., & Capitanio, J. P. (1993). Public reactions to AIDS in the United States: A second decade of stigma. *American Journal of Public Health*, *83*, 574–577.

Johnson, M. O., Chesney, M. A., Goldstein, R. B., Remien, R. H., Catz, S., Gore-Felton, C., . . . & Morin, S. F. (2006). Positive provider interactions, adherence self-efficacy, and adherence to antiretroviral medications among HIV-infected adults: A mediation model. *AIDS Patient Care & STDs*, *20*(4), 258–268.

Kolbasovsky, A. (2008). *A therapist's guide to understanding common medical conditions*. New York: W. W. Norton and Company.

Lee, S. J., Detels, R., Rotheram-Borus, M. J., & Duan, N. (2007). The effect of social support on mental and behavioral outcomes among adolescents with parents with HIV/AIDS. *American Journal of Public Health*, *97*, 1820–1826.

Lesch, A. I. D. S., Swartz, L., Kagee, A., Moodley, K., Kafaar, Z., Myer, L., & Cotton, M. (2007). Paediatric HIV/AIDS disclosure: Towards a developmental and process-oriented approach. *AIDS care, 19*(6), 811–816.

Leserman, J. (2003). HIV disease progression: depression, stress, and possible mechanisms. *Biological Psychiatry, 54,* 295–306.

Lester, D., Aldridge, M., Aspenberg, C., Boyle, K., Radsniak, P., & Waldron, C. (2002). What is the afterlife like? Undergraduate beliefs about the afterlife. *OMEGA-Journal of Death and Dying, 44*(2), 113–126.

Lightfoot, M., Rotheram-Borus, M. J., & Tevendale, H. (2007). An HIV-preventive intervention for youth living with HIV. Behavior Modification, 31, 345–363.

Martire, L. M., Schulz, R., Helgeson, V. S., Small, B. J., & Saghafi, E. M. (2010). Review and meta-analysis of couple oriented interventions for chronic illness. *Annual Behavioral Medicine, 40,* 325–342.

Miller, L. G., & Hays, R. D. (2000). Adherence to combination antiretroviral therapy: Synthesis of the literature and clinical implications. *AIDS Read, 10,* 177–185.

Mitrani, V. B., Prado, G., Feaster, D. J., Robinson-Batista, C., & Szapocznik, J. (2003). Relational factors and family treatment engagement among low-income, HIV positive African American Mothers. *Family Process, 42,* 31–45.

Murphy, D. A., Armistead, L., Marelich, W. D., & Herbeck, D. M. (2015). Parenting deficits of mothers living with HIV/AIDS who have young children. *Vulnerable Children and Youth Studies, 10*(1), 41–54.

Murphy, D. A., Marelich, W. D., Lanza, I., & Herbeck, D. M. (2012). Effects of maternal HIV on children's psychosocial adjustment with peers and their mother. *Vulnerable Children and Youth Studies, 7,* 357–370.

Naar-King, S., Templin, T., Wright, K., Frey, M., Parsons, J. T., & Lam, P. (2006). Psychosocial factors and medication adherence in HIV-positive youth. *AIDS Patient Care & STDs, 20*(1), 44–47.

NCI (2014). Press releases, available at www.cancer.gov/news-events/press-releases/2014.

Nehring, W. M., Lashley, F. R., & Malm, K. (2000). Disclosing the diagnosis of pediatric HIV infection: Mothers' views. *Journal for Specialists in Pediatric Nursing, 5*(1), 5–14.

Núñez, A. E. (2000). Transforming cultural competence into cross-cultural efficacy in women's health education. *Academic Medicine, 75*(11), 1071–80.

Osterberg, L., & Blaschke, T. (2005). Drug therapy adherence to medication. *The New England Journal of Medicine, 353,* 487–497.

Parry, C. D., Blank, M. B., & Pithey, A. L. (2007). Responding to the threat of HIV among persons with mental illness and substance abuse. *Current Opinion in Psychiatry, 20,* 235–241.

Peterson, A. M., Takiyah, L., & Finley, R. (2003). Meta-analysis of trials of interventions to improve medication adherence. *American Journal of Health and Systemic Pharmacy, 60,* 657–665.

Pfaff, C. (2004). Telling a child he is HIV positive: Case study. *South African Family Practice, 46*(9), 35–40.

Qiao, S., Li, X., & Stanton, B. (2013). Disclosure of parental HIV infection to children: A systematic review of global literature. *AIDS Behavior, 17,* 369–389.

Rotheram-Borus, M. J., Flannery, D., Rice, E., & Lester, P. (2005). Families living with HIV. *AIDS Care, 2005,* 978–987.

Rotheram-Borus, M. J., Rice, E., Comulada, W. S., Best, K., & Li, L. (2012). Comparisons of HIV-affected and non-affected families over time. *Vulnerable Children and Youth Studies, 7,* 299–314.

Rotheram-Borus, M. J., Robin, L., Reid, H. M., & Draimin, B. H. (1998). When parents are living with AIDS. *Family Process, 37,* 83–94.

Rotheram-Borus, M. J., Stein, J. A., & Lester, P. (2006). Adolescent adjustment over six years in HIV-affected families. *Journal of Adolescent Health, 39,* 174–182.

Schuster, M. A., Kanouse, D. E., Morton, S. C., Bozzette, S. A., Miu, A., Scott, G. B., & Shapiro, M. F. (2000). HIV-Infected Parents and Their Children in the United States. *American Journal of Public Health, 90,* 1074–1081.

Serovich, J. M., Kimberly, J. A., Mosack, K. E., & Lewis, T. L. (2001). The role of family and friend social support in reducing emotional distress among HIV-positive women. *Aids Care, 13*(3), 335–341.

Smedley, B. D., Stith, A. Y., & Nelson, A. R. (Ed.). (2003). *Confronting racial and ethnic disparities in healthcare*. Washington, DC: Academic Press.

Song, J., Lee, M., Rotheram-Borus, M. J., & Svvendeman, D. (2006). Predictors of intervention adherence among young people living with HIV. *American Journal of Health Behavior, 30*, 136–146.

Squires, K. E. (2007). Gender differences in the diagnosis and treatment of HIV. *Gender Medicine, 4*, 294–307.

Stein, J. A., Riedel, M., & Rotheram-Borus, M. J. (1999). Parentification and its impact on adolescent children of parents with AIDS. *Family Process, 38*, 193–208.

United Nations Programme on HIV/AIDS (UNAIDS). (2008). *Report on the global AIDS epidemic*. Geneva, Switzerland: Author.

U.S. Census Bureau (2011). Income, poverty and health insurance coverage in the United States. Retrieved from http://whereistheoutrage.net/wp-content/uploads/2011/11/us-census-2011-income-poverty-health-insurance.pdf

U.S. Department of Health and Human Services. (2001). *Mental health: Culture, race, and ethnicity*. Rockville, MD: U.S. Department of Health and Human Services.

Waugh, S. (2003). Parental views on disclosure of diagnosis to their HIV-positive children. *AIDS care, 15*(2), 169–176.

Weiss, R. A. (1993). How does HIV cause AIDS? *Science, 260*(5112), 1273–1279.

Wiener, L., Mellins, C. A., Marhefka, S., & Battles, H. B. (2007). Disclosure of an HIV diagnosis to children: history, current research, and future directions. *Journal of developmental and behavioral pediatrics: JDBP, 28*(2), 155–166.

Zhao, J., Li, X., Zhao, J., Zhang, L., & Stanton, B. (2012). Relative importance of various measures of HIV-related stigma in predicting psychological outcomes among children affected by HIV. *Journal of Community Mental Health, 48*, 275–283.

CHAPTER 6

PARENTAL MULTIPLE SCLEROSIS
Karni Kissil

Multiple Sclerosis: About the Illness

Prevalence

Multiple sclerosis (MS), also known as disseminated sclerosis or encephalomyelitis disseminata, affects approximately 2.5 million people worldwide (National MS Society, 2015). The prevalence of MS is twice as high in women (Matthews & Rice-Oxley, 2001), and in recent years there has been an increase in prevalence because of the longer survival rates, which means that women with MS live much longer, as well as an overall increase in the incidence of MS in women worldwide (Koch-Henriksen & Sorensen, 2010). MS is the most common nontraumatic neurological condition in young and middle-aged adults in the Western world, with a clinical onset usually between 20 and 50 years old, although it can also occur in young children and in older adults (Paparrigopoulos, Ferentinos, Kouzoupis, Koutsis, & Papadimitriou, 2010).

MS occurs in most ethnic groups, including African Americans, Asians, and Hispanics/Latinos, but it is more common among Caucasians of northern European ancestry (www.nationalmssociety.org). Hispanic Whites are more likely to have the relapse-remitting form of MS and a younger onset compared to non-Hispanic Whites (Amezcua, Lund, Weiner, & Islam, 2011). African Americans have a greater likelihood of developing vision, transverse myelitis (inflammation of the spinal cord), and mobility problems compared to Caucasians with MS. African Americans also have a more aggressive course of MS compared to Caucasians (Cree et al., 2004).

According to the National Multiple Sclerosis Society (www.nationalmssociety.org), in general, MS is more common in areas farthest from the equator. However, prevalence rates may differ significantly among groups living in the same geographic area regardless of distance from the equator. For example, despite their latitude, MS is rare in some populations, including among Inuit, Yakutes, Hutterites, Norwegian Lapps, Australian Aborigines, and New Zealanders, suggesting that ethnicity and geography interact in complex ways in different parts of the world.

Symptoms and Medical Outcomes

MS is a disease of the central nervous system that is characterized by inflammation, demyelination and axon degeneration. Inflammation occurs when a part of the body becomes reddened, swollen, and painful. Demyelination is when the myelin sheath of neurons is damaged and leads to the impairment of the conduction of signals in the affected nerves. Axon degeneration is a condition in which parts of the nerve cells (called *axons*) break down. These three processes in MS involve multiple functional body subsystems simultaneously and/or progressively (Dutta & Trapp, 2011). MS occurs because of an abnormal reaction of the immune system, wherein it attacks the central nervous system (CNS) (including the brain, spinal cord, and optic nerves). Within the CNS, MS causes the immune system to attack myelin—the fatty substance that surrounds and insulates the nerve fibers—as well as the nerve fibers themselves. This damaged myelin in turn forms scar tissue (sclerosis), which is the origin for the name of MS. When any part of the myelin sheath or nerve fiber is damaged or destroyed, nerve impulses traveling to and from the brain and spinal cord are distorted or interrupted, producing a wide variety of symptoms (www.nationalmssociety.org).

Symptoms of MS vary greatly among patients, and the progression of symptoms is unique to each patient. Symptoms can include the following: (1) transient or persistent visual disturbances; (2) vertigo and dizziness; (3) gait disorders; (4) sensory deficits such as pain, numbness, and tingling; (5) motor deficits such as spasticity (stiff or rigid muscles); (6) weakness; and other more subtle symptoms, such as (7) bladder and bowel dysfunction, (8) sexual problems, (9) mood disturbances, and (10) attention deficits. Fatigue is the most commonly reported symptom that interferes with the daily activities in up to 80% of MS patients, regardless of the degree of their disability (Fattore, Lang, & Pugliatti, 2012). Fatigue is considered by many MS patients to be the most disabling symptom of the disease because it negatively affects their quality of life, mood, and cognitive and social functioning (Schreurs, de Ridder, & Bensing, 2002).

Psychological Comorbidities

Neuropsychiatric symptoms are quite common in MS patients and have been reported to be almost always present (95% of patients), even in early stages or in mild cases of MS (Diaz-Olavarrieta, Cummings, Velazquez, & Garcia de la Cadena, 1999). Major depression is the most common psychiatric disorder that co-occurs, with lifetime prevalence rates close to 50%, which is three times higher than in the general population (Patten, Beck, Williams, Barbui, & Metz, 2003). Symptoms of depression and apathy are linked to higher levels of cognitive impairment (Demaree, Gaudino, & DeLuca, 2003; Feinstein, 2006). Sleep disorders are also more frequent in MS patients than in the general population (reported in over 50% of patients). The most common sleep disorders are insomnia, nocturnal movement disorder (repetitive limb movement during sleep), sleep-disordered breathing, and narcolepsy (overwhelming daytime sleepiness) (Paparrigopoulos et al., 2010). Sleep disorders in MS patients can be primary (disease related) or secondary to pain, spasticity, depression, and medication side effects (Attarian, Brown, Duntley, Carter, & Cross, 2004; Soldatos & Paparrigopoulos, 2005). Less commonly reported psychiatric disorders include bipolar disorder, euphoria, and anxiety (Paparrigopoulos et al., 2010).

Diagnosis and Prognosis

Currently, there are no laboratory tests that can determine whether a person has MS (Polman et al., 2011). Several evaluations are conducted to determine whether a person meets the criteria of MS and to rule out the existence of diseases that mimic MS (e.g., spinal cord lymphoma, lupus, sarcoidosis, stroke, Lyme disease). The criteria for diagnosing MS are referred to as the revised McDonald criteria (Polman et al., 2011), which were last revised in 2010 and include the following three requirements: (1) neurological evidence of lesions or plaques in at least two distinct areas of the central nervous system white matter, (2) evidence that the plaques have occurred at different points in time, and (3) ruling out any other reasonable explanation for these plaques (www.msfocus.org).

A provider first does a thorough medical history and a neurological exam. The three major tools used to determine MS are: (1) an MRI to detect areas of demyelination; (2) evoked potential tests, which are painless procedures where electrodes are placed on the head and body and responses are recorded to determine whether there are delays in nerve transmission; and (3) spinal fluid analysis (spinal tap), where cerebrospinal fluid (the fluid that the brain and spinal cord are bathed in) is taken through a lumbar puncture to check for diseases that mimic MS.

The diagnosis of MS is sometimes obvious and sometimes very difficult. It is highly dependent on the accuracy of the medical history and the physician's examination. Because there is no single test to determine MS, patients can sometime go through several misdiagnoses before being finally diagnosed (www.msfocus.org).

Due to the large number of symptoms, specific experiences with MS can vary. Therefore, the course of MS is impossible to predict because each patient may have a unique illness course. However, studies suggest that being a female, of younger age at onset, and with little disability after 5 years are generally indicative of favorable prognosis (Tullman, 2013).

Types of MS

There are four disease courses of MS and each can be mild, moderate, or severe (www.nationalmssociety.org) (see Figure 6.1).

1   *Relapsing-remitting MS (RRMS).* This is the most common type of MS and is found in approximately 85–90% of patients. It is characterized by early onset in the early 20s and periodic attacks of worsening neurologic function (relapses) followed by partial or complete recovery (remission) with no apparent progression of the disease. The patterns of nerves affected, severity of attacks, and time between remissions vary widely in patients.
2   *Secondary-progressive MS (SPMS).* After 10 to 20 years with the disease, most patients with RRMS will transition to SPMS. This stage is similar to primary progressive MS, with symptoms steadily progressing without relapses or remissions.
3   *Primary-progressive MS (PPMS).* Between 10% and 15% of patients with MS have PPMS, which is characterized by continuous worsening of symptoms from the time of diagnosis without distinct relapses or remissions. The onset for this type of MS is usually around the age of 40. This type of MS usually leads to disability earlier than RRMS and tends to respond poorly to treatment.
4   *Progressing-relapsing MS (PRMS).* This is the least common of the four types of MS disease courses and is characterized by steadily progressing disease from the beginning and occasional exacerbations along the way, with no remissions. People with PRMS may or may not experience some recovery following these attacks.

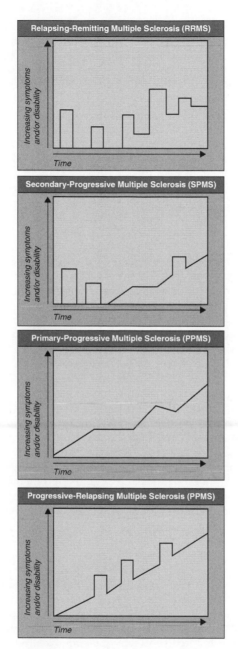

Figure 6.1 Four Types of MS

Source: Holland, N. J., Burks, J. S., & Schneider, D. M. (2010). *Primary progressive multiple sclerosis: What you need to know.* MSAA, Cherry Hill, NJ, and NMSS, New York. Reprinted with permission.

The etiology of MS remains largely unknown, but it is likely caused by a complex interaction between individual genetic susceptibility and environmental factors. Genetic factors appear to play a significant role in MS. For example, among identical twins, if one sibling has MS, the risk for the other twin developing MS is 24%. Among nonidentical twins the risk is 3% (Hansen, Skytthe, Stenager, Petersen, Brønnum-Hansen, & Kyvik, 2005). For first-degree relatives of a person with MS, such as children or siblings, the risk is approximately 2.5–5%, and the risk is potentially higher in families who have several family members with the disease. Among the environmental factors that are currently being studied are demographic variables (e.g., distance from the equator), levels of exposure to sunlight, levels of vitamin D, and smoking. In addition, various viruses and bacteria are currently being investigated to determine whether they play a role in triggering the development of MS (www.nationalmssociety.org).

Treatment

There is currently no cure for MS. However, comprehensive care for MS includes clinical treatment that can help to modify or slow the disease course, treat relapses, manage symptoms, improve function and safety, and address emotional health.

Medications

Medications described in Table 6.1 are often used in MS to modify the disease course, treat relapses, and manage symptoms.

Rehabilitation

Comprehensive treatment of MS includes rehabilitation to improve and maintain activities of daily living (ADLs). At diagnosis and throughout the ongoing treatment, rehabilitation specialists provide education and treatments to reduce fatigue and improve ADLs. The rehabilitation team will target problems with mobility, dressing and personal care, role performance at home and work, and participation in leisure activities. They also provide evaluation and treatment of speech and swallowing difficulties and cognitive problems with thinking and memory. Rehabilitation specialists also include speech/language pathologists, occupational therapists, physical therapists, vocational rehabilitation counselors, and cognitive rehabilitation counselors.

Emotional Support

The comprehensive care of MS should address mental health in addition to physical health issues because mental health professionals can detect emotional problems related to MS such as depression, anxiety, and mood changes. Since MS impacts both patients and their families, mental health professionals should also attend to patients' families by assessing their needs and providing education, support, and treatment tailored to the unique circumstances of each family. For example, some families may need help reorganizing roles and tasks to support the patient, and other families may need help explaining the disease to younger children at home.

Clearly, many healthcare specialists are needed to holistically treat patients coping with MS; therefore, good collaboration and clear communication are essential. Good communication is also essential because of the many medications prescribed and the need to monitor for possible side effects and multidrug

Table 6.1 Medications Used to Treat MS

Category	Function	Available medications
Modifying the disease course	Reduce disease activity and disease progression for many people with relapsing forms of MS.	10 FDA-approved medications: Aubagio (teriflunomide) Avonex (interferon beta-1a) Betaseron (interferon beta-1b) Copaxone (glatiramer acetate) Extavia (interferon beta-1b) Gilenya (fingolimod) Novantrone (mitoxantrone) Rebif (interferon beta-1a) Tecfidera (dimethyl fumarate) Tysabri (natalizumab)
Managing relapses	Medication is used for severe relapses (e.g., loss of vision, or poor balance) that interfere with a person's mobility, safety or overall ability to function. The medication helps to reduce inflammation and shorten the duration of the relapse.	First line of treatment is 3- to 5-day course of high-dose, intravenous corticosteroids. Other options include: • High-dose oral Deltasone (prednisone) • H.P. Acthar Gel (ACTH), for patients who have trouble receiving medication intravenously or tried corticosteroids unsuccessfully or had severe side effects of high-dose corticosteroids
Managing symptoms	Various medications are used to treat MS symptoms.	Following are several examples of MS symptoms and selected medications (nonexhaustive list): • Bladder infections: Cipro (ciprofloxacin) • Fatigue: Amantadine • Pain: Dilantin (phenytoin) • Plasticity: Dantrium (dantrolene) • Tremors: Laniazid, Nydrazid (isoniazid) • Dizziness and vertigo: Antivert (meclizine) • Depression: Prozac (fluoxetine)

interactions. Each patient should have a team of specialists working together to address the various aspects of the disease. It is helpful if this team works within a single center, offering "one-stop shopping." Unfortunately, more often this is not the case and people are referred by their MS physician to other specialists in the community. In most cases, the neurologist functions as the leader of the team. Since MS is a disease of the nervous system, the neurologist is the one who will first diagnose MS, develop a course of treatment, and coordinate with other specialists as needed.

Levels of Uncertainty about the Illness

Because of the myriad symptoms and the unpredictable course of MS (e.g., progression and outcome), coping with it often leads to a lot of uncertainty in patients and their family members. Patients have no way of knowing how quickly the disease will progress and the severity of expected incapacitation. Although the disease can lead to disability, most people living with MS do not become severely disabled. Two-thirds are able to walk, although many will need to use a cane or crutches, and some will use a scooter or wheelchair because of fatigue, weakness, balance problems, or to conserve their energy (www.nationalmssociety.org). By the age of 70, about 25% of MS patients will be restricted to a bed or a wheelchair. Finally, although MS is not a life-threatening disease, it does reduce the life span of patients by 8 years, on average (Olek, 2005).

What Clinicians Need to Know about MS

1   MS is a disease of the central nervous system that can affect multiple systems and functions.
2   MS symptoms are variable and unpredictable. No two people have exactly the same symptoms, and each person's symptoms can change or fluctuate over time.
3   Currently there is no cure. Treatments aim to manage symptoms, modify the course of the disease, and improve general functioning.
4   The disease can lead to various degrees of disability.
5   There is a high level of uncertainty related to the disease.

MS is the most common neurological disorder among young people, with onset often occurring during childbearing years. Consequently, many will have to manage the demands of the disease while parenting their children, which can be challenging depending on the severity of the MS-related symptoms and disability. Indeed, many parents report concerns about the impact of the illness on their children and their parenting abilities (De Judicibus & McCabe, 2004; Pakenham & Cox, 2012). For women, MS plays a role in the decision to become a mother. Many women with MS report seeking advice from multiple sources to ensure that motherhood is possible and will not jeopardize their health. Additionally, preparing for the pregnancy and the first years of parenting requires the careful planning of support and respite to create a balance between the mother's and the baby's needs (Payne & McPherson, 2010). Mothers of younger children report making a conscious effort to set up daily routines that allow them to attend to all their tasks and conserve their energy to avoid a MS relapse. They also report that when they were unable to meet the demands of parenting young children, they were worried about being perceived by others as "bad" mothers (Payne & McPherson, 2010).

Prior studies suggest that mothers with MS are concerned about their children (Harrison & Stuifbergen, 2002; Pakenham, Tilling, & Cretchley, 2012). Mothers report worrying about their children taking on more responsibility at home, needing more emotional support because of their illness, and not fully understanding what is going on with the mother, especially the unpredictable MS relapses (Harrison & Stuifbergen, 2002). Mothers reported being worried and frustrated especially during MS flare-ups because they were unable to: (1) participate in physical activities with their children, (2) transport their children to their activities, (3) help with homework, and (4) be involved in the daily running of the house (Pakenham, Tilling, & Cretchley, 2012). These concerns place mothers with MS at an even higher risk for symptoms of depression (Harrison & Stuifbergen, 2002). However, social support can help mitigate their concerns (Harrison & Stuifbergen, 2002). Thus, mothers with MS can benefit from therapy and psychoeducation to help them develop support systems to ensure their children are receiving practical and emotional support.

People with MS are often cared for by family members throughout the course of their illness. Partners of people with MS often report experiencing a range of negative effects (Knight, Devereux, & Godfrey, 1997; Pakenham et al., 2012). Due to its unpredictable course, caregivers are often confused about MS symptoms, diagnosis, and treatment. They cannot predict relapses, progression of the disease, and the level of daily functioning. Caregivers often have to deal with the patient's emotional changes, anxiety, and/or depression, which are part of the MS symptoms. This uncertainty about the disease and the neuropsychiatric symptoms causes stress for caregivers of people with MS and impacts their adjustment to caregiving and their quality of life (Knight et al., 1997; Lynch, Kroencke, & Denney, 2001; Sherman et al., 2007). The unpredictability of the disease can also disrupt the family hierarchy and family rules because of the sudden need to change priorities, responsibilities, and roles with each relapse and often pull in extended family members to help care for the patient (Halper, 2007). Physical disability and especially motor problems are additional sources of burden on the patient and family (McCabe, Firth, & O'Connor, 2009).

Partners typically report their lives have been significantly constrained by the demands of caregiving and the need to assume additional responsibilities (e.g., housework and child care). Partners report not having enough time for the rest of the family and, at the same time, feeling pressure to spend time with their children, transport them to various activities, and take over responsibilities that otherwise would be shared with the parent with MS. Additionally, coping with MS can put stress on the couple's relationship as evidenced by the higher risk for divorce and separation compared to the general population (Pfleger, Flachs, & Koch-Henriksen, 2010). Interestingly, one study reported a six-fold increase in the risk for divorce when the woman was diagnosed with MS (Glantz et al., 2009).

MS is among the most costly neurological diseases because of its early onset, long duration, and interruption of stable employment for both the patients and their caregivers (Fattore et al., 2012; Kouzoupis, Paparrigopoulos, Soldatos, & Papadimitriou, 2010). In addition to all of the other stressors, families of

MS patients also have to manage financial burdens related to the cost of MS and the loss of work productivity. Not surprisingly, partners of people with MS are at a higher risk for developing depression, anxiety, and distress compared to other caregivers (Buhse, 2008). Thus, clinicians working with families who are coping with parental MS should carefully assess caregivers' well-being and help them develop sources of support (Bogosian, Moss-Morris, Yardley, & Dennison, 2009) as well as find ways to create some stability and structure given the uncertainty of the disease.

Impact of MS on Children and Adolescents

There are mixed findings describing the impact of parental MS on children's well-being. For example, Pakenham and Bursnall (2006) reported that children's greater involvement in family responsibilities was associated with higher levels of depressive and anxiety symptoms and lower positive affect. Yahav, Vosburgh, and Miller (2005, 2007) similarly reported that, compared to the adolescents of "healthy" parents, adolescents of parents with MS felt more burdened and exhibited more fear and anxiety. Yet, a more recent study (Pakenham & Cox, 2014) suggests there are no differences between children of parents with MS and children of healthy parents on a variety of outcomes, including somatization, health, prosocial behavior, caregiving, behavioral-social difficulties, attachment, and family functioning.

Bogosian, Moss-Morris, and Hadwin (2010) conducted a systematic review exploring the impact of parental MS on children across 20 studies. Most studies were conducted with school-aged children (7–11 years old) and showed no negative impact of MS, while the few studies conducted with adolescents (11–18 years old) indicated some negative impact on adolescents' psychological well-being. Studies that did not control for the child's age and included children between the ages of 4 and 25 years old reported that having a parent with MS puts children at an increased risk of developing psychosocial problems. Clearly, age of the child is an important factor in understanding the impact of MS on children, and more studies are needed to clarify our understanding of the interplay between age and other factors in mediating the impact of parental MS on children.

One of the primary effects of parental MS on children is the redistribution of roles and tasks in the family. The wide range of clinical symptoms in MS produces disability in most areas of daily functioning, making it difficult for parents to engage in self-care and ADLs, such as getting dressed, bathing, preparing meals for the family, running errands, and more. Consequently, children of parents with MS often assume caregiving responsibilities more than children of healthy parents do (Pakenham & Bursnall, 2006; Pakenham & Cox, 2012). Research on the impact of increased parental responsibilities on children, however, has been inconclusive.

Some studies have reported that higher levels of caregiving responsibilities are associated with negative child outcomes such as poor adjustment, symptoms of depression and anxiety, and lower positive affect (Pakenham & Burnsall, 2006; Turpin, Leech, & Hackenberg, 2008). In addition, the need to assume more caregiving responsibilities can lead to social isolation because these children feel different than their peers and often are unable to participate in extracurricular activities (Diareme et al., 2006). This isolation is exacerbated by their reluctance to reach out to others for support, believing that their friends cannot understand what they are going through (Pakenham, Bursnall, Chiu, Cannon, & Okochi, 2006).

Other studies (e.g., Bogosian, Moss-Morris, Bishop, & Hadwin, 2011) suggest that caring for a parent with MS can also be beneficial for children. For example, the literature on young caregivers suggests that youth caregiving in a range of family illness contexts (not specifically parental MS) may be associated with positive outcomes including self-perceived maturity, increased confidence in caring, and strengthened relationships (Pakenham, Bursnall, Chiu, Cannon, & Okochi, 2006; Pakenham, Chiu, Bursnall, & Cannon, 2007). There is some evidence suggesting that the impact of caring for a parent with MS is associated with the nature of the caregiving activity. For example, Pakenham and Cox (2012) reported that children who provided higher levels of instrumental care (e.g., scheduling appointments, talking to doctors) and social-emotional care (e.g., keeping parent happy, keeping parent company) showed poorer adjustment, whereas children who provided higher levels of personal-intimate care (e.g., helping parent shower and get dressed) showed better adjustment.

An important issue to consider while working with children of parents with MS is their level of understanding of the disease. MS can be difficult for younger children to understand. Some of the symptoms, such as cognitive changes and fatigue, are invisible and therefore harder to comprehend. A parent's increased impairment, either suddenly or over time, with no apparent precipitator can be confusing to younger children. Children may believe that they have partly caused the disease and wonder whether it is contagious or fatal (Cross & Rintell, 1999). Evidence suggests that children who are not fully informed about the parent's MS have more problems than children who are better informed (Paliokosta et al., 2009). For example, children who were more knowledgeable about the disease experienced less distress and felt that the information about MS helped them to support their parent better (Coles, Pakenham & Leech, 2007).

In a study with a sample of 7- to 14-year-old children of parents with MS, Cross and Rintell (1999) explored children's understanding and experience of parental MS. Their findings suggested that many children were keen observers of their parents; they accurately perceived a variety of their parents' symptoms, including invisible and visible symptoms, affective responses, reduced activity, and stress levels. Most children were aware of the day-to-day variations in the illness. There was a tendency for girls to be more perceptive than boys, especially regarding the more subtle symptoms such as reduced activity and mood changes in their parents. Children's overall understanding of the nature of the disease and its physiology was very limited, and they provided inaccurate information about the disease. Children reported believing that the etiology of MS involved contagion, heredity, fate, or was the result of parents' behavior, such as overwork. Almost half of the children believed their own behavior affected the course of the illness. Even though the children were aware of the day-to-day changes in the disease, none of them reported believing their parent's MS would get worse.

Considering the expected progression of the disease, this is concerning. When a parent's MS gets worse, children who believe their behavior influences the disease may blame themselves. Thus, it is important for clinicians working with children who have a parent with MS to provide them with accurate and developmentally appropriate information about MS. This information may need to be updated and elaborated as the children mature. In addition, children need to hear that they cannot cause or worsen MS.

There is evidence suggesting that children who learn to use positive coping strategies such as problem solving, acceptance, and seeking social support experience less distress, better health, and greater life satisfaction in general

(Pakenham & Bursnall, 2006). Therefore, children of parents with MS can benefit from interventions that focus on facilitation of the development of better coping skills (Horner, 2013).

Impact of MS on Parents and Children: Main Points

1   Parents with MS are concerned about the impact of MS on their children and experience many challenges parenting their children.
2   MS can strain the relationship between the sick parent and his or her partner and significantly burden the caregiving partner.
3   Evidence suggests that parental MS can have both positive and negative effects on children.
4   Research suggests that adolescents are more negatively impacted by MS than younger children.
5   Increased caregiving responsibility can have negative impact on children, and this may be related to the type of caregiving.
6   It is important to provide children with accurate information about MS and to assess whether they attribute changes in the course of illness to their own behavior.
7   Teaching children effective coping strategies such as problem solving and seeking social support can decrease the negative impact of parental MS.
8   Caregivers can benefit from having their own support systems.

Cultural Considerations

Prior research suggests that race and SES are related to various aspects of MS, such as disease progression, comorbidities, prognosis, and treatment (Buchanan, Martin, Wang, & Kim, 2006; Buchanan, Martin, Zuniga, Wang, & Kim, 2004; Buchanan et al., 2010; Cree et al., 2004; Marrie, Horwitz, Cutter, Tyry, Campagnolo, & Vollmer, 2008; Weinstock-Guttman et al., 2003). Several studies reported that African Americans tend to be diagnosed at a younger age, have greater disability with increased disease duration, and demonstrate more rapid cognitive decline and more aggressive course of disease compared to non–African Americans (Cree et al., 2004; Marrie et al., 2008; Weinstock-Guttman et al., 2003). Also, African Americans with MS are significantly younger at admission to a nursing facility and significantly more physically dependent and cognitively impaired than Caucasians with MS at time of admission (Buchanan et al., 2004, 2006).

Buchanan and his colleagues (2010) conducted a study to learn about possible racial and ethnic differences in demographics, MS characteristics and symptoms, and MS treatments among Latinos, African Americans, and Caucasians in the U.S. They analyzed data in an MS registry that was gathered from 35,000 people with MS. They found many racial and ethnic differences among the three groups. Regarding demographic characteristics, a larger proportion of African Americans were female, compared to the other two groups. Also, a larger proportion of

Caucasians were married compared to Latinos and African Americans. Caucasians had significantly higher incomes compared to the other two groups.

Regarding MS characteristics, there were significant differences in the average age of diagnosis and the average age symptoms first appeared, with Latinos experiencing the first symptoms at a younger age (Latinos: 28.6 years old; African Americans: 29.8 years; Caucasians: 30.1 years) and being diagnosed at a younger age compared to African Americans and Caucasians (Latinos: 34.5 years; African Americans: 35.8; Caucasians: 37.4 years). Note that for all three groups, the time from first symptoms to diagnosis is about 6 to 7 years. This translates to years of suffering and seeking medical care for various symptoms and myriad tests and misdiagnoses before arriving at the right diagnosis.

People with MS often have physical comorbidities such as heart problems, various types of cancer, and high blood pressure. Studies report that these differences are also related to race and SES. For example, African Americans have a higher risk for physical comorbidities compared to Caucasians. In addition, having a lower income, less education, and being older than 60 all increase the risk for physical comorbidities (Marrie et al., 2008). Having a low SES was also found to be related to a higher prevalence of adverse health behaviors such as smoking, obesity, and physical inactivity (Marrie, Horwitz, Cutter, Tyry, Campagnolo, & Vollmer, 2009).

Regarding MS treatment, there were significant racial/ethnic differences in MS care, with a smaller proportion of African Americans getting care from an MS specialty clinic or a center compared to Caucasians and Latinos. Less than 50% of all three groups received care from a MS specialty center. Further, more than half of the African Americans in the sample had never been treated by an MS-specialized neurologist, and only about 50% of Caucasians and Latinos have received care from a MS-specialized neurologist (Buchanan et al., 2010).

Since only about half of MS patients receive care in MS specialty centers or from a MS-specialized neurologist, mental healthcare providers will probably meet MS patients in many different clinics. Because of the variety of symptoms and co-morbidities, MS patients receive care from many different experts such as urologists, cardiologists, ophthalmologists, and orthopedics, to name a few, in addition to those who treat them in MS centers. Due to the unpredictable nature of MS and the occasional flare-ups, patients also often end up at the emergency room or hospitalized for various reasons. Thus, mental healthcare providers should actively assess their patients in any of these settings to check whether the specific reason that brought them to the clinic is a standalone illness or part of a diagnosis of MS (e.g., do they suffer from a urinary tract infection, or is the infection part of MS). When working with MS patients, mental healthcare providers should assess the needs of the patients, their primary caretakers, and their children. Mental healthcare providers can educate patients with regard to the possible impact of MS on caregivers and children and help them provide accurate information about MS to their children. Parents also need to clearly tell their children that fluctuations in the parent's condition are part of the course of the illness and are not related to the children's behavior. Providers can help patients create a support system for themselves, their caregivers, and their children to ease the burden, ensure stable daily functioning at home, and prevent a sense of isolation for all family members.

Regarding the impact of MS on children, studies suggest various factors moderate the impact of MS on children. In a review of studies on the impact of MS on children, Bogosian and her colleagues (2010) identified several potential moderating factors. Studies reviewed suggest that parental level of functional impairment and the unpredictability of the parent's disease were related to poorer adjustment in children and to emotional distress (Diareme et al., 2006; Pakenham & Burnsnall, 2006). Another study showed that illness exacerbation was related to mothers' being less affectionate with their children, which in turn triggered anxiety and fear in children (Deatrick, Brennan, & Cameron, 1998).

Family environment can be a protective or a risk factor for children's adjustment to parental MS. Family dysfunction was found to be associated with children's poor adjustment (Diareme et al., 2006). Child coping was also found to be related to how well the healthy partner was functioning (Ehrensperger et al., 2008).

Evidence suggests that there is a gender difference in coping with parental MS. Daughters tend to cope better than sons of parents with MS. Further, healthy mothers and daughters tend to cope better than healthy fathers and sons (Steck, Amsler, Kappos, & Burgin, 2001). In addition, evidence suggests that children are affected more negatively when their mother is sick (rather than the father) (Steck et al., 2007).

Clinical Vignette

The following is a clinical vignette describing a possible clinical presentation of a family coping with parental MS. The vignette is based on a real case. All names and identifying information have been changed to maintain clients' confidentiality.

Daniel, a 4-year-old Asian boy, and his parents were referred to therapy by a family case worker after Daniel was expelled from preschool twice for biting other children. Daniel came to the first therapy session with his mother and father and his 6-month-old baby brother. Daniel's mother, Ting (29-year-old Asian), was diagnosed with relapsing-remitting MS the year before and was currently taking medications. She had flare-ups every few weeks, and during the flare-ups she had to rest in bed for a few days. Her main symptoms during flare-ups were fatigue, loss of bowel control, pain, and forgetfulness. She has also experienced balance problems and fell down a few times. Because of unpredictable presentation of symptoms, she has been afraid to leave the house on her own and has not gone anywhere without being accompanied by a family member. Daniel's father, Jeff (32-year-old Asian), worked for the Army, but he had to quit his job when Ting got sick last year to take care of her and his four young children: Daniel, baby James (6 months old), and their twin daughters (Joy and Faith, 5 years old). Jeff has been looking for a job that will give him more flexibility and time at home to help with caregiving, but so far he has been unemployed for almost a year.

Because of the ongoing family financial difficulties and Ting's illness, they had to move in with Ting's mother. The relationship between Jeff and his mother-in-law was not close, but since they moved in together their relationship has became very contentious. Ting's mother criticizes the way he parents his children; he feels like Ting and her mother are undermining him as a parent and father figure. His mother-in-law often contradicts him in front of the children. He feels excluded from the family and out of place in his mother-in-law's house. Ting agrees that her mother was "meddling" too much in their family affairs but said that she could not challenge her mother because she needed her help.

Jeff wants to look for another affordable apartment, but Ting is hesitant because she does not want to be home by herself when Jeff eventually finds a new job. She was eligible for a few hours a week of home care aid, but she refused to accept it because she wanted to take care of her own children. Both parents are worried about the impact of the MS and stressors on their children.

Did You Know?

- *Sclerosis* is a Greek word meaning hardening of tissue or scars.
- The first documented case of MS is from 1868. Jean-Martin Charcot, a professor at the University of Paris who has been called "the father of neurology," carefully examined a young woman with a tremor of a sort he had never seen before. He noted her other neurological problems, including slurred speech and abnormal eye movements, and compared them to other patients he had seen. When she died, he examined her brain and found the characteristic scars or "plaques" of MS. Dr. Charcot wrote a complete description of the disease and the changes in the brain that accompany it.
- The National Institute of Health (NIH) allocates an average of $115 million per year to funding research on MS.
- The country with the highest prevalence of MS is Hungary, with 176 patients per 100,000 people, followed by Slovenia (150), Germany (149), and United States (135).
- Total healthcare costs for MS in the U.S. (including direct and indirect costs) range from $8,528 to $54,244 per patient per year.
- Some evidence suggests that people who live farther from the equator have a higher risk for developing multiple sclerosis than people who live closer to the equator, and further evidence suggests that moving either closer to or farther away from the equator before the age of 15 can change your risk level. The reasons behind this geographic influence are still unclear.

Conclusions

MS is the most common nontraumatic neurological condition in young and middle-aged adults in the Western world, affecting 2.5 million people worldwide. MS occurs in most ethnic groups, but it is more common in Caucasians of northern European ancestry. MS is characterized by inflammation, demyelination, and axon degeneration of the central nervous system. Symptoms of MS vary greatly among patients and include both physiological and psychological symptoms. The progression of symptoms is unique to each patient. The etiology of MS is unknown. Currently there is no cure to MS, but available treatments help to modify or slow the disease course, treat relapses, manage symptoms, improve function and safety, and address emotional health.

MS can have a negative impact on caregivers and children. Caregivers can feel burdened and constrained by the continuous and unpredictable demands of caregiving. Children can feel burdened by the additional caregiving responsibilities and by social isolation. MS can also strain couple relationships and increases the risk for divorce. Mental healthcare providers working with MS patients should thoroughly assess the needs of all family members and help the family create structure and balance within the unpredictability of the disease as well as create a support system that allows some respite to patients and caregivers.

Test Your Knowledge: True or False

1 MS is the leading cause of death in the U.S.
2 The most common symptom of MS is fatigue.
3 MS impacts more men than women at a rate of 2:1.
4 MS is more prevalent among Hispanics and African Americans.
5 There is no cure for MS.
6 Younger children are more negatively affected by parental MS than adolescents.
7 Increased responsibilities and caregiving in children of parents with MS can have both negative and positive effects.
8 Children sometimes believe that the parent's MS is related to their own behavior.
9 Studies show that children cope better when their mothers are sick than when their fathers are sick.
10 Children's adjustment to parental MS is related to how well their healthy parent is coping with the MS.

Answers: 1-F, 2-T, 3-F, 4-F, 5-T, 6-F, 7-T, 8-T, 9-F, 10-T

Professional Readings and Resources

Kalb, R. (2011). *Multiple sclerosis* (5th ed.). New York: Demos Health.
The Multiple Sclerosis Association of America: www.mymsaa.org/
Multiple Sclerosis International Federation: www.msif.org
Multiple Sclerosis Foundation: www.msfocus.org
Multiple Sclerosis Journal: http://msj.sagepub.com/
Murray, T. J., Saunders, C., & Holland, N. (2012). *Multiple sclerosis: A guide to the newly diagnosed* (4th ed.). New York: Demos Health.
The National MS Society: www.nationalmssociety.org

References

Amezcua, L., Lund, B. T., Weiner, L. P., & Islam, T. (2011). Multiple sclerosis in Hispanics: A study of clinical disease expression. *Multiple Sclerosis, 17*(8), 1010–1016.
Attarian, H. P., Brown, K. M., Duntley, S. P., Carter, J. D., & Cross, A. H. (2004). The relationship of sleep disturbances and fatigue in multiple sclerosis. *Archives of Neurology, 61*, 525–528.
Bogosian, A., Moss-Morris, R., Bishop, F. L., & Hadwin, J. (2011). How do adolescents adjust to their parents' multiple sclerosis. *British Journal of Health Psychology, 16*, 430–444.
Bogosian, A., Moss-Morris, R., & Hadwin, J. (2010). Psychological adjustment in children and adolescents with a parent with multiple sclerosis: A systemic review. *Clinical Rehabilitation, 24*, 789–801.

Bogosian, A., Moss-Morris, R., Yardley, L., & Dennison, L. (2009). Experiences of partners of people in the early stages of multiple sclerosis. *Multiple Sclerosis, 15*, 876–884.

Buchanan, R. J., Martin, R. A., Wang, S., & Kim, M. (2006). Racial analyses of longer-stay nursing home residents with multiple sclerosis. *Ethnicity and Disease, 16*(1), 159–165.

Buchanan, R. J., Martin, R. A., Zuniga, M., Wang, S., & Kim, M. (2004). Nursing home residents with multiple sclerosis: Comparisons of African American residents to white residents at admission. *Multiple Sclerosis, 10*(6), 660–667.

Buchanan, R. J., Zuniga, M. A., Carrillo-Zuniga, G., Chakravorty, B. J., Tyry, T., Moreau, R. L., . . . Vollmer, T. (2010). Comparisons of Latinos, African Americans, and caucasians with multiple sclerosis. *Ethnicity & Disease, 20*, 451–457.

Buhse, M. (2008). Assessment of caregiver burden in families of persons with multiple sclerosis. *Journal of Neuroscience Nursing, 40*(1), 25–31.

Coles, A. R., Pakenham, K. I., & Leech, C. (2007). Evaluation of an intensive psychosocial intervention for children of parents with multiple sclerosis. *Rehabilitation Psychology, 52*(2), 133–142.

Cree, B. A. C., Khan, O., Bourdette, D., Goodin, D. S., Cohen, J. A., Marrie, R. A., . . . Hauser, S. L. (2004). Clinical characteristics of African Americans vs Caucasian Americans with multiple sclerosis. *Neurology, 63*(11), 2039–2045.

Cross, T., & Rintell, D. (1999). Children's perceptions of parental multiple sclerosis. *Psychology, Health, & Medicine, 4*(4), 355–360.

Deatrick, J. A., Brennan, D., & Cameron, M. E. (1998). Mothers with multiple sclerosis and their children: Effects of fatigue and exacerbations on maternal support. *Nursing Research, 47*, 205–210.

De Judicibus, M. A., & McCabe, M. P. (2004). The impact of parental multiple sclerosis on the adjustment of children and adolescents. *Adolescence, 39*, 551–569.

Demaree, H. A., Gaudino, E., & DeLuca, J. (2003). The relationship between depressive symptoms and cognitive dysfunction in multiple sclerosis. *Cognitive Neuropsychiatry, 8*, 161–171.

Diareme, S., Tsiantis, J., Kolaitis, G., Ferentinos, S., Tsalamanios, E., Paliokosta, E., . . . Voumvourakis, C. (2006). Emotional and behavioural difficulties in children of parents with multiple sclerosis. *European Child & Adolescent Psychiatry, 15*(6), 309–318.

Diaz-Olavarrieta, C., Cummings, J. L., Velazquez, J., & Garcia de la Cadena, C. (1999). Neuropsychiatric manifestations of multiple sclerosis. *Journal of Neuropsychiatry and Clinical Neuroscience, 11*, 51–57.

Dutta, R., & Trapp, B. D. (2011). Mechanism of neuronal dysfunction and degeneration in multiple sclerosis. *Progressive Neurobiology, 93*, 1–12.

Ehrensperger, M. M., Grether, A., Romer, G., Berres, M., Monsch, A. U., Kappos, L., & Steck, B. (2008). Neuropsychological dysfunction, depression, physical disability, and coping processes in families with a parent affected by multiple sclerosis. *Multiple sclerosis, 14*(8), 1106–1112.

Fattore, G., Lang, M., & Pugliatti, M. (2012). The treatment experience, burden, and unmet needs (TRIBUNE) study—measuring the socioeconomic consequences of multiple sclerosis. *Multiple Sclerosis Journal, 18*(6, suppl 2), 5–6.

Feinstein, A. (2006). Mood disorders in multiple sclerosis and the effects on cognition. *Journal of Neurological Sciences, 245*, 63–66.

Glantz, M. J., Chamberlain, M. C., Liu, Q., Hsieh, C. C., Edwards, K. R., Van Horn, A., & Recht, L. (2009). Gender disparity in the rate of partner abandonment in patients with serious medical illness. *Cancer, 115*(22), 5237–5242.

Halper, J. (2007). The psychosocial effect of multiple sclerosis: The impact of relapses. *Journal of the Neurological Sciences, 256*, S34–S38.

Hansen, T., Skytthe, A., Stenager, E., Petersen, H. C., Brønnum-Hansen, H., & Kyvik, K. O. (2005). Concordance for multiple sclerosis in Danish twins: An update of a nationwide study. *Multiple Sclerosis, 11*(5), 504–510.

Harrison, T., & Stuifbergen, A. (2002). Disability, social support, and concern for children: depression in mothers with multiple sclerosis. *Journal of Obstetric, Gynecologic, & Neonatal Nursing, 31*(4), 444–453.

Horner, R. M. (2013). Interventions for children coping with parental multiple sclerosis: A systematic review. *Journal of the American Association of Nurse Practitioners, 25*, 309–313.

Knight, R. G., Devereux, R. C., & Godfrey, H. P. D. (1997). Psychosocial consequences of caring for a spouse with multiple sclerosis. *Journal of Clinical and Experimental Neuropsychology, 19*(1), 7–19.

Koch-Henriksen, N., & Sørensen, P. S. (2010). The changing demographic pattern of multiple sclerosis epidemiology. *The Lancet Neurology, 9*(5), 520–532.

Kouzoupis, A. B., Paparrigopoulos, T., Soldatos, M., & Papadimitriou, G. N. (2010). The family of the multiple sclerosis patient: A psychosocial perspective. *International review of psychiatry, 22*(1), 83–89.

Lynch, S. G., Kroencke, D. C., & Denney, D. R. (2001). The relationship between disability and depression in multiple sclerosis: The role of uncertainty, coping, and hope. *Multiple Sclerosis, 7*(6), 411–416.

Marrie, R. A., Horwitz, R., Cutter, G., Tyry, T., Campagnolo, D., & Vollmer, T. (2008). Comorbidity, socioeconomic status and multiple sclerosis. *Multiple Sclerosis, 14*(8), 1091–1098.

Marrie, R. A., Horwitz, R., Cutter, G., Tyry, T., Campagnolo, D., & Vollmer, T. (2009). High frequency of adverse health behaviors in multiple sclerosis. *Multiple Sclerosis, 15*(1), 105–113.

Matthews, W. B., & Rice-Oxley, M. (2001). *Multiple sclerosis: The facts.* Oxford, UK: Oxford University Press.

McCabe, M. P., Firth, L., & O'Connor, E. (2009). A comparison of mood and quality of life among people with progressive neurological illnesses and their caregivers. *Journal of Clinical Psychology in Medical Settings, 16*(4), 355–362.

National MS Society (2015). Who Gets MS (Epidemiology)? Available at www.nationalmssociety.org/What-is-MS/Who-Gets-MS.

Olek, M. J. (2005). Differential diagnosis, clinical features, and prognosis of multiple sclerosis. In *Multiple Sclerosis* (pp. 15–53). Totowa, NJ: Humana Press.

Pakenham, K. I., & Bursnall, S. (2006). Relations between social support, appraisal and coping and both positive and negative outcomes for children of a parent with MS and comparisons with children of healthy parents. *Clinical Rehabilitation, 20,* 709–723.

Pakenham, K. I., Bursnall, S., Chiu, J., Cannon, T., & Okochi, M. (2006). The psychosocial impact of caregiving on young people who have a parent with an illness or disability: Comparisons between young caregivers and non-caregivers. *Rehabilitation Psychology, 51,* 113–126.

Pakenham, K. I., Chiu, J., Bursnall, S., & Cannon, T. (2007). Relations between social support, appraisal and coping and both positive and negative outcomes in young carers. *Journal of Health Psychology, 12,* 89–102.

Pakenham, K. I., & Cox, S. (2012). The nature of caregiving in children of a parent with multiple sclerosis from multiple sources and the associations between caregiving activities and youth adjustment overtime. *Psychology & Health, 27*(3), 324–346.

Pakenham, K. I., & Cox, S. (2014). Comparisons between youth of a parent with MS and a control group on adjustment, caregiving, attachment and family functioning. *Psychology & Health, 29*(1), 1–15.

Pakenham, K. I., Tilling, J., & Cretchley, J. (2012). Parenting difficulties and resources: The perspectives of parents with multiple sclerosis and their partners. *Rehabilitation Psychology, 57*(1), 52–60.

Paliokosta, E., Diareme, S., Kolaitis, G., Tsalamanios, E., Ferentinos, S., Anasontzi, S., . . . & Romer, G. (2009). Breaking bad news: Communication around parental multiple sclerosis with children. *Families, Systems, & Health, 27*(1), 64.

Paparrigopoulos, T., Ferentinos, P., Kouzoupis, A., Koutsis, G., & Papadimitriou, G. N. (2010). The neuropsychiatry of multiple sclerosis: Focus on disorders of mood, affect and behaviour. *International Review of Psychiatry, 22*(1), 14–21.

Patten, S. B., Beck, C. A., Williams, J. V. A., Barbui, C., & Metz, L. M. (2003). Major depression in multiple sclerosis: A population-based perspective. *Neurology, 61,* 1524–1527.

Payne, D., & McPherson, K. M. (2010). Becoming mothers. Multiple sclerosis and motherhood: a qualitative study. *Disability & Rehabilitation, 32*(8), 629–638.

Pfleger, C. C. H., Flachs, E. M., & Koch-Henriksen, N. (2010). Social consequences of multiple sclerosis. Part 2. Divorce and separation: A historical perspective cohort study. *Multiple Sclerosis, 16*(7), 878–882.

Polman, C. H., Reingold, S. C., Banwell, B., Clanet, M., Cohen, J. A., Filippi, M., . . . Wolinsky, J. S. (2011). Diagnostic criteria for multiple sclerosis: 2010 revisions to the McDonald criteria. *Annals of Neurology, 69*(2), 292–302.

Schreurs, K. M., de Ridder, D. T., & Bensing, J. M. (2002). Fatigue in multiple sclerosis: Reciprocal relationships with physical disabilities and depression. *Journal of Psychosomatic Research, 53*, 775–781.

Sherman, T. E., Rapport, L. J., Hanks, R. A., Ryan, K. A., Keenan, P. A., Khan, O., & Lisak, R. P. (2007). Predictors of well-being among significant others of persons with multiple sclerosis. *Multiple Sclerosis, 13*(2), 238–249.

Soldatos, C. R., & Paparrigopoulos, T. J. (2005). Sleep physiology and pathology: Pertinence to psychiatry. *International Review of Psychiatry, 17*, 213–228.

Steck, B., Amsler, F., Grether, A., Dillier, A. S., Baldus, C., Haagen, M., . . . Romer, G. (2007). Mental health problems in children of somatically ill parents, e.g. multiple sclerosis. *European Child & Adolescent Psychiatry, 16*(3), 199–207.

Steck, B., Amsler, F., Kappos, L., & Burgin, D. (2001). Sex specific differences in the process of coping in families with a parent affected by multiple sclerosis. *Journal of Neurology, Neurosurgery, and Psychiatry, 70*(2), 275–275.

Tullman, M. J. (2013). Overview of the epidemiology, diagnosis, and disease progression associated with multiple sclerosis. *American Journal of Managed Care, 19*(suppl 2), S15–S20.

Turpin, M., Leech, C., & Hackenberg, L. (2008). Living with parental multiple sclerosis: Children's experience and clinical implications. *Canadian Journal of Occupational Therapy, 75*, 149–156.

Weinstock-Guttman, B., Jacobs, L. D., Brownscheidle, C. M., Baier, M., Rea, D. F., Apatoff, B. R., . . . Smiroldo, J. (2003). Multiple sclerosis characteristics in African American patients in the New York State Multiple Sclerosis Consortium. *Multiple Sclerosis, 9*(3), 293–298.

Yahav, R., Vosburgh, J., & Miller, A. (2005). Emotional responses of children and adolescents to parents with multiple sclerosis. *Multiple Sclerosis, 11*(4), 464–468.

Yahav, R., Vosburgh, J., & Miller, A. (2007). Separation-individuation processes of adolescents children of parents with multiple sclerosis. *Multiple Sclerosis, 13*(1), 87–94.

CHAPTER 7

PARENTAL SYSTEMIC LUPUS ERYTHEMATOSUS

Karni Kissil

Systemic Lupus Erythematosus: About the Illness

Prevalence

Systemic lupus erythematosus (SLE) is a multisystem autoimmune disease characterized by complex and changing symptoms of the disease. SLE is a chronic autoimmune disease in which a person's immune system mistakenly attacks healthy tissues, cells, and organs (Askanase, Shum, & Mitnick, 2012). The body's immune system normally makes proteins called *antibodies* to protect the body against viruses, bacteria, and other foreign materials (called *antigens*). In an autoimmune disorder such as SLE, the immune system loses its ability to differentiate between foreign substances (antigens) and its own cells and tissues. The immune system then makes antibodies directed against the body itself and attacks healthy cells, tissues, and organs. SLE can affect many parts of the body, including the joints, skin, kidneys, heart, lungs, blood vessels, and brain (Ginzler & Tayar, 2013). Although people with this disease can have many different symptoms, some of the most common symptoms include: (1) a persistent low-grade fever, (2) extreme fatigue, and (3) painful or swollen joints. A common medical sign of SLE is a butterfly-shaped reddish or purplish rash across the bridge of the nose and cheeks (Pettersson et al., 2012).

SLE is characterized by periods of illness, called flare-ups, in which the disease is active, and periods of remission, in which fewer or no symptoms are present (Ginzler & Tayar, 2013). What constitutes a flare-up has been challenging to define because of variability in symptoms and severity (Ruperto et al., 2011). The Lupus Foundation of America (LFA) convened an international working group to reach consensus and define a flare-up. The committee agreed on the following definition: "A flare is a measurable increase in disease activity in one or more organ systems involving new or worse clinical findings, laboratory measurements and/or changes in ADL. It must be considered clinically significant by the assessor and usually there would be at least consideration of an increase in treatment" (Ruperto et al., 2011, p. 456). What constitutes a mild, moderate, or severe flare-up is also not clearly defined and depends on the increase in symptoms and the level of disease activity. A severe flare-up is one that involves a threat to an organ or to life that leads to hospitalization (Ruperto et al., 2011).

Generally, no two people with SLE will have identical symptoms or the same cycle of illness and remission. Some will only have fatigue and kidney problems, such as kidney failure. Others will have heart disease, lung inflammation, and mouth sores. Yet in others, there will be no major organ involvement, just cycles of fatigue, low-grade fever, and joint pain. In addition, some patients have several flare-ups a year while others have one major flare-up and then have no flare-ups for several years (www.lupus.org). The severity and duration of symptoms do vary within and among patients as well (Sterling et al., 2014). For example, fatigue is the most common symptom in SLE, reported by 67–90% of patients (Cleanthous, Tyagi, Isenberg, Newman, 2012), but the frequency, duration, and severity can vary. For some patients, there is a daily or weekly pattern (e.g., fatigue that increases throughout the day, every day) because of one's activity level and having a flare-up. The experience of fatigue ranges from patients experiencing it daily to patients not experiencing it for several years (Sterling et al., 2014). The duration of fatigue also varies and ranges from a few hours to days or months (Cleanthous et al., 2012; Sterling et al., 2014).

Even though the symptoms and course of SLE vary tremendously, some distinct patterns regarding the progression of this disease have been documented in different populations (Alarcón et al., 2006; Andrade, Alarcón, Fernández, Apte, Vilá, & Reveille, 2007; Cooper et al., 2002). Prior studies suggest that men tend to experience more damage from SLE early on and have more kidney involvement compared to women. Minority patients tend to have a more abrupt onset, more severe clinical manifestations, and more active disease compared to White patients (Alarcón et al., 1998, 2006). African American, Hispanic, and Asian SLE patients tend to have more renal (kidney disease), neurological (e.g., seizures), hematological (e.g., anemia), and serosal (inflammation of the heart and/or lungs) manifestations compared to White SLE patients (regardless of age and gender) (Alarcón, McGwin, Petri, Reveille, Ramsey-Goldman, & Kimberly, 2002; Alarcón et al., 1999; Bastian et al., 2002; Pons-Estel et al., 2004). These minority groups also tend to accrue more damage over time and more quickly than White SLE patients (Alarcón et al., 2001; González, Toloza, McGwin, & Alarcón, 2013; Toloza et al., 2004).

An estimated 1.5 million people in the U.S. have SLE, and approximately 16,000 new patients are diagnosed each year (www.lupus.org). Incidence rates of SLE range from 1 to 10 per 100,000 persons per year, and prevalence rates range from 20 to 70 people per 100,000 (Pons-Estel et al., 2010). Epidemiological studies on SLE indicate significant gender, age, racial, ethnic, and socioeconomic variations, which are summarized next (Danchenko, Satia, & Anthony, 2006; Duran, Apte, Alarcón, & LUMINA Study Group, 2007; Fernández et al., 2007; Somers et al., 2014).

There are significant gender differences in SLE prevalence, with higher disease prevalence (10-fold higher) among women compared to men (Pons-Estel et al., 2010; Somers et al., 2014). Age distribution of SLE cases is fairly broad, ranging from children as young as 2 years old to adults 80 years of age and older (Danchenko et al., 2006); however, childhood incidence and prevalence rates are considerably lower than adult rates (Huemer et al., 2001).

There are also substantial differences in disease onset, features, course, and outcome among patients with SLE from the major U.S. ethnic groups, with Hispanic patients (particularly of Mexican ancestry, but not of Puerto Rican ancestry) and African American patients exhibiting more serious progression of this disease at a younger age and with worse outcomes (Fernández et al., 2007). Patients from ethnic minorities tend to develop SLE more frequently, have an acute disease onset, have more disease manifestations, and accrue more disease damage compared to White patients (Alarcón et al., 2006; Fernández et al., 2007; González et al., 2013). For example, African American and Afro-Caribbean females are four times more likely to be diagnosed with SLE compared to White females. African American and Hispanic females tend to be diagnosed at a younger age (Texas Hispanics: 31.4 years old; African Americans: 33.1 years old; Caucasians: 39.8 years old; González et al., 2013) and the disease progresses faster and causes more damage compared to White females (Alarcón et al., 2001, 2004; Bertoli et al., 2008; Cooper et al., 2002; Fernández et al., 2007). SLE incidence, morbidity, and mortality are all much higher among people of African descent, Hispanics, and Asians than among Whites in the United States (Bastian et al., 2007; Fernández et al., 2007; González et al., 2013; Krishnan & Hubert, 2006; Odutola & Ward, 2005).

Prior research suggests that socioeconomic issues, especially poverty, may be more important than race and ethnicity for explaining the current health disparities in SLE (Alarcón et al., 2004; Duran et al., 2007; Fernández et al., 2007; Peschken et al., 2009). Poor SES has been associated with several unfavorable SLE outcomes, including: (1) disease activity, (2) damage accrual, (3) work disability, and (4) mortality (González et al., 2013). Whereas genetic factors are believed to contribute to SLE susceptibility and disease activity at onset, socioeconomic factors such as health insurance, level of education, household income, and social support likely play a major role over the course of the disease (Duran et al., 2007; Fernández et al., 2007; González et al., 2013; Peschken et al., 2009). For example, in prior research, SES (low household income) but not being of African American ethnicity was significantly associated with diminished survival rates (Kasitanon, Magder, & Petri, 2006). In the U.S., low SES is widely associated with ethnic minority status. In addition to poverty, low SES includes lower levels of education, limited or no health insurance, inadequate living conditions, barriers in accessing health care, and, among Hispanics, limited English proficiency. Taken together, these issues can lead to delays in the diagnosis of SLE, poor treatment adherence, and less effective treatment. Under such circumstances, more damage accrual and higher mortality rates tend to occur (Duran et al., 2007; González et al., 2013).

Diagnosis and Prognosis

SLE is a chronic and complex disease. Its symptoms are similar to other types of diseases, which makes it difficult to diagnose SLE (Lateef & Petri, 2012). There is no single laboratory test that can determine if a person has lupus. It can often take months or years after symptoms first appear for a definitive diagnosis to be made. In order to diagnose SLE, a doctor needs to have physical or laboratory evidence for the condition, such as: (1) swelling of joints, (2) protein in the urine, or (3) fluid around the lungs or heart. A person's medical history (and family medical history) is also considered. Additionally, special tests are conducted to rule out other diseases.

The American College of Rheumatology (ACR) developed a list of 11 criteria to help providers diagnose SLE. Having four or more of the following criteria, either at the present time or in the past, indicates a strong chance for a diagnosis of SLE (Hochberg, 1997; Ginzler & Tayar, 2013):

1 *Malar rash*—a rash over the cheeks and nose, often in the shape of a butterfly.
2 *Discoid rash*—a rash that is red, raised, and has disk-shaped patches.

3 *Photosensitivity*—a reaction to sun or light that causes a skin rash to appear or get worse.

4 *Oral ulcers*—sores appearing in the mouth, usually painless.

5 *Arthritis*—joint pain and swelling in two or more joints in which the bones around the joints do not become destroyed.

6 *Serositis*—inflammation of the lining around the heart (pericarditis) and/or lungs (pleuritis).

7 *Kidney disorder*—excessive protein or cellular casts in the urine.

8 *Neurological disorder*—seizures or psychosis.

9 *Blood disorder*—anemia (low red blood cell count), leukopenia (low white blood cell count), lymphopenia (low level of specific white blood cells), or thrombocytopenia (low platelet count).

10 *Immunologic disorder*—antibodies to double-stranded DNA (these are specific antibodies that target specific antigens in the DNA), antibodies to Sm (complex of specific proteins and nucleic acid), or antibodies to cardiolipin (a component of the cell).

11 *Abnormal antinuclear antibody* (ANA)—A positive ANA blood test shows that the immune system is making an antibody (protein) that reacts with components of the body's cells. This is called *autoimmunity,* which is not necessarily harmful. A positive ANA result *may* be associated with an autoimmune illness like lupus, but by itself it does not mean an individual has the disease. Approximately 20% of the population will have a positive ANA test. Positive tests are also seen in other conditions, such as thyroid disease, certain liver conditions, and other autoimmune diseases (www.lupusresearchinstitue.org).

Previously SLE was considered to be a fatal condition; however, today patients can live for decades following the diagnosis (Pons-Estel et al., 2010). Five-year survival rates in most studies conducted in the U.S., Europe, Canada, and Latin America are above 90%, and 15- to 20-year survival rates are approximately 80% (Pons-Estel et al., 2010). Although for some patients SLE can be fatal, individuals who are coping with non-organ-threatening aspects of SLE (e.g., no heart or kidney disease) can anticipate normal life spans if they adhere to their medication regimens and seek help for new manifestations of the disease. Approximately 7% of SLE patients are hospitalized every year, primarily because of organ flare-ups (Lee et al., 2013), and in general most SLE patients rarely require hospitalization.

Types of Lupus

Systemic lupus erythematosus (SLE) is the form of the disease that most people are referring to when they say "lupus." This is a systemic disease that can affect various parts of the body, is the most common, and is the focus of this chapter. However, there are other types of lupus that are less common, which are briefly summarized below and in Figure 7.1 (Shoenfeld & Meroni, 2012; www.lupusresearch.org).

- *Discoid lupus erythematosus* is a chronic skin disorder in which a red, raised rash appears on the face, neck, and scalp. The raised areas may become thick and scaly and can cause scarring. The rash may last for days or years and may recur. In approximately 10% of patients, discoid lupus can evolve into the systemic form of the disease (SLE). This cannot be predicted or prevented. Treatment of discoid lupus will not prevent its progression to the systemic form.

- *Drug-induced lupus* is a form of lupus caused by medications. Many different drugs can cause drug-induced lupus. They include some anti-seizure medications, high blood pressure medications, antibiotics and antifungals, thyroid medications, and oral contraceptive pills. Symptoms are similar to those of SLE (arthritis, rash, fever, and chest pain), and they typically go away completely when the drug is stopped.
- *Neonatal lupus* is a rare disease that can occur in newborn babies of women with SLE, Sjögren's syndrome, or no disease at all. At birth, the babies have a skin rash, liver problems, and low blood counts. These symptoms gradually go away over several months. Neonatal lupus is rare, and most infants of mothers with SLE are entirely healthy.

The etiology of SLE is unclear; however, most agree that it involves a combination of genetic, hormonal, and environmental factors (Zandman-Goddard, Solomon, Rosman, Peeva, & Shoenfeld, 2012). To date, no gene or group of genes has been identified that causes SLE, although the disease does occur in certain families, and some genes have been identified as contributing to the development of SLE (González et al., 2013). Only 10% of SLE patients will have a close relative (parent or sibling) who already has or who may develop this disease. Additionally, only about 5% of the children born to individuals with SLE will develop it (www.lupusinternational.com). In identical twins, if one twin has SLE,

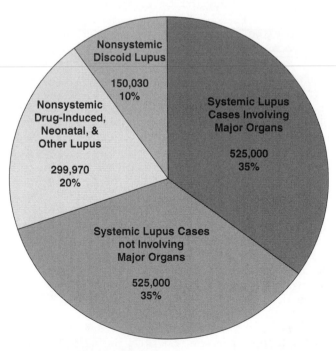

Figure 7.1 Distribution of Types of Lupus

Source: Reprinted with permission from Ellen Illsley. Retrieved from http://lupusadventure betweenthelines.wordpress.com

there is a 25% chance for the other twin to develop the disease, supporting the idea that genetics explain only part of the etiology and additional factors play a role (www.lupus.org).

SLE occurs primarily in women during childbearing ages, which suggests hormones could be involved in the etiology of this disease (Danchenko et al., 2006). In addition, many women have more symptoms before their menstrual periods and/or during pregnancy, which further supports a possible hormonal role in SLE. So far, researchers have been unable to identify specific hormones involved in the development of SLE. Environmental factors are also known to play a role in triggering the disease, such as infections, antibiotics, smoking, ultraviolet light, vitamin D deficiency, certain drugs, and pesticides (Zandman-Goddard et al., 2012).

Treatment

A treatment plan for SLE is typically developed and coordinated by a rheumatologist, who is a doctor that specializes in arthritis and other diseases of the joints, muscles, and bones (www.lupusresearchinstitute.org). Other specialists may join the treatment team and care for a particular patient, based on the patient's symptoms. Thus, if a patient has kidney disease, a nephrologist will likely be involved; if a patient has seizures, a neurologist should be a part of the team. The goals of the treatment plan are to reduce inflammation, suppress the overactive immune system, prevent flare-ups and treat them when they occur, control symptoms like joint pain and fatigue, and minimize damage to organs. It can sometimes take months or years for physicians to find the right combination of medicines to keep a patient's symptoms under control.

There is currently no cure for SLE; however, a wide variety of medications can be used to treat SLE symptoms. Medications described in Table 7.1 are often used to treat SLE symptoms (www.lupus.org).

Psychological Comorbidities

SLE can precipitate mood disturbances such as depression, nervousness, confusion, decreased concentration, and insomnia (Bachen, Chesney, Criswell, 2009; Walker, Smarr, Parker, Weidensaul, Nelson, & McMurray, 2000). The cycle of flare-ups and chronic symptoms caused by SLE can result in an overall decrease in quality of life, both physically and emotionally (Kulczycka, Sysa-Jędrzejowska, & Robak, 2010; Lateef & Petri, 2012). Patients who cope with SLE report being depressed and anxious for the following reasons: (1) pain and physical limitations, (2) changes in appearance (especially hair loss, but also skin problems, swelling of the face, and weight gain), and (3) medication side effects (Beckerman, Auerbach, & Blanco, 2011; Danoff-Burg & Friedberg, 2009; Kuriya, Gladman, Ibanez, & Urowitz, 2008). Additionally, many patients report living with fears of exacerbation of the symptoms and uncertainty about the future course of the disease (Auerbach, Beckerman, & Blanco, 2013; Beckerman et al., 2011; Phillip, Lindner & Lederman, 2009; Moses, Wiggers, Nicholas, & Cockburn, 2005; Seawell & Danoff-Burg, 2005). Several studies have reported that emotional states were associated with the activity and duration of SLE; the more acute the SLE flares were, the more depressed patients became (Bachen et al., 2009; Beckerman et al., 2011; Kulczycka et al., 2010; Phillip et al., 2009; Seawell & Danoff-Burg, 2005).

Table 7.1 Medications Used in SLE Treatment

Category	Function	Examples of Available Medications
Corticosteroids	Help to decrease the swelling, warmth, tenderness, and pain that are associated with inflammation.	Prednisone Hydrocortisone Prednisolone Methylprednisolone (Medrol)
Anti-inflammatories	Help reduce inflammation and pain.	Aspirin Acetaminophen (Tylenol) Ibuprofen (Motrin) Naproxen (Naprosyn)
Antimalarials	Often prescribed for skin rashes, mouth ulcers, and joint pain. They also protect against damage from the sun. It may take months before antimalarial drugs improve SLE symptoms.	Hydroxychloroquine (Plaquenil) Chloroquine
Anticoagulants	Reduce risk of blood clots by thinning the blood.	Heparin (Calciparine, Liquaemin) Warfarin (Coumadin)
Immunosuppressives	Used to control the overactive immune system and reduce inflammation, especially when steroids have been ineffective or when a person cannot tolerate high doses of steroids.	Cyclophosphamide (Cytoxan) Methotrexate (Rheumatrex) Azathioprine (Imuran)
Monoclonal antibody	This medication disrupts B-cell activity (B-cells are responsible for the overaggressive immune system response in SLE).	Belimumab (Benlysta), specifically developed to treat SLE and FDA approved

Women who cope with SLE often describe experiencing acute psychological distress related to a loss of the following: (1) their valued social roles as wives, mothers, sisters, daughters, and friends; (2) physical capabilities; (3) independence; (4) family balance; and (5) the anticipation of additional future losses with the progression of the disease (Beckerman & Sarracco, 2012; Karasz, Ouellete, & Features Submission, 1995). Psychological distress is also related to the continuous uncertainty people with SLE often face. This uncertainty is linked to the course and extent of the illness, future flares, and possible physical, financial, and social limitations. SLE often disrupts an individual's life plans, and its unpredictable course makes it difficult for patients to chart a new trajectory, which can lead to existential insecurities (Beckerman & Sarracco, 2012; Stockl, 2007). Prior research (Auerbach et al., 2013) suggests that social support can mitigate some of this emotional burden for SLE patients. Patients who have friends, for example, are less likely to develop symptoms of depression and anxiety (Auerbach et al., 2013). Thus, helping patients create and maintain social support networks should be an integral part of their treatment plans.

Level of Uncertainty about the Illness

Because of the acuity, chronicity, and unpredictability of SLE, patients often report experiencing high levels of psychological distress and uncertainty (Auerbach et al., 2013). Patients with SLE tend to perceive their bodies as being fragile and unreliable (Mattsson, Möller, Stamm, Gard, & Boström, 2012). Flare-ups can happen suddenly without the patient having any control or understanding of the triggers. There are no patterns to the flare-ups with regard to the frequency or the symptoms. There is also uncertainty about when flare-ups will emerge, with patients not knowing whether their symptoms are related to the SLE, which means another flare-up, or indicative of another co-occurring disease (Mattsson et al., 2012).

What Clinicians Need to Know about SLE

1   SLE is an autoimmune disease in which the body's immune system attacks various cells, tissues, and organs.
2   SLE disproportionally affects women (90% of patients) and ethnic minorities.
3   The most common symptoms include persistent low-grade fever, extreme fatigue, and painful or swollen joints.
4   The disease progresses in cycles of flares and remissions and is highly unpredictable.
5   SLE symptoms mimic many other diseases, and a definitive diagnosis can take years.
6   The 5-year survival rate is approximately 90%.
7   Many SLE patients report experiencing psychological distress related to a profound sense of loss and the ongoing uncertainty about the course and progression of the disease.
8   The etiology of SLE in unknown, although scientists believe that it involves a combination of genetic, hormonal, and environmental factors.
9   There is currently no cure for SLE, but a variety of medications can help to reduce symptoms.

Impact of SLE on Parents

The influence of SLE on parents may begin even before parenting, since SLE can impact family planning and one's ability to have children (Vinet, Pineau, Gordon, Clarke, & Bernatsky, 2008). SLE affects the decision to get pregnant because of the potential risks involved. First, studies report a two- to three-fold increase in disease activity during pregnancy (Cortés-Hernández, Ordi-Ros, Paredes, Casellas, Castillo, & Vilardell-Tarres, 2002). Disease exacerbation can occur at any time during pregnancy until several months after delivery (Clowse, 2007). Second, women with SLE have fewer live births compared to the general population (Vinet et al., 2011). Third, SLE is associated with an increased risk for maternal complications during pregnancy, including preeclampsia (high blood pressure and protein in the urine after the 20th week of pregnancy, which can be fatal if left untreated), hypertension, and thromboembolic events (when a clot that formed in a blood vessel breaks loose and is carried by the blood stream to plug another vessel) (Clowse, 2007). Fourth, women with SLE are about six times more likely to have premature babies compared to healthier women (Yasmeen, Wilkins, Field, Sheikh, & Gilbert, 2001) and to deliver babies who are small for their gestational age (Clowse, 2007).

SLE can cause tension in the couple relationship. Many patients report that the disease has negatively affected the quality of their relationships with their partners (Boomsma, Bijl, Stegeman, Kallenberg, Hoffman, & Tervaert, 2002; Hassett et al., 2012). The challenges of living with SLE cause major career disruptions and often bring heavy financial and emotional burdens (Yelin et al., 2012) for both patients and their partners. People with SLE often have to change careers because of the symptoms of the disease that affect work productivity, and they often work in jobs that are less rewarding and less stable or stop working altogether (Drenkard et al., 2014; Strand et al., 2013; Yelin et al., 2012). The expenses of health care and prescriptions can further exacerbate financial strains and result in increased relationship conflict (Danoff-Burg & Friedberg, 2009). In addition, SLE can negatively affect patients' sex drives and impact the level of intimacy with partners. Many women with SLE have impaired sexual functioning because of physical problems (e.g., pain), emotional problems (e.g., depression), and reduced libido due to disturbances of the hormonal cycle (e.g., as a result of taking steroids), which can reduce one's sex drive and cause additional stress on the relationship (Østensen, 2004).

SLE also significantly affects patients' and their partners' abilities to parent (Backman, Del Fabro Smith, Smith, Montie, & Suto, 2007; Evans & de Souza, 2008; Poole, Rymek-Gmytrasiewicz, Mendelson, Sanders & Skipper, 2012). Mothers who report experiencing fatigue and chronic pain, the most common symptoms of SLE, often report being in too much discomfort to participate fully in family events or to care for their children. Photosensitivity (sensitivity to light) can restrict the amount of time SLE patients are able to participate in outdoor activities with their children (e.g., going to the playground or spending time by the pool). Mothers may miss special events, accomplishments, and important milestones in their children's lives because of debilitating flare-ups.

Mothers with SLE who have younger children (younger than 5 years old) report significant difficulties in daily tasks such as picking up their children, playing with their children on the floor, doing household chores such as cleaning and shopping, and playing with their children outdoors (Poole et al., 2012). They also report having no energy to be patient with and to talk to or listen to their children. Mothers of older children report similar difficulties, such as struggling to do household chores and shopping, and in addition report struggling to maintain discipline with their older children (Poole et al., 2012). Difficulty performing these parenting tasks results in partners assuming most of the child care responsibilities and feeling over-burdened. These difficulties in performing parenting tasks can leave mothers feeling frustrated, angry, guilty, and impatient toward their children (Poole, Hare, Turner-Montez, Mendelson, & Skipper, 2014). In addition, mothers with SLE report being concerned about hereditary issues and worry about the impact of SLE on their children's health, especially their daughters, since SLE is 10 times more prevalent in females (Hale, Treharne, Norton, Mitton, Erb, & Kittas, 2006).

Impact of SLE on Children and Adolescents

Although chronic illness happens to families and not just to individuals, there is scarce research on the psychosocial impact of parental SLE on offspring. Most studies on children of mothers with SLE focus on possible medical and developmental issues these children may develop as a result of the maternal SLE or exposure to SLE medication in utero. For example, many studies investigated possible negative fetal outcomes for women diagnosed with SLE who have flare-ups during their pregnancy, or women who have renal involvement because of the SLE (e.g., Kwok, Tam, Zhu, Leung, & Li, 2011). Children who are born to women who have renal disease during pregnancy are at an increased risk for hospital admissions because of infection (Gayed et al., 2014). Neuropsychological studies of children born to mothers with SLE reported an increased incidence of learning disabilities like dyslexia, dysgraphia, and dyscalculia and an association with a greater risk for autism spectrum disorder (Bomba et al., 2009; Nalli et al., 2014; Ross, Sammaritano, Nass, Lockshin, 2003; Urowitz et al., 2008). Dyslexia seems to be the most frequently reported problem, with a prevalence of 14% in the children of mothers with SLE, versus 2–5% in the general population (Neri et al., 2004). Several studies suggest that sons of SLE mothers are at a higher risk for developing learning disabilities compared to daughters (Neri et al., 2004; Ross et al., 2003). The possible causes for these gender differences are still unclear.

Several studies explored the experiences of children of parents with chronic pain, which is a primary symptom of SLE (Evans & de Souza, 2008; Hoftun, Romundstad, & Rygg, 2013; Kaasbøll, Lydersen, & Indredavik, 2012, 2014). The findings of these studies suggest that adolescent boys and girls whose parents suffer from chronic pain are at an increased risk for developing symptoms of depression and anxiety compared to adolescents whose parents do not have chronic pain (Evans, Shipton, & Keenan, 2006; Kaasbøll et al., 2012). These adolescents are also at a higher risk for experiencing chronic pain themselves (Evans et al., 2006; Saunders, Von Korff, LeResche, & Mancl, 2007).

Adolescents' perceptions of the severity of their parents' illness and how well their parents manage their pain are important factors for understanding their ways of coping (Umberger, Martsolf, Jacobson, Risko, Patterson, & Calabro, 2013). Adolescents who reported that a parent was severely ill and debilitated tended to distance themselves physically and emotionally from the ill parent and to hide their true feelings from the parent to not burden them. They perceived their ill parent as distant and shut down and often wondered if they were loved. In retrospect, these adolescents reported feeling great sorrow and loss because they did not have an attuned and engaged parent and for not having a normal childhood. Adolescents who perceived their parent as able to push through the pain and to be present emotionally for them tended to communicate more with their ill parent about the impact of the parent's illness on the family. These adolescents perceived their ill parent as warm and more available and they had no doubts about being loved (Umberger et al., 2013). Clinicians should tailor family interventions to increase direct communication about the impact of the illness between children and their parents to prevent any mutual emotional distancing.

Prior studies with parents who have children aged 6 to 12 years reported that children who live with maternal chronic pain are at a higher risk for psychosocial and health problems (Evans et al., 2006; Evans, Keenan, & Shipton, 2007; Evans & de Souza, 2008; Stein & Newcomb, 1994). Findings from these studies also suggest that children of mothers who suffer from chronic pain tend to report higher levels of symptoms of depression and anxiety and more aggressive and delinquent behaviors compared to children of healthy mothers. In addition, these children tend to have more compromised health and complain more about pain compared to children of healthy mothers (Evans & de Souza, 2008; Evans et al., 2006, 2007; Schanberg, Anthony, Gil, Lefebvre, Kredich, & Macharoni, 2001). Further, children of mothers with chronic pain tend to show more insecure attachment and become "clingy" compared to children of healthy mothers (Evans et al., 2007; Evans & de Souza, 2008). This is possibly because mothers are inconsistently available (physically and emotionally) to their children because of the unpredictable courses of their illness.

Children aged 6 to 12 years often report being acutely aware of their mothers' health status and search for signs or "red flags" that suggest their mother is not feeling well. They look for signs of pain such as limping, signs of fatigue such as the mother asking the child to make her a cup of tea, and changes in mother's mood and temper. Children often report trying to be "good" during those times to minimize their parent's stress (Evans & de Souza, 2008).

Mothers with SLE report that their children often learn to care for themselves and for the mothers, both physically and emotionally, as well as help with household tasks. These mothers perceived their children as more independent and responsible compared to other children their age (Backman et al., 2007; Evans & de Souza, 2008). Although children often feel proud about their independence and helpfulness, they can also experience a range of negative emotions, such as being angry at their mother's unavailability, frustrated because they are missing out on fun experiences among peers, and feeling deprived of maternal attention. Evidence suggests that mothers with SLE are not always aware of the extent of their children's concerns and anxiety. Clinicians working with families coping with maternal SLE should talk directly to the children in order to get a more accurate picture of their level of distress.

Impact of SLE on Parents and Children: Main Points

1   SLE influences the decision to have children and increases the risk for pregnancy complications.
2   SLE can strain the relationship between the sick parent and his/her partner because of financial concerns, employment problems, sexual problems, and the healthy partner being overburdened with child care.

3   Children and adolescents of parents who suffer from SLE are at risk for experiencing chronic pain, anxiety and depression, and insecure attachment.
4   Children are very attuned to their sick parent's health status and can detect when the parent is not feeling well.
5   The child's perception of how well his/her ill parent manages pain is an important factor in the child's ability to communicate with the parent about his/her feelings.
6   Mothers are not always aware of the extent of their children's concerns and anxiety about their illness.

Cultural Considerations

Mental healthcare providers will typically meet SLE patients in different types of clinics. While most patients are treated by a rheumatologist, due to the variety of symptoms and co-morbidities, SLE patients receive care from different specialists such as nephrologists, dermatologists, and cardiologists. Patients can also end up in the hospital emergency room because of occasional severe or life-threatening flare-ups. Thus, mental healthcare providers should actively assess their patients in any of these clinics to check whether the specific reason that brought them to the clinic is related to an SLE diagnosis.

Mental healthcare providers who work with SLE patients should assess the well-being of the patient and his/her family. Since SLE patients are at a higher risk for psychological distress and their children are at a significant risk for experiencing pain, depression, and anxiety, a thorough family evaluation should assess for these symptoms. Providers should educate patients about the importance of communicating with their children about how the illness may be impacting the family. Patients should also be informed about the association between how their children perceive the way they manage their illness and the children's own adjustment. Since social support can mitigate symptoms of anxiety and depression, providers should help patients create and maintain a support system for the whole family.

In general, SLE is more frequent and severe, with higher disease activity and with more damage accrual among non-White populations compared to White populations (González et al., 2013). Although it is difficult to determine the extent to which these observed differences are caused by genetic or nongenetic factors, scientists believe that genetic factors influence the early course of the disease (e.g., onset), while nongenetic factors play a more salient role over the course of the disease (González et al., 2013). One of the factors that is associated with unfavorable outcomes in SLE is low SES and its related features, such as poverty, difficulty accessing care, no health insurance, inadequate housing, unhealthy behaviors (e.g., smoking), and lower level of education (Alarcón et al., 2004; Duran et al., 2007; Fernández et al., 2007; González et al., 2013). While providers cannot do much about genetic vulnerabilities and some of the socioeconomic factors, they can intervene at the individual and family levels of patients and help ameliorate some of the risk factors. For example, providers can assess what are the systemic barriers for treatment adherence and help patients access the help they need (e.g., child care, transportation). They can educate patients about the importance of social support and changing unhealthy behaviors (smoking, sedentary lifestyle, unhealthy eating habits) in the prevention of SLE co-morbidities and help them access programs to achieve those changes. Finally, providers can help patients learn how to communicate effectively with all their healthcare providers and advocate for what their families need.

Clinical Vignette

The following is a vignette describing a possible clinical presentation of a family coping with parental MS. This vignette is based on a real case. All names and identifying information have been changed to maintain clients' confidentiality.

Suzanna, a 37-year-old Hispanic woman, sought therapy because of concerns about her adolescent daughter, Camilla. Camilla was a junior at the local high school and was a very good student (As and Bs). She was also an excellent athlete and played on the school volleyball team. Camilla and Suzanna have been very close since Suzanna divorced Camilla's father when Camilla was 3 years old. The father went back to his family in Guatemala and has had no contact with them since the divorce. Suzanna never remarried, and Camilla was her only child. Suzanna was diagnosed with SLE 10 years ago, when Camilla was 7 years old. Even though she was consistently monitored by a rheumatologist and was taking medication to control her symptoms and chronic pain, her SLE progressed over the years and her flare-ups became more frequent and more severe. She also developed kidney problems and was receiving dialysis twice a week. Because of her illness, Suzanna had to quit her job as a full-time hairdresser and now she receives social security. Camilla works on the weekends in the local mall and gives all of her salary to her mother to help with their expenses.

Camilla also helps a lot around the house and takes care of Suzanna when she has a flare-up. Although two of Suzanna's sisters live in the same neighborhood, Camilla and Suzanna usually do not ask for their help and manage on their own. Camilla does not have any close friends and spends most of her free time caring for her mother. Camilla is an honor roll student and always talked about wanting to be a doctor. Suzanna is very proud of Camilla and supports her career aspirations. Now that Camilla is a junior in high school, they started looking for a good college to attend. Camilla applied for several colleges and got accepted to almost all of them. She also got accepted to an Ivy League school, on a full scholarship, in another state. Suzanna was excited about her only daughter going to such a prestigious program, only to find out that Camilla has no intentions of going there and plans to stay home and attend a local college she only applied for as a last resort, in case she was not accepted to any of the programs she was interested in. Suzanna tried to convince Camilla to change her mind, to no avail. She felt that Camilla is throwing her career away in order to take care of her, and she did not want her daughter to give up on such an opportunity. Camilla said that taking care of her mother was more important than anything else, and she couldn't trust anyone to make sure her mother was well. After several weeks of tension, arguments, and tears, which exacerbated Suzanna's symptoms and reinforced Camilla's decision to stay close to home, Suzanna suggested that they seek counseling and Camilla agreed.

Did You Know?

1 Treatment for SLE can be expensive. Average annual direct medical costs exceed $20,000, with the average increasing to $63,000 if the kidneys are involved.
2 Women with SLE are at increased risk for loss of bone mass (osteoporosis) and are nearly five times more likely to experience a fracture.
3 SLE patients are strongly encouraged to quit smoking because tobacco products can trigger flares.
4 Lupus was named 130 years ago by a French doctor who thought the rash on the face resembled bites of a wolf. Today the rash is referred to as butterfly-like, but the wolf name persists. *Lupus* is Latin for wolf, and *erythematosus* means reddening of the skin.
5 Cats, mice, and dogs can get lupus, too.
6 SLE can often occur with other autoimmune disorders.
7 The highest incidences of SLE are in Italy, Spain, and Martinique, and the lowest are in Northern Ireland, United Kingdom, and Finland.
8 SLE has been tracked in six continents globally (Europe, North America, South America, Africa, Asia, and Australia).

Conclusions

Systemic lupus erythematosus (SLE) is a multisystem autoimmune disease characterized by complex and changing symptoms of the disease. Common symptoms are fatigue, pain, low-grade fever, and swelling of the joints. SLE is characterized by periods of illness, called *flare-ups,* in which the disease is active, and periods of remission, in which fewer or no symptoms are present. SLE is difficult to diagnose because its symptoms mimic many other diseases and reaching a diagnosis can take years. SLE has no cure, and its symptoms can be managed with medication. Epidemiological studies on SLE indicate significant gender, age, racial, ethnic, and socioeconomic variations, with non-White minorities at the U.S. being diagnosed at younger ages, having more severe manifestations of the disease, having more major organ involvement, and accruing more damage compared to Whites. These differences are attributed to both genetic and nongenetic factors such as low SES. SLE also affects significantly more women than men.

A diagnosis of SLE impacts the patients and their families. SLE patients can experience psychological distress, anxiety, and depression. SLE can cause tension in the patients' relationships with their spouses. SLE can affect the ability to have children and to parent. Children of SLE patients are at a higher risk for developing learning disabilities, having chronic pain, and experiencing anxiety and depression. Mental healthcare providers can help patients and families communicate better about the disease, advocate for better access for care, and adopt a healthier lifestyle to reduce SLE chronic co-morbidities.

Test Your Knowledge: True or False

1 SLE is the leading cause of death in the U.S.
2 The most common symptoms of SLE are pain and fatigue.
3 SLE impacts more men than women at a rate of 9:1.
4 SLE is more prevalent among Caucasians and African Americans.
5 There is no cure for SLE.
6 SLE can put stress on the family due to financial burden, the healthy partner being overburdened with responsibilities, and sexual problems.
7 Communicating with children about the impact of the parental illness can help them adjust better.
8 Children sometimes feel angry and deprived because of a mother's illness.
9 Young children are not really aware of the mother's illness.
10 Children of SLE patients are at a high risk for developing learning disabilities.

Answers: 1-F, 2-T, 3-F, 4-F, 5-T, 6-T, 7-T, 8-T, 9-F, 10-T

Professional Readings and Resources

Lahita, R. G. (n.d) What Is Lupus?: www.lupusinternational.com/About-Lupus-1-1/What-is-Lupus-.aspx

NIH. (2015). Handout on Health: Systemic Lupus Erythematosus: www.niams.nih.gov/health_info/lupus/#Lupus_5

Thomas, D. (2014). *The lupus encyclopedia: A comprehensive guide for patients and families*. Baltimore, MD: Johns Hopkins Press.

Wallace, Daniel J. (2012). The Lupus Book: A Guide for Patients and Their Families. NY, NY: Oxford University Press.

What Causes Lupus?: www.lupus.org/answers/entry/what-causes-lupus

What Is Lupus?: www.lupus.org/answers/entry/what-is-lupus

What Medications Are Used to Treat Lupus?: www.lupus.org/answers/entry/medications-to-treat-lupus

References

Alarcón, G. S., Calvo-Alén, J., McGwin, G., Uribe, A. G., Toloza, S. M., Roseman, J. M., . . . Reveille, J. D. (2006). Systemic lupus erythematosus in a multiethnic cohort: LUMINA XXXV. Predictive factors of high disease activity over time. *Annals of the Rheumatic Diseases, 65*(9), 1168–1174.

Alarcón, G. S., Friedman, A. W., Straaton, K. V., Moulds, J. M., Lisse, J., Bastian, H. M., . . . Reveille, J. D. (1999). Systemic lupus erythematosus in three ethnic groups: III A comparison of characteristics early in the natural history of the LUMINA cohort. *Lupus, 8*(3), 197–209.

Alarcón, G. S., McGwin, G., Bartolucci, A. A., Roseman, J., Lisse, J., Fessler, B. J., . . . Reveille, J. D. (2001). Systemic lupus erythematosus in three ethnic groups: IX. Differences in damage accrual. *Arthritis & Rheumatism, 44*(12), 2797–2806.

Alarcón, G. S., McGwin, G., Petri, M., Reveille, J. D., Ramsey-Goldman, R., & Kimberly, R. P. (2002). Baseline characteristics of a multiethnic lupus cohort: PROFILE. *Lupus, 11*(2), 95–101.

Alarcón, G. S., McGwin, G., Sanchez, M. L., Bastian, H. M., Feslupusr, B. J., Friedman, A. W., . . . Reveille, J. D. (2004). Systemic lupus erythematosus in three ethnic groups. XIV. Poverty, wealth, and their influence on disease activity. *Arthritis Care & Research, 51*(1), 73–77.

Alarcón, G. S., Roseman, J., Bartolucci, A. A., Friedman, A. W., Moulds, J. M., Goel, N., . . . Reveille, J. D. (1998). Systemic lupus erythematosus in three ethnic groups: II. Features predictive of disease activity early in its course. *Arthritis & Rheumatism, 41*(7), 1173–1180.

Andrade, R. M., Alarcón, G. S., Fernández, M., Apte, M., Vilá, L. M., & Reveille, J. D. (2007). Accelerated damage accrual among men with systemic lupus erythematosus: XLIV. Results from a multiethnic US cohort. *Arthritis & Rheumatism, 56*(2), 622–630.

Askanase, A., Shum, K., & Mitnick, H. (2012). Systemic lupus erythematosus: An overview. *Social Work in Health Care, 51*(7), 576–586.

Auerbach, C., Beckerman, N. L., & Blanco, I. (2013). Women coping with chronic disease: The psychosocial impact of Lupus. *Journal of Social Service Research, 39*(5), 606–615.

Bachen, E. A., Chesney, M. A., & Criswell, L. A. (2009). Prevalence of mood and anxiety disorders in women with systemic lupus erythematosus. *Arthritis Care & Research, 61*(6), 822–829.

Backman, C. L., Smith, L. D. F., Smith, S., Montie, P. L., & Suto, M. (2007). Experiences of mothers living with inflammatory arthritis. *Arthritis Care & Research, 57*(3), 381–388.

Bastian, H. M., Alarcón, G. S., Roseman, J. M., McGwin, G., Vilá, L. M., Feslupusr, B. J., & Reveille, J. D. (2007). Systemic lupus erythematosus in a multiethnic U.S. cohort (LUMINA) XL II: Factors predictive of new or worsening proteinuria. *Rheumatology, 46*(4), 683–689.

Bastian, H. M., Roseman, J. M., McGwin, G., Alarcón, G. S., Friedman, A. W., Fessler, B. J., . . . & Reveille, J. D. (2002). Systemic lupus erythematosus in three ethnic groups. XII. Risk factors for lupus nephritis after diagnosis. *Lupus, 11*(3), 152–160.

Beckerman, N. L., Auerbach, C., & Blanco, I. (2011). Psychosocial dimensions of SLE: implications for the health care team. *Journal of Multidisciplinary Healthcare, 4*, 67–72.

Beckerman, N. L., & Sarracco, M. (2012). Listening to lupus patients and families: Fine tuning the assessment. *Social Work in Health Care, 51*(7), 597–612.

Bertoli, A. M., Vilá, L. M., Reveille, J. D., & Alarcón, G. S. (2008). Systemic lupus erythaematosus in a multiethnic US cohort (LUMINA) LIII: Disease expression and outcome in acute onset lupus. *Annals of the Rheumatic Diseases, 67*(4), 500–504.

Bomba, M., Galli, J., Nacinovich, R., Ceribelli, A., Motta, M., Lojacono, A., . . . Tincani, A. (2009). Neuropsychiatric aid in children born to patients with rheumatic diseases. *Clinical and Experimental Rheumatology, 28*(5), 767–773.

Boomsma, M. M., Bijl, M., Stegeman, C. A., Kallenberg, C. G., Hoffman, G. S., & Tervaert, J. W. C. (2002). Patients' perceptions of the effects of systemic lupus erythematosus on health, function, income, and interpersonal relationships: a comparison with Wegener's granulomatosis. *Arthritis Care & Research, 47*(2), 196–201.

Cleanthous, S., Tyagi, M., Isenberg, D. A., & Newman, S. P. (2012). What do we know about self-reported fatigue in systemic lupus erythematosus? *Lupus, 21*(5), 465–476.

Clowse, M. E. (2007). Lupus activity in pregnancy. *Rheumatic Disease Clinics of North America, 33*(2), 237–252.

Cooper, G. S., Parks, C. G., Treadwell, E. L., St Clair, E. W., Gilkeson, G. S., Cohen, P. L., . . . Dooley, M. A. (2002). Differences by race, sex and age in the clinical and immunologic features of recently diagnosed systemic lupus erythematosus patients in the southeastern United States. *Lupus, 11*(3), 161–167.

Cortés-Hernández, J., Ordi-Ros, J., Paredes, F., Casellas, M., Castillo, F., & Vilardell-Tarres, M. (2002). Clinical predictors of fetal and maternal outcome in systemic lupus erythematosus: a prospective study of 103 pregnancies. *Rheumatology, 41*(6), 643–650.

Danchenko, N., Satia, J. A., & Anthony, M. S. (2006). Epidemiology of systemic lupus erythematosus: a comparison of worldwide disease burden. *Lupus, 15*(5), 308–318.

Danoff-Burg, S., & Friedberg, F. (2009). Unmet needs of patients with systemic lupus erythematosus. *Behavioral Medicine, 35*(1), 5–13.

Drenkard, C., Bao, G., Dennis, G., Kan, H. J., Jhingran, P. M., Molta, C. T., & Lim, S. S. (2014). Burden of systemic lupus erythematosus on employment and work productivity:

Data from a large cohort in the Southeastern United States. *Arthritis Care & Research, 66*(6), 878–887.

Duran, S., Apte, M., Alarcón, G. S., & LUMINA Study Group. (2007). Poverty, not ethnicity, accounts for the differential mortality rates among lupus patients of various ethnic groups. *Journal of the National Medical Association, 99*(10), 1196–1198.

Evans, S., & de Souza, L. (2008). Dealing with chronic pain: Giving voice to the experiences of mothers with chronic pain and their children. *Qualitative Health Research, 18*(4), 489–500.

Evans, S., Keenan, T. R., & Shipton, E. A. (2007). Psychosocial adjustment and physical health of children living with maternal chronic pain. *Journal of Pediatrics and Child Health, 43*(4), 262–270.

Evans, S., Shipton, E. A., & Keenan, T. (2006). The relationship between maternal chronic pain and child adjustment: The role of parenting as a mediator. *The Journal of Pain, 7*(4), 236–243.

Fernández, M., Alarcón, G. S., Calvo-Alén, J., Andrade, R., McGwin, G., Vilá, L. M., & Reveille, J. D. (2007). A multiethnic, multicenter cohort of patients with systemic lupus erythematosus (LUPUS) as a model for the study of ethnic disparities in LUPUS. *Arthritis Care & Research, 57*(4), 576–584.

Gayed, M., Khamashta, M., Dimitrov, B. D., Leone, F., Veronica, T., Bruce, I., . . . Gordon, C. (2014). THU0013 Longterm outcomes of children born to mothers with SLE exposed to Azathioprine in pregnancy. *Annals of the Rheumatic Diseases, 73*(suppl 2), 180–181.

Ginzler, E., & Tayar, J. (2013). American college of rheumatology. *Systemic Lupus Erythematosus*. Retrieved from www.rheumatology.org

González, L. A., Toloza, S. M. A., McGwin, G., & Alarcón, G. S. (2013). Ethnicity in systemic lupus erythematosus (SLE): its influence on susceptibility and outcomes. *Lupus, 22*(12), 1214–1224.

Hale, E. D., Treharne, G. J., Norton, Y., Mitton, D. L., Erb, N., & Kitas, G. D. (2006). "Are your hands hurting?": Patients' perceptions of the impact of lupus on their children and grandchildren. *Rheumatology, 45*, I184–I184.

Hassett, A. L., Li, T., Radvanski, D. C., Savage, S. V., Buyske, S., Schiff, S. A., & Katz, P. P. (2012). Assessment of health-related family role functioning in systemic lupus erythematosus: Preliminary validation of a new measure. *Arthritis Care & Research, 64*(9), 1341–1348.

Hochberg, M. C. (1997). Updating the American college of rheumatology revised criteria for the classification of systemic lupus erythematosus. *Arthritis & Rheumatism, 40*(9), 1725–1725.

Hoftun, G. B., Romundstad, P. R., & Rygg, M. (2013). Association of parental chronic pain with chronic pain in the adolescent and young adult: Family linkage data from the HUNT study. *JAMA Pediatrics, 167*(1), 61–69.

Huemer, C., Huemer, M., Dorner, T., Falger, J., Schacherl, H., Bernecker, M., . . . Pilz, I. (2001). Incidence of pediatric rheumatic diseases in a regional population in Austria. *The Journal of Rheumatology, 28*(9), 2116–2119.

Kaasbøll, J., Lydersen, S., & Indredavik, M. S. (2012). Psychological symptoms in children of parents with chronic pain—the HUNT study. *Pain, 153*(5), 1054–1062.

Kaasbøll, J., Lydersen, S., & Indredavik, M. S. (2014). Substance use in children of parents with chronic pain–the HUNT study. *Journal of Pain Research, 7*, 483–494.

Karasz, A., Ouellette, S. C., & Features Submission, H. C. (1995). Role strain and psychological well-being in women with systemic lupus erythematosus. *Women & Health, 23*(3), 41–57.

Kasitanon, N., Magder, L. S., & Petri, M. (2006). Predictors of survival in systemic lupus erythematosus. *Medicine, 85*(3), 147–156.

Krishnan, E., & Hubert, H. B. (2006). Ethnicity and mortality from systemic lupus erythematosus in the US. *Annals of the Rheumatic Diseases, 65*(11), 1500–1505.

Kulczycka, L., Sysa-Jędrzejowska, A., & Robak, E. (2010). Quality of life and satisfaction with life in SLE patients—the importance of clinical manifestations. *Clinical Rheumatology, 29*(9), 991–997.

Kuriya, B., Gladman, D. D., Ibanez, D., & Urowitz, M. B. (2008). Quality of life over time in patients with systemic lupus erythematosus. *Arthritis Care & Research, 59*(2), 181–185.

Kwok, L. W., Tam, L. S., Zhu, T. Y., Leung, Y. Y., & Li, E. K. (2011). Predictors of maternal and fetal outcomes in pregnancies of patients with systemic lupus erythematosus. *Lupus, 20*(8), 829–836.

Lateef, A., & Petri, M. (2012). Unmet medical needs in systemic lupus erythematosus. *Arthritis Research and Therapy, 14*(suppl 4), S4.

Lee, J., Peschken, C. A., Muangchan, C., Silverman, E., Pineau, C., Smith, C. D., . . . Pope, J. E. (2013). The frequency of and associations with hospitalization secondary to lupus flares from the 1000 Faces of Lupus Canadian cohort. *Lupus, 22*(13), 1341–1348.

Mattsson, M., Möller, B., Stamm, T., Gard, G., & Boström, C. (2012). Uncertainty and opportunities in patients with established systemic lupus erythematosus: A qualitative study. *Musculoskeletal Care, 10*(1), 1–12.

Moses, N., Wiggers, J., Nicholas, C., & Cockburn, J. (2005). Prevalence and correlates of perceived unmet needs of people with systemic lupus erythematosus. *Patient Education and Counseling, 57*(1), 30–38.

Nalli, C., Iodice, A., Andreoli, L., Lojacono, A., Motta, M., Fazzi, E., & Tincani, A. (2014). The effects of lupus and antiphospholipid antibody syndrome on fetal outcomes. *Lupus, 23*(6), 507–517.

Neri, F., Chimini, L., Bonomi, F., Filippini, E., Motta, M., Faden, D., . . . Tincani, A. (2004). Neuropsychological development of children born to patients with systemic lupus erythematosus. *Lupus, 13*(10), 805–811.

Odutola, J., & Ward, M. M. (2005). Ethnic and socioeconomic disparities in health among patients with rheumatic disease. *Current Opinion in Rheumatology, 17*(2), 147–152.

Østensen, M. (2004). New insights into sexual functioning and fertility in rheumatic diseases. *Best Practice & Research Clinical Rheumatology, 18*(2), 219–232.

Peschken, C. A., Katz, S. J., Silverman, E., Pope, J. E., Fortin, P. R., Pineau, C., . . . Hudson, M. (2009). The 1000 Canadian faces of lupus: Determinants of disease outcome in a large multiethnic cohort. *The Journal of Rheumatology, 36*(6), 1200–1208.

Pettersson, S., Lövgren, M., Eriksson, L. E., Moberg, C., Svenungsson, E., Gunnarsson, I., & Welin Henriksson, E. (2012). An exploration of patient-reported symptoms in systemic lupus erythematosus and the relationship to health-related quality of life. *Scandinavian journal of rheumatology, 41*(5), 383–390.

Phillip, E. J., Lindner, H., & Lederman, L. (2009). Relationship of illness perceptions with depression among individuals diagnosed with lupus. *Depression & Anxiety, 26*, 575–582.

Pons-Estel, B. A., Catoggio, L. J., Cardiel, M. H., Soriano, E. R., Gentiletti, S., Villa, A. R., . . . Alarcón-Segovia, D. (2004). The GLADEL multinational Latin American prospective inception cohort of 1,214 patients with systemic lupus erythematosus: Ethnic and disease heterogeneity among "Hispanics". *Medicine, 83*(1), 1–17.

Pons-Estel, G. J., Alarcón, G. S., Scofield, L., Reinlib, L., & Cooper, G. S. (2010). Understanding the epidemiology and progression of systemic lupus erythematosus. *Seminars in Arthritis and Rheumatism, 39*(4), 257–268.

Poole, J. L., Hare, K. S., Turner-Montez, S., Mendelson, C., & Skipper, B. (2014). Mothers with chronic disease: A comparison of parenting in mothers with systemic sclerosis and systemic lupus erythematosus. *OTJR: Occupation, Participation and Health, 34*(1), 12–19.

Poole, J. L., Rymek-Gmytrasiewicz, M., Mendelson, C., Sanders, M., & Skipper, B. (2012). Parenting: The forgotten role of women living with systemic lupus erythematosus. *Clinical Rheumatology, 31*(6), 995–1000.

Ross, G., Sammaritano, L., Nass, R., & Lockshin, M. (2003). Effects of mothers' autoimmune disease during pregnancy on learning disabilities and hand preference in their children. *Archives of Pediatrics & Adolescent Medicine, 157*(4), 397–402.

Ruperto, N., Hanrahan, L. M., Alarcón, G. S., Belmont, H. M., Brey, R. L., Brunetta, P., . . . Merrill, J. T. (2011). International consensus for a definition of disease flare in lupus. *Lupus, 20*(5), 453–462.

Saunders, K., Von Korff, M., LeResche, L., & Mancl, L. (2007). Relationship of common pain conditions in mothers and children. *The Clinical Journal of Pain, 23*(3), 204–213.

Schanberg, L. E., Anthony, K. K., Gil, K. M., Lefebvre, J. C., Kredich, D. W., & Macharoni, L. M. (2001). Family pain history predicts child health status in children with chronic rheumatic disease. *Pediatrics, 108*(3), e47–e47.

Seawell, A. H., & Danoff-Burg, S. (2005). Body image and sexuality in women with and without systemic lupus erythematosus. *Sex Roles, 53*(11–12), 865–876.

Shoenfeld, Y., & Meroni, P. L. (Eds.). (2012). *The general practice guide to autoimmune diseases.* Legerich, Germany: Pabst Science Publishers.

Somers, E. C., Marder, W., Cagnoli, P., Lewis, E. E., DeGuire, P., Gordon, C., . . . McCune, W. J. (2014). Population-Based incidence and prevalence of systemic lupus erythematosus: The Michigan lupus epidemiology and surveillance program. *Arthritis & Rheumatology, 66*(2), 369–378.

Stein, J. A., & Newcomb, M. D. (1994). Children's internalizing and externalizing behaviors and maternal health problems. *Journal of Pediatric Psychology, 19*(5), 571–594.

Sterling, K. L., Gallop, K., Swinburn, P., Flood, E., French, A., Al Sawah, S., . . . Nixon, A. (2014). Patient-reported fatigue and its impact on patients with systemic lupus erythematosus. *Lupus, 23*(2), 124–132.

Stockl, A. (2007). Complex syndromes, ambivalent diagnosis, and existential uncertainty: The case of Systemic Lupus Erythematosus (SLE). *Social Science & Medicine, 65*(7), 1549–1559.

Strand, V., Galateanu, C., Pushparajah, D. S., Nikaï, E., Sayers, J., Wood, R., & van Vollenhoven, R. F. (2013). Limitations of current treatments for systemic lupus erythematosus: a patient and physician survey. *Lupus, 22*(8), 819–826.

Toloza, S., Uribe, A. G., McGwin, G., Alarcón, G. S., Fessler, B. J., Bastian, H. M., . . . Reveille, J. D. (2004). Systemic lupus erythematosus in a multiethnic US cohort (LUMINA): XXIII. Baseline predictors of vascular events. *Arthritis & Rheumatism, 50*(12), 3947–3957.

Umberger, W., Martsolf, D., Jacobson, A., Risko, J., Patterson, M., & Calabro, M. (2013). The shroud: ways adolescents manage living with parental chronic pain. *Journal of Nursing Scholarship, 45*(4), 344–354.

Urowitz, M. B., Gladman, D. D., MacKinnon, A., Ibanez, D., Bruto, V., Rovet, J., & Silverman, E. (2008). Neurocognitive abnormalities in offspring of mothers with systemic lupus erythematosus. *Lupus, 17*(6), 555–560.

Vinet, E., Clarke, A. E., Gordon, C., Urowitz, M. B., Hanly, J. G., Pineau, C. A., . . . Bernatsky, S. (2011). Decreased live births in women with systemic lupus erythematosus. *Arthritis Care & Research, 63*(7), 1068–1072.

Vinet, E., Pineau, C., Gordon, C., Clarke, A. E., & Bernatsky, S. (2008). Systemic lupus erythematosus in women: impact on family size. *Arthritis Care & Research, 59*(11), 1656–1660.

Walker, S. E., Smarr, K. L., Parker, J. C., Weidensaul, D. N., Nelson, W., & McMurray, R. W. (2000). Mood states and disease activity in patients with systemic lupus erythematosus treated with bromocriptine. *Lupus, 9*(7), 527–533.

Yasmeen, S., Wilkins, E. E., Field, N. T., Sheikh, R. A., & Gilbert, W. M. (2001). Pregnancy outcomes in women with systemic lupus erythematosus. *Journal of Maternal-Fetal and Neonatal Medicine, 10*(2), 91–96.

Yelin, E., Tonner, C., Trupin, L., Gansky, S. A., Julian, L., Katz, P., . . . Criswell, L. A. (2012). Longitudinal study of the impact of incident organ manifestations and increased disease activity on work loss among persons with systemic lupus erythematosus. *Arthritis Care & Research, 64*(2), 169–175.

Zandman-Goddard, G., Solomon, M., Rosman, Z., Peeva, E., & Shoenfeld, Y. (2012). Environment and lupus-related diseases. *Lupus, 21*(3), 241–250.

CHAPTER 8

PARENTAL DIABETES

Laura Lynch and Maureen Davey

Diabetes: About the Illness

Prevalence

Diabetes has become an epidemic in the U.S. (Aston, 2013). Approximately 18.8 million adults, children, and adolescents have a diabetes diagnosis, and about 7 million are prediabetic or have diabetes but have not yet been diagnosed (CDC, 2011) (see Table 8.1). Additionally, the cost of diabetes (e.g., prediabetes, diagnosed and undiagnosed diabetes, and gestational diabetes) in the U.S. is estimated to be more than $218 billion each year (Dall et al., 2010).

There are two main types of diabetes, type 1 and type 2; type 2 diabetes is much more common than type 1. Type 2 diabetes occurs when the body becomes resistant to the insulin that it produces. Therefore, the body's ability to naturally produce insulin is hindered, which leads to excess glucose build up (Centers for Disease Control and Prevention, 2011). Essentially, there is enough insulin in the body, but the cells are unable to use it. In type 1 diabetes, the body is no longer able to produce insulin at all (Deatcher, 2008). In the U.S., 90% of individuals with diabetes are diagnosed with type 2 (Nolan, Damm, & Prentki, 2011). Given the overwhelming prevalence of type 2 diabetes, we will focus on type 2 in this chapter.

Although type 2 diabetes affects individuals across all races and ethnicities, significant class, racial, and gender-related health disparities currently exist in the U.S. (Carter-Edwards, Skelly, Cagle, & Appel, 2004; Carthron et al., 2010; Chaufan, Davis, & Constantino, 2011; Kramer et al., 2012; Pierre-Louis, Akoh, White, & Pharris, 2011; Rubin & Peyrot, 1998; Samuel-Hodge et al., 2000). African Americans, Hispanic/Latino Americans, American Indians, and some Asian Americans and Pacific Islanders are at a higher risk for developing type 2 diabetes (Centers for Disease Control and Prevention, 2014). African American women at all income levels are especially vulnerable for developing adult-onset type 2 diabetes (Dingfelder, 2013).

Socioeconomic disparities also exist (Connolly, Unwin, Sherriff, Bilous, & Kelly, 2000; Dall et al., 2010). Lower SES is associated with increased diabetes-related mortality rates (Saydah & Lochner, 2010) and overall diabetes risk (Lee et al., 2011). Housing instability and food insecurity, both facets of low SES, negatively affect individuals' abilities to effectively manage their diabetes (Vijayaraghavan, Jacobs, Seligman, & Fernandez, 2011).

Table 8.1 Diagnosed and Undiagnosed Diabetes among People Aged 20 Years and Older

Diagnosed and Undiagnosed Diabetes among People Aged 20 Years or Older, United States, 2010

Group	Number or Percentage Who Have Diabetes
Age ≥ 20 years	25.6 million or 11.3% of all people in this age group
Age ≥ 65 years	10.9 million or 26.9% of all people in this age group
Men	13.0 million or 11.8% of all people in this age group
Women	12.6 million or 10.8% of all people in this age group
Non-Hispanic Whites	15.7 million or 10.2% of all people in this age group
Non-Hispanic Blacks	4.9 million or 18.7% of all people in this age group

Sufficient data are not available to estimate the total prevalence of diabetes (diagnosed and undiagnosed) for other U.S. racial/ethnic minority populations.

Source: Centers for Disease Control and Prevention. (2011). *National diabetes fact sheet: National estimates and general information on diabetes and pre-diabetes in the United States*. Atlanta, GA: U.S. Department of Health and Human Services, Centers for Disease Control and Prevention. Retrieved from www.cdc.gov/diabetes/pubs/pdf/ndfs_2011.pdf

Prognosis and Medical Outcomes

Type 2 diabetes affects glucose, or blood sugar, levels. Glucose levels that are either too low or too high can be dangerous. Hypoglycemia occurs when blood glucose levels drop too low. Symptoms can include the following: (1) shakiness, (2) dizziness, (3) sweating, (4) chills, (5) irritability, (6) confusion, (7) increased heart rate, (8) headache, (9) tingling, (10) weakness, (11) seizures, and (12) unconsciousness (ADA, 2015). Hyperglycemia occurs when blood glucose levels become too high. Symptoms of this condition include an increased thirst and more frequent urination (ADA, 2015). If hyperglycemia is untreated, it can develop into ketoacidosis, a diabetic coma, which can lead to death (ADA, 2015).

Higher blood sugar levels over long periods of time can also damage vital organs (e.g., kidneys, eyes, and nerves). Unless well managed, this can result in numerous medical complications, for example, an increased risk of stroke, heart disease, blindness, renal failure, limb amputations, and nonalcoholic fatty liver disease (Nolan et al., 2011). Individuals diagnosed with diabetes also have a higher risk of developing dental diseases, and in general they are more likely to experience a variety of illnesses (e.g., pneumonia, influenza) (Centers for Disease Control and Prevention, 2011). Among the leading causes of death in the U.S., diabetes was ranked seventh (Centers for Disease Control and Prevention, 2011).

Obesity is a significant risk factor for developing type 2 diabetes. Most individuals diagnosed with type 2 diabetes are overweight, and as the rates of obesity have steadily increased in the U.S., the incidence of type 2 diabetes has also increased (Yaturu, 2011). Most type 2 diabetes diagnoses occur in adulthood. Yet, with the increasing prevalence of childhood obesity in the U.S., it is occurring more frequently among children and adolescents (D'Adamo & Caprio, 2011; Yaturu, 2011). Before individuals develop type 2 diabetes, they often have prediabetes. Prediabetes occurs when blood glucose levels are higher than normal but they are not yet high enough for the definitive diagnosis of type 2 diabetes (Deatcher, 2008).

Type 2 diabetes can be managed, and individuals can lead normal and full lives. Type 2 diabetes management involves maintaining a healthy weight through diet and engaging in regular exercise. If these lifestyle changes cannot be made or maintained, then oral medications (e.g., metaformin) and/or insulin therapy may be used to treat it (Knowler et al., 2002; Nolan et al., 2011; Turkoski, 2006). Insulin therapy is self-administered through insulin injections or an insulin pump, which is worn on the outside of the body and delivers a continuous dose of insulin intravenously (American Diabetes Association, 2015).

Development and Diagnosis of Type 2 Diabetes

Type 2 diabetes can take between 7 and 10 years to fully develop, as the body gradually becomes resistant to insulin and the ability to produce insulin deteriorates (Nisal, Gholap, & Davies, 2012). From patients' and family's perspectives, the onset of type 2 diabetes may seem gradual in some cases and acute in others. It may be more gradual if the diagnosed individual was previously identified as someone at risk for developing type 2 diabetes by a medical provider or was formally diagnosed with prediabetes. Yet families could experience the diagnosis as more acute if they did not know that the family member was at risk for developing type 2 diabetes prior to the formal diagnosis and/or there were no noticeable symptoms prior to the diagnosis. This lack of awareness is quite possible because individuals with type 2 diabetes often do not experience symptoms until the later stages of developing the illness and because a diagnosis during these later stages increases the likelihood of existing diabetes complications (Nisal, Gholap, & Davies, 2012).

Diabetes often runs in families. Prior studies suggest that family history is an important predictor of developing type 2 diabetes (D'Adamo & Caprio, 2011; Knowler et al., 2002; Moses, Mawby, & Phillips, 2013). If an adult patient has type 2 diabetes, then their offspring are at an increased risk of also developing the disease (Ackermann et al., 2011; Bachman, Singhal, Misra, & Foster, 2010; CDC, 2011). It is estimated that individuals with one parent diagnosed with type 2 diabetes have double the risk of developing this type of diabetes, while having both parents diagnosed with type 2 diabetes will increase the risk up to six times (Nolan et al., 2011). The American Diabetes Association estimates that a child has a 1 in 7 chance of developing diabetes if the parent is diagnosed before the age of 50, compared to a 1 in 13 chance if the parent is diagnosed after that age (Nolan et al., 2011).

Another salient risk factor associated with family history is lifestyle (Torpy, Lynm, & Glass, 2009; Yaturu, 2011). Researchers in the United Kingdom and in the U.S. reported that obese and overweight adults were more likely to have a family history of diabetes; overweight adults are almost twice as likely to have diabetes, while obese adults are nearly four times as likely to have it. Despite the mounting evidence, many individuals in the U.S. do not yet believe their family history is a serious risk factor for developing diabetes (Yaturu, 2011). Prior studies suggest that only one-third of parents with diabetes thought it was likely that their children would also develop the disease. Only 38% of brothers and sisters of people who had diabetes, thought they would also develop it. Prior studies suggest that while two-thirds of people know they have type 2 diabetes in their families, only one-third actively seek out family medical history information (CDC, 2011).

Psychological Comorbidities

Diabetes is associated with negative psychological outcomes (e.g., Weinger & Lee, 2006). For example, type 2 diabetes often co-occurs with symptoms of depression (Campayo, Gómez-Biel, & Lobo, 2011). Depression co-occurring with diabetes can negatively affect glycemic and metabolic control and treatment adherence which can lead to complications related to vascular health (Campayo et al., 2011). Campayo and colleagues (2011) noted that "the comorbidity of depression and diabetes is associated with increased morbidity, increased mortality, and higher medical costs" (p. 28). Not only is the rate of depression higher among individuals with type 2 diabetes compared to the general population, there is also some evidence that supports a bidirectional association between diabetes and depression (Renn, Feliciano, & Segal, 2011). This means that depression may act as a risk factor for type 2 diabetes (e.g., by negatively affecting self-care) in some cases and as a consequence of diabetes in others (Renn et al., 2011).

Anxiety has also been associated with type 2 diabetes. Lin and colleagues (2008) analyzed data from the 2006 Behavioral Risk Factor Surveillance System and examined the comorbidity of diabetes and anxiety among U.S. adults. They reported that a diabetes diagnosis was associated with a 20% higher rate of lifetime diagnosis of anxiety than those individuals who do not have diabetes in the U.S. (Lin et al., 2008). A higher association with depression was also confirmed in this study (Lin et al., 2008). Parental diabetes, therefore, can also cause depressive mood, anxiety, and distress in the afflicted parent.

Level of Uncertainty about the Illness

Well-managed or controlled type 2 diabetes presents very differently compared to poorly managed type 2 diabetes. A person with well-managed type 2 diabetes is able to keep his or her blood glucose levels regulated through a combination of dietary changes and regular exercise, and possibly medication. This individual monitors his/her glucose levels (as often as the doctor instructs) by testing the blood with a glucose monitor. This individual also attends medical appointments (typically with a primary care physician or endocrinologist), continually tracks and discusses the illness, and follows the diabetes management plan developed with the doctor. An individual with poorly managed diabetes is not able to regulate his/her blood glucose levels effectively. He or she may not exercise regularly or have a healthy diet. This individual may not keep track of the blood glucose levels as often as the doctor recommends. This individual may also miss diabetes-related medical appointments, and he or she will likely experience periodic episodes of hypoglycemia or hyperglycemia that result from unregulated blood glucose levels.

As discussed earlier in this chapter, type 2 diabetes can cause serious negative health consequences if it is poorly controlled, for example, significant incapacitation like amputated limbs, stroke, coma, or even fatality (Mayo Clinic, 2014). Poor levels of control over the illness can lead to much uncertainty (and fear) in the diagnosed parent as well as in family members.

What Clinicians Need to Know about Diabetes

1   Type 2 diabetes requires consistent management on the part of the patient.
2   Type 2 diabetes can have many negative health outcomes and can ultimately be fatal if not controlled effectively.
3   Type 2 diabetes cannot be cured, but it can be managed with a combination of diet, exercise, and medication.
4   Children of parents with type 2 diabetes are at higher risk for developing the illness themselves.
5   Patients with type 2 diabetes are more likely to have depression or anxiety than the general population.
6   There are significant racial and socioeconomic health disparities associated with type 2 diabetes.

Effects of Diabetes on Parents

As of 2012, there were an estimated 28.9 million individuals aged 20 years or older in the U.S. with diabetes (Centers for Disease Control and Prevention, 2014). According to the United States Census Bureau (2012), there are approximately 24,445,000 two-parent families and 1,859,000 single-parent families in the United States. Based on these statistics, there are likely a considerable number of adults with type 2 diabetes who are parenting school-age children.

If a parent with diabetes is partnered, the couple relationship is inevitably impacted (e.g., Trief et al., 2003). Couples can be affected by and respond to the diabetes in different ways. They may experience the illness as transformative and grow in positive ways, as something they must accept and adapt to, or as something troublesome or scary, which they may attempt to avoid or ignore (Houston-Barrett & Wilson, 2014).

The nondiabetic partner may take on a role in managing the illness. Couples' expectations about the nondiabetic partner's role in the management of diabetes have been found to be associated with the diagnosed partner's diabetes treatment adherence (Seidel, Franks, Stephens, & Rook, 2012). Additionally, the extent to which the diabetes is under control can impact both partners and the quality of the couple relationship. Poorly managed diabetes can act as a relational stressor. Iida, Stephens, Franks, and Rook (2013) found evidence that increased diabetes symptom severity in a partner was related to higher levels of tension and less enjoyment within the couple relationship. Diabetes can also affect a couple's sexual relationship. Erectile dysfunction is significantly more prevalent among men with diabetes than those without it (Jackson, 2004). Sexual dysfunctions such as decreased vaginal lubrication, dyspareunia, and low libido are also more common among women who have diabetes than among nondiabetic women (Meeking, Fosbury, Cummings, 2013). The quality and strength of a couple's relationship inevitably impacts their children; thus, the impact of diabetes on the couple is one path through which parental diabetes can affect children.

Effects of Parental Diabetes on Children

There is limited research examining the psychosocial effects of parental type 2 diabetes on parents and their children, but what little has been done is noteworthy. Laroche, Davis, and colleagues (2008) explored how dietary changes made by African American and Latino parents because of their diabetes influenced how they fed their children at home and how the children experienced these dietary changes. They described four types of family patterns that occur when these changes are enacted. The first pattern includes families in which the parents expected their children to eat the same foods as them and the children did not show much resistance to this parental expectation. In the second pattern, the parents had the aforementioned expectations and the children resisted the dietary changes at home. The third pattern described children who resisted the dietary changes their parents were making and parents who then let their children make other food choices, and finally a fourth pattern described parents who provided their children with food other than what they made for themselves despite no outward resistance from their children. The authors noted that the four different family patterns could be a reflection of cultural differences in parenting styles, because 80% of the African American families were in two of the food patterns and 60% of the Latino families were in the other two food patterns. The authors did not offer any explanation for this difference.

Using data from the same study, Laroche and colleagues (2008) also examined the consumption of (sugary) soda in families where parents were making dietary changes because of diabetes and the effect of these changes on the family's diet. Most parents reported either decreasing or stopping their soda consumption. Some parents tried to reduce or stop their children's consumption of sugar-based sodas and reported that they were met with varying degrees of resistance from their children. Overall, the researchers reported that the level of soda consumption decreased more than the level of any other unhealthy food consumption for many child participants, which was similar for adult participants. They attributed this finding to some families limiting the availability of soda more than other unhealthy foods in their homes. Both of these studies suggest that even the changes parents with type 2 diabetes attempt to make regarding their lifestyles can impact their children in multiple ways.

Laroche et al. (2009) examined the roles of children regarding their parents' type 2 diabetes management. They used the same data from their initial study and included an additional cohort of participants who completed their intervention program. Findings suggest that children's roles included: (1) monitoring parents' dietary intake, (2) helping with shopping and meal preparation, (3) reminding parents to exercise, (4) exercising with parents, (5) reminding parents to take medications, (6) assisting in other diabetes self-management tasks, and (7) tempting adults to stray from their diet for diabetes. The authors noted that the roles children assumed at home were both helpful (e.g., food preparation, medication reminders) and unhelpful (e.g., influencing their diet negatively) for parents as they try to manage type 2 diabetes. They also noted these roles have the potential to both positively affect children (e.g., self-confidence) and to negatively affect them (e.g., isolation and being parentified). The authors did not explore how the children felt about assuming these roles; however, this study demonstrates that children can and often do take an active role in managing their parents' diabetes and that the various roles in turn can affect the parents' experiences of their illness.

Finally, Carthron, Johnson, Hubbart, Strickland, and Nance (2010) studied how the diabetes management of African American grandmothers was influenced by their roles as primary caregivers for their grandchildren. They compared the grandmothers' diabetes management before and after they became the primary caregivers of their grandchildren and compared the grandmothers to another age-matched cohort of grandmothers diagnosed with diabetes who were not primary caregivers for their grandchildren.

The results suggest that grandmothers who were primary caregivers found it harder to maintain a healthy diet and to regularly monitor their blood glucose after they began caring for their grandchildren compared to before they became primary caregivers. The authors suggest that the time and money needed to maintain a healthy diet could have decreased after the primary caregiving of grandchildren began, and the limited finances could have additionally negatively affected their frequency of blood glucose monitoring (which requires costly medical supplies). Findings also suggest that the caregiving grandmother group had less frequent eye examinations compared to the noncaregiving comparison group. The authors concluded that African American grandmothers with diabetes who are primary caregivers could more likely experience diabetes-related negative health consequences because they struggle with effectively managing the diabetes while also caring for their grandchildren. Though this study focused on a very specific population, it illustrates some of the potential ways that type 2 diabetes can make parenting more challenging and shows how parenting responsibilities can affect diabetes management. Parents may tend to their children's needs at the expense of their own, which can have serious health consequences when a parent has diabetes and may need to monitor blood glucose levels, take medication or insulin, exercise regularly, and watch what he/she eats. Also, if a parent's blood glucose levels are too high or too low, he or she will experience physical and/or cognitive symptoms that could temporarily impair parenting (e.g., dizziness, confusion).

Parents who are coping with depression have been shown to be less psychologically available and to struggle with communicating, supervising, and being consistent with parental discipline (Campayo et al., 2011). Since, as mentioned previously, individuals with diabetes often experience depression, diabetic parents are at higher risk of experiencing some of these parenting issues. Additionally, since parental depression has been associated with more internalizing symptoms (e.g., depression and anxiety) in children and adolescents (Fear et al., 2009), depressive symptoms among parents coping with type 2 diabetes may affect their offspring's symptoms of anxiety and depression.

Impact of Parental Diabetes on Parents and Children: Main Points

1 The roles children may take on in the management of their parents' diabetes can impact parents both positively and negatively.
2 Even seemingly small health changes parents with diabetes make, such as improving their diets, can have a significant impact on their children.
3 Parents with diabetes have a higher risk of being depressed, and parental depression can negatively affects children.
4 Parents with diabetes may struggle with balancing their diabetes management tasks along with their parenting responsibilities.

Cultural Considerations

The higher incidence of type 2 diabetes in minority populations suggests the need for more family interventions that are culturally sensitive. More clinical research should examine the role of cultural background and health beliefs on the parental type 2 diabetes experience (Laroche, Davis et al., 2008).

Pierre-Louis et al. (2011) examined the experiences of African American women with diabetes. The women in the study discussed the presence of extreme life stressors, the rising and falling of blood sugars levels together with the stress of trauma and loss, symptoms of depression, lack of connection with health-care providers, food as a source of comfort and stress, blocked energy, and God as a source of strength. Similarly, Lin et al (2008) recommended that health-care providers consider patients' sociocultural backgrounds with regard to how diabetic patients make choices about their treatment and manage their illness. They examined the experience of Taiwanese patients with type 2 diabetes. These patients reported seeking their own culturally sanctioned healing methods and changing their patterns of eating, physical activity, and other culturally bound embedded behaviors. They also said that diabetes had a lot of stigma in their culture and community. Sridhar et al. (2007) examined Indian diabetic patients. They reported that men seem to adjust better to the disease and women had more depressive symptoms, stress, and feelings of guilt. Social support more often came from the nuclear family and specifically from wives. Taken together, these studies highlight the importance of looking at the context of the patients' lives in order to understand the challenges they are facing and to tailor effective interventions for the patients and their families.

Diet and food choices are influenced by a family's culture, so helping families change their dietary habits in ways that take their culture into consideration are important. Parenting styles are also influenced by a family's culture; therefore, helping parents care for their children in culturally sensitive ways is essential. A culturally relevant approach to care is needed among all clinical providers because it has been linked to better provider–client engagement, treatment adherence, and the quality of mental health care (Hark & DeLisser, 2011; Langer, 1999; Núñez, 2000; U.S. Department of Health and Human Services, 2001).

Clinical Adaptation Based on Type of Clinical Setting

Clinicians who work in primary care clinics are most likely to encounter families coping with parental type 2 diabetes, since diabetes is most often diagnosed and treated in primary care. These clinicians have the benefit of having direct access to a diabetic patient's medical provider and should consider collaborating closely with the primary care provider. Ideally, this collaboration can help the mental healthcare professional more fully understand the diabetes diagnosis and medical treatment goals (e.g., weight loss, taking medication consistently), and it will enable the primary care provider to better understand the patient's family support system and any psychosocial stressors that could affect management of the illness. Clinicians who are integrated in primary care settings tend to provide short-term, focused behavioral health interventions that directly impact patient health outcomes. They are likely to be referred families who are coping with type 2 diabetes when the physician is concerned about a patient's management of the diabetes or when a family is having difficulty adjusting to the diagnosis.

When mental healthcare providers first meet with families, they should assess the family using a biopsychosocial framework to determine the following: (1) family's understanding of the illness; (2) how the diabetes has been affecting the patient, partner, and children at home; (3) any psychosocial stressors that may be interfering with management of the illness; and (4) family strengths that can be utilized to promote better coping and management of the diabetes (refer to Chapter 12 for assessments). Using this information, mental healthcare providers can work closely with the family to develop a focused treatment plan that minimizes any barriers to effectively managing the diabetes and that can support any offspring at home who are concerned about the parent's health, which maximizes family strengths and support. Mental healthcare providers can continue to meet with the family as needed throughout the primary care treatment of the illness; however, if there are significant mental health issues or family issues, the clinician will need to make appropriate referrals to community mental health practitioners or mental health practitioners in private practice.

Since they are not co-located with the medical team, mental healthcare providers in more traditional outpatient clinical settings need to be more intentional about collaborating with medical providers who are involved in the care of a parent diagnosed with type 2 diabetes. During an intake session with a family, when it comes up that a parent has diabetes, the provider should ask for permission to contact the primary care physician. The mental healthcare provider should explain that collaboration with medical providers is important to ensure that all of the providers and the family are on the same page regarding the diabetes diagnosis, treatment goals, and any psychosocial stressors. Release of information forms should be reviewed and signed by the patient which will allow for ongoing interdisciplinary collaboration. The mental healthcare provider will need to make a concentrated effort to reach out to medical providers in order to: (1) establish a collaborative relationship and (2) share relevant information to ensure optimal care for the patient and his/her family. In clinical settings, a mental healthcare provider typically has more time than physicians to meet with patients and their families. This helps clinicians explore type 2 diabetes and the surrounding family dynamics in more depth and to address unresolved issues within the family that may not be directly related to the diabetes but could be exacerbated by this stressor.

Clinical Vignette

The following is a clinical vignette describing a possible clinical presentation of a family coping with parental type 2 diabetes.

Ricardo, a 39-year-old Mexican American man, was diagnosed with type 2 diabetes 6 months ago by his primary care physician, Dr. Solano. Over the past year, Dr. Solano has been encouraging Ricardo to increase his exercise and make his diet healthier, as Ricardo has been prediabetic for that length of time. He has recommended that Ricardo lose at least 30 pounds. Ricardo works 50 hours per week as an electrician, and he reports that it is hard to find time to exercise after work. He has a significant family history of type 2 diabetes, including his mother, father, and older sister. Ricardo has expressed that "it's just what happens" to most people in his family as they age. Dr. Solano prescribed Metformin to Ricardo to help manage his glucose levels, which Ricardo takes as prescribed. Ricardo's wife, Gloria, 34, is also Mexican American, and she is an ESL teacher at a local middle school. She currently has no significant health issues, but she has an aunt and a grandmother with type 2 diabetes. Both Ricardo and Gloria prefer to cook and eat traditional Mexican American food, and they consider it to be a significant aspect of their culture that they want to pass on to their daughter. Their daughter, Angie, is 9 years old and, according to her pediatrician, she is slightly overweight for her height. Gloria assists Ricardo in managing his diabetes by reminding him to take his medication and to test his glucose levels. She also suggested that they join the local YMCA to use the gym, but she did not press the issue when Ricardo was uninterested.

Conclusions

Type 2 diabetes impacts all levels of the family system—the patient, the couple, and their children—even when the illness is well-managed and the family has good coping and adaptation skills. Given the prevalence of adult-onset type 2 diabetes, it is likely that clinicians will encounter more families affected by it. Medical providers who care for adults with type 2 diabetes should ask about every patient's family. Ideally, primary care and specialty clinics should have trained mental health clinicians available to assist these patients in performing the critical role of parenting. A therapist can intervene throughout the life cycle of the family and of the disease. For example, providers should regularly assess for depression, anxiety, and eating disorders among individuals coping with type 2 diabetes (Anstoot et al., 2007; Kakleas, Kandyla, Karayianni, & Karavanaki, 2009). They can help families navigate previous psychiatric and behavior issues that are now compounded and magnified by the presence of type 2 diabetes (Anstoot et al., 2007; Kakleas et al., 2009).

It is also important that mental health and medical providers attend to the family's cultural context (Hark & DeLisser, 2011; Núñez, 2000) when addressing the effects of parental type 2 diabetes. For example, as discussed in this chapter, diet and food choices are influenced by a family's culture, so helping families address dietary habits that take into consideration their culture is important. Parenting styles are also shaped by a family's culture, so helping parents diagnosed with type 2 diabetes care for their children in culturally congruent ways is essential.

Did You Know?

1   The estimated cost of diabetes in the U.S. in 2012 was $245 billion.
2   English physiologist Sir Edward Albert Sharpey-Schafer first discovered insulin (produced in the pancreas) in 1910.
3   In 1940, the American Diabetes Association was founded.
4   Individuals with diabetes have a significantly higher risk of having complications from influenza and thus are highly encouraged to get annual flu vaccines.
5   The National Diabetes Prevention Program is currently being led by the Centers for Disease Control and Prevention in collaboration with other federal and private agencies, in an effort to implement a community-based intervention that focuses on promoting lifestyle changes to reduce type 2 diabetes risk in prediabetic individuals.

6   Certified diabetes health educators are health professionals who have had specialized training in diabetes management and prevention and who work in various healthcare settings to help teach and support individuals coping with diabetes so they can effectively manage it.

7   Africa is the region with the lowest prevalence of diabetes.

Test Your Knowledge: True or False

1   Type 1 diabetes is more common than type 2 diabetes.
2   Diabetes can cause significant negative health outcomes.
3   All individuals with diabetes require oral medication or insulin.
4   Type 2 diabetes often runs in families.
5   Type 2 diabetes is typically diagnosed in childhood.
6   Obesity is a significant risk factor in type 2 diabetes.
7   Prediabetes is a condition in which blood glucose levels are higher than normal but they are not yet high enough for a diabetes diagnosis.
8   It is possible for type 2 diabetes to be controlled with diet and exercise.

Answers: 1-F, 2-T, 3-F, 4-T, 5-F, 6-T, 7-T, 8-T

Professional Readings and Resources

American Diabetes Association: http://diabetes.org
International Diabetes Federation: http://idf.org/wdd-index
Joslin Diabetes Center: http://joslin.org
National Diabetes Education Program: http://ndep.nih.gov/

References

Ackermann, R., Finch, E., Caffrey, H., Lipscomb, E., Hays, L., & Saha, C. (2011). Long-term effects of a community-based lifestyle intervention to prevent type 2 diabetes: The DEPLOY extension pilot study. *Chronic Illness, 7*(4), 279–290. doi:10.1177/1742395311407532

American Diabetes Association. (2015). Type 2. Retrieved from www.diabetes.org/diabetes-basics/type-2/

Anstoot, H., Anderson, B. J., Daneman, D., Danne, T., Donaghue, K., Kaufman, F., Rea, R. R., & Uchigata, Y. (2007). Chapter three: Diabetes in children: Psychosocial aspects. In *Pediatric Diabetes, 8* (4, suppl 8), 26–31.

Aston, G. (2013). *Diabetes: An alarming epidemic. Hospital Health Network, 87,* 34–38.

Bachman, E., Singhal, N., Misra, A., & Foster, G. (2010). A School-based intervention for diabetes risk reduction. *The New England Journal of Medicine, 363*(18), 1769–1770.

Campayo, A., Gómez-Biel, C. H., & Lobo, A. (2011). Diabetes and depression. *Current psychiatry reports, 13*(1), 26–30.

Carter-Edwards, L., Skelly, A. H., Cagle, C. S., & Appel, S. J. (2004). "They care but don't understand": Family support of African American women with type 2 diabetes. *The Diabetes Educator, 30*(3), 493–501. doi:10.1177/0145721704030000321

Carthron, D. L., Johnson, T. M., Hubbart, T. D., Strickland, C., & Nance, K. (2010). "Give me some sugar!" the diabetes self-management activities of African-American primary caregiving grandmothers. *Journal of Nursing Scholarship, 42*(3), 330–337. doi:10.1111/j.1547–5069.2010.01336.x

Centers for Disease Control and Prevention. (2011). *National diabetes fact sheet: National estimates and general information on diabetes and prediabetes in the United States.* Atlanta, GA: U.S. Department of Health and Human Services, Centers for Disease Control and Prevention.

Centers for Disease Control and Prevention. (2014). *National Diabetes Statistics Report: Estimates of Diabetes and Its Burden in the United States, 2014.* Atlanta, GA: U.S. Department of Health and Human Services.

Chaufan, C., Davis, M., & Constantino, S. (2011). The twin epidemics of poverty and diabetes: Understanding diabetes disparities in a low-income Latino and immigrant neighborhood. *Journal of Community Health, 36*(6), 1032–1043. doi:10.1007/s10900-011–9406-2

Connolly, V., Unwin, N., Sherriff, P., Bilous, R., & Kelly, W. (2000). Diabetes prevalence and socioeconomic status: A population based study showing increased prevalence of type 2 diabetes mellitus in deprived areas. *Journal of Epidemiology and Community Health, 54*(3), 173–177. doi:10.1136/jech.54.3.173

D'Adamo, E., & Caprio, S. (2011). Type 2 diabetes in youth: Epidemiology and pathophysiology. *Diabetes Care, 34*(suppl 2), S161–S165. doi:10.2337/dc11-s212

Dall, T. M., Zhang, Y., Chen, Y. J., Quick, W. W., Yang, W. G., & Fogli, J. (2010). The economic burden of diabetes. *Health Affairs, 29*(2), 297–303. doi:10.1377/hlthaff. 2009.0155

Deatcher, J. V. (2008). Prediabetes. *The American Journal of Nursing, 108*(7), 77–79.

Department of Health and Human Services Administration on Aging (2001). *Achieving cultural competence: A guidebook for providers of services to older Americans and their families.* Retrieved November 21, 2001, from http://aoa.dhhs.gov/minorityaccess/guidbook2001

Dingfelder, S. (2013). African-American women at risk. *Monitor on Psychology, 44*(1), 56.

Fear, J. M., Champion, J. E., Reeslund, K. L., Forehand, R., Colletti, C., Roberts, L., & Compas, B. E. (2009). Parental depression and interparental conflict: Children and adolescents' self-blame and coping responses. *Journal of Family Psychology, 23*(5), 762.

Hark, L., & DeLisser, H. (Eds.). (2011). *Achieving cultural competency: A case-based approach to training health professionals.* Oxford: John Wiley & Sons.

Houston-Barrett, R. A., & Wilson, C. M. (2014). Couple's relationship with diabetes: Means and meanings for management success. *Journal of Marital and Family Therapy, 40*, 92–105. doi:10.1111/j.1752–0606.2012.00322.x

Iida, M., Stephens, M. A. P., Franks, M. M., & Rook, K. S. (2013). Daily symptoms, distress and interaction quality among couples coping with type 2 diabetes. *Journal of Social and Personal Relationships, 30*(3), 293–300.

Jackson, G. (2004). Sexual dysfunction and diabetes. *International Journal of Clinical Practice, 58*(4), 358–362. doi:10.1111/j.1368-5031.2004.00180.x

Kakleas, K., Kandyla, B., Karayianni, C., & Karavanaki, K. (2009). Psychosocial problems in adolescents with type 1 diabetes mellitus. *Diabetes & Metabolism, 35*(5), 339–350.

Knowler, W. C., Barrett-Connor, E., Fowler, S. E., Hamman, R. F., Lachin, J. M., Walker, E. A., . . . Diabetes Prevention Program Research Group. (2002). Reduction in the incidence of type 2 diabetes with lifestyle intervention or metformin. *The New England Journal of Medicine, 346*(6), 393–403. doi:10.1056/NEJMoa012512

Kramer, H. U., Raum, E., Ruter, G., Schottker, B., Rothenbacher, D., Rosemann, R., . . . Brenner, H. (2012). Gender disparities in diabetes and coronary heart disease medication among patients with type 2 diabetes: Results from the DIANA study. *Cardiovascular Diabetol, 11*, 88.

Langer, N. (1999). Culturally competent professionals in therapeutic alliances enhance patient compliance. *Journal of Health Care for the Poor and Underserved, 10*(1), 19–26.

Laroche, H. H., Davis, M. M., Forman, J., Palmisano, G., & Heisler, M. (2008). What about the children? The experience of families involved in an adult-focused diabetes intervention. *Public Health Nutrition, 11*(4), 427–436. doi:10.1017/S1368980007000791

Laroche, H. H., Davis, M. M., Forman, J., Palmisano, G., Reisinger, H. S., Tannas, C., . . . Heiseler, M. (2009). Children's roles in parents' diabetes self-management. *American Journal of Preventive Medicine, 37*(6), S251–S261. doi:10.1016/j.amepre.2009.08.003

Laroche, H. H., Heisler, M., Forman, J., Anderson, M., & Davis, M. M. (2008). When adults with diabetes attempt to drink less soda: Resulting adult-child interactions and household changes. *Journal of the National Medical Association, 100*(9), 1004–1011.

Lee, T. C., Glynn, R. J., Peña, J. M., Paynter, N. P., Conen, D., Ridker, P. M., ... & Albert, M. A. (2011). Socioeconomic status and incident type 2 diabetes mellitus: Data from the Women's Health Study. *PLoS One, 6*(12), e27670.

Lin, C., Anderson, R. M., Hagerty, B. M., & Lee, B. (2008). Diabetes self-management experience: A focus group study of Taiwanese patients with type 2 diabetes. *Journal of Nursing and Healthcare of Chronic Illness, 17*(5a), 34–42.

Mayo Clinic. (2014, July 24). Type 2 diabetes. Retrieved November 14, 2014, from www.mayoclinic.org/diseases-conditions/type-2-diabetes/basics/complications/con-20031902

Meeking, D., Fosbury, J., & Cummings, M. (2013). Sexual dysfunction and sexual health concerns in women with diabetes. *Practical Diabetes, 30*, 327–331. doi:10.1002/pdi.1805

Moses, A. C., Mawby, M., & Phillips, A. M. (2013). Diabetes prevention. *American Journal of Preventive Medicine, 44*(4), S333–S338. doi:10.1016/j.amepre.2012.12.011

Nisal, K., Gholap, N., & Davies, M. (2012). Type 2 diabetes: Tips and pitfalls in diagnosis and management. *Prescriber, 23*(20), 21–31. doi:10.1002/psb.974

Nolan, C. J., Damm, P., & Prentki, M. (2011). Type 2 diabetes across generations: From pathophysiology to prevention and management. *Lancet, 378*(9786), 169–181. doi:10.1016/S0140-6736(11)60614

Núñez, A. E. (2000). Transforming cultural competence into cross-cultural efficacy in women's health education. *Academic Medicine, 75*(11), 1071–1080.

Pierre-Louis, B., Akoh, V., White, P., & Pharris, M. D. (2011). Patterns in the lives of African American women with diabetes. *Nursing Science Quarterly, 24*(3), 227–236.

Renn, B. N., Feliciano, L., & Segal, D. L. (2011). The bidirectional relationship of depression and diabetes: A systematic review. *Clinical Psychology Review, 31*(8), 1239. doi:10.1016/j.cpr.2011.08.001

Rubin, R. R., & Peyrot, M. (1998). Men and diabetes: Psychosocial and behavioral issues. *Diabetes Spectrum, 11*(2), 81–87.

Samuel-Hodge, C. D., Headen, S. D., Skelly, A. H., Ingram, A. F., Keyserling, T. C., Jackson, E. J., . . . Elasy, T. A. (2000). Influences on day-to-day self-management of type 2 diabetes among African-American women. *Diabetes Care, 23*(7), 928–933.

Saydah, S., & Lochner, K. (2010). Socioeconomic status and risk of diabetes-related mortality in the U.S. *Public Health Reports (Washington, DC: 1974), 125*(3), 377–388.

Seidel, A. J., Franks, M. M., Stephens, M. A. P., & Rook, K. S. (2012). Spouse control and type 2 diabetes management: Moderating effects of dyadic expectations for spouse involvement. *Family Relations, 61*(4), 698–709.

Sridhar, G. R., Madhu, K., Veena, S., Madhavi, R., Sangeetha, B. S., & Rani, A. (2007). Living with diabetes: Indian experience. *Diabetes & Metabolic Syndrome: Clinical Research & Reviews, 1*, 181–187.

Torpy, J. M., Lynm, C., & Glass, R. M. (2009). Diabetes. *JAMA: The Journal of the American Medical Association, 301*(15), 1620. doi:10.1001/jama.301.15.1620

Trief, P. M., Sandberg, J., Greenberg, R. P., Graff, K., Castronova, N., Yoon, M., & Weinstock, R. S. (2003). Describing support: A qualitative study of couples living with diabetes. *Families, Systems, & Health, 21*(1), 57.

Turkoski, B. B. (2006). Diabetes and diabetes medications. *Orthopaedic Nursing / National Association of Orthopaedic Nurses, 25*(3), 227–231. doi:10.1097/00006416-200605000-00015

United States Census Bureau. (2012) America's Families and Living Arrangements. Retrieved from www.census.gov/prod/2013pubs/p20–570.pdf

Vijayaraghavan, M., Jacobs, E., Seligman, H., & Fernandez, A. (2011). The association between housing instability, food insecurity, and diabetes self-efficacy in low-income adults. *Journal of Health Care for the Poor and Underserved, 22*(4), 1279–1291.

Weinger, K., & Lee, J. (2006). Psychosocial and psychiatric challengers of diabetes mellitus. *Nursing Clinics of North America, 41*, 667–680.

Yaturu, S. (2011). Obesity and type 2 diabetes. *Journal of Diabetes Mellitus, 1*(4), 79–95. doi:10.4236/jdm.2011.14012

CHAPTER 9

PARENTAL CARDIOVASCULAR DISEASES

Karni Kissil

Cardiovascular Diseases: About the Illness

Prevalence

Cardiovascular disease (CVD) causes one out of every 2.9 deaths in the U.S. (Lloyd-Jones et al., 2009). CVD is not a singular chronic medical condition but describes a broad range of diseases such as coronary heart disease (e.g., myocardial infarction [heart attack], angina pectoris [chest pain]), high blood pressure, cardiac arrest, and arrhythmia (Shields, Finley, & Chawla, & Meadors, 2012). CVD is currently the leading cause of death in the U.S. and represents approximately 17% of the overall national health expenditures (Lloyd-Jones et al., 2010).

Although CVD remains the leading killer of both women and men in the U.S., there are substantial gender differences in both the prevalence and burden of different types of CVDs (Mosca, Barrett-Connor, & Wenger, 2011). For both women and men, coronary heart disease (CHD) is the largest contributor to CVD morbidity and mortality. The number of women living with and dying from CVD and stroke exceeds the number of men, and the number of hospital discharges for heart failure and stroke is higher for women than for men (Roger et al., 2011). More men are living with and dying of CHD, and they have more hospital discharges for CHD. Gender differences in CVD mortality largely reflect gender differences in the U.S. demographics. Women constitute a larger proportion of the elderly population because women tend to have longer life expectancies compared to men (Mosca et al., 2011).

Additionally, there are ethnic and racial differences in the prevalence of CVD in the U.S., with non-Hispanic Blacks bearing a disproportionate burden of morbidity and mortality rates (CDC, 2005; Heidenreich et al., 2011; Roger et al., 2012). Among women, the prevalence of CVD is 47% for Black women, 34% for White women, and 31% for Mexican American Women (Roger et al., 2011). Noteworthy, the mortality rate of CHD is highest among Black women (122 out of 100,000 compared with 94 out of 100,000 in White women) (Roger et al., 2011).

There are also gender differences in the prevalence of risk factors for CVD (Mosca et al. 2011). Although men and women have a nearly equal prevalence of hypertension (high blood pressure), recent data from the National Health and Nutrition Examination Survey (NHANES) suggest that the prevalence of high blood pressure is greater among women who are older than 65 (National Center for Health Statistics, 2010). The highest rate of hypertension is among Black women (44%), and this is steadily increasing (Hertz, Unger, Cornell, & Saunders, 2005). Diabetes mellitus, another risk factor for CVD, is also more prevalent among women compared to men (Roger et al., 2011).

Lower SES is a well-established risk-factor for CVDs, especially CHD (Albert, Glynn, Buring, & Ridker, 2006; Ruiz, Prather, & Steffen, 2012). Lower SES during childhood is associated with more CHD in adulthood, independently of adult SES (Miller, Chen, Parker, 2011). Lower SES contributes to CVD risk through other risk factors associated with it, such as active and passive smoking (second hand smoking), less education, increased exposure to infectious agents, poorer diets, limited opportunities for physical activity, limited access to health care, and higher levels of stress (Albert et al., 2006; Steptoe & Kivimäki, 2012). For example, more-educated women are less likely to be smokers and are more likely to participate in rigorous physical activities compared to women who have less education (Albert et al., 2006).

Lifestyle risk factors for CVD additionally vary by gender, race, and ethnicity. Cigarette smoking is more common among men compared to women (21.3% vs. 18.1%) (Roger et al., 2011). Non-Hispanic White women have a higher rate of smoking (20.7%) compared to Black women (18.8%) and Hispanic women (9.4%). Rates of physical inactivity are also higher among women compared to men (34.5% vs. 30.3%) (Roger et al., 2011). Obesity and being overweight are highly prevalent among both men and women in the U.S., with two-thirds of Americans being overweight or obese (72% men and 64% women) as defined by body mass index (BMI). (An adult who has a BMI between 25 and 29.9 is considered overweight and a BMI of 30 or higher is obese; Flegal, Carroll, Ogden, & Curtin, 2010). Among women, non-Hispanic Blacks and Mexican Americans are more likely to be obese compared non-Hispanic Whites (50% vs. 45% vs. 33%, respectively) (Flegal et al., 2010).

Types of CVDs

CVD is not a singular chronic medical condition, but encompasses a broad spectrum of diseases and conditions involving the heart and blood vessels (Shields, Finely, Chawla, & Meadors, 2012) (see Figure 9.1). The most common diseases and conditions are (www.heart.org):

1   *Coronary heart disease (CHD)*—describes heart problems caused by a plaque build-up in the walls of the arteries, or atherosclerosis. As plaque builds up, the arteries narrow, making it more difficult for blood to flow to and from the heart, leading to a higher risk for heart attack or stroke.

2   *Heart failure*—condition in which the heart is not pumping blood as well as it should, which results in a limited supply of blood to the cells. An individual with heart failure tends to fatigue easily and becomes quickly out of breath while doing daily activities.

3   *Arrhythmia*—an irregular heartbeat that refers to any change from the normal sequence of electrical impulses to and from the heart. The electrical impulses may happen too fast, too slowly, or erratically, causing the heart to beat too fast (tachycardia), too slowly (bradycardia), or erratically (atrial or ventricular fibrillation). When the heart does not beat properly, it cannot pump blood effectively, which can affect the lungs, brain, and all other organs.

4   *Heart valve problems*—includes several conditions involving malfunctioning heart valves. For example, *stenosis* refers to when the valve does

not open properly and consequently the heart has to work harder to pump blood. *Valve regurgitation* refers to a leaky valve that causes blood to flow back through the valve during heart contractions.

5   *Cardiac arrest*—the abrupt loss of heart functioning in a person who may or may not have been diagnosed with heart disease. Death can occur instantly or shortly after symptoms appear. If cardiopulmonary resuscitation (CPR) is performed and a defibrillator is used to shock the heart and restore a normal heart rhythm within a few minutes, cardiac arrest can be reversed.

6   *Stroke*—when a blood vessel that carries oxygen and nutrients to the brain is either blocked by a clot or bursts (ruptures). When this occurs, part of the brain cannot get the blood (oxygen) it needs, resulting in death of part of the brain.

7   *Cardiomyopathy*—a disease of the heart muscle that can be inherited or acquired. Cardiomyopathy refers to when the heart muscle becomes enlarged, thick, or rigid, causing the heart to weaken and to become less able to pump blood through the body.

8   *High blood pressure (HBP)*—a disease and a significant risk factor for other CVDs. High blood pressure, or hypertension, is often referred to as "the silent killer." Even though it typically has no symptoms, HBP can have deadly health consequences if it is not treated immediately. It is the most common CVD in the U.S. An estimated 78 million people have a diagnosis of HBP. Untreated HBP can lead to stroke, heart attack, heart failure, and kidney damage.

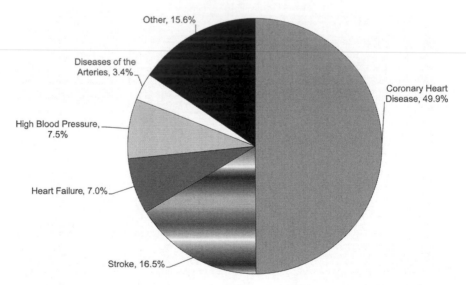

Figure 9.1 Percentage Breakdown of Deaths Attributable to Cardiovascular Disease (United States, 2008)

Source: Roger, V. L., Go, A. S., Lloyd-Jones, D. M., Benjamin, E. J., Berry, J. D., Borden W. B., . . . Turner, M. B. on behalf of the American Heart Association Statistics Committee and Stroke Statistics Subcommittee. (2012). Heart disease and stroke statistics—2012 update: A report from the American Heart Association. *Circulation, 125*, e2–e220. Retrieved from http://circ.ahajournals.org/content/125/1/e2.full.pdf+html. Reprinted with permission.

The risk of developing CVD is the result of the interaction between an individual's genetic inheritance and the physical and social environment he/she lives in over time (Hunter, 2005). Genes provide a "default setting" that predisposes an individual to certain diseases. Yet, modifications of the social and physical environments can lessen the impact that genes have regarding the initiation or progression of a disease (Gluckman & Hanson, 2008; Hasselbalch, 2010). The risk of developing CVD is determined by this complex interplay of modifiable and nonmodifiable factors including but not limited to genes, level of physical activity, nutrition, health status, sedentary behavior, and social circumstances (Archer & Blair, 2011). Twin and familial studies suggest that heredity does not play the most important role in the etiology of CVD because genes contribute only about 30% (Bouchard, Malina, & Perusse, 1997). These genetic studies suggest a substantial role for modifiable environmental factors (Archer & Blair, 2011).

Diagnosis and Prognosis

CVDs can be diagnosed by a primary care provider during a routine annual exam (e.g., high blood pressure), by a cardiologist, or in the emergency room or intensive care unit following a serious cardiac event. Some of the more common symptoms of CVDs are: (1) undue fatigue, (2) labored breathing (called *dyspnea*), (3) heart palpitations (the sensation that the heart is skipping a beat or beating too rapidly), and (4) chest pain.

A healthcare provider can diagnose a CVD based on several assessments. The provider will typically first do a comprehensive medical history, including any family history with CVDs. The provider will then conduct a thorough physical examination and order blood tests (to look for enzymes that indicate a heart attack has occurred). The following diagnostic procedures can be used to diagnose CVD (www.heart.org):

1   *Electrocardiogram* (ECG or EKG)—examines any abnormalities caused by damage to the heart. An ECG is a medical device that makes a graphical record of the heart's electrical activity.
2   *Holter monitoring* or *ambulatory ECG/EKG*—patient wears a heart monitor for several days to record the electrical activity of the heart during daily activities.
3   *Chest X-ray*—determines whether the heart is enlarged or if fluid is accumulating in the lungs as a result of the heart attack.
4   *Echocardiogram*—hand-held device placed on the chest that uses high-frequency sound waves (ultrasound) to produce images of the heart's size, structure, and motion. It can help to detect abnormal rhythm.
5   *Cardiac computer tomography*—refers to several noninvasive, diagnostic-imaging tests (e.g., CT, PET scan) that use computer-assisted techniques to take images of the heart. A computer creates three-dimensional (3-D) images that can show blockages caused by calcium deposits in the coronary arteries.
6   *Exercise stress test*—monitor with electrodes is attached to the skin on the chest area to record the heart functioning (including heart rate, breathing, and blood pressure) while the patient walks on a treadmill.

7   *Cardiac catheterization*—examines the inside of the heart's blood vessels using special X-rays called angiograms. Dye visible by X-ray is injected into the blood vessels using a thin hollow tube called a *catheter*. This procedure is one of the most useful and accurate tools for diagnosing cardiovascular problems. It can detect where arteries are narrowed or blocked, measure blood pressure within the heart and oxygen in the blood, and evaluate heart muscle function.

The prognosis of CVD varies depending on the type of CVD and the risk factors (e.g., obesity, smoking, social isolation). Patients can have full lives after a mild CVD if they make the lifestyle changes needed to reduce person-environment risk factors (e.g., exercise, lose weight). It is beyond the scope of this chapter to fully describe the prognosis for each type of CVD. Instead, some statistics are provided to illustrate the CVD prognosis. The percentages of patients aged 40 years and older who die within a year after a first stroke are 21% for men and 24% for women (Rosamond et al., 2008). The length of time needed to recover from a stroke depends on its severity. Approximately 50–70% of stroke survivors regain their functional independence; however, 15–30% are permanently disabled and 20% require institutional care 3 months after onset (Rosamond et al., 2008). Within 5 years of a first heart attack, among patients who are ages 40 and older, 33% of men and 43% of women will die, 4% of men and 6% of women will have a stroke, and 7% of men and 12% of women will have heart failure (Rosamond et al., 2008).

Several psychosocial factors affect prognosis. For example, social support has been linked to prognosis, with low perceived social support negatively affecting cardiac mortality (Barth, Schneider, & von Känel, 2010). Thus, mental healthcare providers working with CVD patients should assess for available family and social support and facilitate increasing it. In addition, patients' expectations about recovery have been linked to prognosis. Prior studies suggest that patients who have more favorable expectations about their likelihood of recovery tend to have better longer-term survival, regardless of the severity of the CVD illness (Barefoot et al., 2011; Davidson, Mostofsky, & Whang, 2010; Mondloch, Cole, & Frank, 2001). Thus, mental healthcare providers should assess patients' expectations for recovery, instill hope, and help patients modify their expectations as needed.

Treatment

Treatment for CVD can include medication, surgery, and various other procedures such as cardioversion (delivering electrical pulses to the heart to restore normal heart rhythms) or thrombolysis, a procedure that involves injecting a clot-dissolving agent to help restore blood flow in a coronary artery. In Table 9.1 we describe the main medication groups used to treat common CVDs (www. heartandstroke.com).

For some patients, medication is not enough to manage the symptoms of CVD and surgery is required. Some of the more common surgical procedures for treating CVDs include: (1) coronary artery bypass surgery, in which a healthy blood vessel taken from the leg, arm, chest, or abdomen is connected to the other arteries in the heart so that blood is bypassed around the diseased or blocked area; (2) heart valve surgery to repair or replace a heart valve; and (3) surgically inserting a pacemaker, which is the implantation of a small electronic device usually

Table 9.1 Medications Used in CVD Treatment

CVD	Medication Group and Function
Heart attack (also referred to as *myocardial infarction*)	1. *Beta blockers:* Slow the heart rate and reduce blood pressure. 2. *Calcium channel blockers:* Vasodilators that widen the blood vessels and help to lower blood pressure and slow down the heart rate. 3. *Nitrates:* Another group of vasodilators.
Heart failure	1. *ACE (angiotensin-converting enzyme) inhibitors:* Usually given to patients with high blood pressure or heart failure or those with a high likelihood of developing coronary artery disease. They help to control blood pressure and make it easier for the heart to pump. ACE inhibitors help to lower blood pressure by decreasing the amount of angiotensin II the body makes, which makes the blood vessels narrow. 2. *ARBs (angiotensin II receptor blockers):* Used to treat high blood pressure and heart failure. They work as well as ACE inhibitors but may be a better choice for patients who experience side effects after taking the ACE inhibitors. 3. *Beta blockers:* Used to slow the heart rate down and reduce blood pressure. 4. *Aldosterone antagonists:* Mild diuretics that are usually given in combination with other medications. They inhibit the hormone aldosterone, which causes sodium and water retention and raises blood pressure. 5. *Digoxin:* Helps the heart pump stronger and slows down the heart rate to improve its pumping action.
Arrhythmia	*Antiarrhythmic drugs:* Used to treat heart rhythm disorders. They help to bring the heartbeat into a healthy range and also reduce common arrhythmia symptoms such as heart palpitations, irregular heartbeats, fast heartbeats, lightheadedness, fainting, chest pain, and shortness of breath.
Coronary heart disease (CHD)	1. *Anticoagulants:* Also referred to as blood thinners. They help prevent blood clots from forming and growing and thus reduce the risk for heart attack, stroke, and blockages in the blood vessels. 2. *Anti-platelets:* Help to prevent dangerous blood clots from forming. They may be used to reduce the risk of clot-induced heart attack or stroke. Aspirin is the most commonly used anti-platelet.
High blood pressure	Many of the medications used for the other CVDs described are also used to treat high blood pressure, such as beta blockers, ACE inhibitors, diuretics, and calcium channel blockers.

in the chest (just below the collarbone) to help regulate slow electrical problems with the heart.

An important part of CVD treatment includes rehabilitation. During rehabilitation, all of the treatments that address the various risk factors associated with CVD (e.g., smoking, physical inactivity, unhealthy diet) are typically done. Prior studies suggest that people who follow a healthy lifestyle tend to experience a reduced risk of CHD and stroke (Chiuve et al., 2008). Prior studies also suggest that sedentary behaviors (e.g., sitting, reading, screen time) and a lack of physical activity are associated with an increased risk for CVD (Archer & Blair, 2011; Ford & Caspersen, 2012; Thompson et al., 2003). A recent meta-analysis of studies that examined physical activity and risks for developing CVDs concluded that higher levels of leisure time that includes physical activity (e.g., jogging) and moderate levels of occupational physical activity are associated with a reduced risk of CHD and stroke among men by 20–30% and among women by 10–20% (Li & Siegrist, 2012). Thus, an effective rehabilitation plan should include not only a healthy diet and an increase in structured physical activities (e.g., going for a walk, to the gym), but also a decrease in overall sedentary behavior.

Another major risk factor for CVD that can be modified as part of a comprehensive rehabilitation plan is stress. Many studies suggest that exposure to long-term stress is associated with a significant increase in the risk of developing CHD compared to individuals who did not experience long-term stress. Similar results were reported for various types of stress, including: (1) work-related stress, (2) marital problems, (3) death of a child, and (4) caregiving for a sick spouse at home (De Bacquer et al., 2005; Eaker, Sullivan, Kelly-Hayes, d'Agostino, & Benjamin, 2005; Kivimäki et al., 2013; Lee, Colditz, Berkman, & Kawachi, 2003; Li, Hansen, Mortensen, & Olsen, 2002; Orth-Gomer et al., 2000; Yusuf et al., 2004). Social isolation and loneliness have also been reported as common sources of stress (Steptoe & Kivimäki, 2012). Thus, while working with patients who are coping with CVDs, therapists should assess for their levels and sources of stress. The rehabilitation plan should include effective ways to reduce stress, for example, couples therapy for marital problems, increased social interaction to reduce feelings of loneliness, relaxation techniques and mindfulness meditation, support groups and respite for stressed or burnt-out caregivers, and/or a plan to increase physical activity.

Psychological Comorbidities

Depression and psychological distress have long been recognized as significant risk factors for developing cardiovascular disease, for recurrent cardiac events in patients with established cardiovascular disease, for adverse outcomes after coronary bypass graft surgery, and for an increased mortality from other types of cardiac events (Lett, Ali, Whooley, 2008; van Zyl et al., 2009; Wellenius, Mukamal, Kulshreshtha, Asonganyi, & Mittleman, 2008; Whooley, 2006; Whooley et al., 2008). Major depressive disorder is more prevalent among patients coping with coronary heart disease compared to the general population (Kop & Plumhoff, 2011; Poole, Dickens, & Steptoe, 2011) and is associated with subsequent mortality as well as lower functional status (Barth, Schumacher, & Herrmann-Lingen, 2004; Blumenthal et al., 2003). Additionally, evidence suggests that symptoms of depression are not limited to patients. Caregivers can also suffer from depressive symptoms and higher levels of distress in general (Randall, Molloy, & Steptoe,

2009). Depressed patients may experience difficulties with problem solving and coping with challenges, and they can be less compliant with medical therapy and rehabilitation (Grenard et al., 2011); therefore, increased recognition of and treatment for major depression are crucial for patients with CVD and their caregivers.

Levels of Uncertainty about the Illness

Most heart-related illnesses can be life threatening. When patients are first informed of their diagnosis, the realization of having a serious, chronic, and possibly life-threatening illness can generate feelings of powerlessness and helplessness (Roberts, Kiselica, & Fredrickson, 2002). Many patients and partners report experiencing high levels of anxiety and uncertainty about the future (Cameron & Gignac, 2008; Dekel, Vilchinsky, Liberman, Leibowitz, Khaskia, & Mosseri, 2014). The levels of uncertainty can change depending on the diagnosis and prognosis. Surviving a cardiac arrest or a heart attack naturally generates higher levels of anxiety and uncertainty compared to "milder" diagnoses like high blood pressure or an irregular heart beat (arrhythmia).

When the acute phase of first learning about the diagnosis is over and the patient and family begin adjusting to living with a chronic illness, more uncertainty may be experienced by the patient and his/her family (Dekel et al., 2014). Patients often report worrying about losing their partners now that they have been diagnosed with a debilitating condition and they cannot function as well as before the diagnosis (Pruchno, Wilson-Genderson, & Cartwright, 2009). Partners may worry about the stability of the relationship, the asymmetry in the relationship, and the need to adapt to the changing needs of the ill partner (Arrenhall, Kristofferzon, Fridlund, Malm, & Nilsson, 2011).

What Clinicians Need to Know about CVD

1   CVD is not a single illness but describes a broad range of illnesses and conditions involving the heart and blood vessels.
2   CVD is the leading cause of death in the U.S.
3   There are gender, racial, ethnic, and socioeconomic differences regarding the burden of CVDs, with minorities disproportionally burdened with CVD morbidity and mortality.
4   Treatment of CVDs can include a combination of medication, surgery, and rehabilitation that focuses on lifestyle changes that address CVD risk factors.
5   The risks of developing CVD are determined by the interplay of modifiable and nonmodifiable factors that include, but are not limited to, genes, physical activity, nutrition, and health status.
6   Depressive symptoms are prevalent among patients with CVD and are a risk factor for developing CVD in healthy patients.
7   Most CVDs generate feelings of uncertainty and psychological distress in both patients and their partners/caregivers.

Impact of CVD on Parents

Marital status and the quality of relationships are major risk factors for developing CVDs (Smith, Baron, & Grove, 2013). Being married versus being divorced, widowed, or never married has been associated with a reduced CHD risk (Idler, Boulifard, & Contrada, 2012), but strain and disruption in an intimate relationship conversely increase the risk for developing CHD (Smith, Baron, & Caska, 2014) and other CVDs. For example, poor marital quality is associated with higher blood pressure (Holt-Lunstad, Birmingham, & Jones, 2008) and with longer hospital stays for women following coronary bypass surgery (Kulik & Mahler, 2006). CHD progresses more rapidly in women who report experiencing stress in their intimate relationships compared to women who report having happy relationships (Wang et al., 2007). Additionally, more relationship conflict and worries reported by married and cohabiting couples are associated with more CHD in previously healthy individuals (De Vogli, Chandola, & Marmot, 2007), an increased progression of atherosclerosis (Wang et al., 2007), recurrent coronary events, and reduced survival rates in CHD patients (Idler et al., 2012; King & Reis, 2012). On the other hand, higher levels of marital satisfaction were associated with lower levels of depressive symptoms for both patients and their partners (Dekel et al., 2014).

Coping with CVD can lead to significant changes in the relationships of patients and their spouses or partners (Andersson, Borglin, Sjöström-Strand, & Willman, 2013; Dalteg, Benzein, Fridlund, & Malm, 2011; Fransson, Arenhall, Steinke, Fridlund, & Nilsson, 2014; Imes, Dougherty, Pyper, & Sullivan, 2011; Luttik, Jaarsma, Veeger, & van Veldhuisen, 2005). Spouses and partners often report experiencing emotional and physical pressure because they are assuming the responsibilities of caring for their ill spouse, the household, and the rest of the family (Andersson et al., 2013; Arenhall, Kristofferzon, Fridlund, & Nilsson, 2011). Healthy partners may be overwhelmed by constant concerns about the future, their children, and the possibility of another CVD episode (Andersson et al., 2013).

Spouses and partners often report that their lives are "on hold" because of the need to put their own needs aside (Andersson et al., 2013; Arenhall, Kristofferzon, Fridlund, Malm, & Nilsson, 2011; Dalteg et al., 2011). Partners may also feel a sense of loss about the relationship, in particular the loss of the relationship as it was before, and the loss of the partner because of changes in his/her behavior following the diagnosis. Additionally, partners often report less intimacy and sexual activity because of the fear that sexual activity may trigger another cardiac event or exacerbate an existing heart condition (Arenhall et al., 2011; Dalteg, Benzein, Fridlund, & Malm, 2011; López-Medina, Gil-García, Sánchez-Criado, & Pancorbo-Hidalgo, 2014; O'Farrell, Murray, & Hotz, 2000). These changes in parental roles and the marital relationship can affect children with regard to their adjustment and well-being (Diareme et al., 2007).

Impact of Parental CVD on Children and Adolescents

Although chronic illnesses can impact the entire family, few studies have examined the psychosocial impact of parental CVD on offspring. Most studies have focused on how it affects patients, spouses, and the marital relationship. Although many scholars acknowledge that CVD tends to occur among older adults, prevalence studies actually suggest that more than 25% of adults between the ages of 20 and 29 have CVD (data includes CHD, stroke, high blood pressure, and heart failure) (Rosamond et al., 2008).

One type of parental CVD that has been studied is stroke. Researchers conducted several studies assessing children's adjustment to parental stroke from right after the diagnosis and up to 3 years after the stroke (Sieh, Meijer, & Visser-Meily, 2010; van de Port, Visser-Meily, Post, & Lindeman, 2007; Visser-Meily, Post, Meijer, Maas, Ketelaar, & Lindeman, 2005a; Visser-Meily, Post, Meijer, van de Port, Maas, & Lindeman, 2005b). Findings from this longitudinal study suggest that shortly after diagnosis, when the parent has started in-patient rehabilitation, more than half of offspring exhibited externalizing and internalizing problems, either at the clinical or subclinical levels. At the 1-year follow-up, only 29% of children still had these behavioral symptoms. In addition, the healthy parent's depressive symptoms, report of role strain, and negative perception of the marital relationship were significantly associated with their children's well-being (Visser-Meily et al., 2005a, 2005b).

Findings regarding children's adjustment 3 years after the parental stroke suggest similar patterns. Parental depressive symptoms (both for the healthy and the ill parent), life satisfaction of the ill parent, and the quality of the marital relationship were all significantly associated with children's reports of stress 3 years after the parent's stroke (Sieh et al., 2010; van de Port et al., 2007). Two-thirds of the children in this study performed caregiving activities at home and all children did household chores, but the extent of participation in these activities was not significantly associated with children's reports of stress (Sieh et al., 2010; van de Port et al., 2007). Children's functioning was also not significantly associated with the severity of the parent's illness (Sieh et al., 2010; Visser-Meily et al., 2005a). Three years after the parental stroke, children in this study additionally reported some positive changes. More than half of the children reported they felt more mature and needed at home because they had more responsibilities (van de Port et al., 2007).

Taken together, these findings suggest that parental well-being and marital satisfaction following a stroke are important factors for understanding children's adjustment over time. Similar findings were reported in studies on other types of parental chronic illnesses described in this book. In a review of studies on children of somatically ill parents, for example, Roger and his colleagues (Romer, Barkmann, Schulte-Markwort, Thomalla, & Riedesser, 2002) concluded that "the level of emotional stress or psychological maladjustment depended on . . . the subjective perception of the parental impairment" (p. 32). Children's adjustment difficulties can be a direct response to sensing their parents' negative emotional states (e.g., depression, strain, marital dissatisfaction) or a result of the "interrupted parenting" (Armistead, Klein, & Forehand, 1995) they experience due to the healthy parent being burdened by caregiving responsibilities. Mental healthcare providers should attend to the whole family while working with stroke survivors and intervene at the parents' level to promote healthy adjustment for all family members.

Impact of CVD on Parents and Children: Main Points

1　The quality of the marital relationship is associated with CVD risks and recovery from CVDs.
2　A satisfying marital relationship is associated with fewer symptoms of depression following a CVD for both partners.

(Continued)

3   CVD can create significant changes in the marital relationship.
4   Spouses of patients with CVD often feel overburdened and feel a sense of loss.
5   Changes in the marital relationship following a CVD can create interrupted parenting.
6   Children's adjustment to parental CVD is associated with the parents' emotional well-being and marital satisfaction and not with the severity of the illness.

Cultural Considerations

Mental healthcare providers will likely first encounter CVD patients in primary care offices, cardiologist clinics, and emergency rooms or in intensive care units. In any of these clinical settings, mental healthcare providers should first assess the well-being of CVD patients and their families. Since CVD patients and their partners are at a higher risk for psychological distress and depression (Lett, Ali, Whooley, 2008; van Zyl et al., 2009; Wellenius, Mukamal, Kulshreshtha, Asonganyi, & Mittleman, 2008; Whooley, 2006; Whooley et al., 2008), which can impede the patient's recovery (Grenard et al., 2011) and their children's adjustment (Sieh et al., 2010; van de Port et al., 2007; Visser-Meily et al., 2005a; 2005b), a thorough family evaluation should be conducted close to when the parent is diagnosed with a CVD.

Additionally, mental healthcare providers should intervene and help to reduce the CVD risk factors. Improving population-based risk factors has been effective in facilitating a decline in CVD death rates in the U.S. (Heidenreich et al., 2011). Smoking rates have declined since the first surgeon general's report on adverse effects of smoking in 1964. In addition, efforts to reduce dietary fat intake in the 1960s and 1970s, treat hypertension in the 1970s and 1980s, and improve blood lipid levels in the 1980s and 1990s have likely contributed to dramatically reduced CVD death rates through a decline in risk factors (Heidenreich et al., 2011). Thus, mental healthcare providers can intervene with patients who have CVD risk factors before they develop a CVD and do clinical preventions. For example, mental healthcare providers who work in primary care clinics, hospitals, or mental health centers can collaborate with other professionals (e.g., nutritionists, nurses, cardiologists, primary care physicians) to conduct a variety of support groups addressing CVD risk factors. These clinical settings can offer patients who have CVD risk factors comprehensive care that can include mindfulness-based stress reduction programs, smoking cessation using motivational interviewing (Velasquez, Hecht, Quinn, Emmons, DiClemente, & Dolan-Mullen, 2000), and weight loss support groups. Support group preventative programs can reach larger numbers of patients who are at risk for developing CVDs, which could help to offset their health trajectory into a healthier lifestyle.

Racial and ethnic health disparities in the U.S. are well established and have become a concern in health care (Yancy et al., 2011). Racial and ethnic minorities in the U.S. bear a disproportionate burden of disease and higher mortality rates (Yancy et al., 2011). CVD is the leading contributor to this mortality differential, with African Americans being two to three times more likely to die from heart disease compared with Whites at any given age (Mensah & Brown, 2007). Additionally, high blood pressure disproportionally affects African Americans in the U.S. and is prevalent in almost half of African American women (Roger et al., 2011). Additionally, Hispanic Americans diagnosed with heart failure tend to have higher hospital readmission rates and tend to experience multiple barriers to treatment because of language, cultural, and socioeconomic factors that lead to poorer health outcomes (Vivo, Krim, Cevik, & Witteles, 2009).

Recent registry-based research studies confirm a race-based invasive procedure gap, suggesting that people of color and individuals receiving Medicaid are less likely to receive effective treatment and have less access to newer and more costly invasive procedures (e.g., cardiac catheterization, coronary artery bypass graft, implantation of defibrillators) (Cram, Bayman, Popescu, & Vaughan-Sarrazin, 2009; Farmer, Kirkpatrick, Heidenreich, Curtis, Wang, & Groeneveld, 2009; Gaglia et al., 2010). Even though health disparities in CVDs in the U.S. are significant and well-established, healthcare providers are lagging behind in acknowledging this problem. For example, in a survey of cardiologists, approximately one-third acknowledged the existence of racial and ethnic care disparities, and less than 5% acknowledged disparities in their own clinic (Lurie et al., 2005).

Currently, there are various programs attempting to reduce health disparities in cardiac care. For example, in 2009, the American College of Cardiology (ACC) launched the Coalition to Reduce Racial and Ethnic Disparities in CV Outcomes (CREDO), an initiative that gives cardiologists and other healthcare providers who are treating CVDs effective tools to examine disparities in their practice using quality improvement measures to achieve a reduction in cardiac health disparities (Yancy et al., 2011). CREDO disseminates to hospitals effective tools to evaluate their physicians' performance stratified by various patient sociodemographic variables such as race, age, and type of insurance in order to detect gaps in quality of care. CREDO also provides hospitals with tools for cultural competency training for providers as well as patient education and support. Recent studies assessing the effectiveness of these programs report a decrease in cardiac health disparities among participating hospitals (e.g., Chin, Walters, Cook, & Huang, 2007; Cohen et al., 2010; Davis, Vinci, Okwuosa, Chase, & Huang, 2007). Data from these studies support the value of stratified registries, multidisciplinary teams, and community outreach. Mental healthcare providers can advocate for these types of programs in their practice settings and develop multidisciplinary teams to provide culturally competent patient and family-centered quality care to all patients.

Ethnic and racial minorities are also disproportionally affected by CVD risk factors such as smoking and limited physical activity (Kurian & Cardarelli, 2007). These are areas in which therapists are well equipped to intervene. Therapists can meet with patients who have CVD risk factors in various healthcare settings. Therapists who are not working in the medical field may also meet many patients who are not diagnosed with CVD but who have many of the CVD risk factors, such as obesity and smoking. For example, studies suggest an association between childhood sexual and physical abuse and obesity (Gustafson & Sarwer, 2004; Rohde, Ichikawa, Simon, Ludman, Linde, Jeffery, & Operskalski, 2008); thus, mental healthcare providers working with this vulnerable group can help their patients understand some of the reasons behind their obesity as well as provide education and support to prevent the development of CVDs.

Finally, studies suggest that CVD prevention should begin early in life. For example, for individuals who reach middle age with optimal levels of all major risk factors, the remaining lifetime risk of developing CVD is only 6–8% (Lloyd-Jones et al., 2006). Modest improvements in risk factors earlier in life can lead to substantial reductions later in life (Heidenreich et al., 2011). Since children of parents with CVD are at a higher risk for developing CVDs themselves, preventive interventions should address the entire family. These interventions should include psychoeducation for the family. For example, an average 3 gram per person reduction in daily intake of salt (1200 mg of sodium) can reduce the risk of developing CHD by 15% among Black men and women (Bibbins-Domingo et al., 2010). Thus, teaching families about the importance of reducing sodium intake can lead to significant improvements in risk factors for all members of the family and future generations.

Clinical Vignette

The following is a clinical vignette describing a possible clinical presentation of a family coping with parental CVD. This vignette is based on a real case. All names and identifying information have been changed to maintain clients' confidentiality.

Max is a 45-year-old man of Russian origin. He is married to Tara (42 years old). They have two children: Sarah, a junior in high school, and Jack, who is 9 years old. About a year ago, Max started experiencing labored breathing after simple daily activities like walking the dog. He also had difficulty falling asleep because he was experiencing heart palpitations. Tara thought it was because of his anxiety and suggested seeking a mental healthcare provider for therapy. Max visited his primary care physician, who prescribed anti-anxiety medication and mild sleeping pills. Max took the medication for several weeks but still felt no relief. He also started to feel some pressure in his chest a few times during the day. His primary care physician then referred him to a cardiologist. The cardiologist took a comprehensive medical history and Max noted that his brother had a heart attack at the age of 32 and his mother has arrhythmia. The cardiologist ordered some tests and the results showed that Max had blockages in two arteries. Within a few days, he was hospitalized and underwent angioplasty (a procedure in which special tubing with an attached deflated balloon is threaded up to the coronary arteries and the balloon is then inflated to widen the blocked areas). Max had to stay in the hospital overnight for the procedure. He and Tara decided to not tell their two children that Max was undergoing a surgical procedure; instead they told the children he was hospitalized for a routine check-up.

Following the procedure, Max felt better. Max and Tara decided to change their lifestyles. Max started working with a personal trainer to slowly increase his physical activity. Max and Tara changed the family diet and started cooking healthier, low fat meals at home. Max started paying closer attention to what everyone was eating at home. He constantly made comments about his daughter's weight and eating habits. He repeatedly told her that she needed to exercise more and lose weight. Tara kept telling him to back off and saying that he was not being effective since he was hurting Sarah's feelings and creating body image issues for her. Then Tara received an email from Jack's teacher, who expressed her concerns because Jack told her in class that Tara had HIV and that they were moving out of state for treatment. She also wrote that Jack has been distracted in class and seemed somewhat sad. Tara understood that Jack was struggling with the changes at home and with uncertainty and concerns about Tara's health. She realized that he sensed the changes in the house and noticed the secrecy, and without clear information, he imagined the worst case scenario, that she had HIV and not that Max had a heart condition. She talked to Max and they decided to seek family counseling to learn how to cope better with all the recent changes.

Did You Know?

1 Direct medical costs of CVD are estimated to increase to $818 billion by 2030 (from $273 billion in 2010). Indirect costs of CVD, including loss of productivity, are expected to increase to $276 billion by 2030 (from $172 billion in 2010).

2 The American Heart Association was founded by six cardiologists in 1924.

3 In 2008, one in nine death certificates in the U.S. mentioned heart failure.

4 Approximately every second, one American has a coronary event, and approximately every minute, someone dies of one.

5 In 2009, 7,453,000 inpatient cardiovascular operations and procedures were performed in the U.S.

6 A heart beats approximately 100,000 times a day.

7 The beating sound of the heart is the clap of the valve leaflets opening and closing.

8 Heart disease has been found in 3,000-year-old mummies.

9 The blue whale has the largest heart, weighing over 1,500 pounds.

10 A person is more likely to have a heart attack on a Monday morning than on any other day of the week.

Conclusions

CVD describes a broad range of diseases involving the heart and blood vessels, such as coronary heart disease (CHD), stroke, cardiac arrest, and arrhythmia (Shields, Finley, Chawla, & Meadors, 2012). Currently, CVD is the leading cause of death in the U.S. and constitutes 17% of overall national health expenditures (Lloyd-Jones et al., 2010). Common symptoms of CVD include undue fatigue, labored breathing, heart palpitations, and chest pain. There are significant racial, ethnic, socioeconomic, and gender differences in the prevalence and outcome of CVD and in CVD risk factors such as smoking and obesity (Albert et al., 2006; Mensah & Brown, 2007; Rogers et al., 2011, 2012; Vivo, Krim, Cevik, & Witteles, 2009).

Coping with CVD can lead to significant changes in the relationships of patients with their spouses or partners (Andersson et al., 2013; Dalteg et al., 2011; Fransson et al., 2014; Imes et al., 2011). Patients and their spouses and partners are at an increased risk for depression and emotional distress. Partners may feel overwhelmed with responsibility and may feel a sense of loss about the relationship. Prior studies suggest that children's adjustment to parental CVD is associated with the parents' marital satisfaction and emotional well-being and not with the severity of the illness. Mental healthcare providers should attend to the whole family while working with patients diagnosed with CVDs and intervene at all levels of the system to promote healthier lifestyle changes for the patients and their families and to prevent the development of CVD in future generations.

Test Your Knowledge: True or False

1　CVD is the leading cause of death in the U.S.
2　White men are the largest group affected by CVD.
3　Smoking, sedentary behavior, and obesity are some of the risk factors for CVD.
4　CVD patients and their partners are at high risk for developing depression.
5　If your parent has CVD, you will definitely get sick too, since CVD is hereditary.
6　Lowering or eliminating risk factors (e.g., smoking cessation) can help prevent CVD.
7　Partners of patients with CVD may feel burdened and overwhelmed with caregiving responsibilities.
8　Children's adjustment following parental stroke is directly related to the severity of the stroke.
9　Mental healthcare providers can help families reduce risk factors for CVD.

Answers: 1-T, 2-F, 3-T, 4-T, 5-F, 6-T, 7-T, 8-F, 9-T

Professional Readings and Resources

American Heart Association: www.heart.org
Heart Disease Treatment: www.heartandstroke.com
John, K. (2014). *The heart health bible: The 5-step plan to prevent and reverse heart disease*. Boston, MA: Da Capo Lifelong Books.
Franklin, B., & Piscatella, J. C. (2011). *Prevent, halt & reverse heart disease: 109 things you can do*. New York: Workman Publishing Company.
The National Coalition for Women with Heart Disease: www.womanheart.org

References

Albert, M. A., Glynn, R. J., Buring, J., & Ridker, P. M. (2006). Impact of traditional and novel risk factors on the relationship between socioeconomic status and incident cardiovascular events. *Circulation, 114*(24), 2619–2626.
Andersson, E. K., Borglin, G., Sjöström-Strand, A., & Willman, A. (2013). Standing alone when life takes an unexpected turn: Being a midlife next of kin of a relative who has suffered a myocardial infarction. *Scandinavian Journal of Caring Sciences, 27*(4), 864–871.
Archer, E., & Blair, S. N. (2011). Physical activity and the prevention of cardiovascular disease: From evolution to epidemiology. *Progress in Cardiovascular Diseases, 53*(6), 387–396.
Arenhall, E., Kristofferzon, M. L., Fridlund, B., Malm, D., & Nilsson, U. (2011). The male partners' experiences of the intimate relationships after a first myocardial infarction. *European Journal of Cardiovascular Nursing, 10*(2), 108–114.

Arenhall, E., Kristofferzon, M. L., Fridlund, B., & Nilsson, U. (2011). The female partners' experiences of intimate relationship after a first myocardial infarction. *Journal of Clinical Nursing, 20*(11–12), 1677–1684.

Armistead, L., Klein, K., & Forehand, R. (1995). Parental physical illness and child functioning. *Clinical Psychology Review, 15*(5), 409–422.

Barefoot, J. C., Brummett, B. H., Williams, R. B., Siegler, I. C., Helms, M. J., Boyle, S. H., . . . & Mark, D. B. (2011). Recovery expectations and long-term prognosis of patients with coronary heart disease. *Archives of internal medicine, 171*(10), 929–935.

Barth, J., Schneider, S., & von Känel, R. (2010). Lack of social support in the etiology and the prognosis of coronary heart disease: A systematic review and meta-analysis. *Psychosomatic Medicine, 72*(3), 229–238.

Barth, J., Schumacher, M., & Herrmann-Lingen, C. (2004). Depression as a risk factor for mortality in patients with coronary heart disease: A meta-analysis. *Psychosomatic Medicine, 66*(6), 802–813.

Bibbins-Domingo, K., Chertow, G. M., Coxson, P. G., Moran, A., Lightwood, J. M., Pletcher, M. J., & Goldman, L. (2010). Projected effect of dietary salt reductions on future cardiovascular disease. *New England Journal of Medicine, 362*(7), 590–599.

Blumenthal, J. A., Lett, H. S., Babyak, M. A., White, W., Smith, P. K., Mark, D. B., . . . Newman, M. F. (2003). Depression as a risk factor for mortality after coronary artery bypass surgery. *The Lancet, 362*(9384), 604–609.

Bouchard, C., Malina, R., & Perusse, L. (1997). *Genetics of fitness and physical performance*. Champaign: Human Kinetics.

Cameron, J. I., & Gignac, M. A. (2008). "Timing it right": A conceptual framework for addressing the support needs of family caregivers to stroke survivors from the hospital to the home. *Patient Education and Counseling, 70*(3), 305–314.

Center for Disease Control and Prevention. (2005). Health disparities experienced by black or African Americans—United States. *MMWR: Morbidity and Mortality Weekly Report, 54*(1), 1–3.

Chin, M. H., Walters, A. E., Cook, S. C., & Huang, E. S. (2007). Interventions to reduce racial and ethnic disparities in health care. *Medical Care Research and Review, 64*(suppl 5), 7S–28S.

Chiuve, S. E., Rexrode, K. M., Spiegelman, D., Logroscino, G., Manson, J. E., & Rimm, E. B. (2008). Primary prevention of stroke by healthy lifestyle. *Circulation, 118*(9), 947–954.

Cohen, M. G., Fonarow, G. C., Peterson, E. D., Moscucci, M., Dai, D., Hernandez, A. F., . . . Smith, S. C. (2010). Racial and ethnic differences in the treatment of acute myocardial infarction findings from the Get With the Guidelines–Coronary Artery Disease program. *Circulation, 121*(21), 2294–2301.

Cram, P., Bayman, L., Popescu, I., & Vaughan-Sarrazin, M. S. (2009). Racial disparities in revascularization rates among patients with similar insurance coverage. *Journal of the National Medical Association, 101*(11), 1132–1139.

Dalteg, T., Benzein, E., Fridlund, B., & Malm, D. (2011). Cardiac disease and its consequences on the partner relationship: A systematic review. *European Journal of Cardiovascular Nursing, 10*(3), 140–149.

Davidson, K. W., Mostofsky, E., & Whang, W. (2010). Don't worry, be happy: Positive affect and reduced 10-year incident coronary heart disease: The Canadian Nova Scotia Health Survey. *European Heart Journal, 31,* 1065–1070.

Davis, A. M., Vinci, L. M., Okwuosa, T. M., Chase, A. R., & Huang, E. S. (2007). Cardiovascular health disparities: A systematic review of health care interventions. *Medical Care Research and Review, 64*(suppl 5), 29S–100S.

De Bacquer, D., Pelfrene, E., Clays, E., Mak, R., Moreau, M., De Smet, P., . . . De Backer, G. (2005). Perceived job stress and incidence of coronary events: 3-year follow-up of the Belgian Job Stress Project cohort. *American Journal of Epidemiology, 161*(5), 434–441.

Dekel, R., Vilchinsky, N., Liberman, G., Leibowitz, M., Khaskia, A., & Mosseri, M. (2014). Marital satisfaction and depression among couples following men's acute coronary syndrome: Testing dyadic dynamics in a longitudinal design. *British Journal of Health Psychology, 19*(2), 347–362.

De Vogli, R., Chandola, T., & Marmot, M. G. (2007). Negative aspects of close relationships and heart disease. *Archives of Internal Medicine, 167*(18), 1951–1957.

Diareme, S., Tsiantis, J., Romer, G., Tsalamanios, E., Anasontzi, S., Paliokosta, E., & Kolaitis, G. (2007). Mental health support for children of parents with somatic illness: A review of the theory and intervention concepts. *Families, Systems, & Health, 25*(1), 98–118.

Eaker, E. D., Sullivan, L. M., Kelly-Hayes, M., d'Agostino Sr, R. B., & Benjamin, E. J. (2005). Tension and anxiety and the prediction of the 10-year incidence of coronary heart disease, atrial fibrillation, and total mortality: The Framingham Offspring Study. *Psychosomatic Medicine, 67*(5), 692–696.

Farmer, S. A., Kirkpatrick, J. N., Heidenreich, P. A., Curtis, J. P., Wang, Y., & Groeneveld, P. W. (2009). Ethnic and racial disparities in cardiac resynchronization therapy. *Heart Rhythm, 6*(3), 325–331.

Flegal, K. M., Carroll, M. D., Ogden, C. L., & Curtin, L. R. (2010). Prevalence and trends in obesity among US adults, 1999–2008. *JAMA, 303*(3), 235–241.

Ford, E. S., & Caspersen, C. J. (2012). Sedentary behaviour and cardiovascular disease: A review of prospective studies. *International Journal of Epidemiology, 41*(5), 1338–1353.

Fransson, E. I., Arenhall, E., Steinke, E. E., Fridlund, B., & Nilsson, U. G. (2014). Perceptions of intimate relationships in partners before and after a patient's myocardial infarction. *Journal of clinical nursing, 23*(15–16), 2196–2204.

Gaglia, M. A., Torguson, R., Xue, Z., Gonzalez, M. A., Collins, S. D., Ben-Dor, I., . . . Waksman, R. (2010). Insurance type influences the use of drug-eluting stents. *JACC: Cardiovascular Interventions, 3*(7), 773–779.

Gluckman, P. D., & Hanson, M. A. (2008). Developmental and epigenetic pathways to obesity: An evolutionary-developmental perspective. *International Journal of Obesity, 32*, S62–S71.

Grenard, J. L., Munjas, B. A., Adams, J. L., Suttorp, M., Maglione, M., McGlynn, E. A., & Gellad, W. F. (2011). Depression and medication adherence in the treatment of chronic diseases in the United States: A meta-analysis. *Journal of General Internal Medicine, 26*(10), 1175–1182.

Gustafson, T. B., & Sarwer, D. B. (2004). Childhood sexual abuse and obesity. *Obesity Reviews, 5*(3), 129–135.

Hasselbalch, A. L. (2010). Genetics of dietary habits and obesity. *Danish Medical Bulletin, 57*, B4182.

Heidenreich, P. A., Trogdon, J. G., Khavjou, O. A., Butler, J., Dracup, K., Ezekowitz, M. D., . . . Woo, Y. J. (2011). Forecasting the future of cardiovascular disease in the United States: A policy statement from the American Heart Association. *Circulation, 123*(8), 933–944.

Hertz, R. P., Unger, A. N., Cornell, J. A., & Saunders, E. (2005). Racial disparities in hypertension prevalence, awareness, and management. *Archives of Internal Medicine, 165*(18), 2098–2104.

Holt-Lunstad, J., Birmingham, W., & Jones, B. Q. (2008). Is there something unique about marriage? The relative impact of marital status, relationship quality, and network social support on ambulatory blood pressure and mental health. *Annals of Behavioral Medicine, 35*(2), 239–244.

Hunter, D. J. (2005). Gene–environment interactions in human diseases. *Nature Reviews Genetics, 6*(4), 287–298.

Idler, E. L., Boulifard, D. A., & Contrada, R. J. (2012). Mending broken hearts marriage and survival following cardiac surgery. *Journal of Health and Social Behavior, 53*(1), 33–49.

Imes, C. C., Dougherty, C. M., Pyper, G., & Sullivan, M. D. (2011). Descriptive study of partners' experiences of living with severe heart failure. *Heart & Lung: The Journal of Acute and Critical Care, 40*(3), 208–216.

King, K. B., & Reis, H. T. (2012). Marriage and long-term survival after coronary artery bypass grafting. *Health Psychology, 31*(1), 55–62.

Kivimäki, M., Nyberg, S. T., Fransson, E. I., Heikkilä, K., Alfredsson, L., Casini, A., . . . Batty, G. D. (2013). Associations of job strain and lifestyle risk factors with risk of coronary artery disease: A meta-analysis of individual participant data. Canadian Medical *Association Journal, 185*(9), 763–769.

Kop, W. J., & Plumhoff, J. E. (2011). Depression and coronary heart disease: Diagnosis, predictive value, biobehavioral mechanisms, and intervention. In R. Allan & J. Fisher (Eds.), *Heart and mind: The practice of cardiac psychology* (2nd ed., pp. 143–168). Washington, DC: American Psychological Association.

Kulik, J. A., & Mahler, H. I. (2006). Marital quality predicts hospital stay following coronary artery bypass surgery for women but not men. *Social Science & Medicine, 63*(8), 2031–2040.

Kurian, A. K., & Cardarelli, K. M. (2007). Racial and ethnic differences in cardiovascular disease risk factors: A systematic review. *Ethnicity and Disease, 17*(1), 143.

Lee, S., Colditz, G. A., Berkman, L. F., & Kawachi, I. (2003). Caregiving and risk of coronary heart disease in US women: A prospective study. *American Journal of Preventive Medicine, 24*(2), 113–119.

Lett, H., Ali, S., & Whooley, M. (2008). Depression and cardiac function in patients with stable coronary heart disease: Findings from the Heart and Soul Study. *Psychosomatic Medicine, 70*(4), 444.

Li, J., Hansen, D., Mortensen, P. B., & Olsen, J. (2002). Myocardial infarction in parents who lost a child: A nationwide prospective cohort study in Denmark. *Circulation, 106*(13), 1634–1639.

Li, J., & Siegrist, J. (2012). Physical activity and risk of cardiovascular disease—a meta-analysis of prospective cohort studies. *International Journal of Environmental Research and Public Health, 9*(2), 391–407.

Lloyd-Jones, D., Adams, R. J., Brown, T. M., Carnethon, M., Dai, S., De Simone, G., . . . Wylie-Rosett, J. (2010). Heart disease and stroke statistics—2010 update: A report from the American Heart Association. *Circulation, 121*(7), e46–e215.

Lloyd-Jones, D., Adams, R., Carnethon, M., De Simone, G., Ferguson, T. B., Flegal, K., . . . Hong, Y. (2009). Heart disease and stroke statistics—2009 update: A report from the American Heart Association Statistics Committee and Stroke Statistics Subcommittee. *Circulation, 119*(3), e21–e181.

Lloyd-Jones, D. M., Leip, E. P., Larson, M. G., d'Agostino, R. B., Beiser, A., Wilson, P. W., . . . & Levy, D. (2006). Prediction of lifetime risk for cardiovascular disease by risk factor burden at 50 years of age. *Circulation, 113*(6), 791–798.

López-Medina, I. M., Gil-García, E., Sánchez-Criado, V., & Pancorbo-Hidalgo, P. L. (2014). Patients' experiences of sexual activity following myocardial ischemia. *Clinical Nursing Research*. doi:1054773814534440

Lurie, N., Fremont, A., Jain, A. K., Taylor, S. L., McLaughlin, R., Peterson, E., . . . & Ferguson, T. B. (2005). Racial and ethnic disparities in care: The perspectives of cardiologists. *Circulation, 111*(10), 1264–1269.

Luttik, M. L., Jaarsma, T., Veeger, N. J., & van Veldhuisen, D. J. (2005). For better and for worse: Quality of life impaired in HF patients as well as in their partners. *European Journal of Cardiovascular Nursing, 4*(1), 11–14.

Mensah, G. A., & Brown, D. W. (2007). An overview of cardiovascular disease burden in the United States. *Health Affairs, 26*(1), 38–48.

Miller, G. E., Chen, E., & Parker, K. J. (2011). Psychological stress in childhood and susceptibility to the chronic diseases of aging: Moving toward a model of behavioral and biological mechanisms. *Psychological Bulletin, 137*(6), 959.

Mondloch, M. V., Cole, D. C., & Frank, J. W. (2001). Does how you do depend on how you think you'll do? A systematic review of the evidence for a relation between patients' recovery expectations and health outcomes. *Canadian Medical Association Journal, 165*(2), 174–179.

Mosca, L., Barrett-Connor, E., & Wenger, N. K. (2011). Sex/gender differences in cardiovascular disease prevention: What a difference a decade makes. *Circulation, 124*(19), 2145–2154.

National Center for Health Statistics US. (2010). Health, United States, 2009: With special feature on medical technology. Retrieved from www.cdc.gov/nchs/data/hus/hus09.pdf

O'Farrell, P., Murray, J., & Hotz, S. B. (2000). Psychologic distress among spouses of patients undergoing cardiac rehabilitation. *Heart & Lung: The Journal of Acute and Critical Care, 29*(2), 97–104.

Orth-Gomer, K., Wamala, S. P., Horsten, M., Schenck-Gustafsson, K., Schneiderman, N., & Mittleman, M. A. (2000). Marital stress worsens prognosis in women with coronary heart disease: The Stockholm female coronary risk study. *JAMA, 284*(23), 3008–3014.

Poole, L., Dickens, C., & Steptoe, A. (2011). The puzzle of depression and acute coronary syndrome: Reviewing the role of acute inflammation. *Journal of Psychosomatic Research, 71*(2), 61–68.

Pruchno, R., Wilson-Genderson, M., & Cartwright, F. P. (2009). Depressive symptoms and marital satisfaction in the context of chronic disease: A longitudinal dyadic analysis. *Journal of Family Psychology, 23*(4), 573.

Randall, G., Molloy, G. J., & Steptoe, A. (2009). The impact of an acute cardiac event on the partners of patients: A systematic review. *Health Psychology Review, 3*(1), 1–84.

Roberts, S. A., Kiselica, M. S., & Fredrickson, S. A. (2002). Quality of life of persons with medical illnesses: Counseling's holistic contribution. *Journal of Counseling & Development, 80*(4), 422–432.

Roger, V. L., Go, A. S., Lloyd-Jones, D. M., Adams, R. J., Berry, J. D., Brown, T. M., . . . Wylie-Rosett, J. (2011). Heart disease and stroke statistics—2011 update: A report from the American Heart Association. *Circulation, 123*(4), e18–e209.

Roger, V. L., Go, A. S., Lloyd-Jones, D. M., Benjamin, E. J., Berry, J. D., Borden, W. B., . . . Stroke, S. S. (2012). Heart disease and stroke statistics—2012 update: A report from the American Heart Association. *Circulation, 125*(1), 188–197.

Rohde, P., Ichikawa, L., Simon, G. E., Ludman, E. J., Linde, J. A., Jeffery, R. W., & Operskalski, B. H. (2008). Associations of child sexual and physical abuse with obesity and depression in middle-aged women. *Child Abuse & Neglect, 32*(9), 878–887.

Romer, G., Barkmann, C., Schulte-Markwort, M., Thomalla, G., & Riedesser, P. (2002). Children of somatically ill parents: A methodological review. *Clinical Child Psychology and Psychiatry, 7*(1), 17–38.

Rosamond, W., Flegal, K., Furie, K., Go, A., Greenlund, K., Haase, N., . . . Hong, Y. (2008). Heart disease and stroke statistics—2008 update: A report from the American Heart Association Statistics Committee and Stroke Statistics Subcommittee. *Circulation, 117*(4), e25–146.

Ruiz, J. M., Prather, C. C., & Steffen, P. (2012). Socioeconomic status and health. In A. Baum, T. Revenson, & J. Singer (Eds.), *Handbook of health psychology* (2nd ed., pp. 539–567). New York: Psychology Press.

Shields, C. G., Finley, M. A., Chawla, N., & Meadors, P. (2012). Couple and family interventions in health problems. *Journal of Marital and Family Therapy, 38*(1), 265–280.

Sieh, D. S., Meijer, A. M., & Visser-Meily, J. (2010). Risk factors for stress in children after parental stroke. *Rehabilitation Psychology, 55*(4), 391–397.

Smith, T. W., Baron, C. E., & Caska, C. M. (2014). On marriage and the heart: Models, methods and mechanisms in the study of close relationships and cardiovascular disease. In C. Agnew & S. South (Eds.), *Interpersonal relationships and health: Social and clinical psychological mechanisms* (pp. 34–70). New York, NY: Oxford University Press.

Smith, T. W., Baron, C. E., & Grove, J. L. (2013). Personality, emotional adjustment, and cardiovascular risk: Marriage as a mechanism. *Journal of Personality, 62*(6), 502–514. doi:10.1111/jopy.12074

Steptoe, A., & Kivimäki, M. (2012). Stress and cardiovascular disease. *Nature Reviews Cardiology, 9*(6), 360–370.

Thompson, P. D., Buchner, D., Piña, I. L., Balady, G. J., Williams, M. A., Marcus, B. H., . . . Wenger, N. K. (2003). Exercise and physical activity in the prevention and treatment of atherosclerotic cardiovascular disease: A statement from the Council on Clinical Cardiology (subcommittee on exercise, rehabilitation, and prevention) and the Council on Nutrition, Physical Activity, and Metabolism (subcommittee on physical activity). *Circulation, 107*(24), 3109–3116.

van de Port, I. G., Visser-Meily, A., Post, M. W., & Lindeman, E. (2007). Long-term outcome in children of patients after stroke. *Journal of Rehabilitation Medicine, 39*(9), 703–707.

van Zyl, L. T., Lespérance, F., Frasure-Smith, N., Malinin, A. I., Atar, D., Laliberté, M. A., & Serebruany, V. L. (2009). Platelet and endothelial activity in comorbid major depression and coronary artery disease patients treated with citalopram: The Canadian

Cardiac Randomized Evaluation of Antidepressant and Psychotherapy Efficacy Trial (CREATE) biomarker sub-study. *Journal of Thrombosis and Thrombolysis, 27*(1), 48–56.

Velasquez, M. M., Hecht, J., Quinn, V. P., Emmons, K. M., DiClemente, C. C., & Dolan-Mullen, P. (2000). Application of motivational interviewing to prenatal smoking cessation: Training and implementation issues. *Tobacco Control, 9*(suppl 3), iii36–iii40.

Visser-Meily, A., Post, M., Meijer, A. M., Maas, C., Ketelaar, M., & Lindeman, E. (2005a). Children's adjustment to a parent's stroke: Determinants of health status and psychological problems, and the role of support from the rehabilitation team. *Journal of Rehabilitation Medicine, 37*(4), 236–241.

Visser-Meily, A., Post, M., Meijer, A. M., van de Port, I., Maas, C., & Lindeman, E. (2005b). When a parent has a stroke: Clinical course and prediction of mood, behavior problems, and health status of their young children. *Stroke, 36*(11), 2436–2440.

Vivo, R. P., Krim, S. R., Cevik, C., & Witteles, R. M. (2009). Heart failure in Hispanics. *Journal of the American College of Cardiology, 53*(14), 1167–1175.

Wang, H. X., Leineweber, C., Kirkeeide, R., Svane, B., Schenck-Gustafsson, K., Theorell, T., & Orth-Gomér, K. (2007). Psychosocial stress and atherosclerosis: Family and work stress accelerate progression of coronary disease in women. The Stockholm Female Coronary Angiography Study. *Journal of Internal Medicine, 261*(3), 245–254.

Wellenius, G. A., Mukamal, K. J., Kulshreshtha, A., Asonganyi, S., & Mittleman, M. A. (2008). Depressive symptoms and the risk of atherosclerotic progression among patients with coronary artery bypass grafts. *Circulation, 117*(18), 2313–2319.

Whooley, M. A. (2006). Depression and cardiovascular disease: Healing the broken-hearted. *Jama, 295*(24), 2874–2881.

Whooley, M. A., de Jonge, P., Vittinghoff, E., Otte, C., Moos, R., Carney, R. M., . . . Browner, W. S. (2008). Depressive symptoms, health behaviors, and risk of cardiovascular events in patients with coronary heart disease. *JAMA, 300*(20), 2379–2388.

Yancy, C. W., Wang, T. Y., Ventura, H. O., Piña, I. L., Vijayaraghavan, K., Ferdinand, K. C., & Hall, L. L. (2011). The coalition to reduce racial and ethnic disparities in cardiovascular disease outcomes (credo): Why credo matters to cardiologists. *Journal of the American College of Cardiology, 57*(3), 245–252.

Yusuf, S., Hawken, S., Ôunpuu, S., Dans, T., Avezum, A., Lanas, F., . . . Lisheng, L. (2004). Effect of potentially modifiable risk factors associated with myocardial infarction in 52 countries (the INTERHEART study): Case-control study. *The Lancet, 364*(9438), 937–952.

CHAPTER 10

GRANDPARENTS RAISING GRANDCHILDREN

Maureen Davey and Laura Lynch

Introduction

In the last few decades, grandparent-headed households have been steadily increasing (AARP, 2010; U.S. Census Bureau, 2010); therefore, it is important to include a chapter describing the experiences of grandparents who are raising grandchildren, because these caregivers are older and are more vulnerable to developing illnesses. Few grandparents, regardless of race, ethnicity, or social class, choose to parent a second time or to become custodial grandparents in later life (Hayslip & Kaminski, 2008). Custodial grandparenting (CG) happens when a grandparent assumes primary responsibility for parenting a grandchild because parents are not able to care for their child (Hayslip & Kaminski, 2005a; Strom & Strom, 2011; Wilson, 2013). For many grandparents, this unexpected parenting role in later life leads to disruptions in life plans, financial struggles to support their grandchildren on fixed incomes at retirement age (Generations United, 2004), and the need for bigger housing to accommodate school-age children (Strom & Strom, 2011), all while coping with their own health problems in later life (Butler & Zakari, 2005).

Pre-existing health problems can become exacerbated because of the emotional (Conway, Jones, & Speakes-Lewis, 2011) and physical demands (Hinterlong & Ryan, 2008) of childrearing in later life (Brintnall-Peterson, Poehlmann, Morgan, & Shlafer, 2009; Wilson, 2013). Yet, despite the myriad physical health, psychological, and relational challenges, many grandparents report enjoying their roles because they feel positive about keeping their grandchildren out of the formal foster care system, having a second opportunity to parent in a different way, and assuming an important role in their grandchildren's lives (Dolbin-MacNab & Keiley, 2006; Dunifon, 2013; Hayslip & Kaminski, 2005a, 2005b). In this chapter, we deviate from the structure of the previous parental illness chapters to describe the following about CGs: (1) demographic characteristics; (2) economic and legal issues; (3) physical health; (4) psychological health; (5) parenting; (6) children and adolescent outcomes; and (7) cultural considerations, and we also provide a clinical vignette.

Characteristics of Custodial Grandparents

Grandparent-headed households in the U.S. have been steadily increasing since the 1990s (AARP, 2010; Brintnall-Peterson et al., 2009). Approximately 4.9 million children under the age of 18 live in grandparent-headed homes; 915,000 grand-parents in 2010 had primary responsibility for at least one grandchild. Approxi-mately 43% of these grandparents provided care without any assistance from the parents of the grandchild (U.S. Census Bureau, 2010). The most common reasons grandparents decide to raise their grandchildren are parental: (1) substance abuse, (2) abuse and neglect, (3) poverty, (4) incarceration, (5) mental illness, (6) physical illness, (7) teenage pregnancy, (8) abandonment, (9) divorce, (10) military deploy-ment, and (11) death (Bene, 2010; Gibson, 2005; Hayslip & Kaminski, 2005a; Hinterlong & Ryan, 2008; Ruiz, 2008; Simpson & Lawrence-Webb, 2009). Most grandparents decide to raise their grandchildren to prevent formal placements in the foster care system and to help out during the military deployment of parents (Dunifon, 2013; Hayslip & Kaminski, 2005b; Hinterlong & Ryan, 2008).

Grandparents who are raising grandchildren tend to be married (67%), female (58%), and own their own homes (79%), and most are 65 years of age or younger (U.S. Census Bureau, 2010; Wilson, 2013). Approximately one-third also report having a disability. Grandparents who are raising grandchildren are also more likely to be living in poverty compared to grandparents who are not raising their grandchildren; 18% of grandparents aged 60 years and older raising grandchildren lived below the poverty line in 2010 (U.S. Census Bureau, 2010). Although custodial grandparents' ages can range from 41 to 80 (AARP, 2010), approximately one-third (36%) were 60 years old or older in 2010 (U.S. Census Bureau). Grandparent-headed families in the U.S. are racially/ethnically diverse; approximately 50% are non-Hispanic White, 24% are African American, 3% are Asian, 2% are American Indian, and 19% are Hispanic of any race (AARP, 2010; U.S. Census, 2010). Noteworthy, compared to other races, African American grandparents are more likely to assume the role of primary caregivers for one or more grandchildren (Burton, 1992; Gibson, 1999, 2002, 2005).

Within the African American community, there is a historical and cultural tradition of relatives caring for their kin, and maternal grandmothers are the rel-atives who most often become caregivers of their grandchildren (Gibson, 2005; Goodman & Silverstein, 2006). Thus, a disproportionate number of grandpar-ents raising grandchildren in the U.S. are African American (24%) (Conway et al., 2011). Most African American grandparents raising grandchildren are women, single, do not have high school diplomas, receive public assistance, and live below the poverty level (Bene, 2010; Simpson & Lawrence-Webb, 2009); therefore, it is important to consider how structural inequalities can contribute to stressors among African American CGs (Simpson & Lawrence-Webb, 2009). Scholars who have examined informal kinship care among low-income, African American CGs report they often experience: (1) inaccessibility and unresponsiveness from service agencies and (2) destabilizing forces such as drug abuse, violence, and poverty in their communities (Fuller-Thomson & Minkler, 2000, 2005; Jimenez, 2002; Kelley et al., 2013; Minkler et al., 1999, 2005). It is also important to understand the economic and legal issues CGs report experiencing.

Economic and Legal Issues

CGs often struggle to provide adequate housing, food, and clothing because of their fixed incomes and limited financial resources (Hayslip & Kaminski, 2005a). Yet, despite these unexpected financial hardships in later life, most CGs do finan-cially provide for their grandchildren (Generations United, 2004). It is remarkable that they often do this without any formal legal or economic support (compared to the formal foster care system) because they typically have informal custody arrangements to care for their grandchildren (Simmons & Dye, 2003; Simpson & Lawrence-Webb, 2009).

CGs have also reported legal issues regarding obtaining guardianship, enrolling their grandchildren in school, and accessing medical care for their grandchildren (Wilson, 2013). Older CGs have reported experiencing ageism during meetings with school and health staff (Gerard, Landry-Meyer, & Roe, 2006). Some CGs report ongoing custody struggles with other grandparents or their grandchildren's parents (Goodman & Silverstein, 2002). It can be especially difficult for CGs to negotiate relationships with their grandchildren's parents (Hinterlong & Ryan, 2008) because they want to protect their grandchildren, but also allow them to visit with their parents (their adult children) (Gibson, 2005). Consequently, it can be difficult for grandparents to see their adult children fail as parents (Brintnall-Peterson, Poehlmann, Morgan, & Shlafer, 2009).

Some CGs report feeling angry toward their grandchildren's parents, guilty about their own parenting, and shameful of the family structure (AARP, 2010; Conway et al., 2011). Consequently, CGs report experiencing emotional stress because they are sad about their adult child's failure as a parent, and at the same time feel responsible for their adult child not being available to parent his or her own children (Baker & Silverstein, 2008b). As a result of their caregiving responsibilities, CGs reported having less time for their own self-care (e.g., making their own medical appointments) and to spend with their partners, friends, and communities (Dowdell, 2004). Less time to engage in self-care and to receive social support can lead to caregiver burden and more negative physical health outcomes (Dolbin-MacNab, 2006).

Physical Health among CGs

Compared to their noncustodial counterparts, CGs tend to have more physical health problems, including depression, coronary heart disease, physical disabilities, and chronic health conditions like asthma and diabetes (Hadfield, 2014). Hughes, Waite, LaPierre, and Luo (2007) reported that CGs had significantly more depressive symptoms, higher incidence of obesity, and decreased levels of exercise after beginning custodial caregiving. Lee, Colditz, Berkman, and Kawachi (2003) reported a 1.86 times increased risk (age-adjusted) of coronary artery disease among caregiving grandmothers compared to noncaregiving grandmothers. CGs are also more likely to report limitations in activities of daily living, likely due to their older age (Minkler & Fuller-Thompson, 1999).

Raising grandchildren can affect the overall health of CGs because they may neglect their own health care to focus on their grandchildren. One study of African American caregiving grandmothers with diabetes reported that initiating primary caregiving of their grandchildren negatively affected their diabetes management, including the monitoring of their blood glucose levels and diet (Carthron, Johnson, Hubbart, Strickland, & Nance, 2010), which has the potential for long-term health consequences. Baker and Silverstein (2008a) reported that grandmothers who recently took on the primary care of grandchildren were less likely to get their influenza vaccines, cholesterol screenings, and Pap screenings than grandmothers who were not caregivers.

Compared to noncaregiving grandmothers and grandmothers living in multigenerational homes, custodial grandmothers tend to have the worst self-rated physical health (Musil et al., 2011). CGs' overall health-related quality of life (including mental and physical health) has been linked to the number of grandchildren they are caring for, the CGs' level of education, and depression (Neely-Barnes, Graff, & Washington, 2010). Essentially, more grandchildren, lower education level, and higher levels of depression are associated with lower health-related quality of life for CGs (Neely-Barnes et al., 2010).

Yet, other scholars have noted that these differences in health outcomes could be explained by CGs' overall lower socioeconomic status versus the impact of caregiving for grandchildren in later life (Hinterlong & Ryan, 2008). As noted previously, CGs are more likely to have lower incomes, less education, and be part of minority groups, which are also all associated with poorer health outcomes in general (AARP, 2010). Thus, although many studies have reported negative physical health outcomes among CGs, a few studies have reported that becoming a CG can be physically beneficial because this role in later life facilitates a more active lifestyle and healthier meals (Hayslip & Kaminski, 2005a; Leder, Grinstead, & Torres, 2007).

Psychological Health among CGs

Unfortunately, grandparents who have primary responsibility for raising their grandchildren tend to have poorer self-reported mental health outcomes, including experiencing greater parenting stresses and less quality of life compared to grandparents who are not raising their grandchildren (Blustein, Chan, & Guanais, 2004; Butler & Zakari, 2005; Conway et al., 2011). CGs are also more vulnerable to experiencing depressive symptoms, especially among grandmothers raising grandchildren who have behavioral problems (Goodman & Silverstein, 2006).

In a study comparing 86 Caucasian and African American grandmothers raising grandchildren to 86 Caucasian and African American mothers, CGs reported more overall parenting-related stress and distress (Musil, Youngblut, Ahn, & Curry, 2002). Caucasian CGs reported higher levels of parenting-related stress and distress compared to non-CGs (Musil et al., 2002). Blustein et al. (2004) reported that CGs are more likely to experience depressive symptoms compared to when they were not caregiving, and non-White, single caregiving grandmothers are the CG subgroup with the highest likelihood of experiencing depressive symptoms. Parenting can also become stressful for CGs (Dowdell, 2004); CGs may experience caregiving strain, particularly older CGs (Conway et al., 2011). This is not surprising given the multiple stressors CGs report, including financial strain, parenting role strain, and the lack of social support (Butler & Zakari, 2005; Generations United, 2004).

Positive Experiences of CGs

Scholars have noted that the literature focuses too much on negative outcomes among CGs. Many CGs report enjoying their caregiving roles in later life and describe how caregiving gives them a sense of purpose (Hayslip & Kaminski, 2005a, 2005b). There is a long tradition of grandparent involvement in childrearing across cultures in the U.S. (Fuller-Thomson & Minkler, 2005; Gibson, 1999, 2002, 2005; Goodman & Silverstein, 2002). For African Americans, it comes from the extended family traditions to protect children during the deliberate break-up of families during slavery (Jimenez, 2002). Later, great migrations of African Americans from the south moved north to find work and had to leave their children in CGs' care. Extended family and kin needed to work together in the context of racism, poverty, and unemployment (Minkler & Fuller-Thompson, 2005). Today, African Americans at all ages perceive grandparents' roles as important and integral to the family because they provide practical, financial, and emotional support and teach values and religious faith (Kelch-Oliver, 2011; Minkler & Fuller-Thompson, 2005; Ruiz, 2008).

Goodman and Silverstein (2006) compared a sample of African American, White, and Latino grandmothers raising their grandchildren (*n* = 1,058) to examine how cultural norms impact experiences of custodial grandparenting. They reported that African American grandmothers reported the highest well-being compared to the White and Latino custodial grandmothers; White CGs reported the lowest well-being. The authors explain these finding through a cultural lens. As noted earlier, there is a strong African American tradition of grandparents raising grandchildren, which helps to explain their higher scores on well-being. In contrast, Latino custodial grandmothers may experience inner role conflicts because of their cultural expectation of close intergenerational relationships (familism), where typically multiple generations (three generations) of families live together. When Latino grandmothers assume primary caregiving responsibilities of their grandchildren, without their adult children this cultural norm is not fulfilled (Goodman & Silverstein, 2006). Finally White grandparents less often assume custodial grandparenting, so assuming this caregiving role is expected to cause inner conflicts and role strain.

CGs can encounter myriad stressors including strained relationships with birth parents, social and cultural stigma, financial pressure, and their own age-related health issues (Hayslip & Kaminski, 2008). Yet despite these myriad challenges, many CGs report enjoying raising their grandchildren and describe having this role in later life as emotionally fulfilling, which gives them a renewed sense of purpose (Hinterlong & Ryan, 2008). Many children in grandparents' care develop with positive emotional and behavioral outcomes (Pittman & Boswell, 2007).

Parenting among CGs

Given the myriad factors described previously (e.g., possible conflict with child's parents and custody/legal issues, psychological distress, older age and associated health issues, financial issues, role strain), parenting can be challenging for CGs, especially if their grandchildren have social, emotional, or behavioral problems (Hayslip & Kaminski, 2005a, 2005b). Grandparents typically decide to raise their grandchildren because of a disruptive family event (e.g., death of a parent, mental health or substance abuse in a parent); therefore, many grandchildren will understandably have unresolved feelings of loss, sadness, and anger that could be expressed negatively at home, in school, or in the community (Gerard et al., 2006; Strom & Strom, 2011). Thus, CGs not only have to parent children in later life and cope with the parenting failure of their adult children, but they also need to learn how to provide emotional support to vulnerable grandchildren who are coping with the separation from a parent, either temporarily (parent in substance abuse or mental health treatment facility) or permanently (death of a parent) (Dolbin-MacNab & Keiley, 2006).

Grandparents will need to transition from the role of a more traditional grandparent to an active parent who is able to communicate clearly, supervise, discipline, as well as model and reinforce prosocial behaviors (Dolbin-MacNab & Keiley, 2006).

Given the sudden and often stressful circumstances that characterize custodial grandparenting, it is rare to find grandparents whose parental skills are well developed and anchored in current information about: (1) parenting practices, . . . (2) normal developmental changes in their grandchildren's physical, cognitive, and psychosocial, and emotional development, and (3) . . . childhood disorders such as depression, ADHD, drug use, aggression/ acting out behavior, grief at the loss of a parent, self-destructive behaviors, or alcoholism.

(Hayslip & Kaminski, 2005a, p. 158)

Some community centers provide CGs with parent training to help them make this transition. Topics have included: (1) mental health care for themselves and grandchildren; (2) drug use and sexuality; (3) school violence and peer influences; (4) parenting skills (e.g., setting limits); (5) communication skills (how to talk to an adolescent, how to partner with a teacher at school); (6) legal and custodial advocacy; and (7) grief and loss (Hayslip & Kaminski, 2005a; 2005b; Strom & Strom, 2011). Additionally, support groups have been developed and occur at community centers to help CGs cope with their new roles and to find social support from other CGs making this role transition in later life (Gerard et al., 2006). For example, the American Association of Retired Persons (AARP, 2010) has a grandparent information center that maintains a national database of grandparent support groups and has online information describing the emotional, legal, and financial needs of CGs.

Strom and Strom (2011) summarized findings from empirical studies, innovative community initiatives, and case reports to describe what CGs should do to successfully navigate the caregiving transition. The following recommendations are based on their reviews of the literature and empirical studies: (1) modify expectations to fit new conditions (e.g., accept caregiving role and engage new parenting strategies, such as a replacement for corporal punishment, which was more common when they were raising children); (2) cooperate with a parent who shares responsibility for child care; (3) monitor grandchild's emotional, academic, and social progress; (4) become familiar with family rights and social services (advocacy); (5) arrange for respite to have periodic relief from caregiver burden; and (6) spend quality time with grandchild, both in leisure activities and for school-related work (Strom & Strom, 2011).

What Clinicians Need to Know about Custodial Grandparents (CGs)

1   The number of grandparent-headed households has been steadily increasing over the past 20 years.
2   African American grandparents are more likely to become primary caregivers for grandchildren compared to grandparents from other racial/ethnic groups.
3   Becoming a CG can be a positive experience for grandparents.
4   The circumstances surrounding grandparents taking on custody are inevitably stressful and impact the entire family.

(Continued)

5   CGs typically have more-informal custody arrangements that have not been legalized.

6   CGs have to parent children in later life and they also cope with the parenting failures of their adult children.

7   CGs also need to learn how to provide emotional support to vulnerable grandchildren who are coping with the separation from a parent, either temporarily (parent in substance abuse or mental health treatment facility) or permanently (death of a parent).

Children and Adolescents Raised by Custodial Grandparents

Researchers and clinicians have reported that children raised in grandparent-headed families can display developmental (learning disabilities), physical (health problems), behavioral (aggression), academic (poor school performance, learning disabilities, ADHD), and emotional problems (depression, anxiety) because of prior negative experiences with their parents (Dunifon, 2013). As noted previously, the family events that led to the separation from their parents (e.g., substance abuse, abuse, neglect, poverty, death of a parent) are often difficult for school-age children to process and can lead to feelings of grief and loss, which if left unresolved can negatively affect adjustment to being raised by CGs (Smith & Palmieri, 2007).

Children who have been abused or neglected often struggle to establish trust and feel secure in their relationships with CGs (Hayslip & Kaminski, 2005a) and can experience feelings of anger, rejection, and guilt. Relationships among family members can also create stress for grandchildren because visits from parents can be stressful and leave the children feeling hurt, abandoned, and confused (Strom & Strom, 2011). Due to their age difference with CGs, grandchildren could feel disconnected from their grandparents (Edwards & Daire, 2006). Additionally, intergenerational differences regarding household rules and expectations can be a source of tension and conflict between grandchildren and CGs (Hayslip & Kaminski, 2005b). This transition of moving in with CGs often involves moving to a new neighborhood, starting a new school, and getting used to a new home, which can all add to the difficulties in adjustment.

Yet, to date, research findings are mixed regarding the extent to which grandchildren experience problems when they are cared for by CGs (Dunifon, 2013; Edwards & Daire, 2006; Smith & Palmieri, 2007). For example, Smith and Palmieri (2007) conducted a study with grandmothers who were raising adolescent granddaughters and grandsons. Grandmothers reported that boys presented with many more problems compared to girls; boys were more likely to have externalizing behavior problems (e.g., misconduct or acting out). Grandmothers reported that girls were more likely to have internalizing problems (e.g., withdrawal, anxiety, depression) (Smith & Palmieri, 2007).

Similarly, among adolescents living with CGs, Pittman (2007) reported more emotional and behavioral problems compared to other low-income, urban youth living in either single-parent or two-parent traditional families. She explained this finding by suggesting that grandparents are aging and could be struggling with monitoring and setting limits with their grandchildren. Additionally, Pittman (2007) reported that adolescence is a time of identity development and when biological parents are not available to children, this can lead to questioning their own value as a person and lead to depressive symptoms, anxiety, or getting involved in delinquency. In another study with younger children (ages 2 to 6), Pittman and Boswell (2007) reported that very young children who were being raised by CGs were similar to other children regarding emotional functioning, but they were behind their peers in developing academic skills.

According to a systematic review conducted in 2009, compared to two-parent families, children raised by CGs actually had comparable health outcomes but tended to experience more asthma, headaches, accidents, and injuries (Winokur, Holtan, & Valentine, 2009). Behavioral outcomes were also comparable to two-parent families, as the rates of obedience in school and with teachers and the rates of expulsion were comparable. Regarding school outcomes, children raised by CGs were less likely to be rated as above-average students and more likely to repeat a grade compared to two-parent families; however, they were comparable to children in single-parent families on these same academic outcomes (Whitley, Kelley, & Sipe, 2001).

Noteworthy, compared to children in foster care, children raised by CGs were twice as likely to report more positive emotional health (Smith & Palmieri, 2007; Winokur et al., 2009), and only half as likely as foster care children to experience a mental illness. Foster care children were more likely to receive mental health services compared to kinship care children, but the use of physicians was comparable for foster and kinship care children. Regarding safety, kinship care children were less likely to experience a substantiated incident of abuse or neglect while in and out of home placement settings compared to children in foster care; however, kinship families also tended to have lower levels of parental supervision. Children raised by CGs had lower levels of internalizing behaviors (e.g., withdrawn, passive behaviors), lower levels of externalizing behaviors (e.g., aggressive, delinquent behaviors), and higher levels of competence and adaptive behaviors compared to children raised in foster care (Winokur et al., 2009). Thus, it is important to compare outcomes for children being raised by CGs to the appropriate comparison group to fully understand psychological, academic, and social outcomes for grandchildren who are being raised by CGs (Wilson, 2013).

What Clinicians Need to Know about Children Being Raised by CGs

1   Family events that led to separation from their parents are difficult for school-age children to process and can lead to feelings of grief and loss.
2   Relationships among family members can create stress for grandchildren.
3   Intergenerational differences regarding household rules and expectations can be a source of tension and conflict.
4   Compared to children in foster care, children raised by CGs were twice as likely to report more positive emotional health.
5   Young children who were being raised by CGs were similar to other children with regard to emotional functioning, but they were behind their peers in developing academic skills.
6   Children raised by CGs have lower levels of internalizing and externalizing behaviors and higher levels of competence and adaptive behaviors compared to children raised in foster care.

Cultural Considerations

Overall, CG families in the U.S. are ethnically and culturally diverse (U.S. Census Bureau, 2010). Thus, it is important for mental healthcare providers to acknowledge and explore the cultural context of CG families to understand how culture shapes their family functioning and beliefs and to help them cope with a CG's illness.

Single, African American women are the most disproportionally represented group among CGs. Prior research suggests that African American CGs overall have high satisfaction as custodial caregivers to their grandchildren despite the challenges they face as CGs (Kataoka-Yahiro, Ceria, & Yoder, 2004). As previously described, this is related to traditions of custodial grandparenting because of African American families' history of adaptation to racial oppression (Minkler & Fuller-Thompson, 2005). Another study of Filipino caregiving grandparents in Hawaii identified that caregiving was viewed as normative and part of maintaining the values of family closeness and relational reciprocity (Kataoka-Yahiro, Ceria, & Yoder, 2004). Asian American grandparents often live in three-generation homes and participate in caring for their grandchildren alongside parents; however, there are few studies that have examined Asian American CGs (Kataoka-Yahiro, Ceria, & Yoder, 2004). Compared to the general population, CGs are more likely to be immigrants and not speak English as their first language (Population Reference Bureau, 2011). If a language barrier is present, it may serve to increase the isolation that CGs are already likely to experience.

Mental healthcare providers in any setting could encounter a CG family or family member. For instance, a mental healthcare provider integrated in primary care may be referred a CG who is struggling with a mental health issue or who is overwhelmed with stress; they may also be referred a grandchild who presents to the primary care provided with a behavioral issue or emotional distress. An outpatient mental healthcare provider could see the entire CG family who presents in the midst of the initial custody transition or as a result of parenting difficulties, or one CG family member may present in individual therapy. It is essential for providers to fully assess the family structure and custody arrangements to identify CG families and explore the unique stressors they may encounter. CGs and their grandchildren can benefit from supportive counseling or family therapy to help them adapt to the new custody arrangement, help children repair attachment to parents, facilitate children's attachment to CGs, and help children mourn the loss associated with being part of the new family structure.

Family health clinics with integrated mental health that can provide services to both children and older adults are in the best position to facilitate family health care so both CGs and their grandchildren receive coordinated care. When both the CGs and their grandchildren can visit providers on the same day at the same family primary care clinic, barriers to quality health care can be decreased. Clinicians should especially attend to CGs' well-being during caregiving transitions (e.g., when initially taking on custody of grandchildren or returning custody to biological parents), as these are times of increased stress (Baker & Silverstein, 2008a; Baker, Silverstein, & Putney, 2008). Clinicians should also try to connect CGs to support groups whenever possible to provide them with access to other CGs, respite, and increase their social support.

Low-income CGs may qualify for but be unaware of government assistance programs targeting parents and children (U.S. Department of Health and Human Services, 2008). They may benefit from housing programs in order to accommodate their grandchildren in a suitable home; some cities have housing designated for such family caregivers (AARP, 2011). There are also agencies that can provide temporary respite care so CGs can have some relief from their parenting duties (Baker & Silverstein, 2008a; Baker et al., 2008). Clinicians working with CG families should give them relevant practical resources as well as assess and address their mental health and relational issues.

Clinical Vignette

The following is a clinical vignette to help you consider how a family in which a grandparent is raising a grandchild might present.

Mary (age 67) and her husband, Ronald (age 70), are a Haitian American couple who are primary caregivers for their two grandchildren, Marcus (age 12) and Michael (age 11). Mary is a retired elementary school teacher and Ronald is a retired postal worker. Mary and Ronald's daughter (Abigail), the children's mother, died 3 years ago in a car accident. Abigail was a single mother who had sole custody of her children; the two children never had a relationship with their father, who is currently incarcerated in another state. Mary and Ronald were awarded full custody of their grandchildren right after her death. Ronald was diagnosed with colon cancer 3 months ago and is currently undergoing chemotherapy treatment. Mary has had high blood pressure (controlled with medication) and osteoarthritis in her knees (which has been worsening) for the past few years; the arthritis makes it difficult for Mary to get around, and she now uses a cane to walk. Her doctor told her she would benefit from knee replacement surgery; however, she has been putting it off because she worries it would disrupt the family too much, especially given Ronald's current cancer treatment, which debilitates him physically and emotionally. Marcus struggles with anxiety and has been in therapy for the past year. Mary has taken on more of the household and parenting responsibilities since Ronald's diagnosis, and she is feeling stressed and overwhelmed. She is trying to keep things as normal as possible for her two grandchildren so they do not worry much about their grandfather. Yet, Mary is fearful about how the children will handle another loss and how she would care for them alone if Ronald does not survive the cancer.

Conclusions

In this chapter, we described the prevalence of grandparents raising grandchildren and the racial and socioeconomic health disparities (AARP, 2010; Hayslip & Kaminski, 2005b). Additionally, we summarized how being a grandparent who is raising grandchildren affects grandparents physically and psychologically and addressed the various challenges they face. We also discussed how being raised by grandparents impacts grandchildren's mental health and academic functioning. We then described cultural factors to take into consideration (e.g., age, income, race, healthcare setting) when working with grandparents who are raising their grandchildren. Finally, we provided a brief clinical vignette to illustrate how a grandparent-headed home coping with parental illnesses might clinically present.

Test Your Knowledge: True or False

1 Custodial grandparents are grandparents who become the primary caregivers for their grandchildren when parents cannot care for them.
2 Most custodial grandparents are Asian American.
3 Women are more likely to become CGs than men.
4 Children in foster care have better mental health outcomes than children raised by CGs.
5 CGs may be unaware that they qualify for government assistance programs.
6 CGs have a greater likelihood of health issues compared to non-CGs.
7 CG's are typically over the age of 70.

Answers: 1-T, 2-F, 3-T, 4-F, 5-T, 6-T, 7-F

Professional Readings and Resources

American Association of Retired Persons (AARP). (2010). Facts about grandparents raising grandchildren. Retrieved from www.aarp.org/confacts/grandparents/grandfacts.html

Fays, E. (2002). *A grandparent's gift of love: True stories of comfort, hope, and wisdom.* New York: Warner Books.

Hayslip, B., & Hicks Patrick, J. (Eds.). (2006). *Custodial grandparenting: Individual, cultural, and ethnic diversity.* New York: Springer Publishing.

References

American Association of Retired Persons (AARP). (2010). Facts about grandparents raising grandchildren. Retrieved from www.aarp.org/confacts/grandparents/grandfacts.html

AARP (n.d.) GrandFacts. Retrieved from www.aarp.org/relationships/friends-family/grandfacts-sheets/.

Baker, L. A., & Silverstein, M. (2008a). Depressive symptoms among grandparents raising grandchildren: The impact of participation in multiple roles. *Journal of Intergenerational Relationships, 6*(3), 285–304.

Baker, L. A., & Silverstein, M. (2008b). Preventive health behaviors among grandmothers raising grandchildren. *The Journals of Gerontology Series B: Psychological Sciences and Social Sciences, 63*(5), S304–S311.

Baker, L. A., Silverstein, M., & Putney, N. M. (2008). Grandparents raising grandchildren in the United States: Changing family norms, stagnant social policies. *Journal of Sociology and Social Policy, 28*(7), 53–69.

Bene, S. B. (2010). African American custodial grandparents raising grandchildren: A phenomenological perspective of marginalized women. *Journal of Gerontological Nursing, 38*(8), 32–40.

Blustein, J., Chan, S., & Guanais, F. C. (2004). Elevated depressive symptoms among caregiving grandparents. *Health Services Research, 39,* 1671–1689.

Brintnall-Peterson, M., Poehlmann, J., Morgan, K., & Shlafer, R. (2009). A web-based fact sheet series for grandparents raising grandchildren and the professionals who serve them. *The Gerontologist, 49,* 276–282.

Burton, L. M. (1992). Black grandparents rearing children of drug-addicted parents: Stressors, outcomes, and social service needs. *The Gerontologist, 32*(6), 744–751. doi:10.1093/geront/32.6.744

Butler, F. R., & Zakari, N. (2005). Grandparents parenting grandchildren: Assessing health status, parental stress, and social supports. *Journal of Gerontological Nursing, 31*(3), 43–54.

Carthron, D. L., Johnson, T. M., Hubbart, T. D., Strickland, C., & Nance, K. (2010). "Give me some sugar!" the diabetes self-management activities of African-American primary caregiving grandmothers. *Journal of Nursing Scholarship, 42*(3), 330–337. doi:10.1111/j.1547-5069.2010.01336.x

Conway, F., Jones, S., & Speakes-Lewis, A. (2011). Emotional strain in caregiving among African American grandmothers raising their grandchildren. *Journal of Women & Aging, 23*,113–128.

Dolbin-MacNab, M. L. (2006). Just like raising your own? Grandmothers' perceptions of parenting a second time. *Family Relations, 55,* 564–575.

Dolbin-MacNab, M. L., & Keiley, M. K. (2006). A systemic examination of grandparents' emotional closeness with their custodial grandchildren. *Research in Human Development, 3,* 59–71.

Dowdell, E. B. (2004). Grandmother caregivers and caregiver burden. *The American Journal of Maternal/Child Nursing, 29*(5), 299–304.

Dunifon, R. (2013). The influence of grandparents on the lives of children and adolescents. *Child Development Perspectives, 7,* 55–60.

Edwards, O. W., & Daire, A. P. (2006). School-age children raised by their grandparents: Problems and solutions. *Journal of Instructional Psychology, 33,* 113–119.

Fuller-Thomson, E., & Minkler, M. (2000). The mental and physical health of grandmothers who are raising their grandchildren. *Journal of Mental Health and Aging, 6*(4), 311–324.

Fuller-Thomson, E., & Minkler, M. (2005). American Indian/Alaskan native grandparents raising grandchildren: Findings from the census 2000 supplementary study. *Social Work, 50,* 131–139.

Generations United. (2004). Financial assistance for grandparents and other relatives raising children. Retrieved from www.childrensdefense.org/childwelfare/kinshipcare/FinancialAssistance

Generations United. (2011). Family Matters: Multigenerational Families in a Volatile Economy. Retrieved from www.gu.org/LinkClick.aspx?fileticket=L3k2KbjdsqY%3d&tabid=157&mid=606, on Feb. 29, 2012

Gerard, J. M., Landry-Meyer, L., & Roe, J. G. (2006). Grandparents raising grandchildren: The role of social support in coping with caregiving challenges. *International Journal of Aging and Human Development, 62,* 359–383.

Gibson, P. (1999). African-American grandparents: New mothers again. *Affilia, 14*(3), 329–343.

Gibson, P. (2002). African American custodial grandparents as caregivers: Answering the call to help their grandchildren. *Families in Society, 83*(1), 35–43.

Gibson, P. (2005). Intergenerational parenting from the perspective of African American grandparents. *Family Relations, 54*(2), 280–297.

Goodman, C., & Silverstein, M. (2002). Grandmothers raising grandchildren: Family structure and well-being in culturally diverse families. *The Gerontologist, 42,* 676–689.

Goodman, C., & Silverstein, M. (2006). Grandmothers raising grandchildren: Ethnic and racial differences in well-being among custodial and coparenting families. *Journal of Family Issues, 27,* 1605–1626.

Hadfield, J. C. (2014). The health of grandparents raising grandchildren: A literature review. *Journal of Gerontological Nursing, 40*(4), 32–42.

Hayslip, B., Jr., & Kaminski, P. L. (2005a). Grandparents raising their grandchildren: A review of the literature and suggestions for practice. *The Gerontologist, 45,* 262–269.

Hayslip, B., Jr., & Kaminski, P. L. (2005b). Grandparents raising their grandchildren. *Marriage and Family Review, 37,* 147–169.

Hayslip, B., Jr., & Kaminski, P. (2008). *Parenting the custodial grandchild: Implications for clinical practice.* New York: Springer Publishing Company.

Hinterlong, J., & Ryan, S. (2008). Creating grand families: Older adults adopting younger kin and nonkin. *The Gerontologist, 48,* 527–536.

Hughes, M. E., Waite, L. J., LaPierre, T. A., & Luo, Y. (2007). All in the family: The impact of caring for grandchildren on grandparents' health. *The Journals of Gerontology Series B: Psychological Sciences and Social Sciences, 62*(2), S108–S119.

Jimenez, J. (2002). The history of grandparents in the African-American community. *Social Service Review, 76*(4), 523–551.

Kataoka-Yahiro, M., Ceria, C., & Yoder, M. (2004). Grandparent caregiving role in Filipino American families. *Journal of Cultural Diversity, 11*(3), 110–117. Retrieved from http://search.proquest.com/docview/219346704?accountid=10559

Kelch-Oliver, K. (2011). The experiences of African American grandmothers in grandparent-headed families. *The Family Journal, 19*(1), 73–82.

Kelley, S. J., Whitley, D. M., & Campos, P. E. (2013). African American caregiving grandmothers: Results of an intervention to improve health indicators and health promotion behaviors. *Journal of Family Nursing, 19*, 53–73.

Leder, S., Grinstead, L. N., & Torres, E. (2007). Grandparents raising grandchildren: Stressors, social support, and health outcomes. *Journal of Family Nursing, 13*, 333–352.

Lee, S., Colditz, G., Berkman, L., & Kawachi, I. (2003). Caregiving to children and grandchildren and risk of coronary heart disease in women. *American Journal of Public Health, 93*(11), 1939–1944.

Minkler, M., & Fuller-Thomson, E. (1999). The health of grandparents raising grandchildren: Results of a national study. *American Journal of Public Health, 89*, 1384–1389.

Minkler, M., & Fuller-Thomson, E. (2005). African American custodial grandparents raising grandchildren: A national study using the census 2000 American community survey. *The Journals of Gerontology. Series B, Psychological Sciences and Social Sciences, 60*(2), S82–S92.

Musil, C. M., Gordon, N. L., Warner, C. B., Zauszniewski, J. A., Standing, T., & Wykle, M. (2011). Grandmothers and caregiving to grandchildren: Continuity, change, and outcomes over 24 months. *The Gerontologist, 51*(1), 86–100. doi:10.1093/geront/gnq061

Musil, C. M., Youngblut, J. M., Ahn, S., & Curry, V. L. (2002). Parenting stress: A comparison of grandmother caretakers and mothers. *Journal of Mental Health and Aging, 8*(3), 197–210.

Neely-Barnes, S. L., Graff, J. C., & Washington, G. (2010). The health-related quality of life of custodial grandparents. *Health & Social Work, 35*(2), 87–97.

Pittman, L. (2007). Grandmothers' involvement among young adolescents growing up in poverty. *Journal of Research on Adolescence, 17*, 89–116.

Pittman, L., & Boswell, M. (2007). The role of grandmothers in the lives of preschoolers growing up in urban poverty. *Applied Developmental Science, 11*, 20–42.

Ruiz, D. S. (2008). The changing roles of African American grandmothers raising grandchildren: An exploratory study in the piedmont region of North Carolina. *Western Journal of Black Studies, 32*(1), 62–71.

Simmons, T., & Dye, J. I. (2003). *Grandparents living with children: 2000* (Census 2000 Brief Report C2KBR-31). Washington, DC: U.S. Census Bureau.

Simpson, G. M., & Lawrence-Webb, C. (2009). Responsibility without community resources: Informal kinship care among low-income, African American grandmother caregivers. *Journal of Black Studies, 39*(6), 825–847.

Smith, G. C., & Palmieri, P. A. (2007). Risk of psychological difficulties among children raised by custodial grandparents. *Psychiatric Services, 58*(10), 1303–1310.

Strom, P. S., & Strom, R. D. (2011). Grandparent education: Raising grandchildren. *Educational Gerontology, 37*, 910–923.

United States Census Bureau. (2004). 2004 American community survey, S1002, Grandparents. Retrieved from http://factfinder.census.gov/servlet/STTable?_bm=y&-context

U.S. Census Bureau, American Community Survey. (2010). 1-year estimates: Table S1001 and 2005: Table B10001. Retrieved from http://factfinder2.census.gov

U.S. Department of Health and Human Services, Administration for Children and Families, Region IV. (2008). *Grandparents raising grandchildren: A call to action*. Retrieved from http://eclkc.ohs.acf.hhs.gov/hslc/tta-system/health/mental-health/adult-mental-health/Acrobat%20Document.pdf

Whitley, D. M., Kelley, S. J., & Sipe, T. A. (2001). Grandmothers raising grandchildren: Are they at increased risk of health problems? *Health and Social Work, 26*(2),105–114.

Wilson, B. (2013). Grandchildren living in a grandparent-headed household. National Center for Family and Marriage Research. Retrieved from http://ncfmr.bgsu.edu/pdf/family_profiles/file124349.pdf

Winokur, M., Holtan, A., & Valentine, D. (2009). Kinship care for the safety, permanency, and well-being of children removed from the home for maltreatment. *Campbell Systematic Reviews, 1*, 1–171.

PART III

INTERVENTIONS AND CLINICAL CONSIDERATIONS

CHAPTER 11

NEEDS ASSESSMENTS AND CLINICAL TOOLS

Maureen Davey and Brianna Bilkins

Medical providers routinely measure and track physical vital signs (e.g., weight, blood pressure), yet patients are not routinely asked about social and behavioral domains (e.g., emotional distress, impact of patient's illness on family, quality of parent–child relationships) (Pakenham & Cox, 2014; Pakenham & Ireland, 2010). Currently there is no standard regarding which psychosocial assessments providers in primary and specialty medical settings should regularly use and track (Helsing, 2015). Recently, a committee of health experts selected by the Institute of Medicine (IOM) recommended that 12 social and behavioral domains be routinely assessed and recorded in patients' electronic health records; the committee referred to them as "psychosocial vital signs" (Helsing, 2015, p. 8). Based on research suggesting these domains are linked to health outcomes and the availability of reliable and valid tools to measure them, the committee recommended regularly asking about the following 12 psychosocial vital signs: (1) alcohol use, (2) race and ethnicity, (3) residential address, (4) tobacco use and exposure, (5) census tract/median income, (6) depression, (7) education, (8) financial resource strain, (9) intimate partner violence, (10) physical activity, (11) social connections and social isolation, and (12) stress (Helsing, 2015). (See Table 11.1 for list of psychosocial domains and target areas recommended by the IOM committee of health experts.)

We agree with the IOM committee's recommendation that providers routinely assess patients, especially parents coping with an illness and their children's medical *and* psychosocial vital signs. It is important to measure and track psychosocial vital signs at the beginning of a parent's treatment (close to diagnosis) and throughout care, especially the psychological and individual-level social relationships domains and target areas listed in Table 11.1. For example, among ill parents and their children, we recommend the following be routinely assessed: (1) stress levels; (2) negative mood and affect (e.g., depression and anxiety); (3) family routines before and after the parental illness; (4) family communication (direct communication, limited open communication, indirect style of communication, no communication); and (5) quality of child's relationship and attachment to ill parent and, in two-parent families, to the healthy parent (secure, insecure, ambivalent attachment) (Murphy et al., 2009; Sperry, 2005, 2014).

In this chapter we review several valid and reliable assessments (e.g., patient/parental, child/youth, and family assessments) to help providers begin evaluating psychosocial vital signs among families coping with parental illness or to enhance

Table 11.1 Summary of Psychosocial Domains Selected by 2015 IOM Committee

Domain	Target Areas
Sociodemographic	• Sexual orientation • Race/ethnicity • Country of origin/U.S. born or non-U.S. born • Education • Employment • Financial resource strain (e.g., food and housing insecurity)
Psychological	• Health literacy • Stress • Negative mood and affect (e.g., depression, anxiety) • Psychological assets (e.g., conscientiousness, patient engagement/activation, optimism, self-efficacy)
Behavioral	• Dietary patterns • Physical activity • Tobacco use and exposure • Alcohol use
Individual-level social relationships and living conditions	• Social connections and social isolation • Exposure to violence
Neighborhoods and communities	• Neighborhood and community composition characteristics (e.g., socioeconomic and racial/ethnic characteristics)

Source: Helsing, K. (2015). Capturing social and behavioral domains and measures in electronic health records. In *143rd APHA Annual Meeting and Exposition (October 31–November 4, 2015)* (pp. 3–17). American Public Health Association (see p. 8, Table S-1).

an already existing prevention program. First, we describe the importance of doing needs assessments on *all adult patients coping with an illness* in primary and specialty medical settings to find out if they have children at home and if their children are struggling because of their parent's illness. We then review adult assessments developed to evaluate how ill parents and their partners/spouses are feeling and coping. We also describe some self-report child and youth measures to find out how school-age children are managing the parent's illness. Additionally, we describe family assessments and discuss how they can inform a family-centered approach to care. We conclude by providing a clinical case vignette to illustrate the routine use of psychosocial assessments.

Importance of Needs Assessments on All Adult Patients

The diagnosis and treatment of an illness is associated with considerable psychosocial distress for both ill parents and their families (Pakenham & Cox, 2014; Rolland, 1999; Ruddy & McDaniel, 2013). This is especially true during the active treatment phase because ill parents tend to report the following: (1) worries and fears about their health outcomes, (2) changes in physical appearance,

(3) changes in relationships, (4) financial issues, (5) changes in roles and routines at home, and (6) emotional challenges (McDaniel, Doherty, and & Hepworth, 2014; Ødegård, 2005). Both ill parents and their family members report experiencing emotional distress, especially partners/spouses of patients and school-age children (Pakenham & Ireland, 2010).

Assessing how parents are coping with an illness is an important first step for identifying psychosocial issues that may impact treatment and recovery, especially among historically underserved populations (e.g., low income ethnic and racial minority patients) (IOM, 2001; Whaley & Davis, 2007). Psychosocial support programs and services should be informed by what matters to patients so services: (1) respect the patient's and family's values, culture, and needs; (2) provide physical comfort and emotional support; (3) ensure information, education, and communication; (4) involve family and support persons; and (5) remove treatment barriers to improve access to care (IOM, 2001; Sue & Sue, 2008).

Needs assessments are important for program planning because patients do not always communicate their psychosocial concerns to treatment teams (Sperry, 2011) and providers tend to be more focused on treating the illness and not on addressing how patients and family members at home are coping and adapting to it (McDaniel, Doherty, & Hepworth, 2014). Patients have physical, psychosocial, and informational needs during all stages of medical care (Helsing, 2015); therefore, psychosocial support programs should be developed to meet these needs. We recommend providers consider routinely asking about family-based psychosocial support needs and treatment barriers. The first step is to screen all adult patients coping with a chronic or terminal illness in primary, specialty, and community healthcare settings at the beginning of an ill parent's treatment (close to diagnosis), especially if distress is reported or observed in the patient, his/her spouse or partner, and children at home.

For example, in our recently published needs assessment study (Davey et al., 2015), we surveyed a primarily African American sample of parents diagnosed with cancer. We decided to first conduct a needs assessment, because this oncology clinic treats a significant population of low-income racial minority cancer patients who are parenting school-age children. In order to develop culturally relevant family-based services and to remove treatment barriers, we asked patients the following questions in an anonymous self-report needs assessment.

Today's date: _____

Your age: _____

Your gender: ____ Male ____ Female

Your race (you can choose more than one if appropriate):
__Yes __No White
__Yes __No Black/African American
__Yes __No Asian
__Yes __No American Indian or Alaskan Native
__Yes __No Native Hawaiian or Pacific Islander
__Yes __No Other_____

Your ethnicity:
__Hispanic or Latino/Latina
__Not Hispanic or Latino/Latina

Highest level of education you *completed*:
__Less than high school
__High school
__Some college or associate's degree
__Bachelor's degree
__Graduate or professional degree

Your current job status (choose *one* that best describes you):
__Not working or unemployed
__Employed part time
__Employed full time
__Homemaker, raising children, care of others
__Disabled
__Retired

Your current marital/relationship status (choose *one* that best describes you):
__Single, never married
__Currently married
__Divorced or separated
__Not married, but in a relationship

If you are married or in a relationship, do you currently live with your spouse/ partner?
__I am not married or in a relationship
__Yes, I live with my spouse/partner
__No, I do not live with my spouse/partner

Do you have children?
__Yes   __No

If you answered yes, do you have children between the ages of 6 to 18 at home?
__Yes   __No

If you answered no, *you can STOP here*. The remaining questions are for cancer patients who have school-age children at home *and* who are between the ages of ages of 6 to 18.

If you answered yes, please choose one response that indicates your level of concern about the following areas.

How much do you think your children (ages 6 to 18) have been affected by the cancer?

__Not at all __A little __Somewhat __A lot __Very much __The most possible

Because of the cancer I am concerned about . . .

Talking about the illness with one or more children at home.

__Not at all __A little __Somewhat __A lot __Very much __The most possible

Helping/participation in household activities from one or more children at home.

__Not at all __A little __Somewhat __A lot __Very much __The most possible

Coping or emotional well-being of one or more children at home.

__Not at all __A little __Somewhat __A lot __Very much __The most possible

This last section asks about how we can help parents coping with cancer and their school-age children. Please choose one response that indicates your opinion.

How interested are you in your children (ages 6 to 18) receiving support services?

__Not at all __A little __Somewhat __A lot __Very much __The most possible

How interested are you in coming to a family support program where parents and children (ages 6 to 18) come in together?

__Not at all __A little __Somewhat __A lot __Very much __The most possible

Would you rather attend a support program at the hospital where you receive care or at another clinic nearby?

__I would rather attend a support program at the hospital where I currently receive care
__I prefer to attend a support program at another clinic nearby
__It does not matter to me

What are the things you would need to help attend a support program (e.g., child care, tokens for transportation, convenient time)?

We surveyed a convenience sample of adult oncology patients (n = 113; 71.7% African American) in an urban northeastern diverse cancer center (Davey et al., 2015). Findings suggested most patients were parenting school-age children and were worried about them (96%); 86.7% reported they would attend a family support program. Among patients (n = 108 out of 113) who reported currently parenting school-age children at home: (1) 94.7% reported their school age children are somewhat to the most possible affected by their cancer; (2) 91.5% reported that because of the cancer they are somewhat to the most possible concerned about talking about the illness with one or more children at home; (3) 61% reported that because of the cancer they are somewhat to the most possible concerned about how much household/child care help children are providing at home; (4) 92.9% are somewhat to the most possible concerned about coping or the emotional well-being of one or more children at home; (5) 88.5% are somewhat to the most possible interested in receiving support services; and (6) 86.7% are somewhat to the most possible interested in coming to a family support program with their children. Based on these findings, we developed a culturally sensitive family-based prevention program (parents and school-age children meeting together, provided help with transportation and food at each meeting, and located at a convenient place and time) to better meet the needs of minority parents coping with cancer. We recommend providers routinely have adult patients complete a psychosocial needs assessment throughout care, especially close to diagnosis.

Adult Assessments

Providers need to understand how an ill parent and his/her spouse/partner have been coping in order to intervene in helpful ways (Sperry, 2011). Yet, it is understandable that because of financial (billing for family visits to assess psychosocial domains), clinical (lack of knowledge regarding how to assess patients and their families), and productivity issues (time constraints), providers have not routinely assessed patients' and spouses'/partners' psychosocial vital signs (Helsing, 2015). In this section, we review some valid and reliable self-report measures providers can feasibly use to assess parents' psychosocial vital signs at diagnosis and throughout treatment (see Table 11.2 for some recommended adult self-report measures).

The Medical Outcome Study Short Form-36 (Ware et al., 1992) assesses how the diagnosis and treatment impact patients, for example, limitations in activities and social functioning, emotional distress, fatigue, and general perceptions of health. Illness is often described as a traumatic event that leads to significant changes in patients' lives; therefore, it is important to assess for symptoms of depression (Beck Depression Inventory-II: Beck et al., 1996; CES-D: Radloff, 1977 in Table 11.2) and anxiety (State-Trait Anxiety Scale: Spielberger, Gorsuch, Lushene, Vagg, & Jacobs, 1983; Novy et al., 1993 in Table 11.2). Patients and their partners/spouses may feel overwhelmed juggling the demands of treatment, family life, and working. Evaluating perceived stress in patients and their spouses/ partners can facilitate treatment planning (see Perceived Stress Scale: Cohen et al., 1983 in Table 11.2). While many of these self-report assessments can be used throughout treatment, it is appropriate to distribute specific measures at different times (e.g., at diagnosis, during treatment, and follow-up screening).

For example, it is more appropriate to assess for caregiver burden after the partner/spouse has been in that role for a while. The Zarit Burden Interview (Schreiner, Morimoto, Arai, & Zarit, 2006; Zarit & Zarit, 1987 in Table 11.2) is a

Table 11.2 Adult Psychosocial Assessments

Measure	Citation	Description, Validity, and Reliability
Beck Depression Inventory-II	Beck, Steer, & Brown (1996)	The Beck Depression Inventory (BDI-II) measures depressive symptoms in adults (Beck et al., 1996). It includes 21 items, with higher scores indicating more severe depression. Clinical cutoff scores are: 0–13 = minimal, 14–19 = mild, 20–28 = moderate, and 29+ = severe. The BDI-II is a reliable and valid measure of depression that has been used in many clinical settings. BDI-II can be ordered at www.pearsonclinical.com/psychology/ products/100000159/beck-depression-inventoryii-bdi-ii.html#tab-pricing
State-Trait Anxiety Inventory (STAI)	Spielberger, Gorsuch, Lushene, Vagg, & Jacobs (1983) Novy, Nelson, Goodwin, & Towzee (1993)	The State-Trait Anxiety Inventory (STAI) measures anxiety. It includes 20 items (4-point Likert scale), approximately half of which are worded positively (e.g., "I feel pleasant" about anxiety that is absent) and the other half are worded negatively (e.g., "I feel regretful" about anxiety that is present). The STAI is a reliable and valid measure of anxiety that has been used in diverse clinical settings (Novy et al., 1993; Spielberger et al., 1983). STAI for adults can be ordered at www.mindgarden.com/145-state-trait-anxiety-inventory-for-adults
Center Epidemiological Depression Scale (CES-D)	Radloff (1977)	The Center for Epidemiological Studies Depression Scale (CES-D) is a widely used, 20-item self-report valid and reliable scale that measures current levels of depressive symptoms in the general population, focusing on depressed mood during the past week. Scores range from 0 to 60, with higher scores indicating more symptoms of depression. CES-D scores of 16 to 26 indicate mild depression, and scores of 27 or more indicate major depression. CES-D can be found online at www.actonmedical.com/documents/cesd_long.pdf

(Continued)

Table 11.2 (Continued)

Measure	Citation	Description, Validity, and Reliability
Perceived Stress Scale	Cohen, Kamarck, & Mermelstein (1983)	The Perceived Stress Scale assesses a patient's or caregiver's thoughts and feelings about coping, irritability, ability to handle problems, and anger over the past month. Each item is rated on a 5-point Likert-type scale ranging from 0 (never) to 4 (very often), with higher scores indicating higher levels of stress. The scale has good reliability and validity and has been used in diverse medical settings. The Perceived Stress Scale can be purchased at www.mindgarden.com/132-perceived-stress-scale
Medical Outcome Study Short Form-36	Ware & Sherbourne (1992)	The Medical Outcome Study Short Form-36 (MOS SF-36) is a multi-item Likert-type scale that assesses the following eight health concepts in a patient: (1) limitations in physical activities because of health problems; (2) limitations in social functioning because of physical or emotional problems; (3) limitations in usual role activities because of physical health problems; (4) bodily pain; (5) general mental health; (6) limitations in usual role activities because of emotional problems; (7) vitality, such as energy/fatigue; and (8) general health perceptions. Providers need to ask for permission to use the scoring manual. The MOS SF-36 has been shown to have item-discriminant validity as well as scale reliability. It can be found at www.rand.org/health/surveys_tools/mos/mos_core_36item.html
Spiritual Well-Being Scale	Paloutzian & Ellison (1982) D'Costa (1995)	The Spiritual Well-Being Scale is a 20-item measurement with sound psychometric properties that targets a patient's self-reported relationship with God and his or her life satisfaction. Answers provided on the scale will reflect a patient's personal beliefs regarding his/her well-being, with higher scores meaning higher perceptions of well-being and lower scores reflecting lesser perceptions. Likert-type scale items range from "strongly disagree" (score of 1) to "strongly agree" (score of 6), and these items are balanced in terms positive and negative phrases in order to reduce response set bias. The Spiritual Well-Being Scale can be purchased at www.lifeadvance.com/spiritual-well-being-scale.html

Measure	Citation	Description
Herth Hope Index (HHI)	Herth (1992)	The Herth Hope Index (HHI) is a 12-item Likert-type scale (1–4) that measures the following seven hope-fostering categories in patients: (1) interpersonal connectedness, (2) attainable aims, (3) spiritual base, (4) personal attributes, (5) light-heartedness, (6) uplifting memories, and (7) affirmation of worth. It also measures the following three hope-hindering categories that can interfere with maintaining hope: (1) abandonment and isolation, (2) uncontrollable pain and discomfort, and (3) devaluation of personhood. Scores can range from 12 to 48, with higher scores meaning greater hope. The index has been shown to be a reliable measure of hope, with reliability scores ranging from 0.89 to 0.94. A copy of the Herth Hope Index can be found at www.mywhatever.com/cifwriter/content/41/pe1197.html
Zarit Burden Interview (ZBI)	Zarit & Zarit (1987) Schreiner, Morimoto, Arai, & Zarit (2006)	The Zarit Burden Interview was originally developed to assess burden of caregivers of dementia patients, but because there are many similarities in the burden experienced by caregivers of patients with various illnesses, this measure is appropriate. It includes 22 items, 21 of which are Likert-type scale items (0 = never to 4 = almost always) related to health, finances, social life, and interpersonal relationships. A cutoff score of 24–26 has predicative validity for caregivers at risk for depression. Furthermore, the ZBI has also been shown to be a valid and reliable measure with high internal consistency and test-retest reliability. The Zarit Burden Interview can be accessed online at www.aafp.org/afp/2000/1215/p2613.html

useful assessment of caregiver burden; it can help providers find out if caregivers need practical, emotional, and financial support (Schreiner et al., 2006). Similarly, it may be better to assess patient hope using the Herth Hope Index (Herth, 1992; see Table 11.2) and, for those patients who report relying on spirituality to cope, the Spirituality Well-Being Scale (Paloutzian & Ellison, 1982) can be used after the initial shock of the diagnosis has dissipated. Once the patient and partner/spouse have had time to accept the diagnosis and course of treatment, providers can try to understand how to facilitate hope-fostering beliefs (Herth, 1992).

Table 11.2 describes some helpful adult assessments that have been used with parents who are coping with an illness; however, this is not an exhaustive list of adult assessments (see Corcoran & Fischer, 2013, for list of adult assessments).

Child and Adolescent Assessments

If parents report being concerned about their children, then providers should consider asking children to come in for a visit to ask how they are coping with their parent's illness. Young children (under 10 years old) may not be able to complete self-report assessments; however, art or play therapy, which are beyond the scope of this chapter to review, can be helpful nonverbal assessments (see Sperry, 2011). There are many valid and reliable self-report psychosocial measures for school-age children (ages 10 and older). In Table 11.3, we review some of these assessments (depressive symptoms: CDI, anxiety: RCMAS, mood and feelings: MFQ-C/P, impact of parent's illness: PIIS-R, and behavioral health symptoms: BHS) that have been used to assess school-age children who are coping with parental illness. We recommend that, at minimum, providers evaluate depressive symptoms (CDI: Kovacs, 1981), anxiety (RCMAS: Reynolds & Richmond, 1997) and how the child is coping with his/her parent's illness (PIIS-R: Morley et al., 2010; Schrag, Morley, Quinn, & Jahanshahi, 2004).

It is beyond the scope of this chapter to thoroughly review child and adolescent clinical tools. There are many helpful articles and books that review child and adolescent assessments that providers can consider using (see Alderfer et al., 2008; Sperry, 2011).

Family Assessments

If providers observe that parents and children are struggling with open communication, securely attaching to each other, and maintaining family routines because of the parental illness, then we recommend doing family assessments (Sperry, 2011). There are many valid and reliable self-report measures that parents and their school-age children can complete. In Table 11.4, we review some of these family assessments that have been used with families coping with parental illness. We recommend that, at a minimum, providers evaluate parent–child attachment (Security Scale: Kerns et al., 2000), parent–child communication (General Communication: Barnes & Olson, 1985), family routines (FRI: Jenson et al., 1983), and how the family functions (FAD: Miller et al., 1985).

Again, it is beyond the scope of this chapter to thoroughly review all feasible, reliable, and valid family clinical assessments. There are helpful articles and books that review valid and reliable family assessments that providers can consider using (see Pritchett et al., 2011).

Table 11.3 Child and Adolescent Assessments

Measure	Citation	Description, Validity, and Reliability
Child Depression Inventory (CDI)	Kovacs (1981)	The most widely used self-report measure is the Children's Depression Inventory (CDI), which was adapted from the Beck Depression Inventory (BDI) and is reliable and valid for diverse samples of children aged 7 to 18 years (Steele et al., 2006). The CDI includes 27 items that assess behaviors associated with depression (e.g., sleep disturbance, anhedonia, suicidality, and appetite loss). Items are rated on a 3-point scale. Raw scores can vary from 0–54 and are converted to T scores. A cutoff score of 20 indicates severe levels of depressive symptoms. The CDI can be purchased at www.pearsonclinical.com/psychology/products/100000636/childrens-depression-inventory-2-cdi-2.html
Revised Child Manifest Anxiety Scale (RCMAS)	Reynolds & Richmond (1997)	The Revised Children's Manifest Anxiety Scale (RCMAS) includes 37 items that are rated as true or not. A general anxiety factor and three subscales of anxiety have been identified. Extensive reliability (alpha = .85 and adequate internal consistency), validity (e.g., correlation of .85 with State–Trait Anxiety Inventory [STAI] for Children and significant correlation with teacher observations), and normative data have been documented. A cutoff score of 42 indicates severe anxiety. The RCMAS can be purchased at www.wpspublish.com/store/p/2934/revised-childrens-manifest-anxiety-scale-second-edition-rcmas-2
Mood and Feelings Questionnaire Child and Parent Versions (MFQ-C and MFQ-P)	Wood, Kroll, Moore, & Harrington (1995)	The Mood and Feelings Questionnaire is a valid and reliable measure to quickly (takes 5 to 10 minutes to complete) and effectively evaluate core symptoms of depression within the last 2 weeks in children ages 8 to 18. The MFQ is a self-report measure designed for children, adolescents, and their parents; there is a longer 32-item and a shorter 10-item version. The child version (MFQ-C) is completed by the child, and the parent version (MFQ-P) asks the same questions but is completed by the parent about the child's or adolescent's behavior. The MFQ-C and MFQ-P are available at devepi.duhs.duke.edu/mfw.html

(Continued)

Table 11.3 (Continued)

Measure	Citation	Description, *Validity, and Reliability*
Parental Illness Impact Scale-Revised (PIIS-R)	Schrag, Morley, Quinn, & Jahanshahi (2004) Morley, Selai, Schrag, Thompson, & Jahanshahi (2010)	The Parental Illness Impact Scale-Revised is a 51-item reliable and valid self-report measure that youth complete regarding how their parents' illness impacts the following six domains: (1) social development, (2) independence, (3) responsibility, (4) burden of daily help, (5) impact on family functioning, and (6) friends' reactions. Each item is scored from 1 to 5; 5 indicates the best level of functioning. Higher scores indicate better levels of functioning. It has also been adapted for general parental illness and not just Parkinson disease (see Morley et al., 2010). The PIIS-R can be used after contacting the developer of this measure (www.ncbi. nlm.nih.gov/pubmed/19939722).
Behavioral Health Screening Tool (BHS)	Diamond, Levy, Begans, Fein, Wintersteen, Tien, & Creed (2010)	The Behavioral Health Screening Tool is a web-based screening tool developed to evaluate depressive symptoms, suicidality, and behavioral health among youth. This is a valid and reliable online self-report adolescent behavioral health measure that is being used in primary care, emergency departments and health units, mental health clinics, crisis services, and school settings. The BHS evaluates 13 domains (demographic, medical, school, family, safety, substance use, sexuality, trauma, nutrition and eating, psychosis, anxiety, depression, suicide and self-harm) using 54 required items and 34 follow-up items. It takes approximately 7 minutes for adolescents ages 12–18 to complete. Adolescents complete the BHS before meeting with a medical provider, then the web-based system automatically scores a report that the provider reviews. It automatically scores depression, anxiety, suicide, traumatic distress, substance use, and eating disorders and identifies youth strengths. Data can be downloaded into an EMR and aggregated for monitoring quality assurance at clinics. For more information about the BHS, contact the developer directly at guy. diamond@drexel.edu

Table 11.4 Parent–Child and Family Assessments

Measure	Citation	Description, Validity, and Reliability
Security Scale	Kerns, Tomich, Aspelmeier, & Contreras (2000)	The Security Scale is a 15-item valid and reliable measure that assesses children's perceptions of attachment during middle childhood and adolescence. This scale provides a continuous measure of security, evaluating a child's belief in the responsiveness and availability of the attachment figure, the child's use of the attachment figure as a safe haven, and the child's report of open communication with the attachment figure. The Security Scale presents children with descriptions of two types of children and asks which type of child they are most like. Items are scored from 1–4, with greater attachment security represented by a higher score. Scores on the Security Scale have adequate internal consistency and evidence of validity based on security scores correlated with self-esteem, peer acceptance, behavioral conduct, physical appearance, and scholastic competence. For a copy of Kerns Security Scale, contact the developer at kkerns@kent.edu
Short Form Interaction Behavior Questionnaire (IBQ)	Prinz, Foster, Kent, & O'Leary (1979)	The Interaction Behavior Questionnaire (IBQ) is a valid and reliable measure that evaluates agreement and conflict in parent-child dyads. The original IBQ was adapted into a short form consisting of 20 true/false items assessing communication-conflict behavior. Higher scores indicate a more positive relationship with parents. A copy of IBQ can be found at https://books.google.com/books?id=vAPtAgAAQBAJ&pg=PA328&lpg=PA328&dq=Copy+of+Short+Form+Interaction+Behavior+Questionnaire&source=bl&ots=omaaHF1LIF&sig=ui6t72YfqZ9O-6XTJWG-z3hexfk&hl=en&sa=X&ved=0CD4Q6AEwBGoVChMIh4zPy6qmxwIVQVo-Ch2ftgVd#v=onepage&q=Copy%20of%20Short%20Form%20Interaction%20Behavior%20Questionnaire&f=false

(Continued)

Table 11.4 (Continued)

Measure	Citation	Description, Validity, and Reliability
General Communication	Barnes & Olson (1985)	This general communication measure has 10 questions that ask about general communication between a parent and his/her adolescent child. Each question is scored on a 4-point Likert scale ranging from 1 (strongly disagree) to 4 (strongly agree). It is a valid and reliable measure; higher scores indicate better communication. A copy of the General Communication Measure can be found at https://books.google.com/books?id=3LCOAwAAQBAJ&pg=PA330&dq=Copy+of+Short+Form+Interaction+Behavior+Questionnaire&hl=en&sa=X&ved=0CDIQ6AEwAWoVChMIsJO1i6umxwIVil-ACh3KKAsA#v=onepage&q=Copy%20of%20Short%20Form%20Interaction%20Behavior%20Questionnaire&f=false
Family Routines Inventory (FRI)	Jenson, James, Boyce, & Hartnett (1983)	The Family Routines Inventory (FRI) is a 28-item parenting measure that focuses on family routines in the home. It provides information about continuity and predictability in the child's environment. The FRI is rated on a 4-point scale; high scores indicate a high level of routine. It is a reliable and valid measure. The FRI can be found at www.psychwiki.com/dms/other/labgroup/Measufsdsdbger345resWeek1/Elizabeth/Jensen1983.pdf
Family Assessment Device (FAD)	Miller, Epstein, Bishop, & Keitner (1985)	The FAD measures structural, organizational, and transactional characteristics of families. It has seven subscales that assess: (1) affective involvement, (2) affective responsiveness, (3) behavioral control, (4) communication, (5) problem solving, (6) roles, and (7) general family functioning. The measure includes 60 statements that mothers, fathers, and children ages 12 and older can complete. Family members are asked to rate how well each statement describes their own family. The FAD is scored by adding the responses (1–4) for each scale and dividing by the number of items in each scale (6–12). Higher scores indicate worse levels of family functioning. It is a reliable and valid measure that has been adapted for different cultures and used in clinical practice to identify families experiencing problems and evaluate change following treatment.The FAD can be found at http://chipts.ucla.edu/wp-content/uploads/downloads/2012/02/McMaster-FAD-Subscales.pdf

How to Use Clinical Tools to Inform Family-Centered Approaches to Care

Needs and psychosocial assessments should facilitate more open communication by giving patients and their families a chance to openly express their concerns and to identify physical, emotional, and logistical needs (Sperry, 2005, 2011, 2014). Results of needs and psychosocial assessments should be shared with the patient, family members, and his/her healthcare team. Healthcare providers should then develop a family-centered treatment plan and continue to monitor both medical and psychosocial vital signs. Furthermore, the assessments and recommendations should be readily accessible (e.g., in the electronic medical record) to facilitate more open communication between providers, patients, and their family members (Helsing, 2015). Although baseline needs assessments at diagnosis of the ill parent tend to be self-reported, mechanisms for review at several levels (depending on the level of distress or need) should be available and responded to with appropriate treatment. This requires support from trained mental healthcare providers, as well as a formal referral system that is responsive to patients' and their children's needs.

When parents disclose either in the needs assessment or directly to providers they are concerned about how their children/adolescents are adapting to their illness, it is important to ask about the family's functioning prior to diagnosis of the parental illness (McDaniel, Doherty, & Hepworth, 2014). This helps providers understand how the illness has affected family routines, stress, and relationships in the family. Then, a current assessment of family life after the diagnosis should be done with all family members to assess their adaptation. This also validates the family's strengths so that the assessment of family life and routines before and after the illness is a type of intervention. Providers should begin by helping the family develop a timeline of the illness and asking about the family's health history, typically over two to three generations. Family health beliefs can help providers understand how these attitudes and beliefs impact coping and adapting to a chronic illness in a parent (e.g., if the parent also experienced this same illness in his/her family). Drawing out the timeline into the future helps to illicit family members' hopes and fears. This is especially important if the illness is terminal or leads to a permanent change in the ill parent's functioning (see Chapter 12).

Providers should also ask about the timing of the illness in the family's life cycle (Rolland, 1999; see Chapters 3, 12). Medical providers tend to not be as attuned to how illness and the family life cycle (e.g., getting married, birth of first child, raising school-age children or adolescents, launching young adult children) interconnect, so mental healthcare providers can be helpful to both the healthcare team and to the family by talking about how the illness fits into the life cycle of the family (e.g., raising young children, raising adolescents).

Clinical Vignette

The following is a clinical case vignette illustrating how providers can utilize adult, child, and family assessments to help children and adolescents cope with an ill parent.

Joyce, a 40-year-old Latina elementary school teacher, after having a pelvic exam, ultrasound, and biopsy, has just been diagnosed with stage IIA uterine cancer (involves the uterus and surface lining of the cervix). She is married to Alex (43-year-old Caucasian), and they have a 13-year-old daughter, Maria. Alex is also a teacher at a local high school where they live. Shortly after being diagnosed, Joyce and Alex met with her oncologist, Dr. Smith, to discuss options for treatment. Together, they decided Joyce should have a hysterectomy, removal of both ovaries, several months of chemotherapy, and radiation therapy. Dr. Smith's colleague, who is a behavioral healthcare provider at his practice, decided it was important to conduct a needs assessment with Joyce. After she completed the brief needs assessment, the oncology treatment team learned that Joyce is worried about burdening her husband, Alex, and concerned that her daughter, Maria, has become anxious and worried. Joyce and her husband have openly talked to Maria about the cancer diagnosis, course of treatment, side effects, and prognosis. Yet they sometimes share too much information with Maria. Joyce noted that Maria has been having nightmares and does not want to leave Joyce's side, because she worries about her. Upon learning this information, Dr. Smith and the behavioral healthcare provider suggest that she bring her daughter in for a visit and a brief psychosocial assessment.

The following week, Joyce and Maria came to visit Dr. Smith and the behavioral healthcare provider, who warmly introduced themselves to Maria and acknowledged how scary it must be for her mom to be sick, but also reassured her that Joyce is a very strong woman who plans to fight the cancer. After getting to know a little bit about Maria, the behavioral healthcare provider administers the Revised Child Manifest Anxiety Scale (RCMAS) and learns that Maria is quite anxious. Although the cutoff score for severe anxiety is 42, Maria scores a 38, which suggests higher levels of anxiety and a need for further intervention. The provider gives Joyce the contact information of a prevention program that specializes in helping families cope with parental cancer to help Maria communicate more openly to her parents and to help reduce her feelings of anxiety.

After her hysterectomy and two months of chemotherapy, Joyce returns to Dr. Smith for a follow-up appointment. Dr. Smith notices that the optimism and determination Joyce had originally displayed were no longer present. Joyce seems drained, quiet, and depressed. She had to quit her job, feels embarrassed about losing her hair because of the chemotherapy, and does not want her friends and family to see her. She also feels like she lost her identity as a woman and a mother after getting her uterus removed. Dr. Smith decides to have Joyce fill out the Herth Hope Index (HHI), a brief 12-item measure that assesses hope-fostering and hope-hindering beliefs in patients. The HHI suggests Joyce has low interpersonal connectedness, feels like she does not have a purpose or sense of direction, rarely feels lighthearted, has uncontrollable pain and discomfort, and has been isolating herself. Dr. Smith asks Joyce to speak to the behavioral health provider on staff for further assessment of distress and to discuss regular therapy appointments. Furthermore, Dr. Smith invites Joyce's husband and daughter to assess how they are handling Joyce's tough chemotherapy treatment.

At their visit, Dr. Smith and the behavioral healthcare provider first talk to Alex and ask Maria to sit in the waiting room. Similar to Joyce, Dr. Smith notices that Alex seems drained. After learning more about his worries and concerns, they administer the Zarit Burden Interview (ZBI) and learn that Alex is severely burdened by Joyce's cancer treatment. Since Joyce had to quit her job, Alex has had to get a cab driving job four nights a week in addition to his teaching position to pay for the medical bills, and he is rarely home to spend time with Maria. He is participating in few leisure activities or socialization because when he is not working at his two jobs, he is home taking care of Joyce and Maria. Alex scored a 24 on the HHI, which is predictive of a risk for developing depression, so Dr. Smith and the behavioral healthcare provider make referrals to support groups and respite programs for spouses of people with chronic illnesses. They encouraged him to seek respite and to attend the support group.

When Alex was finished, Dr. Smith and the behavioral healthcare provider also assessed how Joyce's chemotherapy treatment has been impacting Maria. They administered the Parental Illness Impact Scale-Revised (PIIS-R), a 51-item measure of the impact that parental illness has on youth. Like Alex, Maria has been negatively affected by Joyce's cancer treatment regarding additional responsibilities, family functioning, and social development. She often feels sad and angry that her mother is not able to attend her school functions, such as the school play that Maria starred in, and she feels embarrassed having friends come to their house because her mother is always in a "bad mood" and does not interact with her friends the way other parents do. Dr. Smith and the behavioral healthcare provider recommend that Maria and her parents meet with a provider to open up communication and find family members who can help to support the family. Dr. Smith explained that it may help the family feel less isolated if they reach out to friends and family for support.

Cultural Considerations

Psychosocial and supportive care interventions should attend to needs regarding the family's structure (e.g., heterosexual married or cohabitating couples, single-parent headed household, same-sex couples, children living with grandparents), race/ethnicity, gender, literacy, and socioeconomic variables. Unfortunately, many minority patients underutilize psychosocial family support programs. Researchers and clinical providers suggest a perceived lack of cultural sensitivity and institutional and structural barriers to participation help to explain the current underutilization of psychosocial support services (IOM, 2001; Whitley, 2007). A better understanding of the psychosocial support needs and barriers to treatment can help to inform the development of culturally sensitive couples and family-based support services. This can improve treatment engagement, retention, and satisfaction among racially and socioeconomically diverse patients and their families (Walsh, 2012). In order to improve service utilization by vulnerable populations, we need to first understand their needs, preferences, and barriers to treatment. Conducting psychosocial need assessments with diverse samples of patients (Davey et al., 2015; Sidani, Guruge, Miranda, Ford-Gilboe, & Varcoe, 2010) is an important first step for developing culturally relevant services; and if available, culturally sensitive measures should be used (Johnson, 2006; Whitley, 2007).

What Clinicians Need to Know about Needs Assessments and Clinical Tools

1   Recently, a committee of health experts selected by the Institute of Medicine (IOM) recommended 12 social and behavioral areas be routinely assessed and recorded in patients' electronic health records; the committee referred to them as "psychosocial vital signs."

(Continued)

2   Providers need to understand how an ill parent and his/her spouse or partner have been coping and their levels of distress and concerns in order to intervene in helpful ways.
3   Child, adolescent, and family psychosocial assessments can help to clarify issues, uncover distress, and identify how best to help children and adolescents cope with an ill parent.
4   It is especially important to measure and track psychosocial vital signs at the beginning of a parent's treatment (close to diagnosis) and throughout care.
5   Psychosocial and supportive care interventions should attend to needs regarding family structure (e.g., heterosexual married or cohabitating couples, single-parent headed household, same-sex couples, children living with grandparents), race/ethnicity, gender, literacy, and socio-economic variables. Unfortunately, many minority cancer patients underutilize psychosocial support programs.

Conclusions

The diagnosis of an illness in a parent followed by diagnostic planning, discussion, and treatment are stressful experiences that affect patients' physical and psychological health and are linked to negative outcomes such as poor treatment compliance, quality of life, and satisfaction with care (Rolland, 1999). In busy medical clinics, patients and families at significant risk for distress will not be identified if they are not routinely screened. Psychosocial screening and needs assessments during acute care have been gaining attention in clinical practices (Sperry, 2014). Patient assessments are especially important among historically underserved populations to facilitate the identification, referral, and retention of patients and families who may respond better to culturally sensitive support services (Schmidt & Bullinger, 2003; Sperry, 2011, 2005). We recommend providers screen all parents coping with an illness and their offspring close to diagnosis and throughout care so both medical and psychosocial "vital signs" are assessed. Routine adult, child/youth, and family psychosocial assessments can help children/youth connect to other available adult figures, improve parent–child communication and attachment, and help to maintain fun activities so children can take a break from their parents' illness, as needed. Assessments also help to identify parents who need emotional and practical support (see Chapter 12 for clinical approaches and Chapter 13 for a review of evidence supported prevention programs).

Professional Readings and Resources

Bray, J. H. (2009). Couple and family assessment. In J.H. Bray & M. Stanton (Eds.), *The Wiley-Blackwell handbook of family psychology* (pp. 151–164). Oxford: Wiley-Blackwell.
Corcoran, K. J. (1994). *Measures for clinical practice: Couples, families, and children* (Vol. 1). New York: Simon and Schuster.
Jacob, T., & Tennenbaum, D. L. (2013). *Family assessment: Rationale, methods and future directions*. New York: Springer Science & Business Media.
Patterson, J., & Williams, L. (2009). *Essential skills in family therapy: From the first interview to termination*. New York: Guilford Press.

References

Alderfer, M. A., Fiese, B. H., Gold, J. I., Cutuli, J. J., Holmbeck, G. N., Goldbeck, L., . . . Patterson, J. (2008). Evidence-based assessment in pediatric psychology: Family measures. *Journal of Pediatric Psychology, 33*(9), 1046–1061.

Barnes, H. L., & Olson, D. H. (1985). Parent-adolescent communication and the circumplex model. *Child Development, 56*(2), 438–447. doi:10.2307/1129732

Beck, A. T., Steer, R. A., & Brown, G. K. (1996). *Manual for the Beck Depression Inventory-II.* San Antonio, TX: Psychological Corporation.

Cohen, S., Kamarck, T., & Mermelstein, R. (1983). A global measure of perceived stress. *Journal of Health and Social Behavior, 24,* 385–396.

Corcoran, K., & Fischer, J. (2013). *Measures for clinical practice and research, Volume 1: Couples, families, and children* (Vol. 1). New York: Oxford University Press.

Davey, M., Bilkins, B., Diamond, G., Willis, A. I., Mitchell, E. P., Davey, A., & Young, F. M. (2015). African American patients' psychosocial support needs and barriers to treatment: Patient needs assessment. *Journal of Cancer Education.* Epub ahead of print.

D'Costa, A. (1995). Review of the spiritual well-being scale. In C. Conoley (Ed.), *Mental measurement yearbook* (12th ed., pp. 983–984). Lincoln, NE: Buros Institute of Mental Measurements, University of Nebraska Press.

Diamond, D., Levy, S., Begans, K. B., Fein, J. S., Wintersteen, M. B., Tien, A., & Creed, T. (2010). Development, validation, and utility of internet-based, behavioral health screen for adolescents. *Pediatrics, 126,* 163–170.

Helsing, K. (2015). Capturing social and behavioral domains and measures in electronic health records. In *143rd APHA annual meeting and exposition (October 31–November 4, 2015)* (pp. 3–17). American Public Health Association.

Herth, K. (1992). Abbreviated instrument to measure hope: Development and psychometric evaluation. *Journal of Advanced Nursing, 17*(10), 1251–1259.

Institute of Medicine. (2001). *Committee on quality health care in America. Crossing the quality chasm: A new health system for the 21st century.* Washington, DC: National Academies Press.

Jenson, E. W., James, S. A., Boyce, W. T., & Hartnett, S. A. (1983). The family routines inventory: Development and validation. *Social Science Medicine, 17,* 201–211.

Johnson, T. P. (2006). Methods and frameworks for cross cultural measurement. *Medical Care, 44,* S17–S20.

Kerns, K. A., Tomich, P. L., Aspelmeier, J. E., & Contreras, J. M. (2000). Attachment-based assessments of parent-child relationships in middle childhood. *Developmental Psychology, 36,* 614–626. doi:10.1037/0012-1649.36.5.614

Kovacs, M. (1981). Rating scales to assess depression in school-aged children. *Acta Paedopsychiatr, 46,* 305–315.

McDaniel, S. H., Doherty, W. J., & Hepworth, J. (2014). *Medical family therapy and integrated care* (2nd ed.). Washington, DC: American Psychological Association Publications.

Miller, I. W., Epstein, N. B., Bishop, D. S., & Keitner, G. I. (1985). The McMaster family assessment device: Reliability and validity. *Journal of Marital and Family Therapy, 11*(4), 345–356.

Morley, D., Selai, C., Schrag, A., Thompson, A. J., & Jahanshahi, M. (2010). Refinement and validation of the Parental Illness Impact Scale. *Parkinsonism Related Disorder, 16*(3), 181–185. doi:10.1016/j.parkreldis.2009.11.001

Murphy, D. A., Marelich, W. D., Herbeck, D. M., & Payne, D. L. (2009). Family routines and parental monitoring as protective factors among early and middle adolescents affected by maternal HIV/AIDS. *Child Development, 80*(6), 1676–1691.

Novy, D. M., Nelson, D. V., Goodwin, J., & Towzee, R. D. (1993). Psychometric comparability of the state-trait anxiety inventory for different subpopulations. *Psychological Assessment, 5,* 343–349. doi:10.1037/1040-3590.5.3.343

Ødegård, W. (2005). Chronic illness as a challenge to the attachment process. *Clinical Child Psychology and Psychiatry, 10*(1), 13–22. doi:10.1177/1359104505048787

Pakenham, K. I., & Cox, S. (2014). The effects of parental illness and other ill family members on the adjustment of children. *Annals of Behavioral Medicine, 48*(3), 424–437. doi:10.1007/s12160-014-9622-y

Pakenham, K., & Ireland, M. (2010). Youth adjustment to parental illness or disability: The role of illness characteristics, caregiving, and attachment. *Psychology, Health & Medicine, 15*(6), 632–645. doi:10.1080/13548506.2010.498891

Paloutzian, R. F., & Ellison, C. (1982). *The spiritual well-being scale.* Nyack, NY: Life Advance.

Prinz, R. J., Foster, S., Kent, R. N., & O'Leary, K. D. (1979). Multivariate assessment of conflict in distressed and non-distressed mother-adolescent dyads. *Journal of Applied Behavior Analysis, 12,* 691–700.

Pritchett, R., Kemp, J., Wilson, P., Minnis, H., Bryce, G., & Gillberg, C. (2011). Quick, simple measures of family relationships for use in clinical practice and research. A systematic review. *Family Practice, 28*(2), 172–187.

Radloff, L. S. (1977). The CES-D Scale: A self-report depression scale for research in the general population. *Applied Psychological Measure, 1,* 385–401.

Reynolds, C. R., & Richmond, B. O. (1997). What I think and feel: A revised measure of children's manifest anxiety. *Journal of Abnormal Child Psychology, 25*(1), 15–20. doi:10.1023/A:1025751206600

Rolland, J. S. (1999). Parental illness and disability: A family systems framework. *Journal of Family Therapy, 21*(3), 242–266. doi:10.1111/1467-6427.00118

Ruddy, N. B., & McDaniel, S. H. (2013). Medical family therapy in the age of health care reform. *Couple and Family Psychology: Research and Practice, 2*(3), 179.

Schmidt, S., & Bullinger, M. (2003). Current issues in cross-cultural quality of life instrument development. *Archives of Physical Medicine and Rehabilitation, 84*(Supp 2), S29–S34.

Schrag, A., Morley, D., Quinn, N., & Jahanshahi, M. (2004). Development of a measure of the impact of chronic parental illness on adolescent and adult children. The Parental Illness Impact Scale (Parkinson's disease). *Parkinsonism & Related Disorders, 10*(7), 399–405.

Schreiner, A. S., Morimoto, T., Arai, Y., & Zarit, S. (2006). Assessing family caregiver's mental health using a statistically derived cut-off score for the Zarit Burden Interview. *Aging and Mental Health, 10*(2), 107–111.

Sidani, S., Guruge, S., Miranda, J., Ford-Gilboe, M., & Varcoe, C. (2010). Cultural adaptation and translation of measures: An integrated method. *Research in Nursing and Health, 33,* 133–143.

Sperry, L. (2005). Case conceptualizations: A strategy for incorporating individual, couple, and family dynamics in the treatment process. *American Journal of Family Therapy, 33,* 353–364.

Sperry, L. (2011). *Family assessment: Contemporary and cutting-edge strategies* (2nd ed.). New York: Routledge.

Sperry, L. (2014). *Behavioral health: Integrating individual and family interventions in the treatment of medical conditions (family therapy and counseling)* (1st ed.). New York: Routledge.

Spielberger, C. D., Gorsuch, R. C., Lushene R. E., Vagg P. R., & Jacobs, G. A. (1983). *Manual for the state-trait anxiety inventory.* Palo Alto: Consulting Psychologists Press.

Steele, R. G., Little, T. D., Ilardi, S. S., Forehand, R., Brody, G. H., & Hunter, H. L. (2006). A confirmatory comparison of the factor structure of the children's depression inventory between European American and African American youth. *Journal of Child and Family Studies, 15*(6), 773–788.

Sue, D. W., & Sue, D. (2008). *Counseling the culturally different: Theory and practice* (5th ed.). New York: Wiley.

Walsh, F. (Ed.). (2012). *Normal family processes: Growing diversity and complexity* (4th ed.). New York: The Guilford Press.

Ware, J. E., Jr., & Sherbourne, C. D. (1992). The MOS 36-item short-form health survey (SF-36): I. Conceptual framework and item selection. *Medical Care, 30,* 473–483.

Whaley, A. L., & Davis, K. E. (2007). Cultural competence and evidence-based practice in mental health services: A complementary perspective. *American Psychologist, 62*(6), 563–574.

Whitley, R. (2007). Cultural competence, evidence-based medicine, and evidence-based practices. *Psychiatric Services, 58*(12), 1588–1590.

Wood, A., Kroll, L., Moore, A., & Harrington, R. (1995). Properties of the Mood and Feelings Questionnaire in adolescent psychiatric outpatients: A research note. *Journal of Child Psychology and Psychiatry, 36,* 327–334.

Zarit, S. H., & Zarit, J. M. (1987). *Instructions for the burden interview.* University Park: Pennsylvania State University.

CHAPTER 12

CLINICAL GUIDELINES FOR WORKING WITH PARENTAL ILLNESS

Laura Lynch

Although parental illnesses vary with regard to onset, course, and prognosis, there are common experiences among families coping with parental illness. Both attachment theory (Bowlby, 1969, 1973, 1980) and the family systems illness (FSI) model (Rolland, 1984, 1987a,b, 1988, 1994a, 1999, 2005) (see Chapter 2) can help providers utilize a family-centered approach to care. In this chapter, we describe general clinical guidelines and recommendations for working with families coping with parental illness, including attending to children's developmental stages, the family's life cycle, and the couple relationship; helping parents talk to children about parental illness; preparing children for hospital visits; using children's books as resources; maximizing social support; collaborating across disciplines, and using a culturally sensitive approach to care.

Child Development

Clinical approaches to help families cope with an ill parent should be informed by children's developmental stages because these will impact their understanding of the illness and coping (Armistead, Klein, & Forehand, 1995; Compas et al., 1994). Similarly, Rolland's FSI model (1984, 1987a,b, 1988, 1994b, 1999, 2005) describes the importance of attending to developmental stages of all family members. Additionally, attachment theory (Bowlby, 1969, 1973, 1980) (see Chapter 2) suggests parental illness will activate attachment behaviors in children, which will vary based on the children's ages and stages of development.

For example, infants often display separation distress by crying (Armsden & Lewis; 1993; Bowlby, 1980; Diareme et al., 2007). Younger children (toddlers and preschoolers) may cry, seek frequent physical proximity to their parents, display hyperactivity, have tantrums, exhibit regression, or even demonstrate aggressive or destructive behaviors when separated from their parents (Armsden & Lewis, 1993; Diareme et al., 2007). Young children may also have difficulty expressing their anger when they are separated from an ill parent; feelings of anger could be expressed behaviorally toward themselves or others (Armsden & Lewis, 1993). School age children's and adolescents' attachment behaviors can include negative behavior at school, increased irritability, or more reckless behavior when they are not feeling connected to a parent. They could also withdraw and appear not concerned by any changes in physical or emotional access to an ill parent; this can occur even among securely attached children (Bowlby, 1980).

As children get older, they tend to want less physical closeness to their parents, but they will still need emotional closeness. Adolescents tend to pursue more autonomy compared to younger children, but they still need a secure parent–child attachment. Secure attachment in adolescence is nurtured with effective and open parent–child communication, including parental sensitivity and responsiveness to adolescents' emotions, which encourages adolescents to more openly express feelings to their parents (Allen, 2008). Secure attachment among adolescents is also improved when parents allow adolescents to have increased independence while still preserving a close relationship (Allen, 2008). Thus, many adolescents with secure attachments will seek out parents for comfort, especially when they are upset or are experiencing distress (Allen, 2008).

In addition to attachment behaviors, children's ages and developmental stages can affect how they express emotions (e.g., anger, fear) about their parent's illness and changes in family routines. For example, children in preschool may believe they are somehow responsible for causing their parent to get sick because of a developmentally appropriate tendency to display magical thinking and a more self-centered view of the world (Diareme et al., 2007). In contrast, adolescents may feel guilty about wanting to spend more time with peers while the family is coping with a parent's illness (Allen, 2008; Diareme et al., 2007). Diareme and

Table 12.1 Child Development Issues Related to Parental Illness

Developmental Stage	Psychological Issues
Infancy	Separation from parent(s)
	Inconsistent physical and emotional care by parent(s)
Toddlerhood	Separation from parent(s) experienced as abandonment or punishment
	Inconsistent provision of attention and limit setting
Preschool	Magical thinking of having caused the parent's illness
	Illness experienced as punishment
	Fun and play perceived as inappropriate
Latency	Irrational fear of causing or exacerbating parent's illness and associated guilt
	Somatic complaints (due to age-expected dependency on parents)
	Guilt for having fun
	Feeling unimportant
Adolescence	Guilt or ambivalence about desire for independence (due to age-expected need for autonomy)
	Somatic complaints (due to age-expected concerns with body image and health-identity formation issues)
	Shame about ill parent (due to age-expected need for peer acceptance)
	Resentment of increased responsibilities at home (due to age-expected need for independent activities)
	Negligence or compromise of own growth and autonomy (due to age-expected guilt for wanting to separate from ill parent)

Source: Diareme, S., Tsiantis, J., Romer, G., Tsalamanios, E., Anasontzi, S., Paliokosta, E., & Kolaitis, G. (2007). Child developmental issues related to parental illness. *Families, Systems, & Health. 25*(1), 98–118 (p. 100). Reprinted with permission of the American Psychological Association.

colleagues (2007) described issues children may face based on their developmental stages. Table 12.1 provides a summary of possible psychological issues among children coping with an ill parent, based on children's developmental stages.

Family Life Cycle

It is helpful to view a family as "a system moving through time" that will experience transitions and have roles and relationship changes at different stages of the life cycle (McGoldrick & Carter, 2003, p. 375). Rolland (1994a, 1994b) also described the importance of attending to a family's life cycle stage. Families with children tend to have similar life cycle tasks regarding having, raising, and launching children; parental illness can impact and/or impede these tasks. McGoldrick, Carter, and Garcia Preto (2015) describe specific tasks among families caring for young children and adolescents. In families with younger children, tasks include: (1) the couple's adjustment as they add children (biological offspring, adoption, step-children) to the family, (2) negotiating parenting, finances, and running the household, (3) adjustment of extended family relationships to accommodate new parenting and grandparenting roles, and (4) adjustment of relationships to accommodate larger systems (work–family balance) based on the new structure of the family (McGoldrick et al., 2015, p. 24).

In families who are parenting adolescents, tasks include: (1) adjustment of parent–child relationships and boundaries to facilitate adolescents' increased autonomy, (2) assistance with adolescents' formation and interaction with relationships in the community (e.g., peers), (3) renewed focus on "midlife couple and career issues," and (4) adjustment to caring for older family members (McGoldrick et al., 2015, p. 24).

Genograms

Multigenerational perspectives (Rolland, 1994a, 1994b) are helpful when working with families coping with parental illness. Using a multigenerational framework is important because extended family may be an untapped source of support or it can lead additional stressors (e.g., caregiving for elderly parents). We encourage providers to assess each family's developmental tasks and goals and consider how the parental illness is impacting them. A good way to accomplish this is by developing a genogram in collaboration with the family (Rolland, 1994a, 1994b). A genogram is a map of two to three family generations and relationships (Gerson & McGoldrick, 1985). Providers can use a genogram to both join and to understand beliefs about parental illness to help the family not repeat unhealthy intergenerational patterns (McDaniel et al., 2014; Rolland, 1994a). Figure 12.1 is an example of a family genogram; later in the chapter we describe a clinical vignette using Figure 12.1.

Couple Relationships

Prior research suggests children are affected by the quality of their parents' relationships (Fear et al., 2009; Riggio, 2004; Spath, 2007; Sturge-Apple, Skibo, & Davies, 2012). Armistead and her colleagues (1995) noted parental physical illness could trigger or exacerbate relationship conflict, which in turn can impact the quality of parenting (Armistead et al., 1995). The authors also described the increased risk of parents experiencing depression, which has been associated with

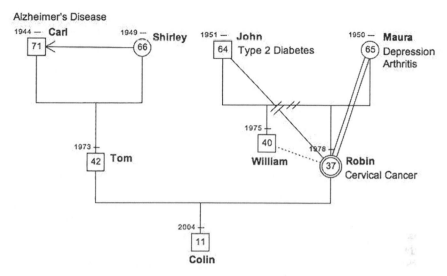

Figure 12.1 Example of a Genogram Identifying Family Illnesses

parental illness (see Chapter 3) (Armistead et al., 1995). When a parent is diagnosed with an illness, providers should assess the couple relationship without children present. If parents are divorced or separated, providers should still try to meet with both the well and ill parent to learn about their relationship history, co-parenting strengths and challenges, and views regarding how the illness has impacted the family. If a couple is distressed, couples therapy or a support group for couples coping with illness in a partner should be discussed as a treatment option (Alati, 2014). Given the risk of depression among individuals coping with chronic illness and their partners (see Chapter 3) and the negative impact depression can have on parenting (Hanington et al., 2012), we recommend that providers screen both partners for depression, at minimum at diagnosis and if possible throughout treatment (see Chapter 11).

Helping Parents Talk to Children about the Illness

Providers working with families coping with an ill parent should facilitate more effective and open family communication, especially about the illness, treatment, and side effects. Parents may worry about telling their children about the illness (e.g., Kennedy & Lloyd-Williams, 2009). Some parents will want to protect their children by disclosing little to no information. Although this is understandable, trying to hide the illness or withholding information is generally not in the best interest of children. Many providers and scholars suggest that helping parents communicate age-appropriate information to their children can be beneficial for both parents and their children (Barnes et al., 2002; Lewis et al., 2015; Paliokosta et al., 2009).

Although children mature in similar ways through each developmental stage, children are unique and may develop at different rates. A child may know more about the illness than parents realize, or a child could have misperceptions about it. Thus, providers should ask children about their understanding, fears, and concerns (e.g., "Do you know what diabetes is? Tell me about it." or "What does cancer mean?") and not assume parents are fully informed about their children's experiences because they are often overwhelmed with the diagnosis, treatment, and many medical appointments.

For example, Myant and Williams (2005) studied illness understanding among children ages 4 to 12 years and reported "the most frequent definition of illness was based upon the presence of symptoms and feeling poorly," even among some of the 4- and 5-year-old participants (p. 118). As children get older, their understandings of illness and health tend to become more complex (abstract thinking) and their knowledge about specific illnesses tends to increase (Myant & Williams, 2005).

Providers should help parents use age-appropriate language when discussing the illness with their children, and parents should not give too many details to younger children because it can be overwhelming and beyond their understanding. Koopman, Baars, Chaplin, and Zwinderman (2004) examined children's development of illness understanding as they got older. They reported that between ages 7 and 11 (corresponding with Piaget's concrete-operational phase), children are able to understand mind–body separation, that is, that illness can be caused from inside of the body and affect parts of the body and can be treated through behavior (e.g., taking medication). At this stage of development, children also begin to understand analogies. The authors recommend that until children reach this level of understanding, adults should explain illnesses using brief, general terms (Koopman et al., 2004). Once children reach this level, parents can also use analogies to help children understand an illness, such as the "heart is a pump" (Koopman et al., 2004, p. 369).

Possible Misperceptions and Fears

When working with the children of ill parents, it is important to ask if they have any worries or concerns and to educate parents about possible fears and concerns their children might be experiencing. As Rolland (1994a) noted, "catastrophic fears and fantasies held silently are far more destructive than realistic concerns that are aired and relieved by the parents" (p. 223). There are many misperceptions children may have about the parent's illness, such as the prognosis of the illness. For example, a child who sees a diabetic parent have a hypoglycemic episode may worry that her parent is going to die. Conversely, a child may not realize the extent to which a parent is ill if he/she is terminal or has a poor prognosis (e.g., in some cases of cancer). Another misperception a child could have is believing the illness is somehow his fault or a punishment for his own bad behavior (Diareme et al., 2007). Preschool-age children might believe they should not play with friends and enjoy themselves while their parent is ill, and adolescents may feel their desire to go out with peers is wrong when their parent is at home not feeling well (Diareme et al., 2007).

Some children worry their parent could die (Maybery & Reupert, 2010). In cases of more advanced or terminal illnesses, this is a realistic fear that should be addressed by providers and parents (see Chapter 14). Yet, for more manageable or chronic illnesses this fear can be addressed by explaining how the illness will be treated and describing the positive prognosis (e.g., "Mom is not going to die. Diabetes is something she can take care of by taking her medicine and eating well; doing these things will keep her healthy" or "Dad's cancer was caught early, which is a really good thing. The doctors think they will be able to help him get better by giving him chemotherapy, which is a strong kind of medicine to fight the cancer"). Younger children may worry about developing the illness from their parent. Providers should help parents explain to their children they will not "catch" the illness from the ill parent and reassure them in developmentally appropriate ways.

Children, especially adolescents, often worry about changes in family functioning and daily routines. They report being concerned about who will take them to extracurricular activities or what will happen during holidays and vacations if, for example, mom or dad is feeling sick because of side effects from the chemotherapy. Older children have reported worrying that family life and routines will never "feel normal" again. Providers can help children express their fears and concerns directly to parents and help parents provide reassurance and accurate information as needed. Some children may feel anxious about expressing their feelings to parents, which depends on the type of relationship parents had with their children prior to the parental illness (e.g., secure attachment, insecure attachment, close, or distant). When children are securely attached to parents, they are more likely to feel comfortable openly expressing their emotions (see Chapter 2).

In addition to experiencing fear, children may experience confusion, sadness, shame, guilt, and anger. Providers should help prepare parents for the range of emotions children could experience and indicate that just because their children are not outwardly expressing distress, it does not mean they are not experiencing any illness-related emotions (Armsden & Lewis, 1993). Any significant change in behavior (e.g., withdrawing, oppositional behavior) can be a sign a child or adolescent is struggling (Armsden & Lewis, 1993). Providers can: (1) help parents model open emotional expression to their children, (2) help parents explore and validate their children's emotions, and (3) help children learn how to identify and express their emotions.

Providers should work with parents and children to help them identify and use healthier ways to express feelings to each other and utilize adaptive coping strategies. After children's understandings of emotions have been assessed, providers can ask children the following questions: (1) "How do you know when you are scared/sad/mad?" (2) "What do you do when you feel this way?" (3) "What could you say to mom or dad to let them know you are feeling this way?" Providers can encourage children and parents to openly talk about adaptive ways to cope with strong feelings. Younger children, for example, may cope with feeling sad by sitting on a parent's lap or cope with feeling angry by running around in the backyard. Older children may talk to a close friend or write in a journal. When parents understand their children's emotions and are aware of their coping strategies, they can be more attuned and responsive to children's needs and facilitate positive emotional coping.

Preparing Children for the Illness

Children will experience their parent's illness in myriad ways, depending on the type of illness and prognosis, their personality, gender, culture, and developmental stage. A child or adolescent may witness a parent experiencing physical symptoms, help with care, or visit a parent in the hospital. Providers should help parents prepare children for these experiences, especially more frightening experiences like visiting a parent in the hospital (Knutsson & Bergbom, 2007). For example, a child of a parent with diabetes should know how to recognize if a parent has become severely hypoglycemic and what to do to help (Rolland, 1994a). A child cared for by a parent at high risk for a stroke or cardiac issues should know what to do if an emergency occurs. Even preschool age children can be taught what constitutes an emergency and how to dial 911. Older school-age children and adolescents may be able to give a hypoglycemic parent a sugary snack or a drink or administer an emergency glucose injection (Rolland, 1994a). Providers should help parents consider possible scenarios regarding how to prepare children in age appropriate ways and facilitate open communication between parents and children.

Some parents may be hospitalized during their illness. What children worry about is often worse than what is actually occurring to their ill parents; visiting parents while they are hospitalized can be comforting for children. Providers should keep in mind that children who do not want to visit a hospitalized parent should not be forced to do so (Clarke & Harrison, 2001). Instead, providers should help parents explore this with their child to see if there are any unaddressed fears or underlying emotions related to the avoidance of the hospital.

Children and adolescents who are uncomfortable visiting a parent in the hospital should be encouraged to still communicate with their ill parent (e.g., over the telephone or Google chat). Infants and toddlers who are too young to understand a parent's hospitalization will not benefit from hospital visits in the same way an older school-age child will; younger children will benefit more from maintaining family routines at home (Clarke & Harrison, 2001). Before a child is brought to the hospital, the well parent (or primary caregiver) should explain what the child might see, including any altered appearance of the parent (e.g., bruising, IVs, monitors), and explain what the child can expect from the ill parent (e.g., "Mommy is very sleepy and will not be able to talk much" or "Dad will be in a hospital bed, but he is feeling good today and is looking forward to hearing about your day at school").

Using Children's Books as Resources

Children's books can be an excellent resource for parents. There are many books about parental illness written for children of various ages. Parental cancer is the most common illness addressed in children's books, but there are also more general books about parental illness. Parents can read books to younger children to help begin illness or death-related conversations (e.g., Gutiérrez, Miller, Rosengren, & Schein, 2014), provide age-appropriate information, and normalize children's experiences. Providers may also consider utilizing (or recommending to parents) children's books that help children identify and express their emotions. This can help children learn how to recognize and talk about their feelings and help parents better understand their children's emotional experiences. At the end of this chapter, we provide a list of books that address parental illness and help children express their emotions.

Maximizing Support Systems

Parental illness can place enormous stress on the family system (Rashi, Wittman, Tsimicalis, & Loiselle, 2015). Providers should help families identify support from the community and extended family members. Given the importance of maintaining family routines, garnering social support is essential. If parents are unable to care for their children because of a physical impairment or a demanding treatment regimen, other trusted family members or friends can provide functional and emotional support (Armsden & Lewis, 1993). Children need consistency; when an ill and well parent feel supported, they can better focus on the needs of their children and be more emotionally available (Armsden & Lewis, 1993).

Grauf-Grounds (2007) described an intervention that can help increase social support. She encourages families to make a list of people who can provide different types of support (e.g., a ride, a meal, emotional support). Then each person on the list is mailed or emailed a brief letter asking them to identify one or two ways they could support the family. The family is then encouraged to place all responses in a visible place so they are reminded of available social support. Providers can also facilitate in-person meetings with family members and possible support persons to help explain the demands of the illness and needs of the family. During this meeting, support persons are encouraged to identify specific ways they can help by providing both practical and emotional support (Grauf-Grounds, 2007).

Guidelines for Diverse Clinical Settings

As mentioned in the earlier illness chapters, mental healthcare providers in diverse practice settings will at some point interact with families coping with parental illness. We hope our recommendations are helpful to all providers (e.g., primary and tertiary care, private practice, community mental health). Yet, there are some differences in the approach to care based on whether a provider is part of an integrated medical setting or works in a mental healthcare setting (e.g., private practice or a community mental health center).

Providers working in medical settings are most likely to be referred a parent coping with a chronic illness. Additionally, since medical care tends to be more patient-centered, ill parents are more likely to be referred for individual therapy. In order to identify the family's needs, we recommend integrated mental healthcare providers first ask if patients are parenting children at home (see Chapter 11). Mental healthcare providers who are integrated in medical settings also tend to provide more short-term support and psychotherapy services. Providers in this role should keep in mind they may need to refer the entire family or some family members for long-term individual, couple, or family therapy if there are more serious mental health or relational issues.

Providers in community mental healthcare or private practice settings are more likely to be referred individuals or families with psychological or relational presenting problems. Yet, clients may not at first talk about experiencing parental illness as part of the presenting problem. Instead, they often describe relationship issues, behavioral issues in children, and emotional distress. We encourage all providers to ask about any past or current illnesses in the family. Additionally, providers in private practice and community mental healthcare centers tend to face greater challenges regarding collaborating with medical providers, which we address in the next section.

Interdisciplinary Collaboration

Families interface with school, healthcare, and government systems. Providers should collaborate and partner with staff in these multiple systems to help support families coping with parental illness. Medical providers can provide mental healthcare providers with important information about the illness (e.g., onset, stage, prognosis). For example, a medical provider may report one prognosis, while family members could have a different understanding. Providers can facilitate improved communication between medical providers and families to help them developed a shared understanding of the illness.

Healthcare teams tend to include multiple providers, so clinicians should be comfortable collaborating with more than one provider (e.g., primary care provider, specialists, nutritionist, nurse navigator, medical social workers) (McDaniel, Doherty, & Hepworth, 2014). Providers who are fully or partially integrated into medical settings tend to have better access to medical providers; they may have joint meetings with the treatment team and the family (McDaniel et al., 2014). Mental healthcare providers in private practice or in community mental healthcare settings will need to be more intentional if they want to collaborate with medical providers. Before contacting them, it is important to first talk about it with the family and obtain written releases of information (McDaniel et al., 2014) (see Chapter 15). After releases of information are signed, providers can initiate contact with medical treatment teams and let them know about their work with the family, as well as offer ongoing collaboration. At the very least, providers should ask about medical providers' views of the illness and, if known, the family's adjustment.

If children are having any problems in school, providers in consultation with parents should contact the school to understand what is happening in the classroom. Providers, with parental permission, may need to inform a teacher about the parental illness. They can coach parents to have more open discussions with their child's teacher regarding their child's needs. If school personnel are aware of the parent's illness, they may be able to provide additional emotional and practical support.

Attending to Culture

In order to effectively work with families, providers should attend to a family's cultural background (e.g., race, ethnicity, SES, language, religion) because it influences how families will cope and adapt. As discussed earlier in the chapter, paying attention to individual and family developmental stages, as well as the larger family system and family illness history, is important. As we explored in the previous illness chapters, providers should also attend to the culture of the family, because beliefs about illness and the illness experience are influenced by families' cultures (e.g., race, ethnicity, SES, spiritual beliefs) (McDaniel et al., 2014; Rolland, 1994a).

Additionally, providers should attend to factors related to the illness. As discussed in Chapter 2, Rolland's (1984, 1987a,b, 1988, 1994a, 1994b, 1999, 2005) FSI model is a helpful way to conceptualize salient illness factors, such as the type of illness onset (e.g., sudden), course of the illness (e.g., relapsing), prognosis (e.g., chronic, terminal), how much incapacitation/disability the ill parent will experience, and the level of unpredictability of the particular illness. Keeping these illness factors in mind will help providers better understand how a particular illness could impact the family. Additionally, providers will be better prepared to address possible illness transitions, which can be particularly stressful for families. For example, understanding the course of a parent's multiple sclerosis could help providers prepare families for illness-related flare-ups. Understanding that a parent's cancer treatment may cause temporary incapacitation can help providers facilitate open family discussions about temporarily shifting roles in the family so they can adapt to the acute phase of cancer treatment. Next we present a clinical case vignette to illustrate the importance of exploring children's understandings and concerns about their parents' illness.

Clinical Vignette

Claire is a family therapist in a private practice who receives a referral from a family medical provider at a nearby primary care practice. The referral is for a family that includes Robin, a middle school teacher (37) of mixed Western European descent; her husband, Tom, an IT director (42) of German-Irish descent; and their son, Colin (11) (see Figure 12.1). The referring provider states that he is concerned about the family's stress level and adjustment to Robin's illness. Six months ago, Robin was diagnosed with cervical cancer and has been undergoing treatment. Robin and Tom talked to Colin about the cancer diagnosis soon after they received it, and they kept Colin informed about the treatment and prognosis. Robin has taken a medical leave from her job to focus on treatment, but she is worried about the family's financial situation if she is not able to return next fall. In addition, Tom's father was diagnosed with Alzheimer's disease over a year ago. His mother is his father's primary caregiver, but Tom is his mother's main emotional support, and he helps to manage their finances and coordinate his father's medical appointments. Although Robin appreciates Tom's dedication to his parents, she feels he has been less supportive to her because he is also caring for his parents. Consequently, she sometimes feels resentful.

Recently, Colin has been experiencing anxiety about going to school; his teacher reported his participation in class has decreased dramatically and he has become more withdrawn from his peers. Robin and Tom are not sure what is going on with Colin; they worry they should not have told him as much about Robin's cancer and treatment. Claire meets with the family. Using a multigenerational lens and a genogram (see Figure 12.1), she quickly identifies the dual stressors the family, and particularly Tom, are facing with Robin's and Tom's father's illnesses. Claire meets with Robin and Tom to first assess the couple relationship; they report they have been arguing more often and both feel misunderstood and not supported by the other. When Claire assesses the family in a joint session, she asks Colin to tell her about what he understands about his mother's illness. While discussing what he knows, Colin begins to cry and admits he looked up cervical cancer online and read his mom could die from it. Robin and Tom are surprised that Colin did not come to them to talk about this; Colin reveals he did not want to make them more sad and upset, especially during his mom's tough treatment regimen. Claire meets with the family to help them communicate more openly with each other, finds caregiving and respite support for Tom and his parents, and meets with the couple to work on supporting each other and more openly expressing their needs.

Conclusions

Parental illness affects all levels of the family system. When providers attend to these multiple levels, they are able to conceptualize and address psychosocial issues for parents and their children. These include attending to children's developmental stages, the family life cycle, the couple, the extended family system, social support, larger systems (e.g., the medical system), and contextual factors (e.g., culture). Providers should help parents more openly talk to their children about the illness. Children will experience a range of emotions throughout the course of a parent's illness; parents can help their children express and cope with their emotions in healthy ways.

What Clinicians Need to Know about Working with Families Coping with Parental Illness

1   Do not assume you fully understand what a child knows about his/her parent's illness; ask the child directly, if possible, or coach the parent to ask the child directly.
2   Educate parents about encouraging emotional expression and encourage them to help their children identify their feelings.
3   Encourage parents to engage in an ongoing open dialogue with their children about the illness.
4   Consider each family member's individual developmental stage, culture, and family life cycle stage.
5   Help families identify and maximize their support systems to decrease parental stress and increase consistency for children.
6   Assess the parent's couple relationship because it can affect not only their ability to cope with an illness but also their children's well-being.

Children's Books about Parental Illness

Ackermann, A. (2001). *Our mom has cancer*. American Cancer Society.
Mills, J.C. (2003). *Gentle willow: A story for children about dying*. New York: Magination Press.
Russell, N. (2001). *Can I still kiss you?: Answering your children's questions about cancer*. Deerfield Beach, FL: Health Communications Inc.
Winthrop, E., & Lewin, B. (2000). *Promises*. Honolulu: University of Hawaii Press.

Children's Books about Emotional Expression

Cain, J. (2000). *The way I feel*. Seattle: Parenting Press, Inc.
Lamia, M. C. (2010). *Understanding myself: A kid's guide to intense emotions and strong feelings* (1st ed.). New York: Magination Press.
Snow, T., & Snow, P. (2007). *Feelings to share from A to Z* (1st ed.). Oak Park Heights, MN: Maren Green Publishing.
Verdick, E., & Lisovskis, M. (2015). *How to take the grrrr out of anger*. Free Spirit Publishing.

References

Alati, R. (2014). Does depression experienced by mothers lead to a decline in marital quality: A 21-year longitudinal study. *Social Psychiatry and Psychiatric Epidemiology*, 49(1), 121–132. doi:10.1007/s00127-013-0749
Allen, J. P. (2008). The attachment system in adolescence. In J. Cassidy & P. R. Shaver (Eds.), *Handbook of attachment: Theory, research, and clinical applications* (pp. 419–435). New York: Guilford Press.

Armistead, L., Klein, K., & Forehand, R. (1995). Parental physical illness and child function-ing. *Clinical Psychology Review, 15*(5), 409–422. doi:10.1016/0272-7358(95)00023-I

Armsden, G. C., & Lewis, F. M. (1993). The child's adaptation to parental medical illness: Theory and clinical implications. *Patient Education and Counseling, 22*(3), 153–165. doi:10.1016/0738-3991(93)90095-E

Barnes, J., Kroll, L., Lee, J., Burke, O., Jones, A., & Stein, A. (2002). Factors predicting communication about the diagnosis of maternal breast cancer to children. *Journal of Psychosomatic Research, 52*(4), 209–214. doi:10.1016/S0022-3999(02)00296-9

Bowlby, J. (1969). *Attachment and loss: Vol. 1: Attachment.* New York: Basic Books.

Bowlby, J. (1973). *Attachment and loss: Vol. 2: Separation.* New York: Basic Books.

Bowlby, J. (1980). *Attachment and loss: Vol. 3: Loss, sadness and depression.* New York: Basic Books.

Clarke, C., & Harrison, D. (2001). The needs of children visiting on adult intensive care units: A review of the literature and recommendations for practice. *Journal of Advanced Nursing, 34*(1), 61–68. doi:10.1046/j.1365-2648.2001.3411733.x

Compas, B. E., Worsham, N. L., Epping, J. E., Grant, R E., Mireauh, G., Howell, D. C., & Malcame, V. L. (1994). When mom or dad has cancer: Markers of psychological dis-tress in cancer patients, spouses and children. *Health Psychology, 13*, 507–515.

Diareme, S., Tsiantis, J., Romer, G., Tsalamanios, E., Anasontzi, S., Paliokosta, E., & Kolaitis, G. (2007). Mental health support for children of parents with somatic illness: A review of the theory and intervention concepts. *Families, Systems, & Health, 25*(1), 98–118. doi:10.1037/1091-7527.25.1.98

Fear, J. M., Champion, J. E., Reeslund, K. L., Forehand, R., Colletti, C., Roberts, L., & Compas, B. E. (2009). Parental depression and interparental conflict: Children and ado-lescents' self-blame and coping responses. *Journal of Family Psychology, 23*(5), 762–766. doi:10.1037/a0016381

Gerson, R., & McGoldrick, M. (1985). *Genograms in family assessment.* New York, NY: WW Norton.

Grauf-Grounds, C. (2007). Increasing social support to manage chronic illness (D. Linville, Ed.). In K. M. Hertlein (Ed.), *The therapist's notebook for family health care: Home-work, handouts, and activities for individuals, couples, and families coping with illness, loss, and disability.* New York: Haworth Press.

Gutiérrez, I. T., Miller, P. J., Rosengren, K. S., & Schein, S. S. (2014). Affective dimensions of death: Children's books, questions, and understandings. *Monographs of the Society for Research in Child Development, 79*(1), 43–61.

Hanington, L., Heron, J., Stein, A., & Ramchandani, P. (2012). Parental depression and child outcomes—is marital conflict the missing link? *Child: Care, Health and Develop-ment, 38*(4), 520–529. doi:10.1111/j.1365-2214.2011.01270.x

Kennedy, V. L., & Lloyd-Williams, M. (2009). Information and communication when a parent has advanced cancer. *Journal of Affective Disorders, 114*(1), 149–155. doi:10.1016/j.jad.2008.06.022

Knutsson, S., & Bergbom, I. (2007). Nurses' and physicians' viewpoints regarding children visiting/not visiting adult ICUs. *Nursing in Critical Care, 12*(2), 64–73. doi:10.1111/j.1478-5153.2007.00209.x

Koopman, H. M., Baars, R. M., Chaplin, J., & Zwinderman, K. H. (2004). Illness through the eyes of the child: the development of children's understanding of the causes of ill-ness. *Patient Education and Counseling, 55*(3), 363–370.

Lewis, F. M., Brandt, P. A., Cochrane, B. B., Griffith, K. A., Grant, M., Haase, J. E., . . . Shands, M. E. (2015). The enhancing connections program: A six-state randomized clinical trial of a cancer parenting program. *Journal of Consulting and Clinical Psychol-ogy, 83*(1), 12–23. doi:10.1037/a0038219

Maybery, D., & Reupert, A. (2010). "Knowledge is power": Educating children about their parent's mental illness. *Social Work in Health Care, 49*(7), 630–646. doi:10.1080/00981380903364791

McDaniel, S. H., Doherty, W. J., & Hepworth, J. (2014). *Medical family therapy and inte-grated care* (2nd ed.). Washington, DC: American Psychological Association.

McGoldrick, M., & Carter, B. (2003). The family life cycle. In F. Walsh (Ed.), *Normal family processes* (3rd ed., pp. 375–398). New York: Guilford Press.

McGoldrick, M., Carter, E. A., & Garcia Preto, N. (2015). The life cycle in its changing context: Individual, family, and social perspectives (E. A. Carter & N. Garcia Preto, Eds.). In M. McGoldrick (Ed.), *The expanding family life cycle: Individual, family, and social perspectives* (5th ed., pp. 1–44). New York: Pearson.

Myant, K. A., & Williams, J. M. (2005). Children's concepts of health and illness: Understanding of contagious illnesses, non-contagious illnesses and injuries. *Journal of Health Psychology, 10*(6), 805–819.

Paliokosta, E., Diareme, S., Kolaitis, G., Tsalamanios, E., Ferentinos, S., Anasontzi, S.,. . . Romer, G. (2009). Breaking bad news: Communication around parental multiple sclerosis with children. *Families, Systems, & Health, 27*(1), 64–76. doi:10.1037/a0015226

Rashi, C., Wittman, T., Tsimicalis, A., & Loiselle, C. G. (2015). Balancing illness and parental demands: Coping with cancer while raising minor children. *Oncology Nursing Forum, 42*(4), 337.

Riggio, H. R. (2004). Parental marital conflict and divorce, parent-child relationships, social support, and relationship anxiety in young adulthood. *Personal Relationships, 11*(1), 99–114. doi:10.1111/j.1475-6811.2004.00073.x

Rolland, J. S. (1984). Toward a psychosocial typology of chronic and life-threatening illness. *Family Systems Medicine, 2,* 245–263.

Rolland, J. S. (1987a). Chronic illness and the life cycle: A conceptual framework. *Family Process, 26*(2), 203–221. doi:10.1111/j.1545-5300.1987.00203.x

Rolland, J. S. (1987b). Family illness paradigms: Evolution and significance. *Family Systems Medicine, 5*(4), 482–503. doi:10.1037/h0089735

Rolland, J. S. (1988). A conceptual model of chronic and life-threatening illness and its impact on the family. In C. Chilman, E. Nunnally, & F. Cox (Eds.), *Chronic illness and disability.* Beverly Hills, CA: Sage Publications.

Rolland, J. S. (1994a). *Families, illness, and disability: An integrative treatment model.* New York: Basic Books.

Rolland, J. S. (1994b). In sickness and in health: The impact of illness on couples' relationships. *Journal of Marital and Family Therapy, 20*(4), 327–347. doi:10.1111/j.1752-0606.1994.tb00125.x

Rolland, J. S. (1999). Parental illness and disability: A family systems framework. *Journal of Family Therapy, 21*(3), 242–266. doi:10.1111/1467-6427.00118

Rolland, J. S. (2005). Cancer and the family: An integrative model. *Cancer, 104*(S11), 2584–2595. doi:10.1002/cncr.21489

Spath, M. L. (2007). Children facing a family member's acute illness: A review of intervention studies. *International Journal of Nursing Studies, 44*(5), 834–844. doi:10.1016/j.ijnurstu.2006.05.008

Sturge-Apple, M. L., Skibo, M. A., & Davies, P. T. (2012). Impact of parental conflict and emotional abuse on children and families. *Partner Abuse, 3*(3), 379–400. doi:10.1891/1946–6560.3.3.379

EVIDENCE-SUPPORTED TREATMENTS FOR PARENTAL ILLNESS

Maureen Davey

The U.S. healthcare system is fragmented, which makes it difficult for patients and their families to navigate it (Blank, 2012) and for providers to coordinate care so they can routinely support families when a parent has a chronic or a life-threatening illness. As we described in the second part of our book, when a parent is diagnosed with an illness, children and adolescents are often reluctant to verbalize their fears and concerns because they do not want to add to their family's burdens (Colletti et al., 2009; Pakenham & Cox, 2012; Worsham et al., 1997). Schools, recreation programs, and other sources of community support are often not aware of the situation or prepared to help children, youth, and their parents at this tough time (Scholten et al., 2013). Many families report struggling to meet the demands of coping with a parental illness, especially single, low-income parents who tend to have fewer resources and less support (Evans & Kim, 2013). Some parents have limited financial resources, minimal respite support, poor communication with the education and healthcare systems, and competing work and family demands (Evans & Kim, 2013). Unfortunately, this can lead to families becoming socially isolated at a time when they most need psychosocial support (Wills & Ainette, 2012).

Throughout this book we have described how different types of parental illnesses can have a profound impact on a child's or adolescent's development, physical and mental health, and well-being (Pakenham & Cox, 2012). We recommend that providers consider using a family-centered approach to care (see Chapter 2) and become familiar with a range of evidence-based and promising (defined as an intervention that is effective but does not yet have enough empirical support to be designated an evidence-based intervention) support services. For example, parent-only, parent–child, child- or adolescent-only, and in-home psychosocial support services should be part of the practice of healthcare providers who have direct contact with families coping with parental illness (Gladstone et al., 2015; Scholten et al., 2013).

There are many different types of support programs and services that are beyond the scope of this chapter to review. In this chapter, we decided to review three promising or evidence-supported prevention programs because they illustrate different modalities (e.g., parent and child sessions, in-home services, and support groups). Most have been evaluated and adapted for diverse populations, and two (Family Talk and Teens and Adults Learning to Communicate) of the three are available online. In this chapter we will review interventions to help families coping with parental: (1) depression (Family Talk: Beardslee et al., 2007), (2) breast cancer (Enhancing Connections Program: Lewis et al., 2006), and

(3) HIV (Teens and Adults Learning to Communicate [TALC]: Rotheram-Borus et al., 2006). We also describe the importance of adapting interventions so they are culturally relevant for diverse populations as well as training to become a culturally competent healthcare provider. Since depression tends to co-occur with experiencing a parental illness, we first review an evidence-based prevention program for families who are coping with parental depression, Beardslee and colleagues' Family Talk Program (Beardslee, 2009; Beardslee et al., 2003, 2007, 2010).

Parental Depression: Family Talk Program

As described in Chapter 3, there are many safe and effective strategies for treating adults diagnosed with depression, including cognitive behavioral therapy, interpersonal therapy, and medication. Yet few researchers and clinical providers report whether the adults treated *are parents* or whether a parent's treatment for depression *affects his or her children* (Beardslee, 2009; Colletti et al., 2009). Some promising preventive intervention strategies for parents coping with depression include treating the parents, providing assistance with parenting, and using a two-generational parent–child clinical approach (e.g., Muñoz et al., 2012). The Institute of Medicine (2009) reported that according to both parent and child reports, parenting programs can be useful and effective (IOM, 2009).

Although promising, we do want to note that this is an area that has some challenges, for example: (1) developing a healthcare system that routinely provides two-generational parent–child treatment for parental depression; (2) responding to the needs of vulnerable populations, especially low income, culturally and ethnically diverse families; (3) responding to families experiencing depression along with other types of family adversity; and (4) developing interventions that build on collaborative and comprehensive service models (Beardslee, 2009; Beardslee et al., 2010). Some additional challenges are the lack of a trained workforce and infrastructure to support the introduction of new prevention programs, not having a payment system to reimburse for these services, and a focus on prevention as opposed to our current focus on treatment in the U.S. healthcare system (Blank, 2012).

Beardslee's Family Talk Program targets the entire family and utilizes a family-centered approach to care (Beardslee, 2009; Focht-Birkerts, & Beardslee, 2000). It is a preventive intervention that was first developed in 1991 in Boston, Massachusetts, for families in which one or both parents had an affective disorder (e.g., depression, bipolar) and were parenting at least one child between 9 and 14 years old (Beardslee et al., 2003; Beardslee, 2009). Beardslee and his colleagues chose this age range because of the increased risk of children developing affective disorders in middle adolescence (Riley et al., 2008). Since the program was first developed 25 ago, it has been used with children between the ages of 4 and 25 in families who have at least one child in early adolescence (Beardslee et al., 2003). This is an evidence-based model that has been evaluated in three separate randomized clinical trials (e.g., Beardslee et al., 2003, 2007) and has been disseminated in diverse practice settings (e.g., primary care, community health centers); it received a 3.5 out of a possible 4.0 in the National Registry of Evidence-Based Programs and Practices for strength of evidence (see http://SAMHSA.org).

Goals of the Family Talk Program

The Family Talk Program is an evidence-based, short-term (6 to 8 sessions), intensive, psychoeducational family-based program with short (1 to 2 weeks) to long-term follow-ups (6 months, 1 year) (Beardslee et al., 2007; Bearsdlee, 2009). Myriad clinical strategies are used to help families cope with parental depression, such as: (1) teaching about depression, (2) assessing all family members and making referrals as needed, (3) helping the family develop a sense of hope about the future, and (4) linking cognitive information (Beck, 1963) to both the individual and family views on affective illness and the life experiences of each family. The main goals are to: (1) inform parents, (2) help parents tap into their resilience and encourage it in their own children, (3) help families plan for the future, (4) help families develop new strategies for talking about the illness, (5) develop new behaviors and attitudes about the illness, and (6) develop new ways to cope that lead to resilience and more open communication between parents and children (Focht-Birkerts & Beardslee, 2000).

Family Talk includes family meetings as well as individual sessions with parents and separate sessions with children (Riley et al., 2008). The number of sessions (6 to 8 sessions) varies depending on the family's needs and the clinical setting. There is a treatment manual available online for diverse provider populations, such as pediatricians, internists, family practitioners, psychologists, psychiatrists, social workers, and family therapists (see web-based training in Family Talk at www.fampod.org/). Completing a training program (online and in-person training, review of cases, reading relevant literature and group discussion, clinical supervision, and evaluation of pilot cases) is recommended by the developers, and this can be tailored to the clinical setting and the population treated. Beardslee and his colleagues also recommend that providers have some prior clinical experience with affective disorders and with children and youth (Beardslee, 2009).

Although the child who is coping with a parent diagnosed with depression is the focus of Family Talk, a primary goal for parents is to more openly communicate about their depression with offspring; the family can then begin to develop a shared understanding and more open communication with each other. Family Talk is built on the premise that the family has untapped resources; the provider's task is to help the family identify and utilize these untapped family resources. Additionally, the provider is considered a facilitator versus an expert who decides what should be done in each session. The main goal of Family Talk is to help family members first better understand the parental depression and each other's views, communicate more openly, and develop a better understanding of parental depression in the context of the cognitive information offered (Beardslee et al., 2003).

Family Talk Modules

There are seven modules in Family Talk that are described next (see Table 13.1 and web-based training in Family Talk at www.fampod.org/).

Session 1

As summarized in Table 13.1 at the conclusion of this section, the first session is an introductory session with the parent(s) that involves: (1) explaining the timing and purpose of the intervention, (2) developing a strong therapeutic alliance with parents, (3) taking a history of the parental depression, (4) identifying the parents' main concerns and defining goals for the family intervention, (5) getting a release of information from the provider treating the parent diagnosed with depression. While taking the history of the parent's depression, questions are first directed toward the ill parent and then providers should ask partners/spouses (when there is a two-parent family) their views about the depression. This facilitates perspective taking and developing a strong therapeutic alliance with both parents.

Session 2

The second session is also with just the parents in order to provide psychoeducation and to ask about their understanding of the family's experiences regarding the parental depression. There are four goals for the second session with parents: (1) continue to ask about the family's experience with depression (affective illness), focusing more on the spouse's/partner's views when there is a two-parent family; (2) present psychoeducational information about the cause, symptoms, and treatment for depression; (3) describe the characteristics of resiliency in children/youth; and (4) help parents consider their children's current levels of functioning and talk about any concerns regarding their adjustment to the parental illness.

Session 3

The third session is a meeting with the children separately, with the parents' permission. There are three main goals for this session: (1) acknowledging the importance of the children's views and developing a strong therapeutic alliance, (2) assessing the children's current levels of functioning and asking questions regarding their understandings of and responses to the parental depression, and (3) helping the children/youth talk more openly to their parents regarding questions or concerns that can be later discussed during the family meeting (fifth session). This latter goal is very important because many children are hesitant to disclose concerns or fears to their parents, but they may be comfortable giving the provider permission to share their concerns and feelings during the family meeting (fifth session). Beardslee (2009) noted that children's responses during the Family Talk sessions will vary depending on their ages, developmental levels, amount of disruption (e.g., parent's irritability, lethargy, lack of responsiveness at home), and tension in the family. It is the provider's job to help children openly express their feelings and help bring these forth in the family meeting so they can have an open and honest discussion with their parents in which any feelings and concerns will be validated by family members.

Session 4

During the fourth session, the provider again meets with parents separately to plan the family meeting (fifth session). There are three main goals for this session: (1) providing parents with an overview of their children's current level of functioning, (2) connecting parents' perceptions of depression with their children's experiences of their affective illness, and (3) asking parents to help plan the family meeting with their children during the fifth session. As the provider and parents plan the family meeting, the provider reviews the psychoeducational information as well as characteristics of resilient children. The provider should also remind parents that they can help their children be resilient by being open to their children's questions during the family meeting without getting defensive or inadvertently shutting down the conversation.

Some parents may decide to talk to their children about a specific incident, for example, when they were hospitalized for severe symptoms of depression; other parents may want to talk in more general terms. It is up to parents to decide the main focus of the family meeting, in consultation with the provider (Beardslee, 2009). Some parents may be reluctant to openly talk to their children because of their feelings of shame as a parent. In these cases, providers may have to take a more active role and ask parents to talk about any fears about having an open discussion with their children and reassure them that coming together as a family to openly share feelings and experiences is a first step toward coping better as a family.

Session 5

The fifth session is when the family meeting occurs with parents and children together. Beardslee describes this session as the most important part of Family Talk (Beardslee et al., 2003, 2007, 2010). The primary goal of the fifth session is to help the family develop a shared understanding of the parental illness and validate parents' *and* children's experiences. The goal is to empower parents to view and present the depression to their children as an illness that may have affected the family but can now be openly discussed and understood. Beardslee (2009) and colleagues suggest there are six principles for a successful family meeting: (1) paying attention to the timing of the meeting, (2) gaining a commitment to the process from the entire family, (3) identifying specific major concerns and addressing them, (4) bringing together and reconstructing the family history, (5) developing a plan to talk more than once, and (6) drawing on all available resources to get through the parental depression together as a family (see Table 13.1). For some families, providers will only need to provide minimal direction; for other families who are reluctant to openly share their experiences and feelings, the provider may have to take a more directive role to facilitate an open discussion between parents and their children.

Session 6

The sixth session is when a 1-week follow-up and check-in with the family occurs. During this session, providers review how family members felt about the family meeting, in particular how the children felt about it, and to help parents consider how to address concerns about their children and questions that their children might still have after the family meeting. This is also when risk factors and how to facilitate resilience in children are reviewed. One of the main goals of this session is to help parents view the intervention as the beginning of an ongoing process. The tasks of the sixth session will reflect what was covered during the previous session, the family meeting (Beardslee, 2009).

Session 7

The seventh session is a long-term follow-up (6 months, 1 year). The purpose of this session is to: (1) encourage the family to use the provider as a resource; (2) review and reinforce what they learned in Family Talk, focusing on the family's unique experiences; and (3) assess the family's functioning since the last intervention session (sixth session). The follow-up typically includes one meeting with parents, but children can be included if parents request it. Additionally, this session reminds parents that the provider is a resource who is available to them in the future (www.fampod.org/). A summary of the seven Family Talk sessions is described in Table 13.1.

We do want to note that not all clinics have the infrastructure and resources to do the sixth and seventh sessions, which require short-term (1 week) and

Table 13.1 Family Talk Sessions

Module	Family Talk Sessions (6 to 8 sessions, 90 minutes to 2 hours each)	Main Tasks
Module 1: Constructing a family history of illness with the parents	Session 1: Parents develop a therapeutic alliance and understand their experiences of recent and past parental depression and share with each other their understandings of the causes and effects of affective disorder. Facilitator begins evaluation of children at home by asking parents questions about the child's past and present.	Introduction, join with parents, parental history, and building consensus. 1. Explain purpose of Family Talk, time frame, and focus of meeting for each session. 2. History taking—ask parent coping with depression about his/her illness, focus on most recent period. 3. Identify family's main concerns and define family goals. 4. Join and establish therapeutic alliance with parents and be empathic and collaborative. 5. Obtain release of information to communicate with provider treating parent coping with depression/affective disorder.
Module 2: Psychoeducation session with parents and understanding the family's story	Session 2: Review experience of first session with parents, ask about non-ill parent's views on spouse's/partner's depression. Cognitive psychoeducation with parents to explore views and beliefs about depression and their child's functioning. Ask about parents' views of child functioning.	Illness experience and cognitive psychoeducation. 1. Ask about non-ill parent's views of spouse's/partner's depression. 2. Cognitive psychoeducation provided to review signs and symptoms of depression, resiliency and characteristics of resilient children and risks, spousal/partner burdens. 3. Ask about parents' views of child functioning focusing on both strengths and areas of concern. 4. Discuss format and preparation for family meeting in the fifth session.

Module 3: Session with the children	*Session 3:* With parents' permission, meet with children alone to explain goal of Family Talk at developmentally appropriate level (ages 4 to 25 but developed for middle adolescents). Assess children's biopsychosocial-spiritual functioning and understanding of parent's depression and understanding of parent's depression and prepare for family meeting in fifth session.	Join with children and explain goal of Family Talk at developmentally appropriate level, assess children across different contexts (e.g., home, school, community), and ask about their concerns. 1. With parents' ideas and guidelines in mind, explain purpose of Family Talk at a conceptual level the children can understand. 2. Assess child functioning in school, outside activities, and peer and family relationships. 3. Assess understanding of parental illness. 4. Ask children about any concerns and questions they want to openly talk about during the family meeting or fifth session.
Module 4: Planning the family meeting with the parents	*Session 4:* Meet with parents alone to plan for family meeting (fifth session) and discuss any questions children wanted to discuss to prepare parents to be open.	Meet with parents to plan family meeting in next session, plan what will be presented, who will present information, and address any concerns or questions children or parents want discussed at family meeting. 1. Review with parents provider's impressions of child functioning based on meeting with children alone. 2. Review with parents any questions children wanted to discuss. 3. Plan format of family meeting: what information to be presented, who will present information, concerns and questions to be discussed at family meeting.
Module 5: Holding the family meeting with parents and children together	*Session 5:* Meeting with parents and children together to facilitate open communication, clarify any different views of parental illness experiences, and improve understanding of each other.	Meeting with parents and children together to facilitate open and nondefensive communication, clarify different views, and facilitate shared family understanding of parental illness experience. 1. Review information about depression and resiliency. 2. Present material as it applies to each family (each family's illness narrative will be unique; need to validate that experience). 3. Facilitate open and nondefensive discussion between parents and children. 4. Help parents and children ask each other questions, encourage sharing individual views, and clarify different perceptions in a nonjudgmental way to promote understanding.

(*Continued*)

Table 13.1 (Continued)

Module	Family Talk Sessions (6 to 8 sessions, 90 minutes to 2 hours each)	Main Tasks
Module 6: One-week follow up and check in with parents and children	Session 6: Review experience of family meeting. Emphasize that Family Talk is the beginning of a process that families can continue. Partner with parents and review goals and what was achieved during Family Talk sessions.	Review and plan for the future. 1. Review family meeting with regard to parents' and children's response to the meeting. 2. Review any information that needs clarification. 3. Emphasize the importance of Family Talk as the beginning of a process that the family can continue. 4. Remind the family of the availability of the facilitator for consultation or referral at any time. 5. Involve parents in review of their goals and accomplishments at time of intervention, focusing on positive aspects and resilience. 6. Review what was not accomplished and address any concerns that were mentioned during the family meeting.
Module 7: Long-term follow-up with parents and with children as needed (6 months, 1 year)	Session 7: Assess family's functioning since last meeting. Address any questions or concerns.	Follow-up meeting with parents reinforcing the tenets of the intervention. 1. Encourage parents to use the provider/facilitator as a resource. 2. Review and reinforce psychoeducation material with a focus on family's illness experience. 3. Assess (formally and informally) family's functioning since last meeting. 4. Ask whether and how participation in the intervention helped the family and what could be improved. 5. Address any questions/concerns.

For more information, see Family Talk: www.fampod.org/

long-term (6 month to 1 year) follow-ups with parents and their children. We do recommend, at minimum, asking how families have been coping since completing the Family Talk program to solidify the changes and to consider doing some booster sessions, as needed (see Chapter 11).

Helping Parents Focus on Their Children

Beardslee and colleagues reported it is important for parents to recognize the impact of the depression on their children/adolescents (Beardslee, 2009). Although it may be difficult for parents to acknowledge that their depression has been stressful for children, worries and fears about causing extreme distress to their children may not be accurate; this is a cognitive distortion that can occur with depression (Beck, 1963). Thus, a more realistic understanding of their children's strengths and problem areas can help to reassure parents. Part of the task for parents in Family Talk is to think about how family experiences with the parental depression have been interpreted by their children. Then the provider can coach the parent(s) to help children openly talk about experiences of the parent's illness, reassuring children they are neither to blame nor responsible for the illness.

Sessions with the parents (see sessions 1, 2, 4 in Table 13.1) explore specific strategies parents can use to help their children cope with the parental illness, such as: (1) clarifying for children what has happened to the parent and to the family; (2) making sure children do not feel responsible for the parent's illness; (3) helping children talk about their own experiences and letting them know they will be not be limited by the parent's depression; (4) identifying supports for children, with particular attention paid to reestablishing those routines that were disrupted by parental illness; (5) discussing current difficulties children are facing; (6) anticipating and seeking treatment for children if needed; (7) identifying the family's resources and adaptive capacities; and (8) emphasizing the need for ongoing open discussions of children's experiences and needs. At the end of these sessions, parents are encouraged to talk about what they hope to accomplish during the family sessions. Then, family sessions are held to present this information to their children.

Help Families Develop Hope for the Future

Family Talk focuses on families' hopes for the future and how they have been affected by parental depression (www.fampod.org/). Providers should ask parents to share thoughts about their children, hopes for the future, and how these hopes have been affected by the illness. Beardslee and colleagues also recommend that providers who are learning Family Talk first examine their own views about raising children (Beardslee et al., 2003; Focht-Birkerts & Beardslee, 2000) to help identify positive and realistic ways to improve children's coping with parental depression.

The principles of Family Talk have also been used in other programs and interventions, including Family Connections (Head Start and Early Head Start teacher training for supporting families facing adversities) and FOCUS (a resiliency program for military families) (Beardslee, 2009; Silverstein et al., 2011). In the U.S., Family Talk has been adapted for single-parent families of color (Podorefsky et al., 2001), single-parent Latino families (Muñoz et al., 2012), and African American families (D'Angelo et al., 2009). Other adaptations have been developed for families in Australia, Costa Rica, Finland, Iceland, the Netherlands, Norway, Rwanda, and Sweden. Treatment manuals are available in English, Dutch, Finnish, German, and Spanish. Materials for Head Start parents and teachers about resilience and depression are available at www.childrenshospital.org/familyconnections. Web-based training in Family Talk and other resources is available at www.fampod.org. Additionally, a tool kit for family service providers is available online at http://store.samhsa.gov/product/SMA14–4878.

Next, we review a promising in-home prevention program that was developed to help mothers coping with breast cancer and their school-age children, the Enhancing Connections Program (Lewis et al., 2006, 2015).

Parental Cancer: Enhancing Connections Program

As described in Chapter 4, an estimated 25% of adults within 2 years of an initial cancer diagnosis are parenting children 18 years of age and younger (ACS, 2015). Parents with cancer tend to understandably be less psychologically available and struggle with communicating, supervising, and being consistent with discipline as they navigate the tough cancer treatment regimen. As parents, they may also display more hostility, irritability, and coerciveness, which are associated with behavioral, social, and self-esteem problems in children (Lewis, 2004; Weaver et al., 2010). Both structured peer support group interventions (Gottlieb & Wachala, 2007) and family interventions (Niemelä et al., 2010; Osborn, 2007) have been developed to provide psychosocial support to children (ages 5 to 18) who are coping with parental cancer, but unfortunately they have rarely informed everyday oncology practice patterns (Deshields et al., 2013).

Peer support group interventions were developed to give children a chance to share feelings about their parent's cancer, improve their understanding and knowledge about the psychosocial aspects of parental cancer, and improve coping strategies (Greening, 1992; Heiney et al., 1996; Taylor-Brown et al., 1993). Two types of children's support group structures have been evaluated: (1) a fixed group for the same child participants with the number of sessions varying from 5 to 10 (Call, 1990; Heiney et al., 1996; Taylor-Brown et al., 1993) and (2) workshops with a changing combination of participants (Bedway & Smith, 1996; Greening, 1992). Both parents and children who have attended support groups have reported improvement in feelings of worry and isolation (Deshields et al., 2013).

Three structured family interventions have been developed and evaluated in the U.S. to help families cope with parental cancer (Davis-Kirsch, Brandt, & Lewis, 2003; Hoke, 1997; Lewis et al., 2006):

1   A short-term psychoeducation intervention (six to eight sessions) was developed to help parents improve family communication and to prevent difficulties among school-age children ages 8 to 16. Only parental outcomes were evaluated and not the impact of the intervention on the children (Hoke, 1997). Parents diagnosed with cancer in this study did improve recognizing their children's concerns and better understood their children's experiences coping with parental cancer (Hoke, 1997).

2   Making the Most of the Moment uses a contextual model of parenthood, coping, and cognitive theory and targets mothers coping with breast cancer (five sessions) to improve communication between mothers coping with breast cancer and their children ages 8 to 12 (Davis-Kirsch, Brandt, & Lewis, 2003). Parental outcomes were evaluated and

suggest mothers improved managing the breast cancer and parenting their children.

3   The Enhancing Connections prevention program, a promising prevention program for mothers coping with breast cancer and their school-age children which is described next (Lewis et al., 2006).

The Enhancing Connections prevention program includes five 1-hour in-home sessions delivered every 2 weeks by a patient educator. Additionally, an interactive booklet about cancer is read by the mother to her child, a mother's workbook is completed by the mother and child together, and a "My Story" child activity book is given to the child to write or draw about his/her mother's diagnosis, treatment, and the child's feelings (Lewis et al., 2006, 2015). This promising prevention program uses a contextual model of parenthood, coping, and cognitive theory to help mothers who are coping with breast cancer improve communication with their school-age children ages 8 to 12 (Lewis et al., 2006, 2015).

Both parental and child outcomes were evaluated in prior studies that included primarily White, well-educated, two-parent, middle class families in six U.S. states (Washington, California, Pennsylvania, Minnesota, Arizona, and Indiana) (Davis-Kirsch et al., 2003; Lewis et al., 2006, 2015) to examine whether the prevention program significantly decreased the mother's depressed mood and anxiety, improved the quality of parenting, and improved the child's behavioral and emotional adjustment to the mother's breast cancer (Davis-Kirsch et al., 2003; Lewis et al., 2006, 2015). A randomized control trial (Lewis et al., 2015) was recently completed to evaluate mothers at 2 and 12 months after the intervention was completed; they were assigned to either the treatment (Enhancing Connections Program) or to a control group (booklet and phone call describing how to communicate and support their child). Findings suggest that compared to the control group, mothers who completed the Enhancing Connections Program had significantly less depressed mood, and 12 months later their children were less depressed compared to the control group of children (Lewis et al., 2015). Yet, Lewis and colleagues (2015) also reported their program did not significantly impact parenting self-efficacy or anxiety among mothers, which should be targeted in future studies.

Conceptual Framework of Enhancing Connections Program

The Enhancing Connections Program was developed 15 years ago from the integration of prior qualitative and quantitative studies with many mothers coping with breast cancer and their school-age children (e.g., Davis-Kirsch et al., 2003; Lewis et al., 2006, 2015) and a developmental-contextual model of parenting, coping theory, and social cognitive theory. Lewis and her colleagues discovered in their earlier descriptive studies that some mothers did not openly prepare or talk to children about their breast cancer diagnosis and treatment, while others disclosed too much information and inadvertently made their children more anxious (Davis-Kirsch et al., 2003; Lewis, 2004). Parents reported they felt ill-prepared to talk to their school-age children and struggled because they had feelings of guilt about how the breast cancer affected their families (Lewis, 2004). Based on these earlier descriptive studies with parents and children, Lewis and her colleagues developed an in-home prevention program to help mothers diagnosed with breast cancer learn how to listen to their school-age children, be more attuned to what their children need to know, and manage their own emotions while talking to children about their cancer diagnosis and treatment (Lewis et al., 2006).

Lewis and her colleagues developed a five-session in-home prevention program, Enhancing Connections, to improve the mother's understanding of her child's perception of and coping with the parent's breast cancer experience and to help the mother support her child's coping. Another goal is to improve the mother's ability to help her school age child by both supporting the child's use of existing coping strategies and broadening the child's use of additional effective coping skills to minimize his/her stress levels. All home-based intervention sessions were developed to improve the mother's parenting skills and self-efficacy in the following areas: (1) managing her own cancer-related anxiety and depressive symptoms so her feelings do not overwhelm the child; (2) helping the mother attentively listen to her child; (3) helping the mother learn how to illicit the child's concerns, feelings, questions, or issues; and (4) helping her improve the child's coping skills and helping the child to better adapt to the parental cancer experience.

Patient educators are trained to provide in-home sessions that include problem-solving skills that are reinforced with homework done by the mother in between the sessions (Lewis et al., 2006). The patient educator provides positive feedback and encouragement in each session.

Enhancing Connections Educational Counseling Sessions for the Mother

Five parts make up the Enhancing Connections Program: (1) five 1-hour in-home patient education sessions every 2 weeks with the mother who is coping with breast cancer, with handouts and assignments; (2) mother–child interactive booklets about cancer; (3) mother's workbook; (4) child's "My Story" booklet; and (5) phone pager number so they can access the treatment team as needed. The five educational in-home counseling sessions were developed and tested for feasibility and acceptability by Lewis and her team in prior studies (Lewis et al., 2006, 2015). The patient educator uses a structured script (see Table 13.2) in each session. Printed handouts are also given to the mother during each home intervention session to highlight the main points of each session.

Session 1
As described in Table 13.2, session 1, anchoring yourself so you can help your child, helps the mother identify what makes her anxious about the breast cancer and avoid transferring her anxieties and concerns to her child. The main goal of the first session is to help the mother identify ways she can take care of herself and help to alleviate stress related to her breast cancer experience. This session helps the mother think of her own experience as distinct from her child's experiences and consider how she can manage her emotions in the presence of her child.

Session 2
Session 2, adding to your listening skills, helps to improve the mother's ability to listen and to not lecture when the child shares his/her thoughts and feelings. The primary goal of this session is to improve the mother's parenting self-efficacy so she can encourage her child to more openly share thoughts and feelings. This session helps the mother more attentively listen and validate her child's thoughts and feelings.

Session 3

Session 3, building on your listening skills, helps the mother identify what she knows about her child's thoughts and feelings. The health educator teaches the mother to use more open-ended questions to, for example, draw out a quiet child and learn about his/her thoughts and feelings regarding the breast cancer experience. This session helps the mother listen to her child share her/his thoughts and feelings while managing her own emotions about the breast cancer experience. The main goal is to teach her how to illicit her child's concerns or feelings in developmentally appropriate and supportive ways, especially the child who is withdrawn and reluctant to talk.

Session 4

Session 4, being a detective of your child's coping, helps the mother observe her child's coping behaviors regarding the breast cancer. Health educators teach the mother how to talk with her child to reinforce or develop adaptive coping skills. This session helps the mother consider observations of her child's coping behavior and how she can improve her child's coping with her breast cancer. This session helps the mother reflect on her child's coping skills and determine what is effective and not effective.

Session 5

Session 5, anchoring skills and celebrating your success, is the final session developed to help the mother transition from the prevention program to ongoing experiences with the breast cancer by helping her reflect on what she learned about herself and her child during the program. The main goal of this final session is to help the mother identify sources of support for maintaining the child's coping skills and the mother–child relationship after the program is completed. This session helps the mother reflect on prior sessions regarding what she learned and did in the program; self-monitoring and self-reflection are parts of parenting self-efficacy. This session also helps the mother identify future resources for ongoing support to maintain both her child's coping and the quality of the mother–child relationship. Table 13.2 summarizes the five in-home sessions.

Mother–Child Interactive Cancer Booklets

The mother–child interactive cancer booklet is a series of three interactive booklets that describe the mother's breast cancer and its treatment. These child-focused booklets describe, in age appropriate ways, breast cancer, surgery for breast cancer, chemotherapy, and radiation therapy. One booklet describes breast cancer and surgical diagnosis and treatment, another describes chemotherapy, and the third booklet describes radiation therapy. Each mother can choose the set of booklets most relevant to her course of treatment, in order to tailor the amount and type of booklet each child is given.

These booklets were designed to be read aloud by the mother and her child together in between sessions; there are specific, open-ended questions in each booklet so the mother and child are guided through an open discussion about the cancer. The built-in questions invite the child to talk about the breast cancer so that the mother can gain a better understanding of her child's views, including any confusion, fears, and misinformation about the cancer; what the child believes caused the cancer; and the child's view of his/her role, if any, in causing the cancer (e.g., the child is not the cause of the parent's breast cancer). Mothers

Table 13.2 Five In-Home Sessions of Enhancing Connections Program

Session Title	Session Structure (five 1-hour in-home sessions every 2 weeks with parents)	Main Tasks
Session 1: Anchoring yourself so you can help your child: Managing your "hot spots"	In-home session with mother diagnosed with breast cancer to help her not over- or underdisclose to her child regarding the breast cancer diagnosis and treatment. Help the mother manage her own emotions and focus on self-care so she can be more attuned to her child's age, development level, and feelings about the breast cancer.	Help mother define her own experience with the breast cancer as separate from her child's experience, manage her own emotions so she does not overwhelm her child, be a more active listener, and focus on her own self-care.
Session 2: Adding to your listening skills	In-home session with mother to help her develop listening skills and better attend to her child's thoughts and feelings in developmentally appropriate ways.	Help the mother to not overdisclose or lecture her child and instead focus on listening to her child's thoughts, concerns, worries, and understanding of the breast cancer experience.
Session 3: Building on your listening skills	In-home session with mother that builds on second session to help her learn how to encourage her child to express concerns or feelings, in particular how to help a more withdrawn child express feelings of worry and concern.	Help mother gain listening skills and learn how to help her child express feelings of worry and concern at developmentally appropriate levels, even when child is reluctant to talk to parent.
Session 4: Being a detective of your child's coping	In-home session with mother to learn how to observe her child's coping behavior related to breast cancer in an open and supportive way.	After mother has learned how to listen and illicit child's concerns, the next step is to help the parent support and reinforce the child's coping behavior to parental cancer experience.
Session 5: Anchoring skills and celebrating your success	Final in-home session to help mother reflect on previous four sessions and on what she learned and to identify future resources and services for ongoing support.	Self-reflective final session helps mothers solidify new skills developed in the program, forging a new view of self as an efficacious parent who can be more attuned, openly communicate in developmentally appropriate ways, and help her child cope with the breast cancer.

For more information, see Lewis, F. M., Casey, S. M., Brandt, P. A., Shands, M. E., & Zahlis, E. H. (2006). The enhancing connections program: Pilot study of a cognitive-behavioral intervention for mothers and children affected by breast cancer. *Psycho-Oncology, 15*(6), 486–497, Table 2.

revealed in prior interview studies they often did not know how to help their children talk about the cancer and did not know how to invite their children to share their thoughts, questions, or feelings about what was happening related to the breast cancer. The scripted, open-ended questions facilitate an open and supportive conversation between the mother and child.

Mother's Workbook

The mother's workbook has session-specific activities and homework assignments that focus on improving the mother's parenting knowledge, skills, and self-efficacy. Behavioral tips are also included in the workbook. For example, one set of behavioral strategies helps her manage interactions with her child in emotionally tough areas that are "hot spots" for the mother, such as addressing the child when she/he asks, "Mom, are you going to die?" All the assignments and the workbook text are designed to involve a feasible amount of time so that the mother is not burdened or asked to do too much.

The Child's "My Story" Booklet

The "My Story" booklet is an interactive booklet developed for the child to write in, draw in, and talk about with the mother in between the five in-home sessions. It provides an opportunity for the mother to positively engage with her child. The content encourages the child to disclose aspects of him-/herself to the mother to help her understand what the child thinks, feels, and does.

Phone Pager Access to Patient Educator

A detailed phone log is kept by the provider to track every phone call from the mothers to the patient educators. The mother is invited in the mother's workbook to call the pager number for support as she completes the homework assignments in between the five in-home sessions or has difficulties talking to her child. Information in the log includes the date and how long the call lasted, the issues discussed by the caller(s), and specific statements made by the patient educators. At this time, information about training and the treatment manuals is not available online, but we encourage providers to contact the developers at the University of Washington (Dr. Lewis) to inquire about future training opportunities in this in-home prevention program for mothers coping with breast cancer and their children.

The third and final program reviewed in this chapter is an evidence-based prevention program (support group format delivered in community settings by two providers or members from the community) developed by Rotheram-Borus and her colleagues first in New York City, and later in Los Angeles and abroad (e.g., Thailand, Zimbabwe, Haiti, South Africa). This is a program for parents (primarily mothers) coping with HIV and their school-age children (ages 11 to 18), Teens and Adults Learning to Communicate (TALC; Rotheram-Borus et al., 2006, 2011).

Parental HIV: Teens and Adults Learning to Communicate (TALC)

Since 1992, the National Institutes of Health (NIH) has funded the development, evaluation, and dissemination of family-focused HIV/AIDS prevention and intervention programs (http://NIH.org). There are now many evidence-based HIV-prevention programs that target the following: (1) parents or children diagnosed with HIV, helping school-age children cope with parental HIV; (2) couples coping with HIV in a partner; and (3) child/adolescent adjustment after parental disclosure of an HIV infection (see a list of evidence-based HIV programs for adults, couples, parents, and children at https://effectiveinterventions.cdc.gov/en/HighImpactPrevention/Interventions.aspx). Additionally, some prevention programs target parenting and healthy communication about sex to prevent HIV in adolescents (e.g., Parents Matter Program by Forehand and colleagues, www.cdcnpin.org/parentsmatter/programDescription.asp).

In this section, we review an evidence-based prevention program called Teens and Parents Learning to Communicate Program (TALC), which has been disseminated and evaluated in community settings with low-income diverse (African American, Latino, Asian) families coping with parental HIV. In 1993, this family-based HIV-prevention program was developed by Rotheram-Borus and her colleagues in New York City, and it was later adapted for families living in Los Angeles (Rotheram-Borus et al., 2012). TALC was developed to help parents (primarily mothers) living with HIV cope with their diagnosis, parent better, and engage in positive and healthy behaviors (Rotheram-Borus et al., 2006). Over the last three decades, Rotheram-Borus and her colleagues have been developing, evaluating, and disseminating TALC and other evidence-based prevention programs both in the U.S. and abroad (e.g., Rotherham-Borus et al., 2011).

TALC was first developed in the early 1990s, before antiretroviral therapies were available. At that time, most parents diagnosed with HIV were expected to die in a year, so sessions originally focused more on helping parents make plans for custody, grief, and loss (Rotheram-Borus et al., 2005). With the development of effective HIV treatment (HAART), as described in Chapter 5, modules and sessions were revised because now parents can expect to live longer and be there to care for their children.

TALC supports parents living with HIV/AIDS and their adolescent children (ages 11–18) using social learning theory (people change their behavior over time in response to opportunities and rewards), cognitive behavioral techniques (positive thoughts and behaviors), and facilitating open communication between parents and their adolescent children (Rotheram-Borus et al., 2006). There are three main areas that TALC targets: (1) parents responding to their serostatus (especially negative emotions of anger, depression, hurt, and hopelessness); (2) parenting while coping with HIV; and (3) post-death adjustment. This family-based program includes two modules (24 sessions, 2 hours/session) designed to be conducted out in the community to improve behavior and mental health outcomes among parents coping with HIV and their adolescent children (Rotheram-Borus et al., 2001, 2011). The first module for a small group of parents (8 sessions) focuses on coping with the HIV illness and disclosure. The second module for parents and their adolescents (16 sessions) focuses on open communication and improving coping with parental HIV (http://chipts.ucla.edu/projects/talc-la/).

The goals of TALC for parents living with HIV are to: (1) improve parenting while ill (e.g., reduce family conflict, improve communication, clarify family roles); (2) reduce mental health symptoms; (3) reduce sexual and drug transmission acts; and (4) increase medical adherence and assertiveness with medical providers (Rotheram-Borus et al., 2003). For adolescents, the goals are to: (1) improve family relationships, (2) reduce mental health symptoms, (3) reduce multiple problem behaviors (e.g., drug use, criminal acts, school problems, teenage pregnancy), and (4) aid school retention (Rotheram-Borus et al., 2006).

TALC has been evaluated in several large randomized control trials with low-income HIV-infected parents in New York City and Los Angeles and their adolescent children (ages 11–18) (e.g., Rotheram-Borus et al., 2012, 2014). Most parents in these studies were low-income African American, Latino, and Asian mothers, and the treatment manual has been culturally adapted for them. Families who completed TALC were compared to families assigned to a control group on mental health and health behaviors, including sexual behavior and substance use. Over 2-, 4-, and 6-year follow-up periods, adolescents assigned to the TALC intervention reported significantly less emotional distress, fewer conduct problems, and fewer family-related stressors and better self-esteem compared to the control group of adolescents (e.g., Rotheram-Borus et al., 2006). Additionally, emotional distress decreased faster among adolescents and parents who completed TALC compared to the families who were assigned to the control group (Rotheram-Borus et al., 2012).

Training TALC Group Facilitators

Two leaders run each group so one leader can focus on the TALC content and the other can focus on group process during sessions. TALC training lasts 2 weeks in order to learn how to implement the program using the treatment manual; the developers also provide ongoing consultations, as needed. Graduate students or members of the community who are positive role models (with no more than a 10th grade education) have been trained in TALC (Rotheram-Borus et al., 2009). The community members are chosen because they are good problem solvers, are parents themselves, and are able to learn basic social learning and cognitive behavioral change techniques. The first week of training focuses on common principles and factors to facilitate behavior change, and the second week is a review of the modules and scripts in the TALC treatment manual. The developers have stated they do not expect exact fidelity to the treatment manual, but at minimum they want group leaders to follow the main principles for each group session (Rotheram-Borus et al., 2009).

Adolescents and Parents Learning to Communicate

Adolescents (ages 11 to 18) are invited to participate in TALC if their parents have already disclosed their HIV-positive status to them. Both parents and adolescents receive a workbook to record their individual goals and accomplishments during the program (Rotheram-Borus et al., 2001, 2003). In order to reduce barriers to treatment, help with transportation, child care, and meals are provided at each of the 24 sessions. Participants who miss a session can complete a makeup. TALC includes a series of small support group sessions out in the community, usually held on Saturdays (a morning 2-hour session and an afternoon 2-hour session for a total of 12 Saturdays or 24 sessions). The scripts for all sessions in the three TALC modules are available online at the Center for HIV Identification, Prevention, and Treatment Services (http://chipts.ucla.edu/projects/talc-la/).

Parents first meet together for eight sessions (module 1) and focus on adapting to their HIV status, maintaining healthy lifestyles, coping with negative feelings regarding the diagnosis, and making decisions about disclosing their status to others. In the next 16 sessions (module 2), parents and their adolescent children are invited to attend sessions; some sessions are with parents and adolescents together and others are sessions with just the parents. The goal of module 2 is to reduce parents' emotional distress, support positive family routines, help their children avoid high-risk behaviors, and make custody plans for their children, as needed. Module 2 was also designed to improve adolescents' coping with the parent's HIV diagnosis and possible death, learn skills to reduce high-risk behaviors (e.g., sexual acts, substance use, and teenage pregnancy), and to reduce emotional distress (Rotheram-Borus et al., 2014). If a parent dies, module 3, which focuses on grief, bereavement, and setting new life goals, can be done with the new caregivers and adolescents. We want to note that it is beyond the scope of this chapter to review module 3 of TALC, but again, all scripts for the three modules can be found online.

TALC Sessions

Module 1: Parents' Curriculum—Taking Care of Myself

The first module includes eight sessions (2 hours/session) with a small group of parents coping with HIV led by two trained members from the community (see Table 13.3 for a summary of the goals for TALC sessions). Here we briefly summarize each of the eight sessions (see http://chipts.ucla.edu/projects/talc-la/ for the 30-page scripts for each session).

Session 1 with Parents

The first parent group session, "Coping With My Illness," has the following six objectives: (1) develop a sense of comfort with the group, (2) establish group rules, (3) learn about coping effectively and helping their children, (4) identify parents' feelings, (5) determine how to help each other, and (6) increase parents' relaxation skills. The goals are first to begin to build group cohesion by openly sharing, developing group rules, and using the tokens to note when they like or appreciate what was shared by others in the group. The second goal is to help parents recognize and accept their feelings, because this is a first step toward better coping with them.

Session 2 with Parents

The second parent group session, "Coping With Fear," has the following five objectives: (1) increase comfort with the group, (2) decrease fears, (3) increase relaxation skills, (4) increase self-esteem, and (5) increase comfort with self-disclosing. In the second session, the goal is to help parents talk about feelings regarding having an HIV diagnosis because it helps them identify and accept their feelings and not feel as isolated. The approach to coping with fear is through repeated exposure (retelling the story and openly sharing feelings of fear) and relaxation.

Session 3 with Parents

The third parent group, "Coping With Anger," has the following six objectives: (1) increase support for each other, (2) identify angry feelings, (3) express angry feelings in a safe environment, (4) increase parents' abilities to tell someone they are angry, (5) increase relaxation skills, and (6) increase self-esteem. Parents living with or recently diagnosed with HIV report feelings of anger, and they often struggle to express the anger in healthy ways, which can lead to somatic complaints or physical illness. In this session, the goal is to help parents identify angry feelings and accept and validate their feelings as understandable. Through role playing, parents practice telling someone else they are angry while being assertive; relaxation techniques are also practiced to help with anger management.

Session 4 with Parents
The fourth parent group, "Coping With Sadness," has the following six objectives: (1) identify feelings of sadness, (2) connect negative thoughts to feelings of sadness, (3) increase ability to alter negative thoughts, (4) increase ability to cope with sadness, (5) use activity schedules to reduce sadness, and (6) increase self-esteem. The goal of this session is to help reduce sadness and depressive symptoms using cognitive behavioral techniques (e.g., describing negative thoughts and irrational beliefs and learning how to counter these thoughts and beliefs). Techniques for reducing sadness are identified, scheduling more pleasant events is practiced, and relaxation and self-esteem exercises are used to increase confidence and to regulate emotions.

Session 5 with Parents
The fifth parent group, "Coping With the Meaning of My Illness," has the following five objectives: (1) clarify life values, (2) develop positive meaning about the illness, (3) determine areas in parents' lives where they can exercise control, (4) project their own future visions; and (5) increase self-esteem. Parents who are coping with a chronic illness tend to search for a meaning in the experience, try to regain mastery over the event, and try to feel good about themselves again despite the illness. These three themes are the focus of this session.

Session 6 with Parents
The sixth parent group, "Coping With Whether to Tell I Have HIV/AIDS," has the following four objectives: (1) learn about concerns regarding disclosure, (2) define disclosure decisions as problems, (3) develop information about the problem, and (4) brainstorm alternative solutions for problems.

Session 7 with Parents
The seventh parent group, "Coping With Telling Others," has the following five objectives: (1) determine advantages and disadvantages of telling others they are living with HIV/AIDS, (2) evaluate different possible actions, (3) learn how to select the best action to take, (4) increase ability to tell someone they are living with HIV/AIDS, and (5) learn about dealing with uncertainty.

Session 8 with Parents
The eighth parent group, "Coping With the Future," has the following three objectives: (1) strengthen vision for a positive future, (2) reduce barriers related to unfinished business, and (3) increase sense of being able to control the future.

Module 2: Parent and Joint Parent and Adolescent Sessions
The second module includes 16 sessions (2 hours/session); eight sessions are with a small group of parents (sessions 1–7, 14) and eight are with a small group of parents along with their adolescent children (sessions 8–13, 15–16); the sessions are again led by two trained providers or members from the community. This module targets both parents and adolescents to help parents consider custody plans, reduce risk, and maintain positive family routines. The parent–adolescent sessions focus on helping youth adapt to their parents' HIV, improving parent–adolescent relationships, and reducing risk behaviors. Here we briefly summarize

the objectives of the 16 sessions (see http://chipts.ucla.edu/projects/talc-la/ for the 30-page script for each session).

Session 1 with Parents
The first session, "What Are My Children's Needs," has the following four objectives: (1) identify needs of their adolescent children, (2) analyze the meaning to an adolescent of possibly losing someone close to them, (3) increase ability to relax, and (4) increase self-esteem. This marks the beginning of the second module of TALC; the first module focused on parents so they could first address their own needs. The second module assumes that after parents have addressed some of their own needs, they can now focus on their adolescent children's needs.

Session 2 with Parents
The second session, "Who Will Take Care of My Children," has the following seven objectives: (1) become more comfortable making plans for someone to take care of their children, (2) identify reasons for and against making a formal custody plan, (3) improve abilities to decide whether it is best for them to keep their children together, (4) identify characteristics they want a guardian to have, (5) identify people who could serve as guardians, (6) evaluate candidates and make a tentative choice of custodian, and (7) identify ways to handle frustration over limited choices.

Session 3 with Parents
The third session, "What Kinds of Arrangements Can I Make?," has the following four objectives: (1) identify feelings about custody planning and effect on self-concept, (2) be able to discriminate between custody options, (3) improve skills in selecting the option that best fits their situation, and (4) increase comfort with custody planning.

Session 4 with Parents
The fourth session, "Preparation Phase: Taking Care of Myself," has the following six objectives: (1) identify feelings of sadness, (2) connect negative thoughts to feelings of sadness, (3) practice ability from module 1 to alter negative thoughts, (4) increase ability to cope with sadness, (5) use activity schedules to reduce sadness, and (6) increase self-esteem. This is a review of what parents learned in the first module as feelings about custody planning may trigger sadness.

Session 5 with Parents
The fifth session, "How Can I Really Listen to My Children?," has the following four objectives: (1) understand how parents talk to their children and whether they listen to their children, (2) distinguish active listening from other kinds of listening, (3) teach parents to listen actively to their children, and (4) overcome obstacles to listening actively.

Session 6 with Parents
The sixth session, "How Can I Tell My Children What I Feel?," has the following four objectives: (1) understand the differences between actively listening and expressing feelings, (2) express feelings directly through *I* statements, (3) increase *I* statements and reduce negative *you* statements, and (4) identify and overcome problems using direct express of feelings.

Session 7 with Parents

The seventh session, "How Should I Deal With Problem Behavior?," has the following five objectives: (1) define adolescent problem behaviors in specific terms, (2) translate negative behaviors into positive behaviors, (3) know the importance of positive reinforcement and how it works, (4) use social reinforcement with adolescents, and (5) become familiar with use of reinforcement programs that include measurement and nonsocial reinforcement.

Session 8 with Parents and Adolescents

The eighth session is the first parent and adolescent group, "How Can We Create a Positive Atmosphere at Home?," and it has the following five objectives: (1) parents and youth will be able to identify positive qualities in each other and express them to each other, (2) parents and youth will become aware of family strengths, (3) parents and youth will have an appreciation for each other's values, (4) parents and youth will be able to give positive messages to each other, and (5) parents and youth will be able to reinforce each other's positive behaviors.

Session 9 with Parents and Adolescents

The ninth session, "How Can We Resolve Conflicts at Home?," has the following six objectives: (1) parents and youth will identify common areas of parent–adolescent conflict, (2) parents and youth will distinguish between parents' and adolescents' responsibilities, (3) parents and youth will identify feelings associated with conflict, (4) parents and youth will review traditional ways of resolving conflict, (5) parents and youth will understand the six-step (no lose, both parent and adolescent win) conflict resolution approach, and, (6) parents and youth will improve their skills in using the six-step conflict resolution approach.

Session 10 with Parents and Adolescents

The 10th session, "How Can We Resolve Conflicts at Home: Part 2?," has the following four objectives: (1) parents and youth will identify obstacles to using the six-step conflict resolution approach and develop ways to overcome them, (2) parents and youth will increase their skills in applying the six-step conflict resolution approach for typical problems at home, (3) parents and youth will set priorities that exist in their family, and (4) parents and youth will apply the six-step method to a low-level conflict between them.

Session 11 with Parents and Adolescents

The 11th session, "How Can We Work Together on Selecting a Custodian?," has the following three objectives: (1) parents will be able to present their custody needs to their teenagers, (2) youth will identify what they want in a custodian, and (3) parents and youth will be able to solve custody issues.

Session 12 with Parents and Adolescents

The 12th session, "How Can We Deal With Drugs and Alcohol?," has the following six objectives: (1) youth and parents will learn how to avoid reinfection from injection drug use; (2) youth will increase their commitments to quit, avoid, or reduce substance use; (3) youth will have an opportunity to learn about disadvantages of substance use from the experiences of others; (4) parents will have an opportunity to make a contributions to their teenagers in substance abuse prevention; (5) youth and parents will increase their dialogue on substance use; and (6) youth and parents will learn how to deal with triggers.

Session 13 with Parents and Adolescents

The 13th session is a parent and adolescent group, "How Do I Prevent Pregnancy and Fatherhood?," has the following four objectives: (1) youth will decrease their motivation to have babies during adolescence, (2) youth and parents will increase their problem-solving skills regarding unwanted pregnancies, (3) youth will decrease attitudes that foster pregnancy, and (4) parents will increase their support of delaying pregnancy until after adolescence.

Session 14 with Parents

The 14th session is a parent-only group, "Where Am I in Making a Custody Plan?," and has the following three objectives: (1) parents who have successfully made custody plans will receive reinforcement for their plans, (2) parents who had difficulty completing their custody plans will receive assistance in overcoming barriers, and (3) parents will receive resources to help them continue to complete their custody plans after the session is over.

Session 15 with Parents and Adolescents

The 15th session is a parent and adolescent group, "How Can Parents Encourage Safer Sex?," and has the following five objectives: (1) youth and parents will increase their knowledge of STDs and HIV, (2) youth and parents will be more able to talk about sex together, (3) youth will be more motivated to seek responsible and mutually caring sexual relationships, (4) parents will be supportive of caring relationships for their teenagers, and (5) youth and parents will increase their skills in problem-solving risky behaviors.

Session 16 with Parents and Adolescents

Finally, the 16th session is a parent and adolescent group, "What Is the Parent's Legacy and the Youth's Goals?," and has the following five objectives: (1) parents will pass on a legacy to their children, (2) parents will feel good about the legacy they have passed onto their children, (3) youth will have a sense of direction for the future and what they want to accomplish, (4) parents will feel secure with their teenagers having a sense of direction, and (5) youth will have an appreciation of the legacy their parents have left them.

Although TALC was designed for two facilitators, the principles can be utilized by individual providers who are working with parents coping with HIV, in particular helping the mother; see Table 13.3 for a summary of the parent and youth topics covered in the 16 sessions.

In addition to these three prevention programs, we also recommend the following resources that summarize other promising interventions to help families cope with parental illness: (1) depression and affective disorder prevention programs (see Muñoz, Beardslee, & Leykin, 2012) and intervention programs (see cognitive behavioral family intervention by Compas, 2014; Compas et al., 2009, 2010, 2011; Riley et al., 2008); (2) parental cancer interventions (see Davis-Kirsch, Brandt, & Lewis, 2003) and oncology support group programs (see Deshields et al., 2013; Gottlieb & Wachala, 2007); (3) HIV (see Parents Matter Program by Forehand et al., 2004; Structural Ecosystems Therapy by Mitrani et al., 2010; CDC list of effective interventions at: https://effectiveinterventions.cdc.gov/en/HighImpactPrevention/Interventions.aspx); and (4) general parental illness interventions (see Scholten et al., 2013).

Table 13.3 TALC Sessions for Parent Module 1 and Parent/Parent–Adolescent Module 2

Session	Parent Topic	Youth Topic
Module 1 with Parents: Coping with Illness, Disclosure		
1 Parents	Coping with illness	
2 Parents	Coping with fear	
3 Parents	Coping with anger	
4 Parents	Coping with sadness	
5 Parents	Coping with meaning of illness	
6 Parents	Deciding to disclose	
7 Parents	Disclosing	
8 Parents	Planning for the future	
Module 2 with Parents and Their Child: Planning a Legacy		
1 Parents	Awareness of my children's needs	Making sense of my parent's illness
2 Parents	Caring for my children	Disclosure of parent with AIDS
3 Parents	Making custody arrangements	Dealing with stigma
4 Parents	Starting my custody plan	Dealing with fear
5 Parents	Listening to my children	Coping with sad feelings
6 Parents	Sharing with my children	Coping with anger
7 Parents	Reducing problem behavior	Acting constructively
8 Parents and Teens	Creating a positive home	Creating a positive home
9 Parents and Teens	Resolving home conflicts (part 1)	Resolving home conflicts (part 1)
10 Parents and Teens	Resolving home conflicts (part 2)	Resolving home conflicts (part 2)
11 Parents and Teens	Selecting a custodian	Selecting a custodian
12 Parents and Teens	Dealing with drugs, alcohol	Dealing with drugs, alcohol
13 Parents and Teens	Preventing pregnancy/ fatherhood	Preventing pregnancy/ fatherhood
14 Parents	Making a custody plan	Make a custody plan
15 Parents and Teens	Encouraging safer sex	Encouraging safer sex
16 Parents and Teens	Setting legacy and the youth's goals	Setting my future goals

Source: Adapted from Rotheram-Borus, M. J., Lee, M. B., Gwadz, M., & Draimin, B. (2001). An intervention for parents with AIDS and their adolescent children. *American Journal of Public Health, 91*(8), 1294–1302.

Cultural Considerations

Differences in attitudes, daily functioning, and levels of distress among different ethnic and racial groups are well-documented, yet most promising and evidence-based psychosocial support services have not been tailored for culturally diverse patient populations (Avis et al., 2008; Bernal et al., 2009). It is important to consider how emotional distress among families coping with parental illness may be exacerbated by poverty, racism, sexism, and homophobia (Castro et al., 2010). Providers should be implementing promising or evidence-based interventions that have been culturally adapted for that population (Flores et al., 2005). In a meta-analysis of 65 studies testing cultural adaptations, Smith et al. (2011) reported that culturally adapted treatments were more effective than nonadapted treatments, and adaptations tailored to specific ethnic/racial groups were more effective than those adapted for a variety of minority groups. Although culturally sensitive approaches to care are recommended across mental health professions (e.g., APA, AAMFT, NASW, AMA), unfortunately there continues to be a gap between cultural competence among providers and culturally adapted interventions designed to help diverse and underserved populations (e.g., ethnic and racial minorities; low-income families; and lesbian, gay, bisexual, and transgender populations) (Whaley & Davis, 2007; Zayas, 2010).

In this chapter, we reviewed two evidence-based interventions (Family Talk for families coping with parental depression: Beardslee, 2009; TALC for families coping with parental HIV: Rotheram-Borus et al., 2003) that were culturally adapted for diverse families, in particular for single parents, as well as for African American and Latino families. The treatment manuals were adapted to tap into resiliency that was culturally relevant and providers were trained to be culturally sensitive (e.g., D'Angelo et al., 2009; Podorefsky et al., 2001; Muñoz et al., 2012). However, most promising and evidence-based interventions have been evaluated with White middle class two-parent families (e.g., Enhancing Connections program) or programs have been evaluated with diverse families but the treatment manual has not been culturally adapted for those families (Bernal et al., 2009).

Cultural adaptation describes the systematic modification of an evidence-based intervention so that it attends to the language, immigration history, culture (race and ethnicity), socioeconomic status, and context of a specific group in order to respect families' cultures and values (Bernal et al., 2009; Griner & Smith, 2006). There are surface-level adaptations that can be helpful, for example, client–therapist racial and/or ethnic matching and providing translated intervention materials to participants. Yet there are also structural adaptations that require a deeper consideration of the role of culture (Zayas, 2010), for example, carefully reviewing how cultural values, traditions, and heritage inform engagement and retention strategies for diverse families coping with parental illness, choosing culturally sensitive assessments (see Chapter 11), and developing treatment manuals that target culturally relevant parenting practices and coping. Finally, it is important to consider how the intervention is disseminated in order to ensure that it is: (1) flexible, (2) efficient, (3) inexpensive, (4) acceptable to diverse populations of patients and their families, and (5) provided in a wide variety of clinical settings, for example, primary care, community health centers, and private practice settings (D'Angelo et al., 2009; Gladstone et al., 2015).

Conclusions

In this chapter, we described one promising (Enhancing Connections: Lewis et al., 2006, 2015) and two evidence-based prevention programs (Family Talk: Beardslee, 2009; TALC: Rotheram-Borus et al., 2001) that use different modalities (e.g., separate parent and child sessions, parent–child sessions, in-home services, and support group formats) to help families cope with parental illness. Interventions and services for families coping with a chronic illness should help parents and children develop adaptive ways to cope with daily life stressors; problem solve; manage feelings of fear, anxiety, and depressive symptoms; and help parents and children have more open communication with each other. Prevention programs should help families decrease emotional distress, have fewer emotional and behavioral problems, and reestablish family routines (Pakenham & Cox, 2012). As described in the second part of our book, illnesses have different courses and produce varying feelings of uncertainty among family members that should also be addressed (e.g., recurrence of cancer or HIV, depressive episode). Finally, we described the importance of providers becoming culturally competent and the cultural adaptation of interventions so that they are relevant for diverse populations of families coping with parental illness.

What Clinicians Need to Know about Evidence-Supported Treatments

1   Consider using a family-centered approach to care and become familiar with a range of culturally sensitive promising and evidence-based support services in different modalities.
2   Beardslee's Family Talk is an evidence-based program that targets the entire family (parents and school-age children) and has been disseminated in diverse practice settings and with diverse populations; it received a 3.5 out of a possible 4.0 in the National Registry of Evidence-Based Programs and Practices for strength of evidence (SAMHSA).
3   Lewis's Enhancing Connections program is a promising in-home prevention program developed to help mothers coping with breast cancer who are parenting school-age children (ages 8 to 12).
4   Rotheram-Borus's Teens and Adults Learning to Communicate (TALC) is an evidence-based group prevention program that has been disseminated to diverse populations of parents coping with HIV and their adolescent children (ages 11 to 18).
5   Cultural adaptation (deep versus surface) describes the systematic modification of an evidence-based intervention so that it attends to the language, immigration history, culture (race and ethnicity), socioeconomic status, and context and so it is culturally relevant and respects families' values.

Professional Readings and Resources

CDC HIV Evidence-Based Prevention Programs: https://effectiveinterventions.cdc.gov/en/HighImpactPrevention/Interventions.aspx
Family Talk: www.fampod.org/
Harpham, W. S. (2011). *When a parent has cancer: A guide to caring for your children.* New York: Harper Collins.
McCue, K., & Bonn, R. (1996). *How to help children through a parent's serious illness.* London: Macmillan.
Parents Matter: www.cdcnpin.org/parentsmatter/programDescription.asp/
Rauch, P. K., & Muriel, A. C. (2006). *Raising an emotionally healthy child when a parent is sick.* New York: McGraw-Hill.
TALC scripts for sessions: http://chipts.ucla.edu/projects/talc-la/

References

American Cancer Society. (2015). *Cancer facts & figures 2015*. Atlanta: American Cancer Society.

Avis, M., Elkan, R., Patel, S., Walker, B. A., Ankti, N., & Bell, C. (2008). Ethnicity and participation in cancer self-help groups. *Psycho-Oncology*, *17*(9), 940–947.

Beardslee, W. R. (2009). *Out of the darkened room: When a parent is depressed: Protecting the children and strengthening the family*. Boston: Little, Brown.

Beardslee, W. R., Ayoub, C., Avery, M. W., Watts, C. L., & O'Carroll, K. L. (2010). Family Connections: An approach for strengthening early care systems in facing depression and adversity. *American Journal of Orthopsychiatry*, *80*(4), 482–495.

Beardslee, W. R., Gladstone, T. R. G., Wright, E. J., & Cooper, A. B. (2003). A family-based approach to the prevention of depressive symptoms in children at risk: Evidence of parental and child change. *Pediatrics*, *112*(2), e119–e131. doi:10.1542/peds.112.2.e119

Beardslee, W. R., Wright, E. J., Gladstone, T. R., & Forbes, P. (2007). Long-term effects from a randomized trial of two public health preventive interventions for parental depression. *Journal of Family Psychology*, *21*(4), 703.

Beck, A. T. (1963). Thinking about depression: idiosyncratic content and cognitive distortions. *Archives of General Psychiatry*, *9*, 324–333.

Bedway, A., & Smith, H. (1996). "For kids only": Development of a program for children from families with a cancer patient. *Journal of Psychosocial Oncology*, *14*(4), 19–28. doi:10.1300/J077v14n04_02

Bernal, G., Jiménez-Chafey, M. I., & Domenech Rodríguez, M. M. (2009). Cultural adaptation of treatments: A resource for considering culture in evidence-based practice. *Professional Psychology: Research and Practice*, *40*(4), 361.

Blank, R. H. (2012). Transformation of the US Healthcare System: Why is change so difficult? *Current Sociology*, *60*(4), 415–426.

Call, D. A. (1990). School-based groups: A valuable support for children of cancer patients. *Journal of Psychosocial Oncology*, *8*(1), 97–118. doi:10.1300/J077v08n01_07

Castro, F. G., Barrera, M., Jr., & Steiker, L. K. H. (2010). Issues and challenges in the design of culturally adapted evidence-based interventions. *Annual Review of Clinical Psychology*, *6*, 213.

Colletti, C. J., Forehand, R., Garai, E., Rakow, A., McKee, L., Fear, J. M., & Compas, B. E. (2009). Parent depression and child anxiety: An overview of the literature with clinical implications. *Child & Youth Care Forum*, *38*(3), pp. 151–160.

Compas, B. E. (2014). Parent and adolescent reports of parenting when a parent has a history of depression: Associations with observations of parenting. *Journal of Abnormal Child Psychology*, *42*(2), 173–183.

Compas, B. E., Champion, J. E., Forehand, R., Cole, D. A., Reeslund, K. L., Fear, J., . . . Roberts, L. (2010). Coping and parenting: Mediators of 12-month outcomes of a family group cognitive–behavioral preventive intervention with families of depressed parents. *Journal of Consulting and Clinical Psychology*, *78*(5), 623.

Compas, B. E., Forehand, R., Keller, G., Champion, J. E., Rakow, A., Reeslund, K. L., . . . Cole, D. A. (2009). Randomized controlled trial of a family cognitive-behavioral preventive intervention for children of depressed parents. *Journal of Consulting and Clinical Psychology*, *77*(6), 1007.

Compas, B. E., Forehand, R., Thigpen, J. C., Keller, G., Hardcastle, E. J., Cole, D. A., . . . Roberts, L. (2011). Family group cognitive–behavioral preventive intervention for families of depressed parents: 18-and 24-month outcomes. *Journal of Consulting and Clinical Psychology*, *79*(4), 488.

D'Angelo, E. J., Llerena-Quin, R., Shapiro, R., Colon, F., Rodriguez, P., Gallagher, K., & Beardslee, W. R. (2009). Adaptation of the preventive intervention program for depression for use with predominantly low-income Latino families. *Family Process*, *48*(2), 269–291.

Davis-Kirsch, S. E., Brandt, P. A., & Lewis, F. M. (2003). Making the most of the moment: When a child's mother has breast cancer. *Cancer Nursing*, *26*(1), 47–54. doi:10.1097/00002820-200302000-00007

Deshields, T., Zebrack, B., & Kennedy, V. (2013). The state of psychosocial services in cancer care in the United States. *Psycho-Oncology*, *22*(3), 699–703.

Evans, G. W., & Kim, P. (2013). Childhood poverty, chronic stress, self-regulation, and coping. *Child Development Perspectives*, *7*(1), 43–48.

Flores, G., Olson, L., & Tomany-Korman, S. C. (2005). Racial and ethnic disparities in early childhood health and health care. *Pediatrics, 115*(2), e183–e193.

Focht-Birkerts, L., & Beardslee, W. R. (2000). A child's experience of parental depression: Encouraging relational resilience in families with affective illness. *Family Process, 39*(4), 417–434.

Forehand, R., Miller, K. S., Armistead, L., Kotchick, B. A., & Long, N. (2004). The Parents Matter! program: An introduction. *Journal of Child and Family Studies, 13*(1), 1–3.

Gladstone, T. R., Beardslee, W. R., & Diehl, A. (2015). Interventions for families when a parent has depression. In A. Reupert, D. Mayberry, J. Nicholson, M. Gopfert, & M. V. Seeman (Eds.), *Parental psychiatric disorder: Distressed parents and their families* (3rd ed. pp. 117–126). Cambridge, UK: Cambridge University Press.

Gottlieb, B. H., & Wachala, E. D. (2007). Cancer support groups: A critical review of empirical studies. *Psycho-Oncology, 16*(5), 379–400.

Greening, K. (1992). The "bear essentials" program: Helping young children and their families cope when a parent has cancer. *Journal of Psychosocial Oncology, 10*(1), 47–61. doi:10.1300/J077v10n01_05

Griner, D., & Smith, T. B. (2006). Culturally adapted mental health interventions: A meta-analytic review. *Psychotherapy: Theory, Research, Practice, and Training, 43*, 531–548.

Heiney, S. P., Bryant, L. H., Walker, S., Parrish, R. S., Provenzano, F. J., & Kelly, K. E. (1996). Impact of parental anxiety on child emotional adjustment when a parent has cancer. *Oncology Nursing Forum, 24*(4), 655–661.

Hoke, L. A. (1997). A short-term psychoeducational intervention for families with parental cancer. *Harvard Review Psychiatry, 5*(2), 99–103. doi:10.3109/10673229709034734

Institute of Medicine. (2009). *Reducing risks for mental disorders.* Washington, DC: National Academies Press US.

Lewis, F. (2004). Family-focused oncology nursing research. *Oncology Nursing Forum, 31*(2), 288–292.

Lewis, F. M., Brandt, P., Cochrane, B. B., Griffith, K. A., Grant, M., Haase, J. E., Houldin, A. D., . . . Shands, M. E. (2015). The enhancing connections program: A six-state randomized clinical trial of a cancer parenting program. *Journal of Consulting and Clinical Psychology, 83*, 12–23.

Lewis, F. M., Casey, S. M., Brandt, P. A., Shands, M. E., & Zahlis, E. H. (2006). The enhancing connections program: Pilot study of a cognitive-behavioral intervention for mothers and children affected by breast cancer. *Psycho-Oncology, 15*(6), 486–497.

Mitrani, V. B., McCabe, B. E., Robinson, C., Weiss-Laxer, N. S., & Feaster, D. J. (2010). Structural ecosystems therapy for recovering HIV-positive women: Child, mother, and parenting outcomes. *Journal of Family Psychology, 24*(6), 746.

Muñoz, R. F., Beardslee, W. R., & Leykin, Y. (2012). Major depression can be prevented. *American Psychologist, 67*(4), 285.

Niemelä, M., Hakko, H., & Räsänen, S. (2010). A systematic narrative review of the studies on structured child-centred interventions for families with a parent with cancer. *Psycho-Oncology, 19*(5), 451–461.

Osborn, T. (2007). The psychosocial impact of parental cancer on children and adolescents: A systematic review. *Psycho-Oncology, 16*(2), 101–126.

Pakenham, K. I., & Cox, S. (2012). Test of a model of the effects of parental illness on youth and family functioning. *Health Psychology, 31*(5), 580.

Podorefsky, D., McDonald-Dowdell, M., & Beardslee, W. (2001). Adaptation of preventive interventions for a low-income, culturally diverse community. *Journal of the American Academy of Child and Adolescent Psychiatry, 40*(8), 879–886.

Riley, A. W., Valdez, C. R., Barrueco, S., Mills, C., Beardslee, W., Sandler, I., & Rawal, P. (2008). Development of a family-based program to reduce risk and promote resilience among families affected by maternal depression: Theoretical basis and program description. *Clinical Child and Family Psychology Review, 11*(1–2), 12–29.

Rotheram-Borus, M. J., Flannery, D., Rice, E., & Lester, P. (2005). Families living with HIV. *Aids Care, 17*(8), 978–987.

Rotheram-Borus, M. J., Lee, M. B., Gwadz, M., & Draimin, B. (2001). An intervention for parents with AIDS and their adolescent children. *American Journal of Public Health, 91*(8), 1294–1302.

Rotheram-Borus, M. J., Lee, M., Leonard, N., Lin, Y. Y., Franzke, L., Turner, E., . . . Gwadz, M. (2003). Four-year behavioral outcomes of an intervention for parents living with HIV and their adolescent children. *Aids, 17*(8), 1217–1225.

Rotheram-Borus, M. J., Lester, P., Song, J., Lin, Y. Y., Leonard, N. R., Beckwith, L., . . . Lord, L. (2006). Intergenerational benefits of family-based HIV interventions. *Journal of Consulting and Clinical Psychology, 74*(3), 622.

Rotheram-Borus, M. J., Rice, E., Comulada, W. S., Best, K., & Li, L. (2012). Comparisons of HIV-affected and non-HIV-affected families over time. *Vulnerable Children and Youth Studies, 7*(4), 299–314.

Rotheram-Borus, M. J., Stein, J. A., & Lester, P. (2006). Adolescent adjustment over six years in HIV-affected families. *Journal of Adolescent Health, 39*(2), 174–182.

Rotheram-Borus, M. J., Stein, J. A., & Rice, E. (2014). Intervening on conflict, parental bonds, and sexual risk acts among adolescent children of mothers living with HIV. *PLoS ONE, 9*(7), e101874. doi:10.1371/journal.pone

Rotheram-Borus, M. J., Swendeman, D., Flannery, D., Rice, E., Adamson, D. M., & Ingram, B. (2009). Common factors in effective HIV prevention programs. *AIDS and Behavior, 13*(3), 399–408.

Rotheram-Borus, M. J., Swendeman, D., Lee, S. J., Li, L., Amani, B., & Nartey, M. (2011). Interventions for families affected by HIV. *Translational Behavioral Medicine, 1*(2), 313–326.

Scholten, L., Willemen, A. M., Last, B. F., Maurice-Stam, H., van Dijk, E. M., Ensink, E., . . . Grootenhuis, M. A. (2013). Efficacy of psychosocial group intervention for children with chronic illness and their parents. *Pediatrics, 131*(4), e1196–e1203.

Silverstein, M., Feinberg, E., Cabral, H., Sauder, S., Egbert, L., Schainker, E., . . . Beardslee, W. (2011). Problem-solving education to prevent depression among low-income mothers of preterm infants: A randomized controlled pilot trial. *Archives of Women's Mental Health, 14*(4), 317–324.

Smith, T., Domenech Rodríguez, M. M., & Bernal, G. (2011). Culture. *Journal of Clinical Psychology, 67*, 166–175.

Taylor-Brown, J., Acheson, A., Farber, J. (1993). Kids can cope: A group intervention for children whose parents have cancer. *Journal of Psychosocial Oncology, 11*(41), 41–44. doi:10.1300/J077V11N01_03

Weaver, K. E., Rowland, J. H., Alfano, C. M., & McNeel, T. S. (2010). Parental cancer and the family. *Cancer, 116*(18), 4395–4401.

Whaley, A. L., & Davis, K. E. (2007). Cultural competence and evidence-based practice in mental health services. *American Psychologist, 62*, 563–574.

Wills, T. A., & Ainette, M. G. (2012). Social Networks and Social Support. *Handbook of health psychology* (p. 465) New York: Psychology Press.

Worsham, N. L., Compas, B. E., & Ey, S. (1997). Children's coping with parental illness. In *Handbook of Children's Coping* (pp. 195–213). New York: Springer.

Zayas, L. H. (2010). Seeking models and methods for cultural adaptation of interventions: Commentary on the special section. *Cognitive and Behavioral Practice, 17*, 198–202.

CHAPTER 14

PARENTAL DEATH AND GRIEF INTERVENTIONS

Karni Kissil

Introduction

In the U.S., approximately 2 million children will lose a parent before the age of 18, and 1 in 20 will lose a parent before graduating from high school (The High Mark Caring Place, 2010; Social Security Administration, 2007). Although the loss of a parent can be devastating at any age, it is among the most stressful life events that a young or school-age child will experience (Dowdney, 2000; Harrison & Harrington, 2001; Torbic, 2011). Children grieve differently than adults, and often their pain is not recognized or understood by adults. Some develop unhealthy patterns of expressing grief, for example, physical complications, depression, antisocial behavior, failure in school, or involvement with the judicial system (National Hospice and Palliative Care Organization, 2012). A parent's death is associated with an increased risk for developing a wide range of problems in childhood and in adulthood, including: (1) anxiety, (2) depression, (3) functional impairment, (4) delinquent behaviors, (5) self-injury, (6) suicidality, (7) health problems, and (8) relationship problems (Cerel, Fristad, Verducci, Weller, & Weller, 2006; Draper & Hancock, 2011; Grenklo, Kreicbergs, Valdimarsdóttir, Nyberg, Steineck, & Fürst, 2013; Jakobsen, & Christiansen, 2011; Kaplow, Layne, Pynoos, Cohen, & Lieberman, 2012; Melhem, Porta, Shamseddeen, Payne, & Brent, 2011; Melhem, Walker, Moritz, & Brent, 2008).

Various factors can affect the process of grieving among children, for example, whether it was the mother or the father who died, if it is a single-parent or two-parent home, gender and age of the child at the time of the parent's death, and whether the death was sudden or drawn out because of a chronic illness (Hope & Hodge, 2006; Howarth, 2011). Parental death can be a traumatic event for children because of the loss of a parent and subsequent changes in multiple domains of children's lives, for example, relocation to a new house, neighborhood, and school; living with extended family or kin if it was a single parent; financial changes; and changes in daily routines and responsibilities (Howarth, 2011; Wolchik, Ma, Tein, Sandler, & Ayers, 2008; Werner-Lin, Biank, & Rubenstein, 2010). The purpose of this book is to help providers support children and families who are coping with parental illness. Sadly, for some families, this will lead to the death of the ill parent. Providers working with families coping with parental illness have an important role and can help families work through anticipatory grief before the loss and mourning after the death of a parent. In this chapter, first the process of anticipatory grief is described (Hibberd, Wamser, & Vandenberg, 2011), which refers to when families are caring for a terminally ill parent.

Anticipatory Grief

For many children and youth, the grieving process begins before the death of a parent (Torbic, 2011). For some it will begin when they first hear about the terminal diagnosis. For others it will start when they first see significant physical and emotional changes in their ill parent. For example, a son may begin to grieve when his father cannot coach his baseball games anymore. This type of grief is called *anticipatory grief*. Anticipatory grief describes grieving that occurs *before* the actual death (Coombs, 2010); it describes the emotional, psychological, and interpersonal processes of confronting the imminent loss of a terminally ill loved one (Hibberd et al., 2011) and is similar to the process of mourning, but occurs in anticipation of the death.

When an individual knows someone is going to die or fears that a loved one may die, it can lead to anticipatory grief that is expressed as feelings, thoughts, and physical symptoms. Some common thoughts among children anticipating the death of a parent are: (1) worry or preoccupation with the parent who is dying and his/her needs or well-being, (2) what will happen to the child when the parent dies, especially in single-parent families, and (3) whether the illness is the child's fault and feeling guilty because the child has done or said something that upset the parent who is dying. Many children experience feelings of sadness, fear, anger, isolation, or loneliness about the imminent loss of a parent and anxiety about when the death will actually occur. Noteworthy, some children will express emotional distress as physical symptoms, for example: (1) headaches, (2) changes in sleeping or eating habits, (3) nausea and stomach pains, (4) muscle aches or tightness in the chest, and (5) difficulty focusing or concentrating in school (Lyles, 2006).

Although anticipatory grief includes stages, every family is unique and will experience anticipatory grief, death, and loss in their own way (Johansson & Grimby, 2012). Anticipatory grief can include the following phases, although not necessarily in this order (Johansson & Grimby, 2012):

- *Phase I.* In this stage, an individual (parent) realizes that death is the outcome of an illness; there is no expectation for a cure. Sadness and depression are often associated with this first stage of grief.
- *Phase II.* The next phase of anticipatory grief is concern for the dying person. Family members (children) may regret arguments or conflicts with the dying parent. For the dying parent, concern is often increased for loved ones, especially children.
- *Phase III.* In this phase, the actual death may be "rehearsed." The physical process of death and what could happen after death are concerns. Funeral arrangements and saying good-bye to loved ones may occur as a result of anticipatory grieving.
- *Phase IV.* During this last phase, loved ones (children) often imagine what their lives are going to be like without the person (parent) who is dying. Dying parents think about the missed rites of passages, for example, proms, weddings, and birthdays. Children wonder what it will be like to lose their parent and who will care for them. The parent who is dying may think about life after death and try to imagine what it will be like for his or her loved ones (children) to live without him or her.

The concept of anticipatory grief has generated some controversy regarding whether it exists, how it is different from post-loss grief, and whether it facilitates or hinders the grieving process after the death of a loved one (Fulton, 2003). Anticipatory grief is different from post-loss grief, because the death is not in the past but is expected in the future; the person being grieved is still alive, albeit terminally ill (Hibberd et al., 2011). Findings have been mixed regarding the effects of anticipatory grief on post-loss mourning (Rando, 2000). Some studies with adults reported possible benefits of forewarning and the opportunity to engage in anticipatory grief; mourners can cherish the time remaining with the dying loved one, help with care, and gradually prepare for navigating life without this person. Other studies suggest anticipatory grief does not significantly decrease post-loss grief (Hibberd et al., 2011; Simon, 2008).

Children may not experience direct benefits from anticipatory grief. For example, younger children, because of their developmental stage, lack the ability to plan and reorganize their lives in preparation for the loss of a parent. They typically do not have opportunities to deepen relationships with their ill parents through caregiving (Hibberd et al., 2011). Additionally, children could be negatively impacted by prolonged exposure to the dying parent, such as witnessing the physical and/or cognitive decline, observing physical manifestations of the illness, and witnessing the anxiety and fear in their dying parent and the caregivers (Saldinger, Cain, & Porterfield, 2003).

Children in families with a terminally ill parent can be negatively affected by the unavailability of adult caregivers (healthy parent or caregiver in single-parent families). Caregivers in the family are often overwhelmed with taking care of the ill parent, along with financial, emotional, and interpersonal issues. Consequently, they may have fewer practical and emotional resources and time to attend to children (Hibberd et al., 2011). Adolescents may be particularly affected because they are often asked to assume adult tasks within the family, for example, taking responsibility for younger siblings and maintaining daily family routines, when the ill parent is too sick or is hospitalized, especially in single-parent families (Rotheram-Borus, Weiss, Alber, & Lester, 2005).

How Children at Different Ages Grieve the Loss of a Parent

The treatment of childhood grief is challenging for both providers and family members because the grieving process is different for children compared to adults. Children mourn differently because their cognitive abilities to grasp and cope with loss are still developing. Depending on the child's age, he/she may not fully understand the concept of death or the finality and permanence of the loss (Howarth, 2011). Among very young children (preschool age and younger), death is perceived as temporary and reversible. Younger children often have magical thinking, believing they can bring back their deceased parent (Tobric, 2011). Due to their emerging verbal abilities, grief reactions in young children can be manifested through behavior, play, and nonverbal expressions (Bugge, Darbyshire, Røkholt, Haugstvedt, & Helseth, 2014). Younger children may also experience somatic symptoms such as headaches, fatigue, stomach aches, difficulty sleeping, restlessness, and loss of appetite (Sood, Razdan, Weller, & Weller, 2006). They could also fear they or others in the family will also become ill or die, or they feel alone and experience fear of separation from their caregivers (Bugge et al., 2014; Dowdney, 2000; Koehler, 2010; National Cancer Institute, 2014). Additionally, young children who are grieving the loss of a parent might regress to more infantile behaviors, such as bed-wetting.

School-age children (6–12 years old) are beginning to understand that death is not reversible and are often curious about the biological process of dying (NCI, 2014). Children at this age are often anxious and fearful about dying and may blame themselves for the death of their parent (Torbic, 2011). Among older children in this age group (age 9 and older), peer relationships are becoming important and they want to fit in. The death of a parent can interfere with the development of their self-esteem if it makes them feel different from their friends, leading to feelings of isolation (Torbic, 2011).

Young adolescents (ages 12–14) experience pubertal physiological changes that can cause significant mood swings and lead to displays of intense emotions as their hormones surge (Robin & Omar, 2014). Egocentric behavior is common; adolescents may begin to withdraw emotionally from the family to establish their independence. Thus, their reactions to the death of a parent may seem self-centered if they are more worried about the impact of the death for them versus other family members (Serwint, 2011). Younger adolescents understand that death is final, yet their primary coping strategy is to protect themselves from emotional pain using denial and limited exposure to painful emotions (thus the intermittent nature of their grief) (Christ, Siegel, & Christ, 2002). Peer relationships are a major priority, which is why young adolescents tend to hide their feelings to fit in with their peers; they often prefer to grieve privately (Christ et al., 2002; Torbic, 2011).

Older adolescents (15–17 years old) use formal operations more consistently, which allows them to integrate past, present, and future. Thus, they are able to understand the enduring consequences of death, acknowledge it more like adults, and confront it before it occurs, understanding the future consequences (Christ et al., 2002; Robin & Omar, 2014; Torbic, 2011). Older adolescents' (age 15–17) grieving processes can resemble adults, with experiences of intense sadness and emotional pain, not wanting to spend time with friends and family, and disturbances in sleep patterns and appetite (Cohen & Mannarino, 2010; Robin & Omar, 2014). Peer support at this age continues to be important as adolescents develop more intimate supportive relationships with peers. These relationships can sometimes facilitate working through the pain. Yet, sometimes peers do not understand the bereaved adolescent's feelings of grief or could even reject him/her (protecting themselves from intense and painful emotions), which can be devastating for the bereaved adolescent (Robin & Omar, 2014).

An important difference between how adults grieve compared to young children and adolescents is the intermittent nature of children's grief. Like adults, children and youth experience "pangs" of grief, which are sudden intense waves of painful feelings of loss. Yet, unlike adults, these feelings tend to appear more intermittently (Christ et al., 2002; Torbic, 2011). This is because of children's developing cognitive abilities and difficulty tolerating intense emotions for long periods of time (Christ et al., 2002). Consequently, it is sometimes difficult for parents and other family members who are also grieving to notice, understand, and respond appropriately to children's intermittent expressions of grief (Bugge et al., 2014; Christ & Christ, 2006; Mannarino & Cohen, 2011; NCI, 2014). Thus, after the loss of a parent, children may actively engage in peer activities (e.g., sports, school clubs) and laugh, which can lead to confusion for adults who could mistakenly believe their children have resolved feelings of grief and have moved on (Dowdney, 2011; Torbic, 2011).

The grieving process for children has been conceptualized as a series of tasks that need to be traversed. In his seminal grief model, Worden (1996) identified the following four tasks: (1) accepting the reality of the loss, (2) fully experiencing the emotional pain resulting from the loss, (3) adjusting to one's environment without the deceased parent, and (4) finding meaning in the parent's death and maintaining a relationship with the parent that supports growth. Scholars have suggested that because the cognitive and emotional abilities of children are not fully developed, they cannot fully resolve the four mourning tasks (Biank & Werner-Lin, 2011; Christ, 2000; Christ, Siegel, & Christ, 2002). For example, the task of accepting the reality of the loss is often challenging for younger children who have not yet mastered the concept of permanence (Davies, 2004). As a result, children may reexperience the loss as they grow older and achieve developmental milestones (e.g., high school graduation, marriage, birth of first child) (Biank & Werner-Lin, 2011; National Cancer Institute, 2014).

Healthy mourning for children tends to occur cyclically and intermittently (Biank & Werner-Lin, 2011; NCI, 2014; Torbic, 2011). As a child develops and matures, she/he will reinterpret the parent's life and death and the relationship with the parent using more mature cognitive and emotional skills. As a result, grief is not resolved but instead periodically renegotiated until adulthood (Biank & Werner-Lin, 2011; Worden, 1996). Consequently, revisiting the loss of a parent helps children more fully understand their parent's death and process their own loss at each development stage or milestone (e.g., attending prom, first relationship, graduating from high school, attending college, marriage, birth of a child). Table 14.1 shows the different ages of children and a summary of how they understand death and express grief.

Complicated Grief

There has been growing recognition of a syndrome of disturbed grief, referred to as *complicated grief* or *prolonged grief disorder* (PGD). While many will recover 12 months after a loss without an intervention (Melhem et al., 2011; Robin & Omar, 2014), 10–15% struggle for months or even years after a loss (Mancini, Griffin, & Bonanno, 2012; Neimeyer & Currier, 2009). There is some debate about the precise constellation of symptoms in prolonged grief (Mancini et al., 2012), but most identify the following symptoms: (1) intrusive and troubling thoughts about the deceased person, (2) intense and persistent yearning for the deceased, (3) numbness and emptiness, (4) difficulty accepting the loss, and (5) hopelessness and purposelessness (Lichtenthal, Cruess, & Prigerson, 2004; Ng, 2005; Prigerson et al., 2009; Shear et al., 2011). Although more often studied in adults, clinical symptoms have also been observed in children and adolescents (Spuij, Dekovic, & Boelen, 2015). Recent studies reported children and adolescents can develop PGD symptoms that can be reliably assessed and are distinct from normal grief, depression, anxiety, and PTSD (Brown & Goodman, 2005; Dillen, Fontaine, & Verhofstadt-Denève, 2008; Spuij, Prinzie, et al., 2012; Spuij, Reitze, et al., 2012).

Melhem and his colleagues (Melhem, Day, Shear, Day, Reynolds, & Brent, 2004) conducted a study assessing grief symptoms in 146 youth exposed to peer suicide. A factor analysis of their reported symptoms identified two dimensions of grief: (1) complicated grief (e.g., finding it painful to recall memories of the deceased, preoccupation with the deceased) and (2) normal grief (e.g., missing the deceased). In this same study (Melhem et al., 2004), complicated grief was

Table 14.1 Grief and Developmental Stages

Age	Understanding of Death	Expressions of Grief
Infancy to 2 years	Not yet able to understand death	Quietness, crankiness, decreased activity, poor sleep, and weight loss
2–6 years	Death is like sleeping Dead person continues to live and function in some ways Death is temporary and not final Dead person can come back to life	Asks many questions (How does she go to the bathroom? How does she eat?) Problems in eating, sleeping, and bladder and bowel control (regression) Fear of abandonment Tantrums Magical thinking (Did I think something or do something that caused the death, like when I said I hate you and wished you would die?)
6–9 years	Death is conceptualized as a person or a spirit (skeleton, ghost, bogeyman) Death is final and frightening Death happens to others; it will not happen to *me*	Curious about death Asks specific questions May have exaggerated fears about school May have aggressive behaviors (especially boys) Some concerns about imaginary illnesses May feel abandoned
9 and older	Everyone will die Death is final and cannot be changed Even I will die someday	Heightened emotions, guilt, anger, shame Increased anxiety over own death Mood swings Fear of rejection, not wanting to be different from peers Changes in eating habits, sleeping problems Regressive behaviors (loss of interest in outside activities) Impulsive behaviors Feels guilt about being alive (especially related to death of a brother, sister, or peer)

Source: Reprinted with permission from the National Cancer Institute.

associated with increased depressive symptoms, suicidal ideation, functional impairment, and symptoms of PTSD among youth. Similar associations were reported by Melhem and his colleagues in another study conducted with parentally bereaved youth (Melhem, Moritz, Walker, Shear, & Brent, 2007) and by Brown and Goodman (2005), who conducted a study with children of parents who were killed in the World Trade Center attacks of September 11, 2001. Brown and Goodman (2005) also conducted a factor analysis and reported two factors that they referred to as *traumatic grief* and *normal grief*. They reported traumatic grief was associated with symptoms of depression, anxiety, and PTSD, as well as poor coping responses (Brown & Goodman, 2005). Since studies on the effectiveness of grief counseling interventions suggest counseling is most effective for children who have significant distress and complicated grief symptoms (Neimeyer & Currier, 2009; Rosner, Kruse, & Hagl, 2010), an accurate assessment of complicated grief is an important first step for providers.

Factors Influencing Adjustment of Bereaved Children: Child Factors

Most scholars conceptualize parental death as a series of stressors related to not only the loss of an important attachment figure but also a decrease in family income, changes in residence, less contact with friends and neighbors, increased responsibilities, and loss of time with the surviving caregiver (Werner-Lin, Biank, & Rubenstein, 2010; Wolchik, Ma, Tein, Sandler, & Ayers, 2008). Parental death can also introduce stressors that limit the surviving caregiver's ability to provide a stable environment, consistent discipline, adequate warmth and support, and open communication with the child (Wolchik, Tein, Sandler, & Ayers, 2006). Thus, bereaved children often have to cope not only with the loss of their parent but also with possible major changes in their environments and daily routines. They may face multiple challenges as they try to mourn the loss of their parent and process changes in their lives, while at the same time mastering the normative tasks of development appropriate for their ages (Biank & Werner- Lin, 2011; Oltjenbruns, 2001; Robin & Omar, 2014). If children become overwhelmed with feelings of grief they may struggle with staying on track developmentally (Biank & Werner-Lin, 2011).

Although the experience of loss is unique in each child, several factors influence the grieving process and a child's adjustment after a parental loss. Some of these factors are child related and some are family related (Hope & Hodge, 2006; Howarth, 2011). Child factors include the child's: (1) gender, (2) age, (3) self-esteem, and (4) developmental stage (Christ & Christ, 2006; Haine, Ayers, Sandler, & Wolchik, 2008; Hope & Hodge, 2006). Girls tend to exhibit more internalizing problems (depressive symptoms, anxiety) after the death of a parent, while boys tend to exhibit more externalizing problems (school problems, delinquency) (Dowdney, 2011; Hope & Hodge, 2006). Prospective longitudinal studies suggest a heightened vulnerability for girls that can persist over time (Schmiege, Khoo, Sandler, Ayers, & Wolchik, 2006). A possible explanation for this gender difference could be that girls tend to take on more household tasks and caring for younger siblings in bereaved families, and as a result they are more burdened and could struggle with staying on track developmentally (Sandler et al., 2003).

Self-esteem is another important factor that can affect bereavement among children and youth (Haine et al., 2003; Wolchick et al., 2006, 2008). Children with higher self-esteem tend to cope better with negative life events; they are also able to integrate stressful experiences with less negative arousal by using more adaptive coping mechanisms (Haine et al., 2003). Additionally, bereavement may result in decreased self-esteem either by having fewer opportunities to engage in activities that improve self-esteem (e.g., social activities, sports, positive interactions with caregivers) or by being exposed to stigma (e.g., parent died of HIV/AIDS, moving to a smaller house in a poorer neighborhood, orphaned because their only parent died) (Haine et al., 2003; Wolchik et al., 2006). Studies that examined the mediating role of self-esteem suggest self-esteem mediates the relationship between life stressors and internalizing and externalizing problems in bereaved children (Haine et al., 2003; Wolchik et al., 2006). Thus, bereaved children who have higher self-esteem tend to experience less internalizing and externalizing problems compared to bereaved children who have lower self-esteem. Consequently, increasing self-esteem has been suggested as one of the important parts of bereavement therapy for children and adolescents (Ayers et al., 2013; Sandler et al., 2010, 2013).

Factors Influencing Adjustment of Bereaved Children: Family Factors

Several family factors can affect the adjustment of children to parental loss. Salient family-level factors include: (1) which parent died (mother versus father), (2) circumstances of the death (sudden or long-term illness), and (3) availability of consistent warm relationships with other caregivers (Dowdney, 2011; Haine et al., 2003, 2008; Hope & Hodge, 2006; Howarth, 2011; National Cancer Institute, 2014).

Which Parent Died

The stability and consistency of the family following parental loss are salient contributors to children's adjustment after parental death (Haine et al., 2008; National Cancer Institute, 2014). Consequently, the gender of the deceased parent is important because this can impact the family stability following death. Earlier studies reported differences between adjustment following maternal versus paternal deaths, suggesting that children tend to have worse outcomes after the deaths of their mothers compared to their fathers. For example, Boerner and Silverman (2001) reported that women who maintained daily routines in the family prior to their husbands' deaths tended to provide more continuity of routines and emotional climate following the husband's death. Thus, in more traditional families, where mothers are in charge of the household, children tend to experience less disruption to their daily routines following the death of a father. Additionally, women's parenting styles tend to be more child centered, so they are often more attuned to children's needs following the loss of a parent. Compared to men raising children, women also tend to seek out professional and supportive communities (Wittouck, Van Autreve, De Jaegre, Portzky, & van Heeringen, 2011).

Bereaved men were often not the primary caregivers in their families before their wives died, and consequently they are not familiar with the practical and emotional parenting of their children (Werner-Lin & Biank, 2012). Men may find it more difficult to garner parenting support because they relied on their wives for support. Since fathers are not always the primary caregivers, they may feel less confident in their parenting abilities (Glazer, Clark, Thomas, &

Haxton, 2010). As a result, some fathers will care more about daily pragmatics (household tasks, homework) and not be as attuned to their children's emotional needs. Other researchers suggest that it is not the gender of the parent that impacts adjustment following parental death but rather the role the parent had in the family (Boerner & Silverman, 2001; Werner-Lin & Biank, 2012). If the deceased parent was the nurturer in the family who was responsible for maintaining daily routines, the family may struggle to regain its sense of safety and stability (Glazer et al., 2010). For any family structure (single parent, two parent), it is important to assess the role of the deceased caregiver to understand the challenges the family will experience adjusting to life after the loss of a parent.

Circumstances of Parental Death

Regarding the cause of death, there have been mixed findings about its impact on children's grief reactions (Cerel, Jordan, & Duberstein, 2008). In some studies, traumatic and sudden parental death (e.g., suicide, homicide) was associated with child PTSD symptoms (e.g., Cerel, Fristad, Weller, & Weller, 2000; Dowdney, 2000), increased risk for depressive disorder up to 2 years post-loss (Brent, Melhem, Donohoe, & Walker, 2009), and an increased risk for suicidal behavior (Hung & Rabin, 2009; Kuramoto, Brent, & Wilcox, 2009). Yet, in a study with children who lost a parent to a violent death (suicide, homicide, and accidents), Brown and her colleagues (2007) reported the cause of death from violence or suicide was not a major predictor of mental health problems in children and was not a useful indicator of bereaved children's needs for intervention (Brown, Sandler, Tein, Liu, & Haine, 2007).

Studies comparing the adjustment to the sudden loss of a parent versus an expected death (from a terminal illness) have also produced mixed results (McClatchy, Vonk, & Palardy, 2009). McClatchy and Vonk (2005) conducted a study with children in bereavement camp and reported that the level of PTSD symptoms among children who lost a parent to an unexpected death was comparable to children who lost a parent to an expected death. In a more recent study, McClatchy, Vonk, and Palardy (2009) compared symptoms of complicated grief and PTSD between children who were bereaved by expected death and children who were bereaved by unexpected death. They reported no significant differences between the two groups. Yet, Pfeffer and her colleagues reported children who were bereaved by sudden death (parental suicide) reported significantly more depressive symptoms and interpersonal problems compared to children who were bereaved because of parental cancer; children were assessed within 18 months of their loss (Pfeffer, Karus, Siegel, & Jiang, 2000). Clearly, more research should be conducted to examine whether the circumstances of the parent's death have a differential impact on children's adjustment.

Availability of Other Caregivers

The caregiver has an important role in helping bereaved children grieve the loss of a parent (Brent et al., 2009; Melhem et al., 2008, 2011). A supportive and nurturing caregiver who models healthy grief and provides opportunities for emotional expression is the biggest protective factor for children and adolescents (Cerel et al., 2006; Hope & Hodge, 2006; Kwok, Haine, Sandler, Ayers, Wolchik, & Tein, 2005; Lin, Sandler, Ayers, Wolchik, & Luecken, 2004; Luecken, Kraft, Appelhans, & Enders, 2009; Luecken & Lemery, 2004; Sandler et al., 2010; Tein,

Sandler, Ayers, & Wolchik, 2006; Werner-Lin & Biank, 2012; Wolchik, Ma, Tein, Sandler, & Ayers, 2008). On the other hand, when the surviving caregiver struggles with his/her own grief, children can be negatively affected (Saldinger, Porterfield, & Cain, 2004; Silverman, Baker, Cait, & Boerner, 2003). For example, in preschool bereaved children, depression in the surviving parent is the most powerful predictor of behavioral disturbances in children (Wolchik et al., 2006).

The loss of a parent can affect the child's caregiver in many ways, especially if the caregiver is the surviving parent, including: (1) intense emotional pain, (2) anxiety, (3) anger, (4) lack of energy, (5) hopelessness, and (6) a lower tolerance to stress (Aho, Tarkka, Astedt-Kurki, & Kaunonen, 2006; Arnold, Gemma, & Cushman, 2005; Werner-Lin & Biank, 2012). Surviving caregivers report increased levels of anxiety and depression, suicidal ideation, and functional impairment, all of which can negatively impact their parenting and availability to bereaved children in their care (Melhem et al., 2008). If the bereaved caregiver is preoccupied with his/her own grief, the absence of the deceased parent will be felt more intensely throughout the family. Additionally, the bereaved child may sense the profound grief of the surviving adult and mask his/her own distress to prevent additional burden on the caregiver (Werner-Lin & Biank, 2012). Sadly, bereaved children may feel more isolated and alone while coping with this loss, losing both caregivers as sources of emotional support.

What Clinicians Need to Know about Children's Grief

1   Early parental death puts children at risk for a wide range of problems in childhood and adolescence.
2   Grief can be expressed differently in children compared to adults and tends to be intermittent.
3   Children tend to experience prolonged grief and reexperience the loss at different developmental stages.
4   In addition to coping with the loss, children often have to face many changes in their environments and daily routines.
5   Many factors influence child adjustment following parental loss, including child and family factors.
6   A supportive and nurturing parent or caregiver is the biggest protective factor contributing to positive adjustment following parental loss.

Grief Interventions

When a parent dies after experiencing a terminal illness, children's difficulties often start before the anticipated death (anticipatory grief). In fact, children's highest levels of distress often occur during the terminal stages of a parent's illness and not immediately following a parent's death (e.g., Cerel et al., 2006; Christ & Christ, 2006; Johansson & Grimby, 2012; Rotheram-Borus et al., 2005). Whenever possible, grief intervention should begin soon after the terminal diagnosis, when the "bad news" is first shared with the parent and family. Mental healthcare providers who work in hospitals, hospice, and other clinics where terminally ill patients are cared for can help families cope with the transition from treating a chronic parental illness to preparing for the loss. There are several strategies providers can use to help children and families through this difficult period.

First, providers can help children and adolescents decide how much they want to be shielded from the reality of the illness and their dying parent. Some children cannot tolerate visits to the hospital. Children should be allowed to choose their level of exposure without feeling guilt or shame; for younger children, it is important to consult with the surviving parent to assess what is best for that child (Saldinger et al., 2003). Second, providers can help to reduce the family's anxiety by providing education about the grief process and validating the range of emotions family members may experience (Haine et al., 2008; Hope & Hodge, 2006; Sandler et al., 2003). Finally, providers can help caregivers regain some sense of order and control by helping them make plans for caring for their children. For example, if the ill parent is a single parent, it is important to discuss alternative caregivers and arrangements for custody.

While there are few evidence-supported interventions for parentally bereaved children, many studies have reported risk and protective factors that can be modified to facilitate healthier adjustment (Ayers, Kennedy, Sandler, & Stokes, 2003; Haine et al., 2008). After first summarizing evidence-supported interventions clinicians can use with bereaved children, we will describe one empirically supported family program for bereaved children and youth (Sandler et al., 2010, 2013) as well as a peer support group program for bereaved children (Metel & Barnes, 2011). First, the following are some recommended therapy components for empirically supported modifiable risk and protective factors (Ayers et al., 2013; Haine et al., 2008; Sandler et al., 2008).

Child Level

1   *Improving child coping skills.* When children actively use coping skills, they tend to adapt better after the loss of a parent (Wolchik et al., 2006). School-age children can be taught specific coping strategies such as problem solving, support seeking, and positive reframing. Even younger children can be taught how to distinguish between problems that are a "child's job" to fix and problems that adults should take care of (Ayers et al., 2013). Additionally, children of all ages can be taught simple strategies to improve problem solving. For example, a common model for teaching positive reframing includes the following four steps: (1) Stop: What am I feeling? (2) Think: First, look outside. What is happening? Then, look inside, any hurtful thoughts? (3) Brainstorm: What helpful thought can I have? (4) Choose: Does the thought make sense to me? And does it feel better? (Ayers et al., 2013). Clinicians can help children increase their coping efficacy by: (1) helping children choose goals and use their coping skills to achieve those goals, (2) providing positive feedback when children make an effort to use their coping skills, and (3) expressing their belief in the children's abilities to successfully cope with their problems (Haine et al., 2008).

2   *Improving child self-esteem.* The loss of positive interactions with the deceased parent or negative interactions with a surviving caregiver (e.g., other parent, grandparents) who is depressed and unavailable can negatively impact children's self-esteem (Haine, Ayers, Sandler, Wolchik, & Weyer, 2003; Wolchik, Tein, Sandler, & Ayers, 2006). Lower self-esteem in parentally bereaved children has been associated with more mental health

problems (Haine et al., 2003; Wolchik et al., 2006). Clinicians can help adolescents reframe negative self-talk (Haine et al., 2008) and help children and youth identify their strengths (Howarth, 2011). Clinicians can also work with parents and caregivers to provide more positive reinforcement and opportunities for children to engage in activities they do well or can easily master to improve children's self-esteem (Haine et al., 2008).

3   *Supporting open expression of emotions.* When children feel they have to inhibit the expression of negative emotions, they are more likely to develop mental health problems (Pennebaker, 2012). Clinicians can engage children in experiential activities that provide opportunities for talking about their feelings following the loss (e.g., using expressive arts such as drawing and painting, talking about favorite memories) (Haine et al., 2008). Clinicians can also work with the child's caregiver to develop a supportive and open relationship so the child feels comfortable openly expressing negative feelings. Children do not have to express negative emotions about the loss, but they need to know they can openly talk to their surviving caregivers about their feelings.

Surviving Parent/Caregiver

One of the most significant contributors to child adjustment following parental loss is positive parenting by the surviving caregiver or other adults that includes open communication and a balance of warmth and effective discipline (Haine et al., 2008; Haine, Wolchik, Sandler, Millsap, & Ayers, 2006; Kwok et al., 2005; Sandler et al., 2008). Clinicians can help bereaved caregivers reduce their own stress so they are more available for their children and can create such positive parenting experiences (Howarth, 2011).

1   *Increasing parental warmth.* Some of the components of parental warmth are expressing affection, conveying acceptance, fostering open communication, and providing emotional support, as well as displaying positive regard (Haine et al., 2008). Clinicians can help caregivers express more warmth toward their bereaved children in consistent and genuine ways.

2   *Helping caregivers reduce stress.* Mental healthcare providers can create supportive and safe spaces for caregivers (e.g., surviving parent, grandparents, foster care parent) to talk openly about their grief and their daily life challenges. They can help caregivers seek self-care while they also grieve the loss.

3   *Teaching caregivers effective discipline.* Clinicians can work with caregivers to increase effective discipline strategies; provide clear rules, expectations, and consequences for misbehaviors; be consistent while enforcing the rules; and use positive reinforcement to increase favorable behaviors (Ayers, Sandler, et al., 1996; Ayers, Wolchik, et al., 1996; Haine et al., 2008).

At the Parent–Child Family Level

1   *Improving caregiver–child communication.* Clinicians can work with caregivers to improve their listening skills and encourage more open communication with their children. Clinicians can also educate caregivers about the importance of having one-on-one time with their

children and providing safe spaces for communication. Caregivers can be encouraged to communicate to their children that it is ok to feel sad or scared or angry about the loss, in developmentally appropriate ways.

2   *Increasing positive family interactions.* Consistent and stable environments lead to healthier adaptation to parental loss (Haine et al., 2008; National Cancer Institute, 2014). Increasing positive family interactions can facilitate more family cohesion and stability. Clinicians can help families schedule a regular time for family rituals and leisure activities (e.g., game night) (Sandler et al., 2003). Having fun together on a regular basis can increase warmth and communication among family members and convey to children that it is acceptable to be happy and have fun together even while grieving.

Providers working with bereaved children or children in anticipatory grief should be direct and honest while discussing death of a parent. Children and adolescents will cope better if they know what is happening and what to expect. Silence about death teaches children this topic is taboo, leaving them isolated and alone with their feelings and fears. Children need to be told the truth based on their developmental levels. Their questions should be answered honestly and directly (Dowdney, 2011; NCI, 2014; Torbic, 2011). Additionally, when talking to children about death, proper words should be used. Euphemisms such as "she passed away" should not be used because they can lead to confusion and misinterpretations, especially among younger children who are very concrete in their thinking (Dowdney, 2011; National Cancer Institute, 2014).

Peer Group Support Groups for Bereaved Children

Peer support groups are a cost effective way to provide grief support for bereaved children and youth (Metel & Barnes, 2011). Some of the most effective work occurs in peer support groups (Berzof, 2011). In a support group, grieving is normalized, leading to less stigma and isolation. Adolescents and children have an opportunity to help others and at the same time master their own losses. Groups facilitate retelling the story of loss over and over again and gaining a sense of coherence and integration. Grief groups offer ways to continue the relationship with the deceased (e.g., photo albums, writing letters, collages) while also connecting with others who have also lost a parent (Berzof, 2011).

Metel and Barnes (2011) conducted a study evaluating the benefits of a peer support group for bereaved children. This program was offered at a community-based charity. Children were divided by age, with a younger group that included children 10 years old and younger and an older group that included children older than 10 years old. Each group was led by a paid staff member and a trained adult volunteer (not necessarily someone who lost a parent). The size of groups ranged between three to eight members. Groups occurred once a week for six to eight weeks and lasted for 90 minutes, with a residential weekend in the middle.

Each peer support group session included an activity designed to facilitate open communication and to help participants express their feelings of grief. For example, in one activity, "Salt Jars," participants reminisced about different times and memories with the deceased parent and gave each memory a color. Then they rubbed colored chalk into salt and poured different colored layers into a jar, which was shared with their peers. In another group activity, "Tesco Tantrum," participants were asked to lie down on the carpet and to think about something they are angry about, punch their fists, stomp their feet, and scream at the top of their lungs until they feel they have had enough.

Metel and Barnes conducted interviews with 23 children (from 17 families) between the ages of 8 and 17 years who participated in this program following the loss of a parent or a sibling. In 16 families the children lost a parent, and in one family children lost an older sibling; parents were also interviewed. The most common perceived benefit reported by both children and parents was the social interaction with peers who also experienced bereavement. Children reported feeling understood by their peers, leading them to feel less isolated and different. This has been reported in other peer support group studies for bereaved children (e.g., Wilkinson, Croy, King, & Barnes, 2007). Children reported the group helped them better manage their emotions and more openly talk about their feelings, especially anger about their parent dying. Yet, parents reported the group did not lead to better parent–child communication about the bereavement at home.

Group Family Bereavement Intervention Program

The Family Bereavement Program (FBP) is an evidence-supported, manualized, grief support group program for parentally bereaved children, adolescents, and their caregivers that was developed by researchers at Arizona State University (Ayers et al., 2013; Hagan, Tein, Sandler, Wolchik, Ayers, & Luecken, 2012; Sandler et al., 2010, 2013). This program is based on a contextual resilience conceptual framework (Sandler, Wolchik, & Ayers, 2007) of family adaptation following parental loss. It was designed to improve family adaptation by encouraging children and surviving caregivers to satisfy their basic needs (e.g., safety, a sense of control, positive evaluation of self) and accomplish developmentally appropriate life tasks. The primary goal is to increase resiliency and facilitate better adaptation (Sandler et al., 2010). It targets skills that increase resiliency such as problem solving and self-esteem to provide bereaved children and their families with strategies to better cope with their losses and life changes.

The program includes 12 two-hour weekly sessions, with separate groups for children and adolescents. Children's groups include children between the ages of 8 and 12 years old. Adolescents groups are for children between 12 and 16 years old. Out of the 12 sessions, eight sessions are for children and caregivers separately and four are conjoint sessions with parents and children together in a multifamily support group. Additionally, in the caregiver program, there are two 1-hour individual sessions to tailor the program to the needs of each family. Each group is led by two master's-level counselors and can include 5 to 11 group members (Ayers et al., 2013).

This program includes a strong psychoeducational component that teaches children and caregivers resilience-promoting coping skills. The caregiver program focuses on: (1) positive parenting, (2) caregiver–child relationship quality, (3) effective discipline, (4) caregiver mental health problems, and (5) negative events (Ayers et al., 2013). Factors targeted in the child and adolescent programs are: (1) caregiver–child relationship quality, (2) positive coping (including active coping and coping efficacy), (3) events that lower self-esteem and threats appraisal, (4) adaptive control beliefs, and (5) adaptive emotional expression (Ayers et al., 2013). These were selected based on salient outcomes in bereaved youth or youth exposed to other major family disruptions (Sandler et al., 2010).

At the beginning of the family program, caregivers and children/youth each identify one personal goal they want to accomplish; throughout the program they practice using skills to accomplish these goals. While teaching program skills, group leaders first solicit group members' experiences and ideas to develop the rationale for using the program skills and to highlight how the skills are relevant to their own experiences. After each skill is described and modeled using role play by the group leaders or by videotape, members then role-play the use of these skills; leaders and other group members give feedback. Families are instructed to practice the new skills between sessions at home and discuss experiences during the next group session.

Each session has a similar structure, as follows: (1) discussion of practice at home, (2) teaching a new skill, (3) practice the new skill, and (4) assignment of activities to practice at home. For example, to work on effective discipline, caregivers are taught to provide clearer rules and expectations, use effective consequences, and be more consistent. Teaching caregivers to improve their relationships with children includes providing one-on-one time with each child, engaging in family leisure activities, and improving their listening skills (Ayers et al., 2013). For more information about the structure and content of this evidence-based program, mental healthcare providers can access treatment manuals (for the children program: Ayers, Wolchik, et al., 1996; for the adolescent version: Ayers, Sandler, et al., 1996).

This manualized program was evaluated using a randomized experimental design that included 156 families who had a total of 244 children and adolescents between the ages of 8 and 16. Participants were randomly assigned to either the FBP program or to a self-study comparison condition in which family members received three books about grief and a syllabus to guide them (Ayers et al., 2013). Participants had to lose a parent 3 to 30 months prior to attending the program. Participants were assessed four times: (1) at the beginning of the program, (2) immediately following the end of the program, (3) 11 months after the post-test, and (4) 6 years after the intervention. Findings suggest the program promotes positive outcomes for both children (e.g., positive coping) and caregivers (increase in positive parenting, decrease in mental health problems) and these are maintained 6 years following participation in the program (Hagan et al., 2012; Sandler et al., 2013).

It is noteworthy that in recent years there has been a lot of debate in the mental health field about the effectiveness of bereavement interventions with children, adolescents, and adults (Bonanno & Lilienfeld, 2008; Currier, Neimeyer, & Berman, 2008; Larson, 2014; Larson & Hoyt, 2007; Neimeyer & Currier, 2009; Rosner, Lumbeck, & Geissner, 2011; Schut, 2010; Spuij et al., 2015). In a meta-analysis of studies examining the effectiveness of bereavement interventions with children, Currier, Holland, and Neimeyer (2007) concluded bereavement interventions for children are no more useful than *not* receiving any intervention. Neimeyer and Currier (2009) examined characteristics of effective bereavement interventions and concluded that grief therapy *can* be helpful for people who experience substantial clinical distress. Similarly, others suggest most bereaved people will not benefit from clinical interventions (Bonanno & Lilienfeld, 2008; Mancini, Griffin, & Bonanno, 2012). "Others with less oppressive and sustained symptoms tend to respond resiliently, even in the absence of intervention, suggesting that grief therapists might adopt an attitude of humble appreciation for what many of the bereaved can achieve without professional assistance" (Neiyemer & Currier, 2009, p. 355). Taken together, these findings suggest mental healthcare providers should first assess all families coping with parental loss so interventions can be tailored for those children and adolescents who can benefit most from professional help—those children and youth who exhibit substantial levels of distress and difficulty following the loss of a parent.

Mental Healthcare Providers in the Medical System

Mental healthcare providers should collaborate with medical providers to help families cope with anticipatory grief and parental death starting at the terminal diagnosis (e.g., collaborating with hospice care providers). Providing timely and accurate information about end-of-life issues (such as prognosis, talking about death, who will care for children in single-parent families) to patients and their families is a challenging task for most healthcare providers. Physicians have reported several reasons for delaying or avoiding these conversations, including: (1) stress, (2) discomfort, (3) lack of training, (4) fear of hurting the recipient of the information, (5) destroying hope, and (6) losing patient trust (Anderlik, Pentz, & Hess, 2000; Baile, Lenzi, Parker, Buckman, & Cohen, 2002; Barclay, Momen, Case-Upton, Kuhn, & Smith, 2011: Friedrichsen & Milberg, 2006; Gordon & Daugherty, 2003; Hancock et al., 2007; Mack & Smith, 2012). This task can be even more challenging for providers when their terminally ill patients have minor children at home.

Providing end-of-life information to patients' children is important for optimal adjustment following parental death (Bylund-Grenklo et al., 2014; Grenklo, Kreicbergs, Valdimarsdóttir, Nyberg, Steineck, & Fürst, 2013). Grenko and her colleagues (2013) conducted a retrospective study with 851 participants who were between the ages of 13 and 16 years old when they lost a parent. The interviews took place 6 to 9 years following the loss. They reported children who did not receive medical information *prior* to the loss of their parents were more likely to experience mistrust of their parent's medical provider compared to children who received information. Children's mistrust of the quality of care provided to their deceased parent was also associated with an increased risk for symptoms of depression (Grenklo et al., 2013).

Mental healthcare providers who work in hospital settings will likely encounter more terminally ill patients; they can be the bridge between medical providers and patient/families by advocating for these important end-of-life conversations. Mental healthcare providers can educate medical providers about the importance of providing this information and how best to deliver the "bad news" to patients and their families. They can also support patients and their families during the terminal stage of the illness. Specifically, they can help families solicit practical and emotional support and make referrals to support groups and other interventions as needed.

Providers can help children and families adapt by providing education about the grief process (Haine et al., 2008; Hope & Hodge, 2006; Sandler et al., 2003). They can collaborate with hospital staff and, in particular, hospice teams by offering a grief education group to families either during the terminal stage or immediately following the loss. The goal of support groups is to normalize the grief and help children and caregivers know what to expect. Some important issues to address are the following: (1) the death is not the child's fault, (2) talking openly about the deceased parent is encouraged, (3) it is normal to feel a wide range of emotions, and (4) it is acceptable to talk to the parent who died and honor his/her memory (e.g., through photo albums, or art projects that preserve their memories) (Sandler et al., 2003).

Since children often express their grief through somatization (Bugge et al., 2014; Sood et al., 2006), providers who work in primary care clinics should be more attuned to the possibility of parental loss among children who present with somatic complaints. Mental healthcare providers can ask caregivers if their children experienced a recent loss that precipitated the somatic complaints. Mental healthcare providers can also educate primary care physicians and pediatricians about the link between parental loss and somatization to increase their likelihood of checking for such experiences and providing a referral for therapy as needed.

Cultural Considerations

The dominant societal discourse about grief is based on the following assumptions: (1) grief follows a distinct pattern, (2) it is time limited and should end, (3) it is linear with specific stages or tasks, and (4) it should be worked through and at the end of the process there is a closure characterized by a detachment from the deceased loved one (Balk et al., 2004; Breen & O'Connor, 2007; Valentine, 2006). Although empirical support for these assumptions is not strong (Balk et al., 2004; Bonanno & Field, 2001; Stroebe & Schut, 2005), they are prevalent and unquestioned in many healthcare settings (Breen & O'Connor, 2007). Empirical evidence suggests various grief service providers (e.g., counselors, clergy, hospice, nurses) still rely on these assumptions while working with the bereaved (Murray, 2002; Valentine, 2006; Walter, 2000, 2006). Breen and O'Connor (2007) suggest these assumptions are not necessarily wrong, but they capture the experiences of primarily White, middle class, and older people (Breen & O'Connor, 2007; Valentine, 2006). These assumptions are less likely to capture the experiences of grief in diverse populations, for example, people bereaved by a stigmatizing death (e.g., HIV) or other cultures beyond the dominant North American culture.

In order to provide culturally sensitive care, providers should be aware of, or at minimum ask about, the cultural beliefs of families and children. This is especially important for grieving families because the failure to observe culturally sanctioned rituals following a death can lead to an experience of unresolved loss (Hardy-Bougere, 2007). Providers should ask families about rituals and traditions, including: (1) beliefs about what happens after death, (2) the roles of family members in coping with death, (3) characteristics of normal expressions of death, and (4) whether there are certain types of death that are more difficult to cope with (Clements et al., 2003). Mental healthcare providers should examine their own beliefs and biases about death so they do not impose their own beliefs on families they serve (e.g., beliefs about the existence of heaven or afterlife) (Hardy-Bougere, 2007). Additionally, providers need to be careful to not impose cultural stereotypes and rather ask whether clients adhere to prevalent cultural beliefs and practices attributed to their cultural group. "While bereavement is a universal phenomenon, the experience of grief is not. Grief is a unique experience that occurs within a historical, social, cultural, and political context" (Breen & O'Connor, 2007, p. 209). All these factors need to be considered when trying to understand the diverse experience of grief.

Although each family is unique, there are some common characteristics typical of the various cultural groups in the United States. Healthcare providers should be familiar with these characteristics when working with diverse groups of bereaved families and children (Hardy-Bougere, 2007). For example, in the

African American community, support of the nuclear and extended family are instrumental in coping with grief and loss. Emotional expressions vary, with some crying and wailing and others being silent and stoic (Smith, 2002). African Americans' cultural beliefs are steeped in religion and spirituality (Van & Meleis, 2003); many believe life exists after death (e.g., heaven). They tend to perceive death as a reflection of God's will or plan, believe the deceased is in God's hands, and believe that they will be united again in heaven after death (Smith, 2002). African Americans tend to rely on inner strength and draw from past experiences while coping with grief or any other major crisis (Hardy-Bougere, 2007). Southern and rural African Americans often have the corpse at the house for the evening before the funeral (Smith, 2002). African Americans could have a mistrust of the healthcare system because of the historical legacy of racism in the U.S., especially regarding advanced directives and end-of-life care (Lobar, Youngblut, & Brooten, 2006; Perkins, Geppert, Gonzales, Cortez, & Hazuda, 2002); they tend to seek help from clergy rather than from healthcare professionals (Lobar et al., 2006).

Latinos in the U.S. represent a large variety of cultures and races. Thus, cultural customs related to grief and loss will vary; no distinct patterns of grief and loss of a loved one have been reported (National Infant and Mortality Review Program, 2005). When working with bereaved Latino families, healthcare providers should familiarize themselves with the concept of *respeto* (rules guiding social interactions). In traditional Latino families there is a strict hierarchy that should be honored, with status going in order from older to younger and from male to female (National Infant and Mortality Review Program, 2005). Religion is also strongly valued, with most Latinos being Catholic and many being Pentecostals. Health is viewed as a gift from God and is highly valued. Faith is enlisted in the prevention of illness through prayers, wearing religious medals, and keeping relics in the home (National Infant and Mortality Review Program, 2005). Grief may be expressed by crying openly; women may wail loudly and men could act according to *machismo*, where there is a belief that men should not show overt emotion (Lobar et al., 2006). The Latino community tends to embrace religion and spirituality; there is a psychological and spiritual continuity between the living and the dead. Thus, families often continue their relationships with the deceased through prayers and visits to the cemetery (Lobar et al., 2006; National Infant and Mortality Review Program, 2005).

In the Asian culture, traditional elaborate funeral ceremonies often mark the passing of souls to the afterlife. Sadness and grief may be expressed as somatic complaints because emotional distress is often considered a disgrace to the family (Lobar et al., 2006). Buddhists tend to view death as an opportunity for improvement in the next life. Dying with a positive state of mind surrounded by family and monks helps the deceased become reborn on a higher level. The body should be handled in a worthy and respectful manner (Dimond, 2004). In Chinese culture, saving face is often an important consideration; in the case of a death, the more people cry for the deceased, the more she/he was loved (Yick & Gupta, 2002). Additionally, filial piety, the responsibility for one's relative, is valued (Lobar et al., 2006). Chinese culture tends to stress the importance of familial obligation to bury the dead and honor the ancestors with religious rites. Traditionally, the most important obligation in life is to perform burial rites appropriately (Klass & Goss, 2014). The Chinese believe in the afterlife and will often burn incense and other symbolic items to ensure the welfare of the deceased's soul in the next life (Klass & Goss, 2014).

What Clinicians Need to Know about Grief Interventions

1 If possible, interventions should start when the parent is at the terminal stage of illness.
2 Education about the grief process can help to reduce anxiety for surviving parents and children.
3 Improving children's coping skills, self-esteem, and abilities to express negative emotions can help them adjust better to parental loss.
4 Helping the surviving caregiver/parent discipline effectively, reduce stress, and increase warmth toward children can help the family adjust better to parental loss.
5 Working with the family to improve communication and positive family interactions can lead to healthier adaptation to parental loss.
6 Providers in medical settings can collaborate with medical staff to provide grief support to families and help physicians deliver accurate information and end-of-life conversations with patients and their families.
7 Grief is a unique experience. Providers should be cautious to not impose preconceived notions about grief on their patients or on patients from different cultures.
8 Most children will recover on their own following parental death and will not need professional help.

Conclusions

The death of a parent is one of the most stressful life events a child can experience, and it significantly increases the risks for a wide range of problems in childhood and adulthood. Parental death can be a traumatic event for children not only because of the actual loss of a parent but also because of the changes it causes in multiple domains of their lives. Due to their developing cognitive and emotional abilities, children understand and express grief differently than adults. Children's grief is intermittent and cyclical as children reexperience their loss as they go through different developmental stages.

The presence of a warm and consistent parent or caregiver and the stability of the environment are strong predictors of children's healthy adaptation to parental loss. Interventions focused on resources that impact resilience can promote better adjustment for children. These interventions can address variables at the child level, such as self-esteem and coping efficacy; at the parent level, such as stress reduction and positive parenting; as well as at the family level, such as communication.

Test Your Knowledge: True or False

1 Young children can express grief through somatic symptoms.
2 Children have to talk about their loss in order to work through their grief.

(Continued)

3   In order to adjust well following parental loss, children have to let go of the deceased parent.

4   Bereaved children revisit their losses as they go through developmental stages.

5   The stability of the family environment is the single most important factor impacting children's adjustment to parental loss.

6   Improving children's coping skills and self-esteem can help them adjust better following parental death.

7   Educating children and their families about the grief process can lower anxiety and improve coping.

8   Grief is a universal experience and therefore the grief process is similar in all cultures.

Answers: 1-T, 2-F, 3-F, 4-T, 5-F, 6-T, 7-T, 8-F

Professional Readings and Resources

Children's Grief Education Association: www.childgrief.org

Cohen, J. A., Mannarino, A. P., & Deblinger, E. (2006). *Treating trauma and traumatic grief in children and adolescents.* New York: Guilford Press.

Lowenstein, L. (2006). *Creative interventions for bereaved children.* Toronto, Ontario: Champion Press.

The National Alliance for Grieving Children: www.nationalallianceforgrievingchildren.org

Rainbows for All Children: www.rainbows.org

References

Aho, A. L., Tarkka, M. T., Astedt-Kurki, P., & Kaunonen, M. (2006). Fathers' grief after the death of a child. *Issues in Mental Health Nursing, 27*(6), 647–663.

Anderlik, M. R., Pentz, R. D., & Hess, K. R. (2000). Revisiting the truth-telling debate: a study of disclosure practices at a major cancer center. *The Journal of Clinical Ethics, 11*(3), 251–260.

Arnold, J., Gemma, P. B., & Cushman, L. F. (2005). Exploring parental grief: Combining quantitative and qualitative measures. *Archives of Psychiatric Nursing, 19*(6), 245–255.

Ayers, T. S., Kennedy, C. L., Sandler, I. N., & Stokes, J. (2003). Bereavement, adolescence. In *Encyclopedia of primary prevention and health promotion* (pp. 221–229). New York: Springer.

Ayers, T. S., Sandler, I. N., Lutzke, J. R., Twohey, J. L., Li, S., Losoya, S., & Kriege, G. (1996). *Family Bereavement program: Group leader intervention manual for adolescent program.* Tempe, AZ: Prevention Research Center, Arizona State University.

Ayers, T. S., Wolchik, S. A., Sandler, I. N., Twohey, J. L., Weyer, J. L., Padgett-Jones, S., . . . Kriege, G. (2013). The Family Bereavement Program: Description of a theory-based prevention program for parentally-bereaved children and adolescents. *OMEGA—Journal of Death and Dying, 68*(4), 293–314.

Ayers, T. S., Wolchik, S. A., Weiss, A., Sandler, I. N., Jones, S., Cole, E., & Barrow, S. (1996). *Family Bereavement program: Group leader intervention manual for parent program.* Tempe, AZ: Prevention Research Center, Arizona State University.

Baile, W. F., Lenzi, R., Parker, P. A., Buckman, R., & Cohen, L. (2002). Oncologists' attitudes toward and practices in giving bad news: An exploratory study. *Journal of Clinical Oncology, 20*(8), 2189–2196.

Balk, D., Cook, A. S., Doka, K., Hansson, R. O., Klass, D., Neimeyer, R. A., . . . Weiss, R. S. (2004). Report on bereavement and grief research. *Death Studies, 28*, n.4917575.

Barclay, S., Momen, N., Case-Upton, S., Kuhn, I., & Smith, E. (2011). End-of-life care conversations with heart failure patients: A systematic literature review and narrative synthesis. *British Journal of General Practice, 61*(582), e49–e62.

Berzof, J. (2011). The transformative nature of grief and bereavement. *Clinical Social Work Journal, 39*, 262–269.

Biank, N. M., & Werner-Lin, A. (2011). Growing up with grief: Revisiting the death of a parent over the life course. *OMEGA—Journal of Death and Dying, 63*(3), 271–290.

Boerner, K., & Silverman, P. R. (2001). Gender specific coping patterns in widowed parents with dependent children. *OMEGA-Detroit Then New York, 43*(3), 201–216.

Bonanno, G. A., & Field, N. P. (2001). Examining the delayed grief hypothesis across 5 years of bereavement. *American Behavioral Scientist, 44*(5), 798–816.

Bonanno, G. A., & Lilienfeld, S. O. (2008). Let's be realistic: When grief counseling is effective and when it's not. *Professional Psychology, 39*(3), 377–380.

Breen, L. J., & O'Connor, M. (2007). The fundamental paradox in the grief literature: A critical reflection. *OMEGA—Journal of Death and Dying, 55*(3), 199–218.

Brent, D., Melhem, N., Donohoe, M. B., & Walker, M. (2009). The incidence and course of depression in bereaved youth 21 months after the loss of a parent to suicide, accident, or sudden natural death. *The American Journal of Psychiatry, 166*(7), 786–794.

Brown, A. C., Sandler, I. N., Tein, J. Y., Liu, X., & Haine, R. A. (2007). Implications of parental suicide and violent death for promotion of resilience of parentally-bereaved children. *Death Studies, 31*(4), 301–335.

Brown, E., & Goodman, R. F. (2005). Childhood traumatic grief following September 11, 2001: Construct development and validation. *Journal of Clinical Child and Adolescent Psychology, 34*, 248–259.

Bugge, K. E., Darbyshire, P., Røkholt, E. G., Haugstvedt, K. T. S., & Helseth, S. (2014). Young children's grief: Parents' understanding and coping. *Death Studies, 38*(1), 36–43.

Bylund-Grenklo, T., Kreicbergs, U., Uggla, C., Valdimarsdóttir, U. A., Nyberg, T., Steineck, G., & Fürst, C. J. (2014). Teenagers want to be told when a parent's death is near: A nationwide study of cancer-bereaved youths' opinions and experiences. *Acta Oncologica*, 1–7.

Cerel, J., Fristad, M. A., Verducci, J., Weller, R. A., & Weller, E. B. (2006). Childhood bereavement: Psychopathology in the 2 years postparental death. *Journal of the American Academy of Child & Adolescent Psychiatry, 45*(6), 681–690.

Cerel, J., Fristad, M. A., Weller, E. B., & Weller, R. A. (2000). Suicide-bereaved children and adolescents: II. Parental and family functioning. *Journal of the American Academy of Child & Adolescent Psychiatry, 39*(4), 437–444.

Cerel, J., Jordan, J. R., & Duberstein, P. R. (2008). The impact of suicide on the family. *Crisis: The Journal of Crisis Intervention and Suicide Prevention, 29*(1), 38–44.

Christ, G. H. (2000). *Healing children's grief: Surviving a parent's death from cancer.* New York: Oxford University Press.

Christ, G. H., & Christ, A. E. (2006). Current approaches to helping children cope with a parent's terminal illness. *CA: A Cancer Journal for Clinicians, 56*(4), 197–212.

Christ, G. H., Siegel, K., & Christ, A. E. (2002). Adolescent grief: It never really hit me . . . until it actually happened. *Jama, 288*(10), 1269–1278.

Clements, P. T., Vigil, G. J., Manno, M. S., Henry, G. C., Wilks, J., Das, S., . . . Foster, W. (2003). Cultural perspectives of death, grief, and bereavement. *Journal of Psychosocial Nursing and Mental Health Services, 41*(7), 18–26.

Cohen, J. A., & Mannarino, A. P. (2010). Childhood traumatic grief. In M. D. Dulcan (Ed.), *Textbook of child and adolescent psychiatry* (pp. 505–516). Washington, DC: American Psychiatric Publishing.

Coombs, M. (2010). The mourning before: Can anticipatory grief theory inform family care in adult intensive care? *International Journal of Palliative Nursing, 16*, 45–51.

Currier, J. M., Holland, J. M., & Neimeyer, R. A. (2007). The effectiveness of bereavement interventions with children: A meta-analytic review of controlled outcome research. *Journal of Clinical Child and Adolescent Psychology, 36*(2), 253–259.

Currier, J. M., Neimeyer, R. A., & Berman, J. S. (2008). The effectiveness of psychother-apeutic interventions for bereaved persons: A comprehensive quantitative review. *Psychological Bulletin, 134*(5), 648.

Davies, D. (2004). *Child development; A practitioner guide* (2nd ed.). New York: Guilford.

Dillen, L., Fontaine, J. R., & Verhofstadt-Denève, L. (2008). Are normal and complicated grief different constructs? A confirmatory factor analytic test. *Clinical Psychology & Psychotherapy, 15*(6), 386–395.

Dimond, B. (2004). Disposal and preparation of the body: Different religious practices. *British Journal of Nursing, 13*(9), 547–549.

Dowdney, L. (2000). Annotation: Childhood bereavement following parental death. *Journal of Child Psychology and Psychiatry, 41*(7), 819–830.

Dowdney, L. (2011). Children bereaved by parent or sibling death. In D. Skuse, H. Bruce, L. Dowdney, & D. Mrazek (Eds.), *Child psychology and psychiatry* (2nd ed., pp. 92–99). Hoboken, NJ: Wiley & Sons.

Draper, A., & Hancock, M. (2011). Childhood parental bereavement: The risk of vulnerability to delinquency and factors that compromise resilience. *Mortality, 16*(4), 285–306.

Friedrichsen, M., & Milberg, A. (2006). Concerns about losing control when breaking bad news to terminally ill patients with cancer: Physicians' perspective. *Journal of Palliative Medicine, 9*(3), 673–682.

Fulton, R. (2003). Anticipatory mourning: A critique of the concept. *Mortality, 8*(4), 342–351.

Glazer, H. R., Clark, M. D., Thomas, R., & Haxton, H. (2010). Parenting after the death of a spouse. *American Journal of Hospice and Palliative Medicine, 27*(8), 532–536.

Gordon, E. J., & Daugherty, C. K. (2003). 'Hitting you over the head': Oncologists' disclosure of prognosis to advanced cancer patients. *Bioethics, 17*(2), 142–168.

Grenklo, T. B., Kreicbergs, U. C., Valdimarsdóttir, U. A., Nyberg, T., Steineck, G., & Fürst, C. J. (2013). Communication and trust in the care provided to a dying parent: A nationwide study of cancer-bereaved youths. *Journal of Clinical Oncology, 31*(23), 2886–2894.

Hagan, M. J., Tein, J. Y., Sandler, I. N., Wolchik, S. A., Ayers, T. S., & Luecken, L. J. (2012). Strengthening effective parenting practices over the long term: Effects of a preventive intervention for parentally bereaved families. *Journal of Clinical Child & Adolescent Psychology, 41*(2), 177–188.

Haine, R. A., Ayers, T. S., Sandler, I. N., & Wolchik, S. A. (2008). Evidence-based practices for parentally bereaved children and their families. *Professional Psychology: Research and Practice, 39*(2), 113–121.

Haine, R. A., Ayers, T. S., Sandler, I. N., Wolchik, S. A., & Weyer, J. L. (2003). Locus of control and self-esteem as stress-moderators or stress-mediators in parentally bereaved children. *Death Studies, 27*(7), 619–640.

Haine, R. A., Wolchik, S. A., Sandler, I. N., Millsap, R. E., & Ayers, T. S. (2006). Positive parenting as a protective resource for parentally bereaved children. *Death Studies, 30*(1), 1–28.

Hancock, K., Clayton, J. M., Parker, S. M., Butow, P. N., Carrick, S., Currow, D., . . . Tattersall, M. H. (2007). Truth-telling in discussing prognosis in advanced life-limiting illnesses: A systematic review. *Palliative Medicine, 21*(6), 507–517.

Hardy-Bougere, M. (2007). Cultural manifestations of grief and bereavement: A clinical perspective. *Journal of Cultural Diversity, 15*(2), 66–69.

Harrison, L., & Harrington, R. (2001). Adolescents' bereavement experiences. Prevalence, association with depressive symptoms, and use of services. *Journal of Adolescence, 24*(2), 159–169.

Hibberd, R., Wamser, R., & Vandenberg, B. (2011). Anticipatory grief. In S. Goldstein & J. A. Naglieri (Eds.), *Encyclopedia of child behavior and development Vol. 2* (pp. 111–112). New York: Springer.

The Highmark Caring Place. (2010). Spirals of grief. Retrieved from www.highmark caringplace.com/cp2/pdf/spiralgrief_part2.pdf

Hope, R. M., & Hodge, D. M. (2006). Factors affecting children's adjustment to the death of a parent: The social work professional's viewpoint. *Child and Adolescent Social Work Journal, 23*(1), 107–126.

Howarth, R. A. (2011). Promoting the adjustment of parentally bereaved children. *Journal of Mental Health Counseling, 33*(1), 21–32.

Hung, N. C., & Rabin, L. A. (2009). Comprehending childhood bereavement by parental suicide: A critical review of research on outcomes, grief processes, and interventions. *Death Studies, 33*(9), 781–814.

Jakobsen, I. S., & Christiansen, E. (2011). Young people's risk of suicide attempts in relation to parental death: A population-based register study. *Journal of Child Psychology and Psychiatry, 52*(2), 176–183.

Johansson, A., & Grimby, A. (2012). Anticipatory grief among close relatives of patients in hospice and palliative wards. *American Journal of Hospice and Palliative Medicine, 29*, 134–138.

Kaplow, J. B., Layne, C. M., Pynoos, R. S., Cohen, J. A., & Lieberman, A. (2012). DSM-V diagnostic criteria for bereavement-related disorders in children and adolescents: Developmental considerations. *Psychiatry, 75*(3), 243–266.

Klass, D., & Goss, R. E. (2014). Asian ways of grief. In K. J. Doka, & J. D. Davidson (Eds.). *Living with grief: Who we are how we grieve* (pp. 13–26). London and New York: Routledge.

Koehler, K. (2010). Sibling bereavement in childhood. In C. A. Corr, & D. E. Balk (Eds.), *Children's encounters with death, bereavement, and coping* (pp. 195–218). New York: Springer.

Kuramoto, S. J., Brent, D. A., & Wilcox, H. C. (2009). The impact of parental suicide on child and adolescent offspring. *Suicide and Life-Threatening Behavior, 39*(2), 137–151.

Kwok, O. M., Haine, R. A., Sandler, I. N., Ayers, T. S., Wolchik, S. A., & Tein, J. Y. (2005). Positive parenting as a mediator of the relations between parental psychological distress and mental health problems of parentally bereaved children. *Journal of Clinical Child and Adolescent Psychology, 34*(2), 260–271.

Larson, D. G. (2014). Taking stock: Past contributions and current thinking on death, dying, and grief: A review of beyond Kübler-Ross: New perspectives on death, dying and grief. *Death Studies, 38*(5), 349–352.

Larson, D. G., & Hoyt, W. T. (2007). What has become of grief counseling? An evaluation of the empirical foundations of the new pessimism. *Professional Psychology: Research and Practice, 38*(4), 347.

Lichtenthal, W. G., Cruess, D. G., & Prigerson, H. G. (2004). A case for establishing complicated grief as a distinct mental disorder in DSM-V. *Clinical Psychology Review, 24*(6), 637–662.

Lin, K. K., Sandler, I. N., Ayers, T. S., Wolchik, S. A., & Luecken, L. J. (2004). Resilience in parentally bereaved children and adolescents seeking preventive services. *Journal of Clinical Child and Adolescent Psychology, 33*(4), 673–683.

Lobar, S. L., Youngblut, J. M., & Brooten, D. (2006). Cross-cultural beliefs, ceremonies, and rituals surrounding death of a loved one. *Pediatric Nursing, 32*(1), 44–50.

Luecken, L. J., Kraft, A., Appelhans, B. M., & Enders, C. (2009). Emotional and cardiovascular sensitization to daily stress following childhood parental loss. *Developmental Psychology, 45*(1), 296.

Luecken, L. J., & Lemery, K. S. (2004). Early caregiving and physiological stress responses. *Clinical Psychology Review, 24*(2), 171–191.

Lyles, M. M. (2006). Anticipatory grief. Retrieved from http://childgrief.org/documents/AnticipatoryGrief.pdf

Mack, J. W., & Smith, T. J. (2012). Reasons why physicians do not have discussions about poor prognosis, why it matters, and what can be improved. *Journal of Clinical Oncology, 30*(22), 2715–2717.

Mancini, A. D., Griffin, P., & Bonanno, G. A. (2012). Recent trends in the treatment of prolonged grief. *Current Opinion in Psychiatry, 25*(1), 46–51.

Mannarino, A. P., & Cohen, J. A. (2011). Traumatic loss in children and adolescents. *Journal of Child & Adolescent Trauma, 4*(1), 22–33.

McClatchy, I. S., Vonk, M. E., & Palardy, G. (2009). The prevalence of childhood traumatic grief—a comparison of violent/sudden and expected loss. *OMEGA—Journal of Death and Dying, 59*(4), 305–323.

McClatchy, R. S., & Vonk, M. E. (2005). An exploratory study of post-traumatic stress disorder symptoms among bereaved children. *OMEGA—Journal of Death and Dying, 51*(4), 285–300.

Melhem, N. M., Day, N., Shear, M. K., Day, R., Reynolds III, C. F., & Brent, D. (2004). Traumatic grief among adolescents exposed to a peer's suicide. *American Journal of Psychiatry, 161*(8), 1411–1416.

Melhem, N. M., Moritz, G., Walker, M., Shear, M. K., & Brent, D. (2007). Phenomenology and correlates of complicated grief in children and adolescents. *Journal of the American Academy of Child & Adolescent Psychiatry, 46*(4), 493–499.

Melhem, N. M., Porta, G., Shamseddeen, W., Payne, M. W., & Brent, D. A. (2011). Grief in children and adolescents bereaved by sudden parental death. *Archives of General Psychiatry, 68*(9), 911–919.

Melhem, N. M., Walker, M., Moritz, G., & Brent, D. A. (2008). Antecedents and sequelae of sudden parental death in offspring and surviving caregivers. *Archives of Pediatrics & Adolescent Medicine, 162*(5), 403–410.

Metel, M., & Barnes, J. (2011). Peer-group support for bereaved children: A qualitative interview study. *Child and Adolescent Mental Health, 16*(4), 201–207.

Murray, J. A. (2002). Communicating with the community about grieving: A description and review of the foundations of a broken leg analogy of grieving. *Journal of Loss & Trauma, 7*(1), 47–69.

National Cancer Institute. (2014). Grief, bereavement, and coping with loss. Retrieved from www.cancer.gov/cancertopics/pdq/supportivecare/bereavement/HealthProfessional/page1

National Hospice and Palliative Care Organization. (2012). 2011 Edition, NHPCO facts and figures. *Hospice care in America.* Alexandria, VA: Author.

National Infant and Mortality Review Program. (2005). Customs and values that may affect Latino grief. *The American College of Obstetricians and Gynecologists,* 1–3.

Neimeyer, R., & Currier, J. (2009). Grief therapy: Evidence of efficacy and emerging directions. *Current Directions in Psychological Science, 18,* 352–356.

Ng, B. Y. (2005). Grief revisited. *Annals of the Academy of Medicine, Singapore, 34*(5), 352–355.

Oltjenbruns, K. A. (2001). Developmental context of childhood: Grief and regrief phenomena. In M. S. Stroebe, R. O. Hansson, W. Stroebe, & H. Schut (Eds.), *Handbook of bereavement research: Consequences, coping, and care* (pp. 169–197). Washington, DC: American Psychological Association.

Pennebaker, J. W. (2012). *Opening up: The healing power of expressing emotions.* New York: Guilford Press.

Perkins, H. S., Geppert, C., Gonzales, A., Cortez, J. D., & Hazuda, H. P. (2002). Cross-cultural similarities and differences in attitudes about advance care planning. *Journal of General Internal Medicine, 17*(1), 48–57.

Pfeffer, C. R., Karus, D., Siegel, K., & Jiang, H. (2000). Child survivors of parental death from cancer or suicide: Depressive and behavioral outcomes. *Psycho-Oncology, 9*(1), 1–10.

Prigerson, H. G., Horowitz, M. J., Jacobs, S. C., Parkes, C. M., Aslan, M., Goodkin, K., . . . Maciejewski, P. K. (2009). Prolonged grief disorder: Psychometric validation of criteria proposed for DSM-V and ICD-11. *PLoS Medicine, 6*(8), e1000121.

Rando, T. (2000). On the experience of traumatic stress in anticipatory and post death mourning. In T. Rando (Ed.), *Clinical dimensions of anticipatory mourning: Theory and practice in working with the dying, their loved ones and their caregivers* (pp. 155–221). Ottawa, Canada: Research Press.

Robin, L., & Omar, H. A. (2014). Chapter 11: Adolescent bereavement. In J. Merrick, A. Tenenbaum, & H. A. Omar (Eds.). *School, adolescence and health issues* (pp. 97–108). Hauppauge, NY: Nova Science Publishers Inc.

Rosner, R., Kruse, J., & Hagl, M. (2010). A meta-analysis of interventions for bereaved children and adolescents. *Death Studies, 34*(2), 99–136.

Rosner, R., Lumbeck, G., & Geissner, E. (2011). Effectiveness of an inpatient group therapy for comorbid complicated grief disorder. *Psychotherapy Research, 21*(2), 210–218.

Rotheram-Borus, M. J., Weiss, R., Alber, S., & Lester, P. (2005). Adolescent adjustment before and after HIV-related parental death. *Journal of Consulting and Clinical Psychology, 73*(2), 221.

Saldinger, A., Cain, A., & Porterfield, K. (2003). Managing traumatic stress in children anticipating parental death. *Psychiatry, 66*(2), 168–181.

Saldinger, A., Porterfield, K., & Cain, A. C. (2004). Meeting the needs of parentally bereaved children: A framework for child—centered parenting. *Psychiatry, 67*(4), 331–352.

Sandler, I. N., Ayers, T. S., Wolchik, S. A., Tein, J. Y., Kwok, O. M., Haine, R. A., . . . Griffin, W. A. (2003). The family bereavement program: Efficacy evaluation of a theory-based prevention program for parentally bereaved children and adolescents. *Journal of Consulting and Clinical Psychology, 71*(3), 587–600.

Sandler, I. N., Wolchik, S. A., & Ayers, T. S. (2007). Resilience rather than recovery: A contextual framework on adaptation following bereavement. *Death Studies, 32*(1), 59–73.

Sandler, I. N., Wolchik, S. A., Ayers, T. S., Tein, J. Y., Coxe, S., & Chow, W. (2008). Linking theory and intervention to promote resilience of children following parental bereavement. In M. Stroebe, R. O. Hansson, H. Schut, & W. Stroebe (Eds.), *Handbook of bereavement research: Consequences, coping, and care* (pp. 531–550). Washington, DC: American Psychological Association.

Sandler, I. N., Ma, Y., Tein, J. Y., Ayers, T. S., Wolchik, S., Kennedy, C., & Millsap, R. (2010). Long-term effects of the family bereavement program on multiple indicators of grief in parentally bereaved children and adolescents. *Journal of Consulting and Clinical Psychology, 78*(2), 131–143.

Sandler, I. N., Wolchik, S. A., Ayers, T. S., Tein, J. Y., & Luecken, L. (2013). Family bereavement program (FBP) approach to promoting resilience following the death of a parent. *Family Science, 4*(1), 87–94.

Schmiege, S. J., Khoo, S. T., Sandler, I. N., Ayers, T. S., & Wolchik, S. A. (2006). Symptoms of internalizing and externalizing problems: Modeling recovery curves after the death of a parent. *American Journal of Preventive Medicine, 31*(6), 152–160.

Schut, H. (2010). Grief counselling efficacy: Have we learned enough?. *Bereavement Care, 29*(1), 8–9.

Serwint, J. R. (2011). Separation, loss, and bereavement. In R. M. Klcigman, R. B. F. Stanton, J. W. St. Geme, N. F. Schor, & R. Behrman (Eds.), *Nelson textbook of pediatrics* (19th ed., pp. 45.e6–45.e11). Philadelphia, PA: Elsevier Saunders.

Shear, M. K., Simon, N., Wall, M., Zisook, S., Neimeyer, R., Duan, N., . . . Keshaviah, A. (2011). Complicated grief and related bereavement issues for DSM-5. *Depression and Anxiety, 28*(2), 103–117.

Silverman, P. R., Baker, J., Cait, C. A., & Boerner, K. (2003). The effects of negative legacies on children's adjustment after parental death. *Omega: Journal of Death and Dying, 64*, 359–376.

Simon, J. L. (2008). Anticipatory grief: Recognition and coping. *Journal of Palliative Medicine, 11*(9), 1280–1281.

Smith, S. H. (2002). " Fret no more my child . . . for I'm all over heaven all day": Religious beliefs in the bereavement of African American, middle-aged daughters coping with the death of an elderly mother. *Death Studies, 26*(4), 309–323.

Social Security Administration (SSA). (2007). *Beneficiary data: Social security administration*. Washington, DC: Author.

Sood, A. B., Razdan, A., Weller, E. B., & Weller, R. A. (2006). Children's reactions to parental and sibling death. *Current Psychiatry Reports, 8*(2), 115–120.

Spuij, M., Dekovic, M., & Boelen, P. A. (2015). An open trial of 'Grief-Help': A cognitive–behavioural treatment for prolonged grief in children and adolescents. *Clinical Psychology & Psychotherapy, 22*(2), 185–192.

Spuij, M., Prinzie, P., Zijderlaan, J., Stikkelbroek, Y., Dillen, L., Roos, C., & Boelen, P. A. (2012). Psychometric properties of the Dutch inventories of prolonged grief for children and adolescents. *Clinical Psychology & Psychotherapy, 19*(6), 540–551.

Spuij, M., Reitz, E., Prinzie, P., Stikkelbroek, Y., de Roos, C., & Boelen, P. A. (2012). Distinctiveness of symptoms of prolonged grief, depression, and post-traumatic stress in bereaved children and adolescents. *European Child & Adolescent Psychiatry, 21*(12), 673–679.

Stroebe, M., & Schut, H. (2005). To continue or relinquish bonds: A review of consequences for the bereaved. *Death Studies, 29*(6), 477–494.

Tein, J. Y., Sandler, I. N., Ayers, T. S., & Wolchik, S. A. (2006). Mediation of the effects of the Family Bereavement Program on mental health problems of bereaved children and adolescents. *Prevention Science, 7*(2), 179–195.

Torbic, H. (2011). Children and Grief: But What About the Children?. *Home Healthcare Now, 29*(2), 67–77.

Valentine, C. (2006). Academic constructions of bereavement. *Mortality, 11*(1), 57–78.

Van, P., & Meleis, A. I. (2003). Coping with grief after involuntary pregnancy loss: Perspectives of African American women. *Journal of Obstetric, Gynecologic, & Neonatal Nursing, 32*(1), 28–39.

Walter, T. (2000). Grief narratives: The role of medicine in the policing of grief. *Anthropology & Medicine, 7*(1), 97–114.

Walter, T. (2006). What is complicated grief? A social constructionist perspective. *OMEGA—Journal of Death and Dying, 52*(1), 71–79.

Werner-Lin, A., & Biank, N. M. (2012). Holding parents so they can hold their children: Grief work with surviving spouses to support parentally bereaved children. *OMEGA—Journal of Death and Dying, 66*(1), 1–16.

Werner-Lin, A., Biank, N. M., & Rubenstein, B. (2010). There's no place like home: Preparing children for geographical and relational attachment disruptions following parental death to cancer. *Clinical Social Work Journal, 38*(1), 132–143.

Wilkinson, S., Croy, P., King, M., & Barnes, J. (2007). Are we getting it right? Parents' perceptions of hospice child bereavement support services. *Palliative Medicine, 21*(5), 401–407.

Wittouck, C., Van Autreve, S., De Jaegere, E., Portzky, G., & van Heeringen, K. (2011). The prevention and treatment of complicated grief: A meta-analysis. *Clinical Psychology Review, 31,* 69–78.

Wolchik, S. A., Ma, Y., Tein, J. Y., Sandler, I. N., & Ayers, T. S. (2008). Parentally bereaved children's grief: Self-system beliefs as mediators of the relations between grief and stressors and caregiver–child relationship quality. *Death Studies, 32*(7), 597–620.

Wolchik, S. A., Tein, J. Y., Sandler, I. N., & Ayers, T. S. (2006). Stressors, quality of the child–caregiver relationship, and children's mental health problems after parental death: The mediating role of self-system beliefs. *Journal of Abnormal Child Psychology, 34*(2), 212–229.

Worden, J. (1996). *Children and grief: When a parent dies.* New York: Guilford Press.

Yick, A. G., & Gupta, R. (2002). Chinese cultural dimensions of death, dying, and bereavement: Focus group findings. *Journal of Cultural Diversity, 9*(2), 32–42.

CHAPTER 15

ETHICAL CONSIDERATIONS

Karni Kissil

In this chapter we describe some common ethical issues that may occur while working with families who are coping with parental illnesses in diverse practice settings (e.g., primary care, specialty care, private practice). Most mental healthcare providers will collaborate with medical providers and staff, such as physicians, nurses, or hospice staff. Some are behavioral healthcare providers who work in integrated primary care clinics and are embedded in the treatment team. Others work in private practice, but they need to collaborate with healthcare providers to improve the quality of medical and psychosocial care for their clients and families. The following common ethical issues are described in this chapter: (1) informed consent, (2) collaborating with medical providers, (3) confidentiality, (4) documentation, (5) working with the family as a unit of treatment, (6) contacting school personnel, and (7) self of the therapist and managing professional/personal boundaries. We describe these common ethical issues using two case examples.

Ethical Case Example 1: Mental Healthcare Provider Embedded in a Medical Setting

Donna is a 42-year-old Caucasian woman. She is a single mother of two children, 15-year-old Audrey and 11-year-old Kory. Donna was diagnosed with breast cancer 4 years ago, had a double mastectomy, and received chemotherapy; she has been cancer free for 2 years. Yet, 2 years ago she was diagnosed with cervical cancer, had surgery and chemotherapy, and went into remission. Six months ago, during a follow-up screening, the oncologist found cancer in her liver, possibly metastasized from her cervical cancer. Donna again had surgery; her providers discovered the cancer metastasized to her liver, small intestines, and ovaries. After the surgery, Donna's oncologist shared the bad news and told her there was not much to do at this point because the cancer had spread throughout her body. He reassured her that the treatment team would do everything they could to make her comfortable.

While she was sick, Donna's mother moved in to take care of her and to help with her two children. Additionally, her older sister, who lived nearby and was very close to Donna, came over every day to help Donna maintain a daily routine for her children. Both Donna's mother and sister accompanied her to all of her medical appointments, waited for her during chemotherapy treatments, and were informed of her diagnoses and all treatments. Donna signed a release of information form allowing both her mother and sister to communicate with her oncology treatment team. At first Donna did not share her cancer diagnosis and treatment with her children. Yet, after she got sick the second time (2 years ago), she disclosed the diagnosis to her 15-year-old daughter, but not to her 11-year-old son, because she felt he was too young and sensitive. Kory, her son, knew that his mother was sick but did not know she now had terminal cancer.

After receiving the terminal diagnosis, Donna consulted with a clinical social worker in the oncology department whom she met during her previous hospitalizations. She wanted to tell her sister about the terminal diagnosis so she could start preparing for her death and ensure her children would be safe and cared for; however, she did not want to tell her mother she was dying because her mother had a history of alcohol abuse and she did not want to jeopardize her recovery. She also did not want to tell her younger son, hoping he would have a few more months to experience a "normal childhood." When she got out of her session with the social worker, she found her mother sitting in the hospital waiting room area. Her mother was talking to the nurse, asking about Donna's new treatment plan after the surgery. When her mother saw Donna and the social worker, she approached them to ask the social worker about the change in Donna's medications. In the next section we describe common ethical considerations and apply them to this case example, in which a mental healthcare provider (social worker) is embedded in a medical setting (oncology).

Informed Consent

Informed consent describes the process of providing information to a patient *prior* to treatment regarding their rights as well as information needed to make informed medical decisions (Giampieri, 2012; Hudgins, Rose, Fifield, & Arnaut, 2013). It can also include an authorization to release information to outsiders; these are specific forms and processes of securing a patient's consent to release protected health information for a specific purpose and to whom (e.g., primary care provider, therapist, family members). Additionally, in settings where medical care is provided by multiple providers, informed consent can include identifying one's professional identity prior to treating a patient/client as well as explaining the risks, limitations of confidentiality (e.g., all members of the team can access information shared in this medical setting because the team is the provider), and the patient's ability to discontinue treatment at any time (Hudgins et al., 2013).

The process of obtaining informed consent should be a routine procedural issue in integrated care settings, especially regarding when, how, and from whom informed consent is obtained (Barnett, 2007; Hudgins et al., 2013). For example, should the patient sign informed consent that covers the entire treatment team (including mental healthcare providers) at the beginning of treatment? Should there be two separate informed consent forms, one for medical treatment and one for mental healthcare treatment? If there is one comprehensive consent form, which member of the treatment team should be in charge of providing all of the information to a new patient?

Many recommend that informed consent should be an *ongoing process,* especially while treating patients who are coping with medical and mental health issues (Barnett, 2007; Giampieri, 2012; Striefel, 2009). The term *process* means informed consent should be openly *discussed* with patients (Giampieri, 2012; Mammucari et al., 2014). This can be challenging because some medical clinics provide patients with only written documents that can be read when patients first begin care, which some patients may not fully understand or thoroughly read. There could be language or literacy barriers that prevent patients from fully understanding informed consent and its implications for sharing their health information and care (Hodgson et al., 2013). When there are multiple providers and myriad treatments (medical, mental health), in addition to written consent, we also recommend clearly explaining each type of treatment and the roles of providers and clarifying who will have access to the patient's medical and mental healthcare information. Additionally, in healthcare settings that have electronic medical record systems (EMR), patients should be informed of what type of health information will be documented in their medical record and who will have access to it (e.g., a patient may want to know if what happens during psychotherapy sessions will be documented and available to every provider on the medical team).

Further, an *ongoing process* for obtaining informed consent means it should be revisited throughout treatment and not just at the beginning of care (Hudgins et al., 2013). This is important because over time treatment options may change, policies and clinical practices could be revised, as could the utilization of health-related technologies (e.g., portals, emails) (Hodgson et al., 2013). Patients' preferences for sharing information could also change (e.g., following a divorce or after the prognosis changes). For example, following her last surgery, Donna's prognosis and treatment plan changed. This would be an important time to revisit informed consent to ensure Donna understands her options for treatment and prognosis and has the opportunity to ask questions and clarify who will currently have access to her health information.

Confidentiality

According to HIPAA's Privacy Rule (45 CFR 164.506, U.S. Department of Health & Human Services, 1996), *confidentiality* describes the federal protection of personal health information balanced with avoiding the creation of unnecessary barriers to the delivery of quality health care (Hodgson, Mendenhall, & Lamson, 2013). Confidentiality seems like a straightforward issue when addressing patients one-on-one in an outpatient office or in the exam room, but it can become more complicated when multiple providers and family members are involved in care and when using EMRs. Especially in integrated care settings, electronic record systems were developed to facilitate access for multiple providers, but this also increases the risk for confidentiality breaches unless precautions are taken (e.g., tracking who can access a medical record) (Robinson & Reiter, 2007). Additionally, integrated care teams often include professionals from diverse disciplines (e.g., clinical psychologists, social workers, family therapists, medical providers) who follow different codes of ethics (Hudgins, Rose, Fifield, & Arnault, 2014). In order to ensure confidentiality is managed appropriately, treatment teams should meet regularly and closely collaborate with each other regarding honoring ethical guidelines and protecting patients' health information (Hudgins et al., 2014).

Nonmedical providers (e.g., social workers, counselors, marriage and family therapists) who are part of an integrated care team may find themselves in challenging situations. They may be unsure whether they should follow the code of ethics of their professional organizations (e.g., APA, AAMFT, NASW) or the code of ethics of the American Medical Association (AMA) that governs policies and regulations in medical settings. Providers may discontinue collaborating with each other because they are concerned about confidentiality. While respecting confidentiality of our patients is very important, having separate medical and mental health records and treatment plans can hinder continuity of care (Hodgson et al., 2013; Kathol, Butler, McAlpine, & Kane, 2010; von Esenwein & Druss, 2014). As integrated care becomes more commonly practiced, it is important to find an ethical and careful way to merge these two ways of practicing (Gould, 2013; Hodgson et al., 2013; Hudgins et al., 2014; Rigby et al., 1998).

In case example 1, confidentiality was at risk when Donna's mother was talking to the nurse in the waiting room. Since Donna has been in and out of the oncology department for 4 years, she, her sister, and her mother have developed close working relationships with the oncology treatment team. So, it was not unusual for her mother to casually talk to the nurses and the physicians who were caring for Donna. Yet, at this time, Donna did not want her mother to know about the terminal diagnosis, which she discussed with the social worker during the session that day. When multiple family members are involved, providers have to maintain a delicate balance between being supportive and maintaining confidentiality of their patients. Hodgson and her colleagues (2013) advise that open spaces such as hallways and waiting areas should be designated for non-work-related and nonconfidential information, and closed-door spaces should be reserved for confidential conversations about patient care.

Some professional disciplines have addressed the issue of confidentiality while working with several family members. For example, the APA code of ethics describes the importance of clarifying the relationship of the therapist with each family member at the beginning of treatment, that is, who is being identified as the patient and how information will be shared among family members (APA standard 10.2 [APA, 2010]). The AAMFT code of ethics also recommends clarifying the limits of confidentiality at the beginning of treatment and describes the importance of protecting patients' privacy, for example, requiring written consent for disclosures between participating family members (http://aamft.org, principle II: confidentiality).

In the clinical example described previously, the therapist should immediately record the change in Donna's preferences for release authorizations and her decision to exclude her mother from being informed about her terminal diagnosis. Since Donna's mother is currently at the clinic and asking questions in the waiting room, the therapist has to make a judgment call regarding whether she should just note this change in Donna's medical record and trust team members will review the EMR before speaking to Donna or her family members or to immediately reach out to team members to inform them about this recent change. If all team members follow the recommendation to restrict hallway conversations to nonconfidential material, it is likely the nurse will tell Donna's mother to address her question the next time she accompanies Donna to her appointments, and with Donna present.

Noteworthy, it is not uncommon for patients to bring a support person during medical appointments. While it may be the responsibility of the patient to inform the provider what can be shared with a support person, providers should also explore this issue before starting the session or medical examination (Gould, 2013). Many confidentiality breaches and patient grievances can be prevented by being more cautious throughout care.

Scope of Practice

Most professional disciplines' codes of ethics describe the scope of practice. Providers are advised to be aware of that scope, to continue getting education in their areas of expertise, and to treat problems within the boundaries of their competence (e.g., APA standard 2.01, boundaries of competence [APA, 2010]; NASW standard 1.04, competence [NASW, 2008]). Mental healthcare providers who practice in integrated care settings should provide care cautiously in several ways. First, mental healthcare providers may have access to patients' medical information, such as test results, which they do not have the medical expertise to interpret. Yet, they may be asked by patients to explain this information even though it is beyond their scope of practice. Second, mental healthcare providers have access to patients' medical records and may have information that the patient is not yet aware of (e.g., recent test results). Thus, mental healthcare providers should always defer to medical providers when medical questions are asked by patients (Rosenberg & Speice, 2013). In case example 1, Donna's mother asked the social worker about Donna's change of medication. In addition to the issue of confidentiality discussed previously, this question is beyond the scope of practice for the social worker, so she should tell Donna's mother to bring this up the next time she accompanies Donna to the medical appointment.

Scope of practice is important not only regarding the intersection of mental and medical spheres but also within each of these areas. For example, let's suppose the social worker asked Donna why she did not want her mother to know about her terminal diagnosis. Donna then shares with the social worker that her mother is a recovering alcoholic who has been sober for 20 years, but she recently relapsed and Donna did not want to further burden her. The social worker, who has known Donna for 4 years and feels very close and comfortable with the family, may feel "tempted" to help Donna's mother work on her alcohol abuse issues. Yet, this is not within the boundaries of her expertise and not part of her responsibilities on the oncology treatment team. The right thing to do in this case is to provide Donna's mother with a referral to alcohol abuse counseling.

Changes in care settings are another issue to consider. Where care is provided may change during treatment. For example, in Donna's case, she may be transferred to a hospice clinical setting as her cancer progresses, or she may decide to stay home and receive home-based hospice care. Quality of care should be provided with the best interest of the patient in mind, wherever it is needed, regardless of location. Donna's therapist should collaborate with the hospice team and help them provide end-of-life care, and she should be able to visit Donna at the hospice setting and at home to ensure the continuity of high quality of care.

Documentation

Every professional discipline addresses providers' responsibilities to maintain accurate, timely, and adequate documentation (e.g., APA standard 6.02 [APA, 2010]; AMA opinion 7.025 [AMA, n.d.]). While mental healthcare providers have prioritized and advocated for patients' privacy, often at the expense of optimal shared care in the past (Rosenberg & Speice, 2013), when working in an integrated treatment team, providers should recognize the value of having a comprehensive biopsychosocial-spiritual understanding of patients with regard to the provision of quality care and effective treatment planning (Kathol et al., 2010; von Esenwein & Druss, 2014).

In integrated care settings, where there is typically one comprehensive shared medical record, ethical dilemmas can arise. Mental healthcare providers should use discretion when documenting sensitive information about patients and their family members (Hodgson et al., 2013; von Esenwein & Druss, 2014). Family members' privacy is an important factor to consider; minimal identifying information should be used in the medical record. Only information that is essential for the provision of quality of care should be included (von Esenwein & Druss, 2014), because patients can obtain their own medical records.

Continuing with Donna's case, the provider should use discretion when documenting the therapy sessions. She should describe Donna's request to not tell her mother about the terminal diagnosis, but exclude information about her mother's alcohol abuse issues to protect her mother's privacy. Yet, the fact that Donna's mother had recently relapsed may impact her ability to support Donna as her cancer progresses, so it could be important to help Donna find additional social support. Thus, the therapist should consider noting in the medical record the possible scenario (that her mother will become less available for her) without describing too many details that compromise her mother's health information and privacy.

Working with the Family as the Unit of Treatment

While many providers, researchers, and organizations (e.g., American Academy of Nursing, JCAHO, Institute of Medicine, Institute for Family Centered Care) have supported the importance of family members' involvement to improve patients' clinical outcomes, many collaborative care models, including the patient-centered medical home, place little emphasis on engaging family members as part of the healthcare team (Agency for Healthcare Research and Quality, 2008). At the same time, many of today's behavioral healthcare providers and physical healthcare providers lack training regarding how to interview, intervene, and respond to more than one person in the room efficiently and effectively (Martire, 2005; Martire et al. 2004). As described in Chapter 2, family-centered care is a paradigm shift and a change in culture for many healthcare providers and clinics. We recommend considering a family-centered approach to care, especially while working with parents who are coping with an illness and their families. Thus, it is important to also consider how working with the family as a unit of treatment will impact ethical guidelines.

Responsibility

A therapist's primary responsibility is to his/her client. Yet, the family is the client when using a *family-centered approach* to medical care, which is defined as a healthcare delivery approach endorsing the support and participation of family members (Shields, 2010). When working with a family, there could be more than one individual in treatment, so it may be difficult to choose an appropriate treatment or intervention. For example, an intervention that best helps one family member might not always be optimal for other family members. In the case of Donna, her decision to not disclose her terminal diagnosis to her mother and to her younger son may help her feel good about protecting her mother and her child, but it may not be the optimal choice for them. Being unaware of Donna's terminal diagnosis denies her family members of the opportunity to prepare for her death and cherish the remaining time they have together. Although we recommend respecting the choices of the parent who is ill, the mental healthcare provider working with Donna should help Donna explore what would be the most appropriate psychosocial intervention (see Chapters 2 and 14) benefitting the well-being of all family members.

Confidentiality

Providers working with families may encounter ethical issues regarding confidentiality because, when implementing a family-centered approach to care, the identified client is more than one person (AAMFT, 2001; AMA, n.d.). Therapists should be transparent and inform family members at the beginning of treatment of their rights to confidentiality and the limits of confidentiality when working with more than one client. Some providers agree to not disclose to other family members any information an individual family member decides to share in private. Other providers believe that this policy limits their effectiveness and take a position of no secrets among family members, meaning that even information that was disclosed in an individual session can be discussed in family sessions. In order to avoid a potential breach of confidentiality, some providers refuse consultations with individual family members unless all agree the provider will not keep secrets from other family members. Whatever position a provider takes, it is important to discuss it with the family prior to beginning therapy to prevent a scenario in which different family members function under different assumptions about confidentiality. In case example 1, if Donna would like to have a few sessions with her mother to discuss issues in their relationship, the therapist has to discuss with Donna the confidentiality around her terminal diagnosis.

Informed Consent

Informed consent is another important ethical consideration for providers who are working with families. The process of informed consent should take place with every member of the family participating in therapy (age 14 and older in most U.S. states), even if some members join at a later stage. Thus, if Donna wants to have a few therapy sessions with her daughter, Audrey, to discuss the changes at home due to Donna's illness and address Audrey's concerns about the future, the mental healthcare provider has to discuss informed consent with Audrey.

It is often the case that some family members are not so eager to participate in family therapy as other members. This highlights the issue of voluntary participation. Donna's daughter, Audrey, has to consent to treatment. Coercing someone, either by the therapist or other family members, to attend therapy is unethical. However, mental healthcare providers can strongly encourage reluctant family members to attend one session to find out if therapy can benefit them in any way.

Case Example 2: Mental Healthcare Provider in Private Practice

Kim is a 35-year-old African American woman. She was recently diagnosed with multiple sclerosis (MS) following 2 years of suffering from various symptoms and going to different providers in search of a definitive diagnosis. She is a professional dancer, and up until 3 months ago she worked for a well-known dance company. Due to the unpredictability and severity of her symptoms, especially the flare-ups, she had to quit her job. Kim is married to Jordan, a 36-year-old African American man. Jordan works as a human resource manager in a big hotel. The couple has three young children: 9-year-old Vanessa, 5-year-old Aaron, and 3-year-old Tasha.

Kim sought therapy following her MS diagnosis. Her primary care physician thought she was depressed and needed some professional help navigating the impact of the diagnosis on her life and family. He was also concerned because Kim told him sometimes she was too tired to get out of bed and take her medications. He referred Kim to a mental healthcare provider who specializes in medical family therapy and whose office was in the same building as the clinic. During her therapy sessions, Kim talked about her struggle accepting the MS diagnosis, hoping to wake up one day realizing it was just a bad dream. She talked about feeling depressed regarding the loss of her dancing career, concerns for her husband who has to work so hard at work and at home when she has her flare-ups, and financial difficulties following the loss of her job as a dancer. She also talked about struggling to be consistent in taking care of her children, especially when her symptoms were incapacitating. She was worried about becoming a neglectful mother when her symptoms "take over." Kim did not tell her children about her diagnosis, because she felt that they were too young to understand.

Collaboration with Medical Providers

Kim has several providers involved in her MS care. She has a primary care physician, who referred her for therapy. She also sees a neurologist, who diagnosed her with MS and referred her to a rehabilitation specialist who is part of the neurology department at the local hospital where the neurologist works. The rehabilitation specialist helps her find effective ways to reduce feelings of fatigue and adjust to living with MS.

Since Kim has several providers, good communication amongst all of them is essential for optimal continuity of care. She is taking several medications that will change as her condition progresses, so every member of the treatment team needs to be aware of all medications; frequent communication is recommended. At the beginning of treatment, the provider should openly discuss release authorization for each provider involved in Kim's care. The counselor should describe the benefits of communicating with Kim's providers as well as the risks. A provider should be specific about the type and extent of information that will be shared. With Kim's signed releases of information, her counselor can contact her providers to explain his role and ask for information that will improve his work with her. With Kim's permission, he can report any helpful information back to the treatment team. Mental healthcare providers should be cautious about maintaining Kim's privacy and only report information that will benefit Kim's treatment. This information should not be as detailed as the therapy notes in the EMR.

Confidentiality

Differing from a mental healthcare provider who is embedded in a medical setting, Kim's therapist is in a private practice office located in the same office building as her provider, so there are no shared medical records. Confidentiality rules are more straightforward and easy to follow since mental healthcare providers have to follow the codes of ethics of their professional disciplines (e.g., ACA, AAMFT, NASW). While in integrated care mental healthcare providers are encouraged to document only information that is essential to the patient's continuity of care, providers in private practice can write detailed psychotherapy notes that include interpretations, dynamic processes, and relational information (Hudgins et al., 2013). Mental healthcare providers have to be mindful when sharing information with other providers that they obtain release authorization and have clearly discussed with their patients the extent and type of information to be shared.

Contacting School Personnel

Let's continue with the story of Kim. As described, Kim did not want her children to know about her MS diagnosis. Yet, a few weeks later, Kim learned that Vanessa, her older daughter, was having problems in school. Her teacher reported that Vanessa seemed distracted, sad, and withdrawn. Her class participation recently decreased, which negatively impacted her grades, and she has been sitting alone during recess. Kim wondered if she should disclose her illness to Vanessa's teachers so they are more caring and sensitive toward her, and she wondered if this means that Vanessa understands what is going on and perhaps she should disclose her illness to Vanessa.

Deciding whether and when to contact school personnel should be decided by the patient in consultation with his or her spouse or partner. The mental healthcare provider should discuss this option with Kim and her husband and help her address questions such as: What is the purpose of contacting the school? Is it better to do it in person or send a letter? How much is she comfortable disclosing? Would she and her husband like any kind of intervention from the school (e.g., having the school counselor talk to Vanessa, including Vanessa in a support group in school). Kim should also decide whether she would like to sign a release of authorization to open up communication between the school and her mental healthcare provider. If Kim prefers that the provider contact the school directly, they have to discuss the specific information the provider is allowed to share with the school; all communication and interactions with the school should be documented in Kim's record.

Mental healthcare providers should remember the scope of their practice and intervene accordingly. For example, Kim and the provider might agree that a few family therapy sessions with her two older children, Vanessa and Aaron, will be helpful. If the provider is experienced in a family-centered approach to care, he can conduct these sessions. Alternately, he can provide Kim with a referral to a family therapist for these sessions and continue to work with Kim in individual sessions.

Self of Therapist and Managing Professional and Personal Boundaries

Let's continue with the story of Kim. When Kim meets with the mental healthcare provider and tells him about her daughter's school problems and her dilemma regarding disclosing the MS diagnosis to her, the provider responds impatiently and tells her she has to disclose the diagnosis to all of her children as soon as possible because secrets are always harmful. The provider immediately notices the hurt reaction on Kim's face and realizes the way he responded was unlike his usual therapeutic style. When the provider reflects on his behavior, he realizes the situation was tough because of his own personal history with parental illness. The mental healthcare provider lost his father to a chronic illness when he was a child. His family kept the father's illness a secret from him for several years. The provider was told about it a few days prior to his father's death. At that time, he also found out that his older siblings knew all along about their father's illness. He was resentful toward his family about the way his father's illness was handled and felt that they should have told him sooner. When Kim brought up her struggle in deciding whether she should tell her own children, he was responding from a vulnerable and hurt position, identifying too much with Kim's three young children. After realizing that he was becoming reactive, the provider reminded himself that this is not his family. He took a deep breath and was able to reengage in a conversation with Kim, this time letting her express her own concerns about how, when, and with whom to disclose her MS diagnosis and how to answer questions that may arise when she talks to her children.

This case example illustrates that, as mental healthcare providers, we bring all of who we are into the therapy room. Our histories, life experiences, personalities, and personal values shape how we interact with our clients. While having had similar experiences as our clients can help us identify with their struggles and better understand their pain (Aponte & Kissil, 2014; Elkaim, 1997), we have to be able to differentiate ourselves from our clients and their issues (Aponte & Kissil, 2014). We have to make sure we work with our clients to find the best course of action that fits *their* circumstances and not impose what we believe are the solutions we needed when we struggled with similar issues.

Working with clients and families who are coping with medical illnesses can bring up family-of-origin medical issues among mental healthcare providers (McDaniel, Doherty, & Hepworth, 2014). These can include beliefs about health and illness, experiences of illness and loss, family patterns of interacting around illness and loss, as well as experiences of interacting with health providers (McDaniel, Doherty, & Hepworth, 2014). These experiences can help providers connect to their clients, better understand their struggles, and understand how to best help them (Aponte & Kissil, 2014). In order for therapists to utilize their own experiences during clinical encounters, they have to be comfortable accessing those experiences and memories when needed. At the same time, in order to differentiate themselves from their clients, providers have to be skilled at tracking their own reactions during sessions to notice when they get triggered, and then take the appropriate steps to maintain their professional boundaries. Being reflective and using supervision and/or consultation as needed can help mental healthcare providers effectively manage their professional selves and remain client centered (Rosenberg & Speice, 2013).

Professional Readings and Resources

Curtis, R., & Christian, E. (Eds.). (2012). *Integrated care: Applying theory to practice.* New York: Taylor & Francis.

Dziegielewski, S. F. (2013). *The changing face of health care social work: Professional practice in managed behavioral health care* (3rd ed.). New York: Springer.

Hanson, S. L., Kerkhoff, T. R., & Bush, S. S. (2005). *Health care ethics for psychologists: A casebook.* Washington, D.C.: American Psychological Association.

McDaniel, S. H., Doherty, W. J., & Hepworth, J. (2014). *Medical family therapy and integrated care.* Washington, D.C.: American Psychological Association.

References

Agency for Healthcare Research and Quality. (2008). Multidisciplinary family clinic increases access to care for inner city residents, leading to improved outcomes and high patient satisfaction. Retrieved from www.innovations.ahrq.gov/content.aspx?id=2186

American Association for Marriage and Family Therapy. (2001). AAMFT code of ethics. Retrieved from www.aamft.org/iMIS15/AAMFT/Content/Legal_Ethics/Code_of_Ethics.aspx

American Medical Association. (n.d.). Code of medical ethics of the American Medical Association. Retrieved from www.ama-assn.org/ama/pub/physician-resources/medical-ethics/code-medical-ethics.page

American Psychological Association. (2010). Ethical principles of psychologists and code of conducts. Retrieved from http://apa.org/ethics/code/index.aspx

Aponte, H., & Kissil, K. (2014). "If I can grapple with this I can truly be of use in the therapy room": Using the therapist's own emotional struggles to facilitate effective therapy. *Journal of Marital and Family Therapy, 40*(2), 152–164. doi:10.1111/jmft.12011

Barnett, J. E. (2007). Seeking an understanding of informed consent. *Professional Psychology: Research and Practice, 38*, 179–182.

Elkaim, M. (1997). *If you love me, don't love me: Undoing reciprocal double binds and other methods of change in couple and family therapy*. New York: Jason Aronson.

Giampieri, M. (2012). Communication and informed consent in elderly people. *Minerva Anestesiologica, 78*(2), 236–242.

Gould, D. A. (2013). Primary care provider reflections on Common Themes from Special issue on ethical quandaries when delivering integrated primary care. *Families, Systems, and Health, 31*(1), 49–51.

Hodgson, J., Mendenhall, T., & Lamson, A. (2013). Patient and provider relationships: Consent, confidentiality, and managing mistakes in integrated primary care settings. *Families, Systems, & Health, 31*(1), 28–40.

Hudgins, C., Rose, S., Fifield, P. Y., & Arnault, S. (2013). Navigating the legal and ethical foundations of informed consent and confidentiality in integrated primary care. *Families, Systems, & Health, 31*(1), 9–19.

Hudgins, C., Rose, S., Fifield, P., & Arnault, S. (2014). The ethics of integration: Where policy and practice collide. In J. Hodgson, A. Lamson, T. Mendenhall, & T. R. Crane (Eds.) *Medical family therapy: Advanced applications* (pp. 381–402). New York: Springer.

Kathol, R. G., Butler, M., McAlpine, D. D., & Kane, R. L. (2010). Barriers to physical and mental condition integrated service delivery. *Psychosomatic Medicine, 72*(6), 511–518.

Mammucari, M., Lazzari, M., Maggiori, E., Gafforio, P., Tufaro, G., Baffini, S., . . . Sabato, A. F. (2014). Role of the informed consent, from mesotherapy to opioid therapy. *European Review for Medical and Pharmacological Sciences, 18*(4), 566–574.

Martire, L. M. (2005). The "relative" efficacy of involving family members in psychosocial interventions for chronic illness: Are there added benefits to patients and family members? *Families, Systems, and Health, 23*, 312–328.

Martire, L. M., Lustig, A. P., Schulz, R., Miller, G. E., & Helgeson, V. S. (2004). Is it beneficial to involve a family member? A meta-analysis of psychosocial interventions for chronic illness. *Health Psychology, 23*, 599–611.

McDaniel, S. H., Doherty, W. J., & Hepworth, J. (2014). *Medical family therapy and integrated care*. Washington, D.C.: American Psychological Association.

National Association of Social Workers. (2008). *NASW code of ethics (Guide to the everyday professional conduct of social workers)*. Washington, DC: Author.

Rigby, M., Roberts, R., Williams, J., Clark, J., Savill, A., Lervy, B., & Mooney, G. (1998). Integrated record keeping as an essential aspect of a primary care led health service. *BMJ, 317*(7158), 579–582.

Robinson, P., & Reiter, J. (2007). *Behavioral consultation and primary care: A guide to integrating services*. New York: Springer.

Rosenberg, T., & Speice, J. (2013). Integrating care when the end is near: Ethical dilemmas in end-of-life care. *Families, Systems, & Health, 31*(1), 75–83.

Shields, L. (2010). Questioning family-centered care. *Journal of Clinical Nursing, 19*(17–18), 2629–2638.

Striefel, S. S. (2009). Ethical behavior in medical settings. *Biofeedback, 37*(4), 119–122.

U.S. Department of Health and Human Services. (1996). Health insurance portability & accountability act. Retrieved from www.hhs.gov/ocr/privacy

von Esenwein, S. A., & Druss, B. G. (2014). Using electronic health records to improve the physical healthcare of people with serious mental illnesses: A view from the front lines. *International Review of Psychiatry, 26*(6), 629–637.

INDEX

Note: Page numbers with *f* indicate figures; those with *t* indicate tables.